Law School Survival Kit

by Jeff Adachi, Esq.

Law School Survival Kit

by Jeff Adachi, Esq.

Published by:
Survival Series Publishing Company
P.O. Box 77313
San Francisco, CA 94107
(415) 979-6785 tel., (415) 664-6463 fax
www.survival-series.com

Author:	Jeff Adachi, Esq.
Copy Editor:	Robert Uchida
Layout/Graphics:	Romeo Carambas, Larry Roberts
Original Cover Illustration:	Hiroki Asai
Original Illustrations:	Joseph L. Phillips & Stanley Adachi
Original Word Processing:	Kathy T. Asada, Esq.
Permission to reprint questions:	California State Bar, Committee of Bar Examiners

Other books by the Survival Series Publishing Co:
Bar Exam Survival Kit
Bar Cards
Complete Bar Cards
Bar Breaker
MBE Survival Kit
Jury Chart
For more information, visit www.survival-series.com

Law School Survival Kit

Table of Contents

I. Introduction to the First Year of Law School • 1

Overview 3
Preview of the First Year Curriculum 5

II. Introduction to the Law School Learning Experience • 21

Reading and Analyzing Cases 25
Classroom Instruction 31
Briefing the Case 34
Organizing the Cases and Materials 38
Outlining 40
Developing the Problem Solving Approach 44
Applying the Problem Solving Approach 48

III. Law Charts • 69

Torts 71
Criminal Law 79
Contracts 83
Contract Remedies 91
Civil Procedure 95
Real Property 103

IV. How To Write Law Shool Examination Essay Answers • 115

Ten Rules to Write By 118
How to Answer a Torts Problem 127
How To Answer a Criminal Law Problem 175
How To Answer a Contracts Problem 197
How To Answer a Civil Procedure Problem 240
How To Answer a Real Property Problem 266

V. Preparing for Midterms and Final Examinations • 281

Law School According to Garth 283
Ten Major Downfalls of Final Examinations 283
How to Memorize the Law 286
A Question of Time 293
Developing a Study Schedule 298
A Final Word 300

VI. Appendix • 303

Case Briefing Forms 305
Glossary of Abbreviated Terms 309
Glossary of Terms by Subject 310

Introduction to the First Year of Law School

Part I

Overview of the Survival Kit

Preview of the First Year Curriculum

Torts

Criminal Law

Contracts

Civil Procedure

Property

Legal Writing & Research Skills

give you a significant advantage over your colleagues ... with this knowledge.

what you have learned.

Part Three of this book contains the *Law Charts* for each of the first year subjects: Torts, Criminal Law, Contracts, Civil Procedure and Property. In Part Three, you will be taught how to use the *Law Charts* in this book, and how to ...

Overview

Welcome to the *Law School Survival Kit.* This book is designed to provide you with the tools needed to succeed in law school. The *Law School Survival Kit* is packed from start to finish with proven strategies, techniques and practical survival tips that will help you attain your goals. This book will show you how to prepare for law professors' Socratic method of teaching, to read and brief cases, outline and organize the law and prepare for examinations. The information in this book will give you a significant advantage over your colleagues who enter law school without this knowledge.

Part One of this book begins with a preview of the first year courses. Each first year subject is discussed individually, focusing on the "big picture." After viewing the law from the big picture, you will see how it all fits together.

In Part Two, you will receive a guided tour through the "Law School Learning Experience." First, you will learn how to read and analyze a case. Second, you will be introduced to the Socratic method used by law professors in teaching the law. Third, you will learn how to "brief" a case. Fourth, you will learn the different ways case materials are organized. Fifth, you will learn how to "outline" – the process of organizing reading materials and other information into a running diary of what you have learned.

Part Three of this book contains the *Law Charts* for each of the first year subjects: Torts, Criminal Law, Contracts, Civil Procedure and Property. In Part Three, you will be taught how to use the *Law Charts* in this book and how to apply them to solving law school exam problems.

Law Charts contain the checklists of questions or issues you must ask yourself in solving law school examination problems. While commercial and student outlines contain the general principles of law, i.e., the "black letter law," *Law Charts* provide you with the next critical step in the law school learning process – that of organizing, applying and memorizing the law for purposes of exam taking. The *Law Charts* are often the "missing link" in the law school learning experience. Unfortunately, only too rarely is the student taught exactly how to develop and use a problem-solving approach.

The *Law Charts* in this book will apply regardless of the law school you attend. However, if your instructor emphasizes a specific law particular to your state, you should obviously know the rule. Likewise, if there is a conflict between a rule of law or concept as explained by your professor and the rule as stated in this book, follow your professor's rule, for it is your professor who will grade your final examination.

In Part Four, you will learn how to write examinations in each of the five first-year subjects. We will take you through actual law school exams and show you how to answer these problems by using *The Six Steps of Exam Taking.* Then, in Part Five, we will provide you with some important tips that will help you prepare for midterms and final examinations. You will also find case briefing forms and an essential glossary of terms in the Appendix of this book.

The *Law Charts* in this book is based on the common body of law taught in most first year law school programs. Although the teaching style and curriculum of different professors will vary, the law you will learn during law school is based on a theoretical "universal" law common to all states. Of course in real life, the laws of each state may vary considerably, and a lawyer looks to the law of the jurisdiction in which he or she practices. In law school, however, the law is taught as if the same law applied universally throughout the country.

There are two important reasons for this. First of all, the first year curriculum is designed to give you a general introduction to the study of law as a concept, not simply the specific law of your state. You will, therefore, be expected to know rules of other jurisdictions and states where appropriate. The second reason is grounded in economics; most professors rely on casebooks that are distributed nationally and contain cases and commentaries from all the states. While your instructor will no doubt from time to time supplement the case book studies with local law, the law you will learn as a law student in Florida, for example, will not differ substantially from the law taught in California, or Cowabunga for that matter.

As you begin your journey into the labyrinth of legal education, remember that you are being trained to be a problem solver. The basic purpose of law school, and hence this book, is to teach you how to solve legal problems. An attorney's function is to use the law to solve real-life problems and disputes. Each of the skills you will learn in law school, whether it be reading or briefing cases, or participating in the Socratic Method, is designed to train you to be a problem solver. Initially many of these exercises may seem a bit tedious, but you must have faith that mastering each step in the law school learning process will make you a better lawyer in the years to come.

Throughout your legal education, this book will serve as an important reference guide that you will refer to again and again as you become better acquainted with the law school learning process and as you improve your problem solving skills. As you do with any reference guide, you should scrutinize the information in this book and use those tips you find helpful.

I will be your personal coach and tutor during law school studies. Like an athletic coach, I will give you the methods and strategies that will help you attain your goals, whether your objective is to receive top grades or to improve your learning and studying skills. At the same time, I will often point out the obvious and remind you of things you already know. Together, we will tackle the exciting challenges that await you in law school.

Preview of the First Year Curriculum

The required courses during the first year in law school are remarkably uniform around the country. With few exceptions, the first year curriculum typically includes courses in Torts, Criminal Law, Civil Procedure, Property and Contracts. In addition to these "substantive" courses, the first year curriculum usually includes a course designed to teach legal research and writing skills.

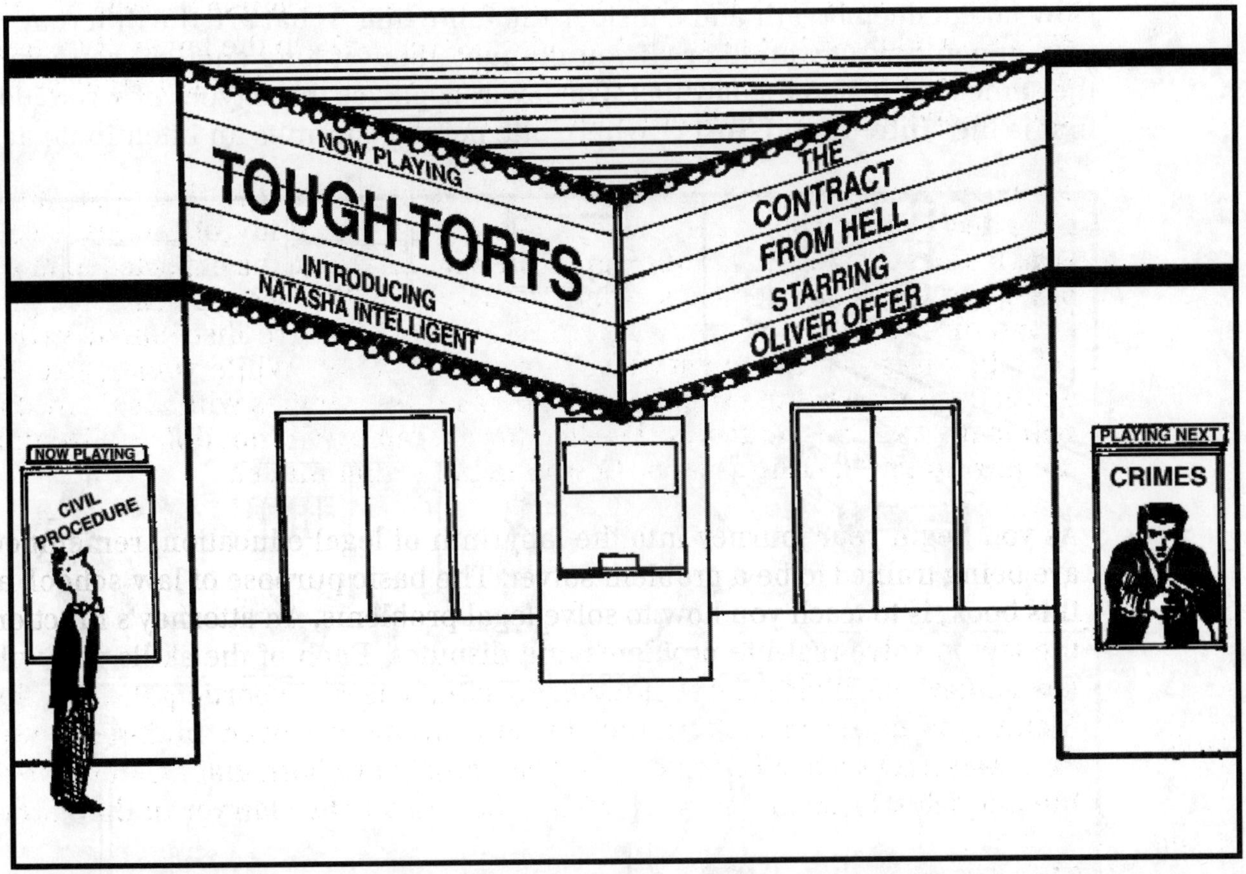

It is imperative that you view the substantive courses from the big picture. Seeing the "big picture" means that you not only understand each individual rule of law, but also understand how those rules of law fit together. All too often, the law is taught in myopic, tiny slivers, and the student, focusing on the detail of the law, cannot see the forest through the trees. It is, therefore, appropriate to take a few moments to discuss what you will be learning in each course, from the vantage point of the "big picture."

Please note that as with any summary the purpose of this brief discussion is not to teach or preach the law, but only to give you a quick overview of what to expect in each of your first year classes.

TORTS

Often hailed as the easiest of the first year subjects, the law of Torts concerns itself with private wrong. When one party commits a wrongful act against another, the law of torts provides a cause of action and remedy. If your neighbor picks up a rock and throws it at your new car, a private wrong is committed, and you have a tort action against your neighbor.

Now take a deep breath and consider the following. What are the different ways one person could wrong another? If you thought about it long enough, you would reach the same conclusion the law has. The law recognizes three types of wrongdoing. The first is the "**Intentional Torts,**" where one person commits an intentional act against

another. The second is "**Negligence**" where one person acts carelessly toward another. The third is "**Strict Liability,**" where liability is imposed regardless of any mental intent or negligence.

After pondering the subject of intentional conduct, you may come up with seven ways one person might intentionally act to injure another. The first might be touching another in a harmful or offensive manner. Call that a "**battery.**" No, not the Energizer battery that keeps on going, but a battery. The second might be causing another person to be in apprehension of harmful or offensive touching. Call that an "**assault.**" The third would be restraining another's liberty, known as "**false imprisonment.**" The fourth would be causing another to suffer emotional distress aptly named "**intentional infliction of emotional distress.**" The fifth might be entering another's land without the owner's consent by committing "**trespass to land,**" and the sixth and seventh might be damaging or destroying another's property, known respectively as "**trespass to chattels**" and "**conversion.**"

Holy Toledo! There you have the seven intentional torts! Each of these torts is a "cause of action" made up of numerous "elements" which must be proven. For example, a battery is defined as: (1) an affirmative act, (2) with the intent to touch another, (3) resulting in harmful or offensive contact. Each "element" of battery must be proven in order for the party bringing the law suit to recover. The tort of false imprisonment is: (1) an act or omission (2) with the intent to confine another, (3) resulting in actual confinement of the plaintiff and (4) either awareness of the confinement or injury resulting from such confinement. Again, the "rule" of false imprisonment consists of various "elements" and "requirements" that must be proven. If a plaintiff proves each of the "elements" of false imprisonment, she is said to have proved a "prima facie" case of false imprisonment.

The subject of intentional torts is taught through a series of cases and examples demonstrating how each element of each tort is "applied" to a different set of facts. You will learn how the various rules of law have evolved and developed throughout time. You will learn the rationales underlying the rules and the effect and influence of public policy.

If a cause of action appears to exist, that is each element is proven, the next step is to determine whether a **defense** applies. These defenses include **consent, defense of others, defense of property, self-defense, necessity and the privilege of arrest.** A defense is a legally recognized justification that will absolve or release the defendant from liability for committing the tort. For example, self-defense is a defense to a battery. If a person commits a battery in self-defense, his act is said to be privileged, and he is not liable for the battery. How do you know if self-defense applies in a given case? The same way you were able to determine whether a battery existed --- you run though a checklist of elements. For self-defense, you must ask: (1) Did D reasonably believe she was in danger from P? (2) Was the force necessary to prevent the harm?

(3) Was deadly force used?

This dichotomy between the cause of action and the defenses is one that will appear in other areas of law. For example, in criminal law, once you have determined that the elements of a crime have been proven, you turn to the issue of whether a potential defense exists. Similarly, in contracts law, once you have determined that a legal or contractual relationship exists, you then determine whether any "defenses to a contract" apply.

The next theory of liability in tort law is that of **negligence.** Negligence is careless conduct by a defendant causing injury to another. The definition of negligence is a breach of duty of due care that is the actual and proximate cause of plaintiff's injury.

In order to prove negligence, again certain "elements" must be met, just as in the area of intentional torts. For example, the plaintiff must demonstrate that the defendant owed him/her a duty of due care, that is a duty to exercise due care toward her, that the defendant breached the duty and the breach caused the plaintiff's injury. If each "element" is met, then the plaintiff is said to have proved a "prima facie" case of negligence.

As with intentional torts, you will learn the defenses to negligence: **contributory negligence, comparative negligence, assumption of the risk and the last clear chance doctrine.** Each defense either partially or completely bars plaintiff's recovery for negligence. For example, the defense of contributory negligence bars the plaintiff's recovery where the plaintiff himself acted in a negligent manner, contributing to his injury. You will learn the elements of each defense and how to apply each defense to determine whether it applies or not.

The third category of tortious conduct involves **strict liability,** in which a defendant is held liable in tort for her conduct, regardless of the presence or absence of intent. Strict liability involves abnormally dangerous activities, such as possessing a dangerous pet or engaging in dangerous activities, such as transporting nuclear waste.

Other areas commonly covered in first year torts in varying degree include products liability, defamation, privacy torts, nuisance, business torts, misrepresentation and malicious prosecution.

The area of **products liability** is made up of five different torts: misrepresentation, breach of express warranty, strict products liability, implied warranty and negligence. Each tort provides the plaintiff with a separate ground of relief when a plaintiff suffers injury caused by a product, and each tort is made up of a checklist of elements that must be fulfilled before a cause of action is said to exist. For example, Misrepresentation requires that there be a misrepresentation of a material fact, that the plaintiff relied upon the misrepresentation in using the product, that the representation was actually made by defendant, who is a commercial supplier of goods, and that the representation was intended and expected to reach a class of persons of which the plaintiff was a member. This tort protects a consumer from misrepresentation made by a retailer or a manufacturer. As with all torts, each cause of action is accompanied by a checklist of defenses that must be considered.

The law of **defamation** determines when a person may successfully sue for injuries caused by words of another. Defamation is the publication or announcement to a third party by defendant, that in fact defames or ridicules plaintiff, that is capable of being understood by the third party, and that causes damage to plaintiff's reputation. Again, each "element" of a defamation action must be met, and again, defenses such as "truth as a complete defense," must be considered.

The **privacy torts** protect a plaintiff from invasions of privacy perpetrated by a defendant. The four privacy torts are: intrusion, public disclosure of offensive private facts, placing plaintiff in a false light in the public eye and misappropriation of plaintiff's name or likeness. Each privacy tort addresses a different type of harm. For example, the tort of false light may apply where plaintiff's picture is placed next to a defamatory headline, even though the headline concerns another person.

The tort of **nuisance** is of two types, private and public; both torts involve substantial interference with the public or private use of land, such as when your neighbor constantly plays loud music or engages in activity that creates a foul smell and air pollution. **Harm to a plaintiff's business** is governed by the torts of injurious falsehood, interference with contract and interference with an economic advantage: Apart is the tort of **misrepresentation**, which can be either intentional or negligent, when a defendant misrepresents a past or present fact to be true, and the plaintiff justifiably relies on the representation. Lastly, the torts of **malicious prosecution,** abuse of process and wrongful civil proceedings, protect a defendant from vexatious litigation or improper civil and criminal proceedings.

You will also learn "**general considerations**" in tort law, or general principles applying to all torts. These principles should be considered in analyzing any tort problem. General considerations include the concept of vicarious liability, statutory immunity, wrongful death, multiple defendant problems and statute of limitations issues. For example, in the area of vicarious liability, you will learn when parents are held liable for the tort of their child, or when an employer is liable for the tort of his or her employee. Again, you will learn a series of elements or tests that must be met before the rule is said to apply.

As you can see, the law of torts involves a myriad of different causes of action, allowing one person to sue another for wrongful conduct. If you keep in mind that the overriding issue in torts is whether a tort has been proven, and if so, what defenses and general considerations apply, you will be well on your way to seeing the big picture.

CRIMINAL LAW

Your studies in criminal law will center on whether a crime has been committed and if so, what defenses may apply. Each crime requires both a **mens rea,** which is the intent requirement, and **actus reus,** the accompanying criminal act. In substantive criminal law, the issue is always whether a particular person is guilty of a particular crime, i.e., have the elements of the charged crime been proven? The second issue is what defenses may apply.

There are two primary parties in a criminal case. The person charged with a crime is known as the **defendant.** The party bringing the action is usually the state or the United States government, known as the **prosecutor.** While a tort provides private parties with a remedy for wrongful conduct, the law of crimes provides a penal sanction, such as incarceration, for one who violates society's criminal laws.

You will learn the various crimes a defendant could be charged with: the **inchoate crimes** of solicitation, attempt and conspiracy; **crimes against the person,** including battery, false imprisonment, mayhem, assault, rape, kidnaping, and robbery; **crimes against property,** such as larceny, arson, burglary, extortion, false pretenses, uttering, receiving stolen property, embezzlement, larceny by conversion, and forgery. These are known as the common law crimes, which existed in old England.

Each crime is made up of certain "elements" that must be met before a defendant is said to be "guilty" of a crime. For example, the common law crime of burglary required that there be a trespassory breaking and entering into the dwelling house of another at nighttime with the specific intent to commit a felony or larceny therein. The mens rea requires that the defendant have the specific idea in his/her mind at the time of the entry that he/she intends to commit a theft or felony offense inside the structure. The actus reus requires a breaking and entering into a structure. Each element of burglary must be fulfilled before a defendant may be convicted. Each crime you will learn is likewise made up of "elements" that must be met before one may conclude that a crime has been committed.

Standing apart is the **crime of homicide**, which involves a multi-level analysis. A homicide charge encompasses murder, manslaughter, the statutory degrees of murder, and the felony murder rule. Even though each of these possible charges involve a criminal homicide or killing, each represents a different level of culpability and punishment, depending on the state of mind of the perpetrator.

For example, at common law, murder was defined as the intentional killing of another with malice aforethought. Malice aforethought was said to exist at common law when the actor actually expressed an intent to kill or seriously injure another, or when the actor performed an act that evidenced a depraved heart. Throughout time, the judges, who were dissatisfied with the all or nothing approach of murder, developed lesser gradations of homicide, known as manslaughter. One type of manslaughter was deemed voluntary manslaughter. These were killings where the act was performed intentionally, but without malice aforethought. A second type of manslaughter is known as involuntary manslaughter, where a person unintentionally kills another.

At modern law, the crime of murder itself is divided into degrees. First degree murders are those killings which are premeditated and deliberate, as where poison or bombing is used as the instrument causing death. Second degree murders generally include all murders which are not of the first degree. You will also learn the felony murder rule, which supplants the intent requirement of murder when a person commits a homicide during the course of an inherently dangerous felony.

The defenses to crimes are similar to but different from the defenses you will learn in torts: insanity, drunkenness or intoxication, entrapment, mistake of fact/mistake of law, age, necessity, duress, crime prevention, defense of others, defense of property, and self-defense. Each defense is made up of certain elements or requirements that must be fulfilled before a defense is said to either justify or excuse a criminal act.

For example, the defense of entrapment requires, under the majority rule, that the criminal act is instigated by the police and that the defendant is not criminally disposed to commit the crime. Thus, in most jurisdictions, the court or jury examines the defendant's actual motivation in committing the crime, and whether the defendant was predisposed to commit a crime. However, in a minority of jurisdictions, the test is just the opposite. The court looks to the effect that the police conduct would have upon the average law-abiding citizen. Thus, under this test, it is irrelevant what the defendant actually thought or whether the defendant was predisposed to commit the crime. If entrapment is determined to exist, then the crime is "excused" and the verdict is not guilty.

The key to criminal law is learning the vocabulary, understanding the role of mens rea and actus reus, and being able to identify the crimes and defenses in a given fact pattern.

CONTRACTS

The law of contracts begins with the concept of a legal or contractual relationship – that is, a relationship between two or more parties giving rise to legal rights and obligations. There are three requirements to a legal relationship. They are known as "offer," "acceptance" and "consideration."

The source of contract law includes the common law, the Uniform Commercial Code, that sets forth the law involving the sale of goods, the Restatement of Contracts One and Two (like movies, law books have sequels as well), a model code of contracts law, and of course, the law of your state.

Let's take an example. If you want to purchase a beautiful, original Picasso painting at the local store, what do you do? First, you might make or respond to an offer. An **offer** is simply words, oral or written, which indicate a promise or willingness to perform an act, i.e., "I'll take that painting for $5!" There are certain criteria by which to decide whether an "offer" was made. Generally, the law looks to the language used in the offer, the certainty and definiteness of the terms employed, the inclusion of terms such as price, quantity, time, and place for performance, and whether the offer was communicated to the party intended. These "elements" are similar to the elements of a battery or burglary in that the elements represent requirements that must be proven before an offer is said to exist.

Now, how must your offer to purchase the Picasso be **accepted** in order to form a contract? Again, there is a checklist of elements that must be met for an acceptance to be valid. The accepting party must have known about the offer, the offer must have been communicated to the accepting party, the acceptance must be unequivocal and must be accepted by the offer's terms. If each of these elements are met, a party is said to have accepted the offer.

Also, an offer may be **terminated** or ended before it is accepted. Once again there is a checklist of items to consider: where the offer is rejected, taken back or "revoked" or terminated by law. For example, you may revoke your offer to purchase the painting for $5 by telling the seller, "Deal's off," before the seller accepts. The seller may "reject" your offer of $5 for the Picasso by saying, "I would rather burn this beautiful Picasso than sell it to you for $5"; or, if the Picasso was a forgery, the law would terminate the offer on the grounds of illegality.

Consideration is also required for a legal relationship. Consideration means that both parties must give something up, or change their positions in some way as a result of the transaction entered. In the example above, the seller is parting with a painting, which has value, and the purchaser is giving up $5. Thus both the seller and buyer suffer a legal detriment and receive a legal benefit.

After it is determined that a legal relationship exists, you then consider **defenses to a contract,** including illegal and fraudulent contracts, mistakes made in contracting, when one of the parties is a minor or is insane, unconscionable contracts and the statute of frauds. Like the defenses in contracts or criminal law, the existence of such a defense will "bar" the legal relationship. Each defense is made up of elements that must be proven or disproven through legal reasoning, just like "self-defense."

Thus, if the seller of the Picasso was insane when he sold the painting for $5, the defense of lack of capacity could be raised to "bar" or void the contract. If a mistake was made, that is instead of $5 million the contract erroneously read $5, then under certain circumstances the defense of mistake could be raised. If, on the other hand, the buyer put a gun to the seller's head and said, "I just made you an offer you can't refuse," the defense of coercion or duress might apply. With each defense, the facts must be evaluated to determine whether a given defense applies.

The next area of law involves "conditions." A **condition** is a circumstance that must occur before a duty to perform arises. For example, the buyer of the painting might condition his purchase of the Picasso upon the verification that the painting is authentic. In the event that the condition does not occur, i.e., the painting is determined to be a forgery, the seller is released from the contract.

Conditions may be **excused** in a number of instances, such as where performance is intentionally or negligently hindered, when one party repudiates the intention to perform, when a party knowingly accepts defective performance, the party is disabled or estopped from performing the contract, or when performance become impossible.

Thus, in the example above, if the seller intentionally prevents the buyer's art expert access to the Picasso, thereby precluding a determination of its authenticity, the seller's conduct might be said to "hinder" performance, and the buyer would be released from performing her obligation under the contract. If, on the other hand, the buyer learned that the Picasso was a forgery but insisted on purchasing the painting anyway, the seller has "knowingly accepted defective performance," and the condition that the painting be authenticated would be excused.

Once any conditions have been fulfilled, or have otherwise been satisfied or excused, then it must be determined if the duty to perform has been **discharged.** The list of circumstances where discharge occurs includes: impossibility, frustration of purpose, subsequent agreement of parties, impracticality and the occurrence of a condition subsequent.

Employing the same example, if the painting were destroyed in a fire, then the circumstance of impossibility might operate to discharge the buyer's duty to perform, since the subject matter of the contract no longer exists. Taking a second example, if the seller and buyer mutually agree to call off the deal, then both parties are discharged from their duty to perform.

Less frequently taught in significant detail during first year contracts is the law of **third party beneficiaries, assignment and delegation.** Each of these areas of law sets forth the legal requirements where a party seeks to assign or delegate the duty to perform or the right to receive performance to another party.

If buyer and seller entered a contract for the purchase of the Picasso, seller could assign his right to receive the $5 to another party under certain circumstances. The buyer could delegate his duty to perform, that is pay the $5, under certain circumstances. If, on the other hand, a third party such as an art museum was to benefit from the contract and certain other requirements were met, a third party beneficiary contract might exist. The significance of determining a contract to be a valid assignment, delegation or third party beneficiary contract is that such a finding will decide which parties have legal rights or liabilities under the contract, and which parties do not.

The law of contracts comes full circle with the areas of **breach of contract** and **remedies.** Contract remedies are usually the subject of a more in depth course taken in your second or third year of law school, but your professor will no doubt touch upon what some of the remedies for breach are during your first year.

On the subject of remedies, if the seller of the Picasso failed to deliver the painting as agreed, she would be in "breach" and could be sued for money damages or specific performance. Specific performance is an example of a "remedy" that would entitle the buyer to receive the painting if certain requirements were met. Other contract remedies include rescission or cancellation of the contract, restitution or out-of-pocket damages and reformation or re-writing of a contract.

For some odd reason, the law of contracts is rarely taught in chronological order, that is from offer to breach. Some professors begin the course with remedies, a seemingly bizarre place to start, since one can hardly appreciate the need for a remedy without understanding what a contract is. Another instructor may begin with a discussion of consideration. Regardless of the order in which the material is presented, however, remember how each concept fits in the big picture.

CIVIL PROCEDURE

Civil Procedure is best described as the nuts and bolts of civil practice. You will learn how a law suit is brought and what procedures are required to bring a law suit.

While the order in which your professor will teach each legal concept will vary, it is not uncommon to begin first year Civil Procedure with the concept of jurisdiction. Jurisdiction simply refers to the power of the court. In order to bring a law suit in a particular court, the court must have power over the parties, known as **personal jurisdiction,** and power to hear the subject matter of the case, known as **subject matter jurisdiction. Notice** and **venue** requirements must also be met, which means that the party sued must know about the law suit, and the law suit must be held in a convenient location.

Again, at the risk of oversimplifying the complexities of jurisdiction and its many rules and exceptions, consider the following. If you order another to come over to where you are standing, that person might respond, "No. Make me." Your power to make that person come to where you are standing is similar to the concept of "jurisdiction." The law says that a court may exercise power over a person only if certain requirements must be met. "Subject matter jurisdiction" is the subject of your dispute or discussion. "Notice" is roughly akin to your proclamation demanding that the person come over to where you are standing. "Venue" requires that your meeting occur in a location convenient and practical to both parties.

"Your Honor, I object on the grounds of lack of personal jurisdiction, lack of subject matter jurisdiction, improper venue, inadequate notice, failure to state a claim, untimely amendments, failure to join an indispensable party and I move to interplead, implead, file a class action and remove this case to another court!"

Each of these concepts – jurisdiction, notice and venue – comes with a checklist of issues or questions that must be resolved before any one component may be said to exist. For example, personal jurisdiction requires that either one of the five traditional requirements of jurisdiction be present, or that the defendant have certain "minimum contacts" with the state in which the lawsuit is heard. In analyzing a civil procedure problem, you must also consider whether the case is being brought in state or federal court, since different rules of procedure apply to each.

Other areas of study include the choice of law, i.e., which state's law applies in a given case, joinder of parties and claims, class action suits, intervention, interpleader and impleader.

Some professors begin Civil Procedure with the subject of **pleadings,** encompassing the actual filing of a law suit, from the plaintiff's complaint, challenges to the complaint, the defendant's answer, amendments to the pleadings, discovery devices such as depositions, admissions of facts, documents, interrogatories, mental or physical examinations of the parties, and the subpoena duces tecum.

Civil Procedure also exposes the student to **the trial**, from the demand for a jury trial, pre-trial motions and the pretrial conference, jury selection and jury verdicts, post-trial motions and relief, appellate rights and the doctrines of collateral estoppel and res judicata.

PROPERTY

The law of real property brings with it a unique vocabulary of strange and awkward new words and phrases and the challenge of identifying property interests and their attendant characteristics.

"I'll trade you two easements for a fee simple absolute."

Think about your most treasured possession – a house, car or piece of jewelry, perhaps. If you own it free and clear, it belongs to you. In the language of real property, it would be said that you owned that property in "fee simple" or "fee simple absolute." If that property was to pass upon death only to your children and their children or issue, you would own the property in "fee tail." If you owned the item only for your lifetime, then you would have a "life estate." If you owned the item for a time period measured by another's lifetime, you would own the property "pur autre vie." If on the other hand, you owned the item but it was subject to the possibility of being taken away by another, you would own a "fee simple defeasible." These are examples of the new labels you will learn in real property. Each "label" or term represents a manner or method of holding title in real property.

There are five major categories of ownership interest in land.

The first is land that is **presently owned** or **possessed,** including fee simple absolute, fee tail, life estates, life estates pur autre vie, and fee simple defeasible. The second is known as **leasehold** interests, including various types of landlord-tenant lease agreements and the rights and duties of both the tenant and the landlord. The third major area involves estates that are owned at the same time by more than one person, i.e., "joint tenancy," "tenancy by the entirety" and "tenancy in common." For example, in a joint tenancy, each co-owner owns the whole estate, and the surviving owner takes the entire estate upon the death of the other co-owners. Similar to the study of landlord-tenant law, you will the learn the rights and duties of co-tenants who jointly own such property interests.

Somewhat mystical is the fourth area, called "**future interests,**" which represents land not presently owned, but subject to ownership in the future. Future interests include reversions, remainders, executory interests, contingent remainders and the right of re-entry. For example, if A gives B a life estate in Pinkacre, and upon B's death, the land goes to C, then C is said to own a "remainder." While C does not own Pinkacre while B is alive, C has a future interest in Pinkacre, since he will own Pinkacre upon B's death. Future interests are subject to certain rules limiting the transferability of such land interests: the Doctrine of Merger, the Rule in Shelly's case, the Doctrine of Worthier Title, and the Rule Against Perpetuities.

Incorporeal or **use interests** in land form the fifth area. These include the law of easements, covenants, equitable servitudes, implied reciprocal servitudes and profits. For example, an easement is the right to use another's land, such as having the legal right to use your neighbor's driveway to obtain access to your property.

The final area concerns the law of **fixtures,** or personal property physically connected to the land.

Most introductory real property courses also cover zoning laws, land sale contracts and deeds, recording acts, and adverse possession. **Zoning laws** divide land into districts where certain uses of land are permitted or prohibited. **Land sale contract** law will teach you the requirements of a land sale transaction, and how land is transferred from one party to another. **Recording acts** are laws which require a grantee of land to publicly record his or her interest in land, in order to protect the grantee from other claims on the land. The doctrine of **adverse possession** permits an occupier of land to obtain legal ownership of that land when certain requirements are met.

Do not panic because you are not yet familiar with these terms. That is why you a paying for a legal education. Instead, focus on the big picture and enjoy the previews.

LEGAL WRITING AND RESEARCH SKILLS

As mentioned above, the first year curriculum usually includes a course of legal writing and research skills. In general, these courses teach the student how to begin the meticulous process of researching legal precedent and how to wade through the labyrinth of the law. The student is taught to write like a lawyer, to frame arguments and to cite legal authority. In terms of the written work product, the course assignments may involve writing a demand letter, a memorandum of points and authorities, a motion, an appellate brief, or other document requiring both research and writing skills.

Introduction to the Law School Learning Experience

Part II

Reading and Analyzing the Cases

Example: People vs. Madonna

Example: People vs. Perry

Classrooom Instruction

Briefing the Case

Example: People vs Bart

Example: People vs. Letterman

Example: People vs. Michael

Organizing the Cases and Materials

Outlining

Why Should I Outline?

How to Outline

Developing a Problem Solving Approach

What is a Problem Solving Approach?

Understanding the Law

How to Develop a Problem Solving Approach

Example: Burglary Problem Solving Approach

Applying the Problem Solving Approach to Law School Examinations

Using the "IRAC" to Write Law School Examinations

The Six Steps of Exam Writing

- Reading the Question
- Visualizing the Problem
- Determining How Much Time Per Question
- Determining What Questions are Presented
- Writing Out the Answer
- Reaching A Conclusion

Introduction to the Law School Experience

"Now which shell is the law under?"

The *Law School Learning Experience* is a strange new animal to which most first year students have never been exposed. The teaching process in law school differs radically from that of undergraduate studies in most academic areas. Perhaps the most common teaching method in undergraduate studies is the rote memory process of teaching. The student listens to and absorbs the lectures of his or her professor, jots down notes, reads the texts and is then tested on what was "learned" in class. This learning method requires the student to memorize information and then regurgitate the information relevant to answering the question. Often the answer is black or white, e.g., "How far is the sun from the moon?"

In law school, you are given bits of information, called "rules" or "the law," and then bombarded with a flurry of different factual situations to analyze. This is the often feared "Socratic" method of teaching employed during class. You will be asked to read countless "cases," involving lawsuits brought by real-life litigants, decided by courts of law throughout the centuries, recorded and now used for legal precedents. More often than not, the "rules of law" will conflict with one another, and the reasoning of the court deciding the case will appear as fickle as the weather. The rules of law and cases will be written in a strange new language known as legalese, a hybrid language consisting long, little-known words and fancy Latin phrases.

Rather than be the talisman of the storm, your law school professor will often confuse you by testing you with even more questions, rules of law and exceptions to the rules to consider. This is known as "hiding the ball." While most professors will deny any such intent, law has traditionally been taught in this manner. Instead of handing the student each sacred rule of law on a silver platter, the instructor poses questions about how the law has been applied in various situations. The student is then expected to glean the rules of law from these Socratic lessons. It's very similar to reading one of Aesop's fables, and then asking yourself what the moral of the story was.

Add to this the fact that the "questions" posed by the professor are answered by those sitting along side of you, who usually know as much or less than you do. Finally, you are told that at some point in time, you will sit for a mysterious midterm and final examination that will determine whether you will be a good lawyer, or at least, whether you will make it through the first year of law school.

Sound confusing? Now factor in anxiety, fear, disorganization, lack of confidence (or even worse, blind arrogance), and a host of other negative mental states that prey on the human psyche, and yes, you are in for a strange and unique experience.

This is not meant as a scare tactic or to suggest that your first year studies are unduly difficult or un-doable. Thousands of law students have done it before you, and thousands will do it long after you have become a lawyer. Everyone who graduates from law school learns how to organize the great mass of materials into a problem-solving approach and how to use the approach to solve final exam problems. The key is to have that system at your fingertips <u>before</u> you take the final examinations. Unfortunately, many law students discover the "key" to law school exam writing <u>after</u> their first year of law school, and in some cases, not until they sit for the bar examination.

By now, you may have begun to question the law school learning process. You may wonder why it must be as it is. As you read through this introductory section, remember that law school is designed to teach you **how** to think, not **what** to think. One task of a lawyer is to examine a factual situation and to apply the law and legal reasoning to that situation to reach a conclusion. What better way to teach one to think than by asking him/her again and again to explain himself/herself, to explain "why" a certain conclusion should be reached. While it may sometimes appear illogical, the law school learning process often mirrors the legal challenges you will face as a lawyer.

Now that we have defined the challenge, what is the solution? The solution is that first, you must understand the learning process you will be engaged in for the next three to four years, and then develop a system to digest the great mass of materials into an approach that can be used to solve exam problems. You may be thinking, why not just skip this section and go right to the *Law Charts*, memorize the approaches, and take the examinations? Such a shortcut would short circuit your legal education, because each step in the learning process is critical and builds upon the previous step. Thus, you must master each step in the learning process and build a strong foundation before going onto the next task. Although certain exercises and assignments may seem useless at times, everything has a purpose.

But first, an overview. This chart summarizes the steps involved in the Law School Learning Experience:

A good study plan has seven steps:

READING AND ANALYZING THE CASES

BRIEFING THE CASES

CLASSROOM INSTRUCTION

ORGANIZING THE CASES AND MATERIALS

SECONDARY SOURCES:
Commercial Outlines; Hornbooks; Restatements of Law

DEVELOPING A PROBLEM SOLVING APPROACH

TAKING EXAMINATIONS

Now, a few words about each.

Reading and Analyzing the Cases

One of your first tasks in law school will be to read the class assignments. So what's so mysterious about reading?

While you obviously know how to read, reading the law is a little different from reading a newspaper, magazine or hot romance novel. For one, you are dealing with a new language, i.e., "legalese." Legalese is a strange brew of Latin, old English and altogether strange and foreign words of seemingly unknown origin.

The language of the legal profession is very different from the language lay people use in everyday conversations. No one says, "I contend that your vehicle proceeded into the intersection in a northwesterly direction at a speed in excess of the legal limit!" Most people would say, "Hey, your car was going too fast!" But "legalese" is a language of precise meaning, and you will have to learn this new language in order to understand what judges and legislators are saying in their decisions. This is not to say that you will spend the rest of your life speaking a language that no one understands. Most lawyers do not use legalese when talking to each other or anyone else. But if you are to learn the law, you must learn the language. Keep a legal dictionary handy, and take the time to learn the terminilogy now.

Remember that language is your tool as a lawyer. Words, their use, and more importantly their power are the staples of a lawyer's trade, and much of your career as a lawyer will be spent reading documents, reports, cases, etc. as a trained reader. At the same time, remember that the objective is not to speak in a secret code that no one else understands. You will not impress clients or jurors with fancy ten-dollar words. Your job as an attorney is to make the law accessible to lay people, and that means being able to translate the gobblegook of the law into clear, understandable, common English.

Remember also that a lawyer is a trained reader. A lawyer might read a business contract 15 times with a magnifying glass to make sure it is right. You too, must learn how to be a "trained reader" who not only can read a document quickly, but also determine what information is relevant to solving whatever problem is before you. A lawyer also makes judgment calls about information he or she is reading in deciding what information is relevant or irrelevant to solving whatever problem is at hand.

As you read through cases, you will encounter words you do not understand. Stop and look up each word in a legal dictionary and memorize the definition. If your memory fails you, write the word down, along with an easy-to-remember definition. For example, if you are not familiar with the word "negligence," you might jot down the definition next to it in your notebook. You can then later go back to your notebook and review the new terms that have become part of your "legal" vocabulary.

The appendix of this book contains a glossary of the words and definitions you will need to know, arranged by subject matter. While this list is by no means exhaustive, it will give you a good head start to learning legalese.

Now, a few words about how to read a case.

First of all, what is a case? A case is simply an opinion of a court, explaining what problem or "issue" it had to solve, what rules of law it applied to solving the problem, the reasoning process employed in solving the problem and the conclusion reached. The case involves a dispute, law suit or action between two parties that has been litigated in the court system.

While reading through any case, you will find a number of things, including:

(1) **FACTS:** What happened in the case.
(2) **ISSUES:** What questions the court has to decide.
(3) **RULES:** What the relevant principles of law are.
(4) **APPLICATION OF THE RULES TO THE FACTS:** The legal reasoning of the court and the rationale for its decision.
(5) **CONCLUSION OF THE COURT:**
What the court decides.
(6) **PROCEDURAL HISTORY OF THE CASE:** How the case got to the court which is deciding it.

You should look for each of these components while reading a case. Keep each component in mind and ask yourself, "Is this a fact, issue, rule, etc.?"

Let's take an example:

PEOPLE v. MADONNA
999 Cal.App.3d 666
(1867)

This is an appeal from the trial court after final judgment by court trial. The issue is whether Madonna is guilty of a burglary. On April 14, 1866 at midnight, Madonna went to visit her boyfriend, Sean Penniless. She went into his apartment and found that he was not home. She missed him so much that she broke into his apartment by breaking the window and sliding through the window.

At common law, a burglary is the trespassory breaking and entering into the dwelling house of another at nighttime with the specific intent to commit a felony or larceny therein. At the time of the breaking and entering, the burglary must have the specific intent to commit a felony (i.e., robbery, rape, murder, arson, mayhem, etc.) or a theft within the dwelling house.

The trespassory requirement is met, since there is no evidence that Madonna had the true owner's consent. The breaking and entering element is met here, because Madonna broke a window in order to gain entry and entered Penniless' apartment. Secondly, the "dwelling house" requirement is met since Penniless lives at the place which was the subject of Madonna's act. The "nighttime" requirement is met, because Madonna broke in at midnight. However, the "specific intent" requirement is missing, since Madonna broke into Penniless' apartment to see Penniless because she missed him. There was no intent by Madonna at the time of the entry to commit a felony or a theft.

Madonna was not guilty of burglary. Thus, the judgment and sentence entered by the trial court must be reversed.

First, notice the heading. The heading will tell you a great deal about a case. The name of the case is People v. Madonna. That title immediately tells you that the case is a criminal law case, because criminal cases are ordinarily brought by the "state" or the "People of the state" or "U.S." Because this action was brought by the "People," this is a criminal case in which the defendant, Madonna, was charged with a crime. Next, notice the strange numerals underlying the case. That is known as a case citation or "cite." If you ever collected baseball cards, you probably had some system for organizing your collection. The same is true of "cases." Each case is assigned a "citation." The citation tells you the volume in which the case appears, the name of the series or books it appears in, and the page number. For example, here we have volume 999, the California Appellate Decisions 3rd Series, page 666. Were this a real case, you could look in volume 999, page 666 in the California Appellate Decisions 3rd Series, and you would find People v. Madonna. Finally, the date the case was decided is included in the citation. This case was therefore decided in 1867.

Now, let's look for each of the components of this case, discussed above.

(1) FACTS: **What happened in the case?** The court or author of the case decision outlines the "facts" of the case. You are told that on April 14, 1866, at midnight, a person by the name of Madonna went to visit her boyfriend, Mr. Penniless, but found he was not home. Madonna then broke into his apartment because she missed him, and presumably was arrested and charged with a crime.

(2) ISSUES: **What questions the court has to decide?** The question or "issue" which the court must decide is whether Madonna is guilty of the common law crime of burglary.

(3) RULES: **What the relevant principles of law are.** The court explains that the "rule" of burglary is the trespassory breaking and entering into the dwelling house of another at nighttime with the specific intent to commit a felony or larceny therein. A rule consists of certain requirements or elements which must be proven in order for the rule to be applied. The elements of a common law burglary are: (1) trespassory entry, without the true owner's consent; (2) breaking and entering; (3) dwelling house belonging to another; (4) at nighttime; (5) with the intent or idea of committing a crime amounting to a felony or a theft inside. Each of these elements must be met in order for Madonna to be guilty of a burglary.

(4) APPLICATION OF THE RULES TO THE FACTS: **The legal reasoning of the court and the rationale for its decision.** The court takes each one of the "elements" of the rule and "applies" or compares it to the facts. First, the court says that Madonna's entry was trespassory and without the owner's (Sean's) consent. Next, the court considers whether Madonna did in fact commit a breaking and entering. Thirdly, the court decides whether the dwelling and nighttime requirements are met. Finally, the court "applies" or "analyzes" the intent requirement.

(5) CONCLUSION OF THE COURT: **What the court decides.** After "applying" the rule and its requirements to the facts, the court concludes that Madonna is not guilty of burglary.

(6) PROCEDURAL HISTORY OF THE CASE: **How the case got to the court that is deciding it.** The court tells the reader that the case was decided after a court, or non-jury trial, and that the defendant Madonna is appealing her burglary conviction.

You may be thinking, wow, what a strange way to learn about a rule of law. Why not just tell me what the rule of law is rather than to couch it in an old, moldy case about what happened to Madonna way back in 1866?

As noted above, however, there is a reason for everything. American law is based on stare decisis, which literally means to "stand by" what has already been decided, i.e., "Stand by the law." When people commonly refer to precedent, they are invoking the

legal principle of stare decisis. This also means that in deciding a question or issue, courts will apply or at least consider earlier principles of law, so as to reach a consistent decision. This is especially true when a lower court is bound to follow the decision of a higher court. Thus, studying cases allows the student to study the history and development of a particular rule.

Let's take another example:

People v. Perry
77 Cal.App.3d 22
(1899)

Dela-Street, Chief Justice, writing for the majority:

This is an appeal after Perry's conviction for burglary. The facts are undisputed. Mason Perry was angry at Burger Hamilton and decided to get even. At 3:00 p.m. on January 1, 1896, Perry broke into Hamilton's residence, intending to steal a valuable Criminal Law case book which belonged to Hamilton. Once inside Hamilton's house, Perry was arrested. At trial, Perry was convicted of burglary. On appeal, Perry argues that no burglary was committed because he committed the act during the daytime hours and at most is guilty of trespass. The burglary statute in question states: "Burglary is the trespassory breaking and entering of the dwelling house of another with the specific intent to commit a theft or felony therein."

The issue we must decide is whether Perry committed a burglary.

Burglary is the breaking and entering of a dwelling house of another with the specific intent to commit a theft or felony. At common law, the act constituting a burglary must have occurred at night. However, at modern law, this is no longer required.

Appellant is correct in asserting that at common law, the act constituting burglary must have occurred at night. However, most states – including California – applying modern law, have deleted the "nighttime" requirement. The rationale of the nighttime requirement was that burglars operated only under the cover of night. Because this is not a valid presumption today, we uphold Perry's conviction under the statute. In addition, Perry claims that the statute afforded him inadequate notice, since the statute does not specify nighttime or daytime. We reject this argument because the statute clearly proscribes the conduct forbidden under law.

Further, the state Supreme Court in People v. Earl E. Rizer (1894) 72 Cal.App.3d 111 held that the state legislature intentionally omitted the word "nighttime" from the statutory definition of a burglary. The court recognized that the legislature intended to attach criminal liability to a burglary, whether committed during daylight or nighttime, because of the dangerous nature of the act, and that the common law distinction was no longer valid.

Thus, Perry's conviction is affirmed.
This example demonstrates the principle of "stare decisis." In solving the problem before it, the court refers to a previous case decided by the state supreme court and follows the ruling of the higher court. This example also shows how a court may overrule or reject a principle of law, i.e., the common law definition of burglary, in this case relying on legislative intent.

A second reason why you learn the law through reading cases is that each case will demonstrate various principles of law. Like Aesop's fables, each case may "apply" or analyze one or two or fifty different issues of law. Each legal analysis serves as an example of how someone, i.e., a judge, decided a legal question. Thus, you learn by way of example.

Reading a case is like learning to ride a bike. As you practicing, reading more and more cases, the faster and easier it will be to grasp the essence of the case. Take the time early on to carefully read all assigned cases so as to foster good case reading skills.

Classroom Instruction

Classroom instruction in law school differs significantly from what you have experienced in your previous education. The primary cause of this difference, often identified as a source of discomfort and fear in the hearts and minds of young law students, is the "Socratic Method" of teaching law.

Anyone who has seen the popular law school movie "The Paper Chase" or who has studied Plato's Republic or Greek Socratic dialogues will recall this teaching method.

The Socratic Method is named after Socrates, one of the most admired figures in world history, who taught his disciples by using particular facts to illustrate a general idea. This process, which usually took the form of a conversation between two or more people, would begin with the assumption that each person knew the definition of a concept, idea or rule. That assumption would be challenged through the application of various factual situations.

The Socratic Method effectively exposed the ignorance of those who participated in the process, because each participant's interpretation of the concept, idea or rule was constantly challenged by the others, who insistently asked, "But what if ..."

First year students often fear the Socratic Method of teaching because it is different and it requires intimate student participation. All too often, it is the risk of embarrassment and humiliation that causes the student to dislike the Socratic Method.

For those who would rather jump off a bridge than face the Socratic method, be assured that your fears are unfounded. First, remember that embarrassment and humiliation exist in the mind of the beholder. So what if you cannot answer a question put to you. If you could answer each and every legal question that will be put to you, you'd have a brain the size of the moon, and certainly would not be in need of a legal education. Also, humiliation and hurt pride are a small price to pay for not knowing the answer. When you become a lawyer, the ante for not knowing the answer will rise significantly. It could mean the difference between winning an acquittal or a life sentence for your client, or a million dollar verdict. Because there are no such penalties attached to your success or lack thereof in class discussions, try to participate in Socratic discussions.

As a lawyer, you will often find yourself "thinking on your feet," or "flying by the seat of your pants," when asked a unexpected question by an impatient judge or adversary. The best experience is the kind that's free in the classroom.

Even if you cannot answer the question and somehow feel that you are the worst example of a Socratic victim in all of legal history, humiliation and embarrassment are often our best teachers. Also remember that you will not be graded on your class performance; rather, most law school professors evaluate your performance based solely on a year-end test which is graded anonymously. You are not graded on your ability to answer questions put to you in class.

Of course, no one wants to look like a fool in front of his or her peers. The only solution is to be prepared; after reading the following section on briefing cases, you will know exactly what to do to avoid anxiety and fear over being "called on" in class.

But first, let's take an example of the Socratic Method of teaching.

PROFESSOR: "Well, Mr. Noel Itall, we have discussed the rule of burglary. What does the case of People v. Perry tell us about the nighttime requirement?"

STUDENT ITALL: "The Perry case held that the nighttime requirement of a burglary at common law was no longer a statutory requirement under the State's new burglary statute.

PROFESSOR: "And what did the court base its reasoning upon?

STUDENT ITALL: "Actually two things. The court first recognized that people often commit burglaries in the daytime as well as at night and that the common law requirement that the burglary occur at night was therefore no longer a valid distinction. Secondly, the Legislature intentionally omitted the nighttime requirement in defining the crime of burglary."

PROFESSOR: "Very good, Mr. Itall. I see that you have read the Perry case very closely. But now, let me ask you to assume that the nighttime requirement is still in effect. What if it were dusk? What result would you have in the Perry case if he committed the burglary of Hamilton's residence at dusk?

STUDENT ITALL: "Uh, uh, uh, uh, ooooooohhhhhh, uh, I don't know."
PROFESSOR: "Ah hah, Ms. Smart, please save us from this dilemma!"

STUDENT SMART: "Well, under common law, the time of day would be a question of fact for the jury. Just as there are different shades of gray, there are different shades of dusk. If the hour of dusk was say, darker than daylight, then the nighttime requirement would be present; if, on the other hand, the daylight was more prevalent than the dark, the opposite result could be found."

PROFESSOR: "You don't really believe that babble do you? But let's assume just for purposes of discussion that we assume Ms. Smart to be correct. What if, Mr. Rapp, the burglary occurred during a total eclipse?

STUDENT RAPP: "I don't know. My mind is dark!"

PROFESSOR: "Well, EXCCCCUUUUUSSSE ME for breathing. Ms. Brainz?"

STUDENT BRAINZ: "It would depend on the timing of the burglary relative to the total or partial eclipse . . ."

While the above example certainly exaggerates the ordinary dynamics of a Socratic chat, the principle is illustrated.

Do your best to prepare for class, and when and if you are called upon, participate. Do not be intimidated by the Socratic Method; instead, use it to stretch your mind. If it helps, pretend that you are one of the contestants on a game show, and that the prize is a hot new red Ferrari.

For those of you who abhor the Socratic method of teaching and think it an ineffective means of teaching the law, remember that Socrates himself was put to death in 399 B.C. after he had two opportunities to talk his way out of it. Also, if worse comes to worse – which it won't – and you cannot utter a sound, you can always say, "I pass." This is one difference between law school in the real world, because you cannot say "pass" when asked a question in court. Look upon your participation in the Socratic method as a challenge that will improve your wit, rap and public speaking skills.

Remember that no one was ever born a great public speaker. Public speaking is an acquired skill that improves with time and practice. Famed trial lawyer Ellis Rubin had to overcome a childhood stuttering problem that was so severe that he could not even say his own name. Yet Mr. Rubin prevailed over his handicap through hard work, preparation and practice, and became a maverick defense attorney who has been involved in over three thousand trials.

Briefing the Case

If there is any one rule about briefing a case, it is this: there is no magic method by which to brief a case. The key is finding **A** method, not **THE** method. Keep in mind the purpose of briefing a case: to aid as a study guide in organizing class assignments, to provide a "running" outline or record of cases you have read, and to prepare for class recitation. Also keep in mind that different minds will brief differently; some students will find it necessary to brief in greater detail than others, depending on how one's mind and memory works.

The objective in briefing cases is to organize the facts, issues, rules, application, and conclusion components noted above into a "brief" understandable format. The rationale for briefing is that it is both undesirable and unnecessary for the student to go back and re-read the entire case word for word either before class or before exams. It is much more practical and convenient to have the essence of a case in an organized, succinct, accessible brief.

Remember that a brief is a study tool to be used by you. You will refer to the brief when called upon in class and questioned about a case you read. You may refer to the brief when studying for examinations, or even when drafting your outline or problem-solving approaches. Thus, the brief should be written in a manner that can be understood and used by you.

Probably the most common method of briefing involves separating each component of a case into a simple FIRAC format. FIRAC refers to the components of a legal analysis which you have already learned: Facts, Issue, Rules, Application and Conclusion. In your case brief, you would also include the procedural history of the case and any concurring or dissenting opinions. A concurring opinion is one in which the author agrees with the ultimate conclusion of the majority decision, but writes a separate decision; a dissenting opinion is one in which the author disagrees with the majority and writes a separate opinion to voice his or her opinion.

Because case opinions are written in essay format, it is necessary to search for each of the F-I-R-A-C components. Your goal in briefing a case is to put together a brief summary of the decision in a format that will allow you to instantly refresh your memory as needed.

In identifying the F-I-R-A-C components when reading a case, make sure that you take the time to distinguish between each component. Ask yourself: where are the facts of the case? What is the issue or issues the court must decide? What are the rules of law and so on. These are the same questions a lawyer asks himself or herself when reading a case. As an attorney, you will read thousands of cases in your legal career. It will serve you well to learn how to read cases carefully and correctly.

As you brief more cases, reading a case will become second nature to you, like riding a bicycle. In fact many second and third year students abandon formal case briefing and instead employ a technique frowned upon by many instructors. This technique, known as "book briefing," refers to the method of briefing a case in the margins aligning the text of the case. This method should not be used until the student is well familiar with the process of reading, briefing, and analyzing cases.

Here are a few examples of case briefs, again using "burglary" as an example. This example briefs a simple, single issue case decision:

CASE BRIEF EXAMPLE #1: People v. Bart

FACTS: Bart and Lisa were living together in Homer's castle. One evening, Bart lost his house keys and gained entry into Homer's castle by climbing up the ivy and crawling through an open window. Bart is charged with burglary.

ISSUE: Did Bart commit burglary?

RULE: A burglary is the breaking and entering of the dwelling house of another at nighttime with the specific intent to commit a felony or larceny therein. In order to constitute a burglary, the place which is the subject of the burglary must belong to one other than the burglar.

APPLICATION: A burglary requires that the dwelling house that is the subject of the burglary belong to someone other than the burglar. Here, there is no burglary because Bart resides in Homer's castle and cannot be convicted of burglarizing his own residence.

CONCLUSION: No burglary.

Now let's take a brief which includes procedural history and a dissenting opinion:

CASE BRIEF EXAMPLE #2: People v. Letterman

PROCEDURAL HISTORY: The case is on appeal from Letterman's conviction in the trial court.

FACTS: Letterman broke into Leno's house. He kicked in the door, intending to steal Leno's television. However, Leno was home, watching the "Tonight Show" and scared off Letterman. Letterman fled and never entered Leno 's home and did not take the television. Letterman is apprehended and charged with burglary.

ISSUE: Did Letterman commit a burglary?

RULE: A burglary is the breaking and entering of the dwelling house of another with the specific intent to commit a felony or larceny therein. A burglary is not committed unless there is a breaking or entering. However, the burglar need not actually physically enter the premises. A breaking with the slightest entry, made with the intent to commit a felony or theft, is sufficient.

APPLICATION: Letterman committed a burglary. Letterman's act of kicking in the door constituted a breaking into Leno's residence. The issue here is whether there was an entry. The rule is that the slightest entry is sufficient and that actual physical presence of the burglar is not required. Here the evidence shows that at least Letterman's leg entered Leno's apartment and that is sufficient. That Letterman did not actually carry out his intent to steal is immaterial, as the intent to steal need not be carried out in order to constitute burglary.

CONCLUSION: Conviction affirmed.

DISSENT: (Justice Differently) Dissent, led by Justice Differently, argues that because the trial record is silent as to whether Letterman's leg actually entered the apartment, there is insufficient evidence to uphold the conviction, and the court should reverse the judgment. Dissent notes that while the evidence is on appeal viewed in the light most favorable to the prosecution, inferences cannot be made in the absence of evidence.

Now, let's take a case brief involving more than one issue:

CASE BRIEF EXAMPLE #3: People v. Michael

FACTS: Michael, a musician, rented a studio from Motown for $5.00 a night, from 5:00 to 9:00 p.m. One evening, after leaving the studio, Michael realized he left his glasses at the studio. Not having a key, Michael broke the back window of the studio and took the glasses. Unbeknownst to Michael, he accidentally took Bubble's glasses. Michael is charged with burglary.

ISSUE: Did Michael commit burglary?

RULE: A burglary is the breaking and entering into the dwelling house of another at nighttime with the specific intent to commit a felony or larceny therein.

APPLICATION: It is clear that a trespassory breaking and entering occurred by virtue of Michael's act of breaking into the studio. Michael did not have the owner's consent to be in the studio after his rental time had expired. The studio, however, at common law, would not qualify as a dwelling house since no one resided there. Because the studio was a commercial structure, at common law there would be no burglary. Most states have abrogated this requirement, but provide for a lesser penalty where a burglary of a commercial building is concerned. The nighttime requirement is met, since the breaking occurred in the evening. However, all states have abrogated this requirement. Likewise, the requirement that the structure belong to another is met, since the structure did not belong to Michael. However, the main issue in the case is whether Michael had the specific intent to commit a larceny or felony once he was inside the studio. The specific intent of burglary requires that the defendant intend to commit a felony or larceny inside the structure at the time of the entry. Michael intended to recover his glasses which he had left there, not to steal anything. His act of taking Bubble's glasses clearly constitute a "mistake of fact," which is a defense to the specific intent requirement of burglary.

CONCLUSION: Because of the lack of specific intent, Michael is not guilty.

In each of the examples above, the case brief is structured similarly, listing the facts, issues, rules, application and conclusion. Where the court has more than one issue to decide, the issues are considered and discussed one at a time.

Case brief forms are provided in the Appendix. Case brief form "A" may be used to brief a simple one or two issue case, while case brief form "B" is designed to brief more complicated, multi-issue cases.

Organizing the Cases and Materials

In your quest to understand the law, you will be exposed to an endless supply of books and materials. Case books, horn books, statutes, codes, restatements and commercial outlines are just a few of the new silent friends you'll meet in the years to come. Each source has a role to play and can be used and abused. Thus, a word about each:

CASE BOOKS: These books weigh about ten pounds each and cost an arm and a leg and a foot, but are the "required reading" for the course. If you notice that your arms are getting longer as the semester wears on, it's probably caused by carrying these books from class to class. Case books contain an edited version of cases in a particular subject matter, followed by commentaries, which usually discuss the significance of the case, and other applications of the rules of law. Case books teach by example, that is, by feeding you examples of real-life cases where law was applied. You will ordinarily receive a reading assignment and may be required to read as many as 30-40 pages to prepare for each class. The majority of this reading will involve reading cases.

CLASS NOTES: Some people are better note takers than others, but most people find it necessary to keep notes of their professors' lectures for future reference. Of course, this depends on your professor and the significance your professor places on class material. Some professors test students primarily on what is discussed in class, while others do not. You are, therefore, well advised to find out what your professor expects from you in terms of class attendance as well as knowledge of materials discussed in class. Keep your class notes well organized; it is suggested that you purchase a few notebooks for this purpose. Your class notes will obviously come in handy when determining what your professor expects you to know for the final examination.

HORNBOOKS: Hornbooks are legal treatises, written by recognized experts in the field. Most hornbooks present an in-depth conceptual presentation of the law, including the rules of law, the history or development of the rule and numerous examples of cases and applications of the rules. Rather than relying solely on cases to illustrate a rule of law, hornbooks focus on the concepts underlying the law.

STUDENT OUTLINES: As a first year student, you will be enticed to seek out the winning outlines of those who have gone before you. Students often go to great lengths to create outlines incorporating class materials, cases and lectures; you may even hear whispers about a special "Holy Grail" outline that guarantees any student who sets eyes upon it an "A" grade or better. While a well-written outline may be of assistance in your studies, remember that it is the process of writing an outline that teaches you. It is the mental struggle which accompanies the process of writing out the concepts of law in an organized manner that teaches, not the end product. In other words, writing an outline should be viewed as an essential part of the law school learning process.

COMMERCIAL OUTLINES: Commercial outlines are often denigrated by academicians as a cheap and lazy short cut to learning the law. The first year student is often "warned" not to use outlines and, instead told to read the case book. In reality, commercial outlines are neither "the big bad wolf," nor a substitute for class materials. A commercial outline is merely the substantive law organized in an outline format. Outlines generally contain a conceptual approach to the law, case summaries and examples. If you find outlines helpful, then use them; if on the other hand, you find them unnecessary, or you if prefer to write your own outlines, then do not use them. If you decide to purchase a commercial outline, take the time to find an outline best suited to your needs.

CANNED BRIEFS: "Canned briefs" refer to case briefs of case books, conveniently packaged for student use. The idea behind these briefs is that instead of re-inventing the wheel and briefing cases yourself, you can buy pre-written canned briefs that will save you the trouble. While use of canned briefs are again a personal choice, remember that canned briefs are no substitute for learning how to read and brief cases on your own.

STATUTES AND CODES: Books containing statutes and codes are used primarily as reference materials during the first year of law school, since most instructors rely on the casebook rather than books containing statutory law. The two major sources of law are state law and federal law, although most cities and municipalities also have their own law and codes as well.

RESTATEMENTS: Restatements of the law are exactly that -- restatements of what the law is. These restatements represent the work of educators and lawmakers who have drafted a statement of the law; in many instances, portions of these works have been adopted by the states. These works are highly regarded and are often consulted as reference works.

Given the many different sources you have at your disposal, it is no wonder that the learning of law has been characterized as a "paper chase." Every individual will find some sources more or less helpful than others, so do not feel that you must somehow rely on all or any of the above reference works. The only rule of thumb is that you should use those resources which are helpful and reject those which are not. Do not fall victim to the belief that you must read every single legal book on a given subject in order to truly understand it. Such a mentality will send you on an endless paper chase into oblivion.

Trust your own common sense. Fellow students as well as second and third year students may swear that one given book or outline is "a must" for law school. The problem with such advice is that everyone's advice is generally different, depending on the experience and level of success that the individual has had.

Do not buy every outline or book in existence. Even the best book is useless if it is not read. Carefully scrutinize the materials available to you and only purchase what you really need. In the case of Restatements, Hornbooks and Codes, you usually will find these books at your local law library.

Outlining

An outline is a tool which is used to organize and record your legal studies. Think of an outline as a diary or journal of your daily progress in law school. Outlines will normally contain summaries of cases, notes and quips from your professor's lectures, passages from hornbooks and other secondary sources, and any other miscellaneous information which you think important and relevant.

Why Should I Outline?

Because you will be exposed to a great deal of materials and information, it is extremely helpful to keep a running record of what you have learned. The purpose of outlining is to organize the materials for purposes of exam taking. Your task is to take the materials available to you and reduce them into a form which is easily understood by you and will serve to refresh your memory about what you have learned. Outlining is part of the funneling process of transferring the great bulk of materials into a well-organized summary. This summary will assist you in reviewing what you have learned in preparation for exam taking.

How to Outline

When outlining, remember that there is no right or wrong way to outline. The method by which you outline will be determined by your own thinking process and course curriculum. For example, one person may require a great deal of detail in order to remember a point discussed in class, while another might need only a phrase or word to recall the same point.

Along these same lines, more is not always better. An outline is a summary, not a re-writing of your casebook, and you should strive to be concise and "to the point." Many law students brag about the length of their outlines as if quality were determined by the pound. In the case of outlines, smaller is generally better.

Also, remember that outlining itself is part of the learning process, and no outline, in and of itself, supplies all the answers. Outlining aids you in organizing your understanding of the law; it's like putting a jigsaw puzzle together. The law tends to fit into well defined areas, "tests" and "rules and exceptions." The key is not simply to produce an outline, but to understand how all the pieces of law fit together.

Although no two outlines produced by different people will be identical, there are proven tips which will assist you in drafting an outline that will work for you:

1. USE HEADINGS IN YOUR OUTLINE: If your instructor supplies you with a syllabus, use the syllabus as the headings for your outline; if not, then you may find the table of contents in your casebook a helpful guide to use as headings. Headings are the main subject areas that you will cover in class. Examples of headings for the subject area of "Torts" might be:

I. THE INTENTIONAL TORTS

(A) BATTERY
(B) ASSAULT
(C) FALSE IMPRISONMENT
(D) INTENTIONAL INFLICTION OF EMOTIONAL DISTRESS
(E) TRESPASS TO LAND
(F) TRESPASS TO CHATTELS
(G) CONVERSION
(H) DEFENSES TO INTENTIONAL TORTS

II. NEGLIGENCE

(A) DUTY
(B) BREACH
(C) STANDARD OF CARE
(D) ETC.

III. STRICT LIABILITY

IV. PRODUCTS LIABILITY

V. DEFAMATION

Find a logical way to divide the area of law that you are outlining. The general headings in the examples above would be I- V, representing the various bases of liability in tort law. The sub-headings would be (A)-(D). For example, the subheading for intentional torts represents the various torts where liability is based on intentional conduct.

2. OUTLINE BY SECTION: It may be effective for you to outline by section, as it is sometimes necessary to first gain the overall idea of a particular area of law before you begin outlining. For example, you might outline the INTENTIONAL TORTS section after you have completed reading the entire section. You will have a better idea as how each tort fits into the "big picture" of intentional torts after you have read and studied the entire area of law. But also remember that outlining is an ongoing process, and you should not wait until a few weeks before the exams to begin outlining.

3. BE DISCRIMINATING IN DECIDING WHAT MATERIAL TO INCLUDE: When outlining, do not write a hornbook. You need not include everything anyone in the world has said about a particular rule of law in your outline. Economy of words is always the rule. At the end of the quarter or semester, you do not want a one thousand page outline to review.

4. OBTAIN FEEDBACK ON YOUR OUTLINE: From time to time, you will want to know whether you are on the right track in outlining the materials. Befriend a trusted second or third year student and ask him or her to review your outline to insure that you are not omitting important information in your outline.

5. PERIODICALLY REVIEW YOUR OUTLINE: The purpose of your outline is to provide you with a personalized study aid, so use it! Even the best outline is useless if unused.

Now let's take an example of an outline, again using "burglary" and the cases which we have read in this section.

EXAMPLE OF AN OUTLINE OF BURGLARY:

I. CRIMES AGAINST PROPERTY

A. BURGLARY

1. DEFINED: At common law, a burglary is the trespassory breaking and entering into the dwelling house of another at night with the specific intent to commit a felony or larceny therein.

2. Cases on burglary:

• <u>People v. Madonna</u>:
Court held that no burglary where D entered apartment because she missed her boyfriend. No intent.
• <u>People v. Perry</u>:
Court rejects C/L requirement that burglary must be committed at night; recognizes that modern law abrogated nighttime requirement because burglars do not only operate at night.
• <u>People v. Bart</u>:
Structure which is the subject of the burglary must belong to one other than the burglar.
• <u>People v. Letterman</u>:
Court held that "slightest entry" of D's foot sufficient to constitute "entry" for burglary conviction. Dissent argues insufficient evidence.
• <u>People v. Michael</u>:
Court holds that commercial structure can be the subject of a burglary under modern law; also holds no burglary where D made a mistake of fact, believing that eyeglasses taken belonged to him.

3. Class Lectures: Professor Lurch said that all states have abrogated the "dwelling house" requirement, and instead have laws that give a lesser penalty for commercial or non-residential burglaries.

Professor Lurch also raised questions about possible defenses to burglary:
Voluntary intoxication might be a defense to burglary, since burglary is a specific intent crime.
Mistake of fact, as in the <u>Michael</u> case is a defense as well.
Reclaiming of property is also a defense.
Class discussion: a burglar cannot be convicted of both burglarizing and receiving the same property.

4. Hornbook: LaFave & Scott Criminal Law hornbook - summer home not lived in year-round is considered a "dwelling house."

While your outline will vary in terms of the amount of detail contained in it, it would likely include the same information as the above outline: the rules of law, examples of cases analyzed, important points discussed in class and any other appropriate information.

Although outlines serve a very important role in the law school learning process by providing a tool to keep a running tab of what you have learned, outlines will not give you the ultimate tool you will need to solve law school examinations. For this, you must develop a problem-solving approach.

Developing a Problem-Solving Approach

What is a Problem-Solving Approach?

By now, you're probably wondering what all the fuss over a problem-solving approach is. You may be thinking, geez, what's the big deal? Why is the problem-solving approach shrouded in mystery? Why don't they just tell me how to solve a legal problem?

This final step, and probably the most important step, is rarely discussed in class. As a law student, your class time is spent adrift in the Twilight Zone of the law, reaching and exploring new heights in the application of the law. Flying the fascinating skies of the law is fun as an intellectual pursuit, and is a necessary step in your legal training. But for exam purposes, you will be expected to solve a legal problem. You will be required to "apply" the law that you have learned to a new fact pattern. And all too often, no one will have explained to you the rules of the exam game.

The rules of the exam game are not readily apparent: You will be asked to analyze a new set of facts within a finite time period. It will be your responsibility to ask yourself the questions you will answer, i.e., the issues which are presented. The questions which you are required to answer will not appear on the examination. When writing an essay answer, you must communicate and articulate your answer in an organized, disciplined and logical analysis, stating the applicable rules of the law. You must apply the facts to the law in a lawyer-like fashion and reach a well-reasoned conclusion. Sound vague enough?

The problem-solving approach provides the questions you must ask yourself when presented with a new factual situation.

When you are confronted with a problem, you normally ask yourself a series of questions in order to resolve the problem. For example, if you ask yourself, "What kind of movie do I feel like watching tonight?" you would ask yourself a series of questions to answer that question. First you would consider the facts, that is, "What movies are playing at the local cinema?" After reviewing the titles, you might ask, "Should I see a comedy, drama, romance or action picture?" After that question is resolved, you might also consider who the actors in each movie are. You might go a step further and apply **stare decisis**, and you might base your decision on other movies you have seen involving the same actor or director. After considering various factors, including the time that the movie is being shown, you would reach a conclusion.

This is not to suggest that anyone going to the movies necessarily asks each of these questions, but we are constantly engaged in the process of asking ourselves questions. This same concept applies to the problem-solving approach.

Legal reasoning is such that everyone solving a legal question necessarily asks themselves the same questions. Regardless of whether you are studying law in Anchorage, Alaska or Palm Springs, California, if you were solving a burglary problem, you would necessarily ask yourself the same series of questions regarding whether each of the elements of a burglary were proven. In the exam room, everyone solving the same legal problem should ask themselves the same, identical questions in solving that problem. That is because the law, as it is taught to you during your first year, is a constant. While your response to the question will vary from that of your colleagues, the questions you will ask yourself are identical.

The Law Charts containing the problem-solving approaches in Part III of this book are "checklists" of those questions or issues you would ask yourself in solving any legal problem. Now let's move on to the question of how to develop a problem-solving approach.

Understanding the Law

How do you develop this blueprint to solve any legal problems in a particular subject area? How do you know when you have it right? How do you determine where the rules and exceptions go?

First, you must understand the law conceptually. What this means is that you understand what the rule of law means, what the key elements of the rule are and how to apply the rule to a new set of facts.

For example, consider the common law crime of burglary. What is a burglary? A burglary is one of the crimes in the area of criminal law. A crime requires two things: an "evil" mind, (**mens rea**) and an act (**actus reus**).

The "act" required in a burglary is the trespassory breaking and entering of a dwelling house of another at nighttime. There are five questions that must be asked to determine whether the "act" occurred. First, the defendant must commit trespass. "Trespass" means that the defendant enter the land without the true owner's consent. Second, there must be a breaking, that is, the defendant must physically break into the structure. Third, there must be an entry, however slight. Fourth, at common law, the structure must have been a dwelling house or a place where people lived and slept. But at modern law, a burglary can be committed against a commercial building, and usually a lesser penalty results. Fifth, at common law the burglary must have occurred at night. However, under modern law, this element has been abolished.

The "evil mind" or intent requirement is the specific intent to commit a felony or larceny inside the structure. This means at the time of the entry, the defendant must have the specific idea in his or her mind to commit a felony offense or to steal something inside the house.

If you are able to articulate and understand the above, then chances are you conceptually understand what a burglary is. You are now ready to develop your problem-solving approach.

How to Develop a Problem-Solving Approach

You have read cases on the crime of burglary. You have read about poor Mason Perry, the romantic intent of Madonna, Letterman's slight entry, Bart's search for his house keys, etc. Your professor has taken great pains to give you numerous examples of what is and isn't a burglary. You may have even arisen in the middle of the night, thinking about the crime of burglary. It is now time to put all that you know about burglary into a formula that will solve any burglary problem that may come your way:

Example - Problem Solving-Approach (from Torts Law Chart, Part III)

ISSUE TO BE SOLVED: IS D GUILTY OF A BURGLARY?

WHAT'S THE RULE: **A burglary is the trespassory breaking and entering into the dwelling house of another in the nighttime with the specific intent to commit a felony or larceny therein.**

WHAT **ELEMENTS** MUST BE PROVEN?

(1) Is the entry **trespassory**?

•The entry must be trespassory or without the true owner's consent.

(2) Is there a **breaking** and **entering**?

•There must be some physical entry, however slight, by the perpetrator.

(3) Is the subject of the burglary a **dwelling house**?

•Under common law, the structure had to be a dwelling house where people lived or no burglary was committed.

•Under modern law, a burglary may be committed even though the structure was not a place where people lived (i.e., warehouse, commercial business). However, many states still retain the dwelling house requirement but provide for a lesser penalty where a commercial structure is involved.

(4) Did the structure belong to **one other** than the defendant?

•No burglary is committed if the structure belongs to defendant.

(5) Did the alleged burglary occur **at night**?

•At common law, a burglary could only be committed at night.

•At modern law, the nighttime requirement has been abolished.

(6) Did the defendant have the **specific intent to commit a felony or larceny** inside the structure at the time of the entry?

•Burglary is a specific intent crime, which means that the perpetrator must possess a certain criminal intent when the crime is being committed at the time of the entry.

•The burglary must intend to either commit a felony, such as rape, robbery, murder, mayhem, arson, etc. or a theft in order to be guilty of burglary.

These are the questions you or anyone else must ask in solving the question: "Is the defendant guilty of a burglary?" Each of these six elements represents a question or issue to be resolved before a burglary can be committed.

You will find that every rule of law is made up of issues or questions which must be resolved before the rule is said to apply. Whether you are analyzing a crime, a tort or a contract problem, each rule you apply is made up of a series of questions that must be analyzed in order to reach a solution. The problem-solving approach is simply a checklist of these issues or questions.

As you read through each of the problem-solving approaches contained in the Law Charts in this book, notice the similarities in how each approach is structured. Each approach contains a series of broad questions, which are, in turn, divided into sub-issues, and sub sub-issues. For example, in contracts, the first broad issue is whether there is a legal relationship between the parties. In order to answer this question, it must be determined whether there is a valid offer, acceptance and consideration. In order for an offer to be found, three elements must be met: there must be an objective intent to contract, the offer must be certain as to its terms and the offer must be communicated to the offeree. Likewise, acceptance and consideration require that certain elements be met before a legal relationship is said to exist.

These questions must be asked whenever one is confronted with the issue: "Is there a legal relationship?"

Instead of merely stating the principles of law, the problem-solving approaches present a step-by-step strategy or formula. The problem-solving approach is a formula which can be used to solve any law examination problem.

While the *Law Charts* in this book contain excellent problem-solving approaches, it is highly recommended that you develop your own approach, tailored to the specifics of your professor's curriculum. As with outlining, the value in a problem-solving approach lies in the learning process involved in creating an approach that works for you.

Developing your problem-solving approach is only half the fun. The real challenge is applying the problem-solving approach to a new factual situation, which, by the way, is exactly what you are required to do on most law school examinations.

Applying the Problem-Solving Approach to Law School Examinations

Examinations, are important insofar as your success on them will determine your final grade. This section will show you not only how to apply problem-solving approaches (contained in your *Law Charts*) to an exam question, but also how to articulate a written answer.

Using "IRAC" to write law school examinations

You must become accustomed to an entirely new kind of testing mechanism -- the law school examination. The law school examination is typically a fact pattern that must be analyzed to determine which legal issues are raised. This is known as an "essay-type" examination. Occasionally, students are given short-answer or multiple-choice examination questions as well. However, regardless of the format of the examination, the process of problem-solving is the same.

Essay examinations require a well-organized, logical analysis, which correctly identifies and analyzes each legal issue raised. The writing structure most commonly used both in law school and in practice is known as "IRAC." Like "FIRAC, " "IRAC" stands for:

ISSUE: What is the issue presented for analysis?
RULE: What is the applicable rule of law?
APPLICATION: Apply the rule of law to the relevant facts.
CONCLUSION: Reach a conclusion.

Now let's take an example. Assume that you are deciding what movie to see this weekend. An "IRAC" analysis would read something as follows:

The issue is what movie I should see this weekend. The rule is that I enjoy comedies the best, because they make me laugh and I always have a good time. Applying the rule, the movie, "It's a Wonderful Life" is a comedy. Because it is a comedy, it will make me laugh and I'll have a good time. In conclusion, I will see that movie.

Of course most people do not articulate this type of reasoning when making each and every decision. But on a law school examination, you are expected to explain your reasoning, no matter how tedious or obvious that reasoning might sound. You must take great pains to explain each and every step in your analysis, and articulate all your reasons for reaching a particular conclusion.

This "IRAC" writing structure will force you to cover each and every component of a legal analysis and help you compartmentalize your discussion of each issue presented. "IRAC" will prevent you from forgetting to discuss issues that appear obvious but are necessary to a good exam answer. If you are not a proficient writer, by all means use "IRAC."

You might notice almost immediately when reviewing other model answers that "IRAC" is not followed in every model answer. That is because many students are able to organize and write without the use of structure. This does not mean, however, that you should abandon a formal structure in favor of anarchy. Once again, if you are having difficulty writing an organized analysis, rely on "IRAC" to get you there.

Number one on your list of priorities, right next to waking up in the morning, should be obtaining copies of your professor's past examinations. Try asking the law school librarian for assistance, as most instructors keep their past examinations on file. By the time you sit for your midterm and/or final examinations, you should be well acquainted with your professor's preferred exam writing style.

To become a proficient exam writer, take examinations, again and again and again. Like riding a bike, examinations become easier with time. You will find that with each examination you take, your confidence level and ability will rise.

Remember that there is a world of difference between reading an exam answer and writing out your own answer to a question. It is the process of writing out exam answers that teaches you how to solve problems. It is therefore advisable to write out exam answers to each of the questions presented in this book. After you have attempted to write out your answer, compare your answer with the model answer in this book. Only in this way will you learn how to apply the strategies and techniques in this book.

Now let's turn to an exam question, using the problem-solving approach from the Torts Law Chart and IRAC to solve it:

Mattie and David worked at the Blue Moon detective agency. David and Mattie had their offices in the one story flat, and David sometimes slept in the back room on those days that he was too tired to go home. They had rented the building for nearly six years from Don Smith. Both Mattie and David were licensed private investigators.

One day, Maria Corleone came to the office and asked to speak with Mattie and David. She told them that she had just married a man she was very much in love with, but was somewhat concerned because he led a very mysterious life. She told them that he associated with various "mafia" people and was very secretive about his life. She was beginning to believe that perhaps he was not an insurance agent, as he had told her.

Later that afternoon, during lunch, Gifford Gangster was called by Vito Corleone, who told him to break into the Blue Moon detective agency and steal his wife's file. Vito had learned of his wife's visit to the agency, and feared that she had "talked." Gifford agreed to do the job that night.

At 6:00 p.m., Gifford reached the Blue Moon agency. He had with him the "iron" hand, a mechanical device which could be inserted through a hole in a window and be manipulated by the operator to pick up items and retrieve them.

Gifford went to the window, and cut a hole one foot in diameter with a glass cutter and inserted the "iron" hand.

Using the "iron" hand, Gifford found Maria's file and retrieved it. He brought the file to Corleone, and to their surprise, they found a copy of the video tape of "Godfather Part VI" which belonged to Vito Corleone.

Subsequent investigation by Blue Moon revealed that Don Smith was really Vito Corleone, their landlord.

Is Gifford guilty of burglary?

The "issue" or question raised by this problem is whether Gifford Gangster is guilty of burglary. You must ask yourself each of the questions necessary to determine if each of the elements of a burglary are proven. In articulating your answer, you state each issue, each rule, and then apply the facts to the law explaining your reasoning. Finally, reach a conclusion and then go on to the next issue.

Each issue is discussed separately. Make sure to compartmentalize your discussion of each issue. For example, the first issue is whether there was a trespassory entry by Gifford. This issue should be discussed separately and apart from your discussion of the other elements of a burglary. Students commonly make the mistake of trying to discuss more than one issue at once since issues often overlap or seem too trivial to discuss alone. Though it may appear painfully obvious, take each issue individually, one at a time.

Now how do we apply the facts to the law? The answers to the questions raised by the Torts problem-solving approach are in the facts. Ask yourself, "what do the facts say about this element of burglary?" For example, the second element of burglary requires a breaking and entering. The question presented by these facts is whether Gifford's act of using the glass cutter and iron hand to obtain Maria's file constitutes a breaking and entering. More importantly, application is the process of explaining why a particular conclusion is or is not justified. Now think about it. Is there a breaking? Does Gifford's act of using the glass cutter to cut a hole in the glass constitute a breaking? Why or why not? Because when a person cuts a hole in a structure, the structure is violated, right? Application means that you must explain the reasoning behind your conclusion.

In the following model answer, focus on the application, which is set forth in **bold** type:

<u>PEOPLE v. GIFFORD GANGSTER</u>

<u>Is Gifford guilty of a burglary?</u>

The issue is whether Gifford is guilty of burglary.

Burglary is the trespassory breaking and entering into the dwelling house of another in the nighttime with the specific intent to commit a felony or larceny therein.

(1. Trespassory requirement) The first issue is whether the entry was trespassory. In order to be trespassory, the entry must be without the true owner's consent. **Gifford could claim that no trespass occurred because he entered the office with the building owner's consent. He would argue that because the building was owned by Vito Corleone, also known as "Don Smith," any entry was not only consensual, but at the direction of the true owner. However, because the offices that Gifford entered had been rented to the Blue Moon detective agency, their possessory interest in the premises would be superior to Corleone's. Therefore, because Gifford did not have the tenants' consent, he could not escape a burglary conviction on this basis**. Therefore, this element is met.

(2. Breaking and entering) The second issue is whether there was a breaking and entering. Burglary requires that there be an actual breaking and entering, however slight. **Gifford's act of cutting a hole in the office window with a glass cutter is sufficient to constitute a breaking because he penetrated the structure. As to the entry requirement, while the extent of Gifford's physical entry into Blue Moon's office is limited to the insertion of the "iron" hand, the iron hand was an extension of Gifford's arm. In order to constitute an entry, even the slightest physical entry is sufficient. Here the "iron hand" entered the room, and hence the entry requirement is met.** Thus this element is met.

(3. Dwelling house) The third issue is whether the structure was a dwelling house. Common law burglary requires that the structure be a residence, where people live and sleep. **Gifford would argue that the structure is a commercial building where people work, not sleep. However, the facts indicate that David sometimes slept in the back room on those days that he was too tired to go home. While it is a close question, many courts have held that summer homes and other temporary residences qualify as dwelling houses, and under such a view, this element would be met.** It should be noted that while the dwelling house element was required at common law, most states have eliminated this requirement, or have provided for a lesser penalty where a commercial structure is involved. Therefore the dwelling house requirement is met.

(4. Dwelling House of Another) The fourth issue is whether the structure belongs to another. **Again, the fact that Corleone, Gifford's boss, owns the structure, would not preclude Gifford's liability for burglary since David and Mattie, as tenants, have superior rights to the office.** This element is met.

(5. Nighttime requirement) The fifth issue is whether the "nighttime" requirement is met. At common law, a burglary could only be committed at night. **This might present some problem here, depending on when the sun went down in Los Angeles on the date in question. Here the burglary occurred somewhere around 6:00 p.m. which could mean that it was day, night or dusk.** However, under modern law, the nighttime requirement has been abolished and therefore the absence of this element would not bar Gifford's conviction for burglary.

(6. Specific intent requirement) Lastly, burglary is a specific intent crime, which means that the perpetrator must possess a certain criminal intent when the crime is committed. Stated simply, the perpetrator must not only intend the acts he or she is committing, but also must possess a certain criminal intent while committing the acts.

The specific intent requirement of burglary is that the burglar must intend either to commit a felony, such as rape, robbery, murder, mayhem, arson, etc. OR a theft at the time of the entry. **Gifford did not intend to commit any felony at the time he entered the premises. However, he did intend to commit a theft. Earlier he had been told by Vito Corleone to break into the office and steal Maria Corleone's file, and he did exactly what he was told. Theft was his very purpose in entering the office. His intent is further evidenced by his relationship with Corleone and the use of tools such as the iron hand in perpetrating the burglary.**

Gifford could conceivably claim that no theft was committed, since the only item he found in the file was the video tape, which belonged to his boss Vito. However, he would lose on this issue since he need only have the specific intent to commit a theft at the time of the entry. At the time of the entry, Gifford intended to commit theft by taking the file, and was unaware of the contents of the file.

Because Gifford intended to steal the file at the time of the entry, this element is met.

In conclusion, Gifford would be found guilty of burglary, since all the requirements have been fulfilled.

When reading the model answer, focus on the structure of the question. Each issue is clearly identified, and each element is discussed in a separate paragraph. Each issue is discussed separately, one at a time, and is compartmentalized from the discussion of other issues. The same "IRAC" format is followed relentlessly for each issue.

Also note the use of crutches. "Crutches," like glue, hold the analysis together. Phrases such as "the first issue is," or "the second issue is," assist the writer in organizing the analysis. They also help the writer "get going" when faced with writer's block.

The Six Steps of Exam Taking

The next question you might be asking is how do I get from reading the exam to writing out an answer?

Six Steps of Exam Taking

(1) **READ THE QUESTION** - Read the question carefully for content and determine what facts are relevant to solving the problem.

(2) **VISUALIZE THE PROBLEM** - See the fact pattern come to life and commit these facts to memory.

(3) **DETERMINE WHAT QUESTIONS ARE PRESENTED, APPLY THE PROBLEM SOLVING APPROACH AND CREATE AN OUTLINE** - Determine what particular issues are presented by the problem, apply the problem solving approach (or LAW CHART) and organize your analysis (e.g., outlining).

(4) **MAKE A QUICK JUDGMENT CALL AS TO HOW MUCH TIME TO SPEND DISCUSSING EACH ISSUE** - Divide the number of issues by the available time according to the relative importance of each issue.

(5) **WRITE OUT YOUR ANSWER** - We will focus on basic I-R-A-C to express your answer.

(6) **REACH A CONCLUSION, MOVE ON TO THE NEXT PROBLEM/ISSUE** - Always conclude one way or another; don't be wishy-washy! Also, once you have completed the problem, move on to the next issue or problem once your allotted time is up.

This section focuses on how to articulate your answer in a clear and concise fashion by following the six steps of exam taking:

These steps best represent the most efficient method to solve a law school examination. These six steps will give you a consistent strategy to follow in solving law school questions. Use these six steps to develop a system that works, and once you have mastered the system, follow it religiously.

Now, let's review each step carefully:

(1) READING THE QUESTION

How to Read a Law School Examination

In reading a law school examination, apply the same "how to read" principles discussed earlier. At the risk of reiterating what has already been said, a lawyer possesses the intensity of a trained reader and a scrupulous eye that misses nothing. This principle must be applied with particular vigor and exacting skill when reading law school examinations. Misreading a fact pattern can produce fatal results on a law school examination, because even the smallest error can take the analysis far off course. Even when you become a trained reader, you will still read a law examination problem two or three times in order to master the facts. You must read a law school examination as if your life and happiness depended upon it.

As an attorney, your ability to investigate and ascertain the facts will often determine the success of your case. Every lawyer will go through the facts of a case hundreds of times before presenting his/her case to a jury. Indeed, it is quite difficult to begin solving a problem until all pertinent facts are known to the problem solver.

The typical essay examination will consist of two parts: a fact pattern and interrogatories. The fact pattern consists of a factual situation to which the law is applied. The interrogatories tell the student what issues to focus upon or solve.

Law school examinations typically have interrogatories that raise only the most general issues. For example, in a torts examination, the interrogatory might read, "Please discuss the rights and liabilities of each party" or "What causes of actions exist and what defenses will be raised?" Interrogatories in a criminal defense essay examination might ask, "What crimes were committed and what defenses will each defendant raise?" or "Please discuss the criminal liability of all parties and the defenses which apply, if any." These are "general interrogatories" asking the reader to analyze all legal issues presented by the fact pattern. Of course, your professor may give you specific issues or interrogatories to analyze as well, i.e., "Please determine whether the defense of consent applies."

There are different theories on how to read a law school examination. Some would suggest that the student read the interrogatory first to get a grasp of what is being tested. Others maintain adamantly that the student begin at the top and read straight down to the interrogatories. The point here again is to select a method that works for you and to follow it. If you find that reading the interrogatories helps calm your nerves before reading the narrative portion of the question, then do it! On the other hand, if you are better able to comprehend the question reading from top to bottom, then by all means do it!

Whether you read the question backwards or forwards or sideways, you must learn how to read the question carefully. With each examination you are exposed to, you will find that the speed with which you are able to read through the facts will increase. In time, you will be quite surprised to find that your ability to read and digest information will be quite superior to that of a person without your training and expertise.

What to Read For in a Law School Examination

While the above heading may sound a bit awkward, it means exactly that – when reading a law school examination, you must READ and look for certain things. Remember that reading a law school examination is much different than reading the "National Enquirer." Not only must you read the exam carefully, as noted above, but you must also constantly make judgment calls about the importance and significance of the facts before you. Is this fact relevant, or is it a red herring, i.e., an irrelevant factor thrown in to distract the student? What area of law is this fact relevant to?

As a lawyer, you will be called on constantly to make judgment calls about what is and what is not important, what represents a decision of major significance and what represents a trivial issue. Lawyers are not paid exorbitant hourly rates to recite the law; lawyers are trained to make decisions and judgments based on logical and informed reasoning.

It is best that you begin making these "judgments" and "decisions" immediately. Do not worry if your decisions are not always right. It is better to make a hundred "mistakes" in judgment than never to make any judgment calls at all. Remember, when solving a law school exam problem, you have a problem to solve and must determine which facts are important to solving your problem.

Think of an experienced attorney who is investigating a murder case. The attorney would review each document carefully, looking over police reports, autopsy reports, ballistic reports, and perhaps hundreds of other documents, carefully culling each fact to determine which ones might be relevant to defending or prosecuting the accused. The attorney would visit the scene of the crime and might even re-enact the incident, looking for evidence and other relevant information relating to how the crime may have occurred. The attorney would speak with each available witness to determine what relevant information a witness possessed.

Likewise, you will be called upon to make the same type of judgment calls as you read through a law school exam question. Perhaps every word, every phrase and every sentence is critical to solving the problem; perhaps not. The key is that it is you who must make that determination, no one else.

How Many Times to Read a Law School Examination

The simple answer is, "as many times as necessary." If you must read the exam question fifty times in order to understand it, then read it fifty times. As noted above, speed will come with time. However, it is important that you struggle in the early stages to become accustomed to reading law school examinations.

Even the most learned exam taker may find it necessary to read the exam more than once. Read it once purely for content, to familiarize yourself with the parties and the events that unfold, then read the question again, and ask yourself which facts are relevant to solving the problem.

Remember that what counts is not how many times you read the examination, but whether the facts sink into your memory and thought process as you read it. When reading a lengthy fact pattern, you will invariably find that it takes a great deal of concentration to read it carefully and absorb the information it contains. What you wish to avoid is wasting time referring back to the fact pattern while you are writing out your answer, because you do not have a strong grasp of the facts. Ultimately, it is the quality of the reading, not the quantity, that counts.

How Much Time to Spend Reading the Examination

The obvious answer is, "it depends." But you should devote whatever time is necessary to obtain a firm grasp of the facts. For a one-hour essay examination, you may be well advised to spend from 10-15 minutes reading the question, and another 10 minutes outlining the question, before you begin writing. That would leave approximately 40 minutes to write the examination answer, which in most instances should be more than sufficient time to complete the exam, assuming, of course, that the exam can be completed in an hour's time.

What is important here is that you set aside a certain amount of time that you will spend reading the examination and stick to it. For example, if you are given a three hour examination, with three parts, each of which will require an hour to write, you might decide to spend no more than 20 minutes reading each of the three questions.

Be disciplined. Set time limitations and stick to them like a fly on flypaper.

(2) VISUALIZING THE PROBLEM

The old saying goes, “a picture says a thousand words.” If you look at the cartoons in this book, you may find that the message contained therein is much better conveyed by the illustration than the text that accompanies it. This is because what we think is based on images in our heads, not words. When you think about what you did today, what comes into your mind? Are they words, such as “I went to my Torts class this morning?” or do you have an image of yourself, sitting in your Torts class, scrupulously taking notes?

Unless you are a human version of Webster’s dictionary, you see pictures in your mind. The same principle must be applied to law school exams. You have to see the problem in order for you to truly understand what is going on. Even when you are reading an exciting novel, while the words convey meaning to you, your mind, coupled with your imagination, paints a mental picture. You must consciously apply this same concept to law school examinations.

This step is commonly overlooked by law students, largely due to the students’ unfamiliarity with the exam process and the effect of anxiety, fear, and other emotional states affecting the logical method to solve a problem. You must see the problem occur right in front of you, in the eye of your mind.

This example illustrates the importance of VISUALIZING the problem:

Jed, a millionaire oil tycoon, wanted to buy a special gift for Grannie. He sent for a shipment of killer bees from South Africa, because these bees produced the sweetest honey, which was Grannie’s favorite dessert.

The carrier of the bees, Trans-Bay International, transported the bees from South Africa to Los Angeles. Trans-Bay International specialized in the transportation of exotic animals and insects and used specially designed cages for the transport of these deadly bees. However, on the day that Jed’s bees were shipped, Trans-Bay had depleted their supply of the special cages and instead used a cage intended for local transport of ordinary honey bees.

The wire mesh on these cages had larger holes and were not usually used for the domestic transport of the smaller killer bees.

The bees arrived safely at Los Angeles International Airport. Jed was somewhat concerned because he was aware of section 1233 of the California Health and Safety Code which provides that "any person who transports, attempted to transport, sold or offered to sell or possessed or received" killer bees could face up to 1 year in the county jail and/or a $1000 fine.

Jed's nephew Jethro picked up the shipment of bees at the airport and placed the cage in the back of his van. As he drove home, Mr. Drysdale accidentally rear ended Jethro's van. As a result, the bee cage flew through the front window, and because the holes in the wire mesh that enclosed the bees were too big, the bees escaped. The bees, upon being released from the cage, stung a cat, Bessie, about a block away from the accident, and Bessie, in an insane, rabid rage resulting from the fatal African killer bee venom, bit two-year-old Jonathan. Jonathan's mother, Annie Mae, who was standing only a few feet away from, fell into unconsciousness, striking her head on a rock after witnessing the traumatic event. Normally, such a fall would not have injured a person with a skull of ordinary strength and hardness, but because Annie Mae had weak bone structure, her skull was smashed. Her falling was witnessed by Jane Hathaway, who after hearing Annie Mae cry out for help, simply laughed at Annie Mae and walked away, since she hated Annie Mae. A city ambulance responded immediately, but Annie Mae's injuries were compounded when the ambulance ran out of gas one mile away from the hospital. Later investigation revealed that the gasoline attendant had not filled the tank of gas as requested by the ambulance driver.

Please analyze the rights of <u>all</u> parties, and the defenses that may be raised by each party.

Now isn't that a mouthful? How are you going to remember what is going on? How will you keep the parties straight? How will you compartmentalize each of the many incidents?

There is only one way you will remember: you must see the characters come to life. If you do not know anyone named Jed, imagine that Jed is an actual breathing and living person, who is doing the things stated in the problem. Visualize Jed ordering the bees for Grannie and watch Transbay International as they ship the buzzing bees to this country. See Mr. Drysdale as he crashes into the van driven by Jethro. Watch poor Annie Mae fall to the ground as she watches Bessie bite Jonathan.

Law school professors typically use nondescript names such as "A" or "Mrs. Jones" and "Mr. Smith" in drafting law school exam problems. In visualizing the fact pattern, it helps immensely to think of real live characters in visualizing the fact pattern. Instead of seeing a one-dimensional "A" character, see a living, breathing person named "Andy" or "Art" or "Aardvaark."

Now read the problem again, and visualize each scenario in the problem. After you have visualized each event, commit that event to memory and move onto the next fact. Do not be discouraged if you initially have difficulty remembering each fact, because speed and accuracy will come with time. Think of a face as you see each character, and commit that face to your memory.

Fact visualization is not a concept that is limited to law school examinations. Visualization is an essential tool of any lawyer who is arguing a case to a jury. A courtroom is often devoid of the actual environment in which an event at issue occurred, with the exception of photographs and other demonstrative evidence. How does a lawyer assist a jury in understanding what really happened in a particular case?

A good attorney will not only visualize the problem herself, but will also help the jury see the event through their minds' eyes. Compare the following closing arguments:

"In this case, Annie Mae was injured. She was injured when she saw a cat bite Jonathan. This observation caused her to fall, hitting her head on the ground."

"Annie Mae first looked in front of her, seeing a rabid cat who had been bitten by defendants' deadly bees. The cat was frothing at the mouth, and in a fit of rabidity, lashed out at two-year-old Jonathan, Annie Mae's son. As the cat's teeth bit into Jonathan's flesh, Annie May, feeling the instantaneous fear that her son was in danger, fainted. As she fell from the shock of what she had witnessed, her head violently smashed on the hard sidewalk below her with a tremendous thud."

SEE THE DIFFERENCE? (no pun intended)

One description is as dry as a micro-waved Salisbury steak TV dinner, while the other is as exciting as a dripping, gooey, chocolate sundae with a bright cherry and fluffy whipped cream on top.

This is not to say that you should use visualization as a poetic license to add facts to the fact pattern. Remember that legal problem-solving is not the same as creative writing; a lawyer is strictly limited to the facts before him. A lawyer cannot "make up" facts to suit her case, and the facts of the case are limited by the evidence. Do not add facts to make the fact pattern more interesting or easier to remember.

(3) DETERMINE WHAT QUESTIONS ARE PRESENTED, APPLY THE PROBLEM SOLVING APPROACH AND CREATE AN OUTLINE

After you have read the problem, determined which facts are important to solving the problem, and visualized the problem, the next step is to figure out what questions or legal issues are raised.

As discussed earlier, in solving a legal problem, it is you who must ask yourself what issues of law are presented. How do you know what issues are presented by a particular fact pattern? How do you ask the right question?

As I'm sure some wise person once said: "There are two ways to ask the right question. You can ask the right question, or you can ask every question."

Unless you are Oliver Wendell Holmes reincarnated, or a legal whiz, chances are that you will not always ask the right question when solving a legal problem. What do you do? Do you scream and throw up your hands? Yes. But after you do that, do exactly what is suggested in this book: ask every question, by applying a problem-solving approach.

A problem-solving approach is a checklist of the questions or issues you must ask when confronted with a particular type of legal question. The *Law Charts* in Part III of this book contain problem-solving approaches for each of the five first year subjects. Because the law is a constant, you apply the same law to different fact patterns. While each fact pattern is different, the law which you apply is a constant.

For example, in answering an intentional torts problem, what would be the first question you would ALWAYS ask? You would always ask, "Gee, I wonder what intentional torts may exist?" The second question you would ask is, "Hmm. What torts? Battery? Assault? False Imprisonment? Intentional Infliction of Emotional Distress? Trespass to Land? Trespass to Chattels? Conversion? These are the questions you would ask in answering an intentional torts problem. If you concluded that a battery might have occurred, you would then ask, "Is each element of a battery met?" First, you would determine if an affirmative act occurred. In order to determine that, you would ask whether the defendant acted voluntarily, or whether the defendant's act resulted from coercion, duress or involuntary forces. Secondly, you would ask whether the intent requirement was met. In this regard, you would ask two questions: Did the defendant actually intend to make contact with the plaintiff, or was the defendant substantially certain contact would occur. Thirdly, you would ask whether or not the contact was harmful or offensive to the reasonable person. Fourthly, you would ask if there was actual contact between the defendant and plaintiff, or something closely connected to the plaintiff's person.

Anytime a battery issue was presented, you would ask these questions. It may appear strange to ask each and every question relentlessly. It may seem easier to simply look at the problem and pluck whatever issue is raised from it. However, a lawyer's job is to comprehensively and carefully analyze each and every issue. If you were relying upon an attorney's judgment, you would want your lawyer to consider each and every element of a potential cause of action or defense. In solving an exam problem, you are required to perform a comprehensive analysis.

As your ability to analyze the law improves, you will begin to see the law as a series of tests that must be proven in order for the law to apply. Law is a general rule applied to specific situations. A doctor who is operating on a patient follows a general procedure. The patient might first be anesthetized. Then the doctor checks the patient's readings, and so on. Although the results and solutions might be different depending on the patient, the same procedures are followed in every operation. Like the procedures of an operation, the law is applied step by step, point by point.

The key to learning and understanding how to use the law are the problem-solving approaches. While this book contains *Law Charts* with excellent examples of problem-solving approaches, try to tailor your own, using the approaches in this book as examples. The objective of this exercise is to place the law learned into a problem-solving approach that will solve any legal problem involving that particular area of law. Like the mechanic who cannot learn to fix a car without actually working on one, you cannot truly learn and appreciate the law without applying the law to the legal problems. As you master each subject area, you will feel a great sense of accomplishment and mental prowess. Try it! You will like it!

(4) MAKE A QUICK JUDGMENT CALL AS TO HOW MUCH TIME TO SPEND DISCUSSING EACH ISSUE

Most exams are administered under strict time constraints. Whether you have thirty minutes or three hours to answer a question, you must learn how to allocate your time. Here is a quick and easy plan to follow which will ensure that you complete the exam within the available time.

Before you begin writing out your answer, quickly review your outline and decide how much time you can afford to discuss each issue. Remember that all issues are not created equally, and that some issues are more important than others. Exams test your judgment and your ability to distinguish between minor, medium and MAJOR issues. Get in the habit of categorizing all issues as being minor, medium and MAJOR issues. This will help you prioritize the issues you must discuss in your answer. Then apply the rule of relativity: the relative importance of the issues dictates how much time you will spend discussing that particular issue.

For example, if you only have 45 minutes to answer a particular question, look at the outline and break that 45 minutes among each legal issue you will discuss. If the major issue is whether a battery occurred, you might spent 15 minutes on that issue alone. If a minor issue is whether the defendant consented to the battery, you might limit the time you spend answering that issue to 5 minutes.

By sticking to the time estimates you set, you will learn how to answer any question within the time allotted.

(5) WRITE OUT YOUR ANSWER

Once you have created an outline, you now have a road map to follow. Like a set of good directions, your outline will provide the blueprint for your answer. You should know exactly what you want to say in your answer before you begin writing it. This is because you have already fully analyzed the answer in your outline. Writing out your answer is much easier when you know exactly what it is you want to say.

There are two components to a winning answer: strong application coupled with each of the I-R-A-C components.

Using I-R-A-C

Learning how to integrate each of the I-R-A-C components in your analysis is so important that we have devoted an entire chapter to it. In Part IV, you will learn how to write law school examination answers. You will see that I-R-A-C is the basic building blocks of a good legal analysis.

Remember that your analysis should reflect each of the I-R-A-C components. You should always clearly state the issue, even when it is obvious. This is because you must define the questions you are addressing. The rule must always be included, as you must demonstrate that you can recite the applicable legal principles. Application is really the meat and potatoes of your analysis, so let's take a few moments to discuss this important concept.

What is Application?

Time for another deep breath. You have read the problem carefully, determined what facts are relevant to solving the problem, and determined what questions are presented by the problem by asking the questions in your problem-solving approach. Now you must organize your analysis, apply the relevant facts to the issues presented and articulate an answer. While this sounds nice and easy, application is a skill earned through experience. Applying the facts to the law is the stuff that good lawyers are made of. Application is a skill you must master. But it will take time. You will not become Clarence Darrow, Johnnie Cochran or Clara Foltz overnight.

"TELL ME WHY!"

Application is often portrayed as a mysterious concept that appears only when the magical words, "Abracadabra" are murmured. It is much simpler than that. Application is the process of explaining why the facts in your case demand a certain conclusion. The operative word is "why." Application traces your thought process by explaining WHY the facts either support or do not support a particular conclusion.

Application is often the most difficult concept for students to grasp because most people are not in the habit of explaining themselves. Suppose a friend asks you to the movies. Usually, you will respond in a conclusory fashion, saying either yes or no. Most people do not demand a full, rational and logical explanation for every decision made. However, if you were asked to explain your reasoning, you might say something like this:

The issue is whether I should go to a movie with you. The rule is that I have gone to a movie before with you and did not enjoy myself. The reason why I did not enjoy myself is (1) you had already seen the movie and kept spoiling the suspense by telling me what was going to happen; (2) you kept talking throughout the movie; (3) you didn't share your bon-bons. Therefore, in conclusion, I will not go to the movies with you."

Of course, you would not ordinarily speak in this fashion. But this is what application means. You must explain your reasoning point by point, and you are to presume nothing. Pretend as if you are speaking to a child, who is demanding, "Tell me why!"

One of the most common criticisms of first year exam papers is that a particular analysis is "conclusory," meaning that the student reaches a conclusion without explaining the legal reasoning supporting the conclusion.

Compare the following examples:

An offeree in Arnold's shoes would not consider Roxanne's words to be an offer BECAUSE Roxanne stated that she "might be interested" in selling her car to Arnold for the "right" price. The use of the word "might" indicates indecision and uncertainty. Roxanne would have used command language such as "shall" or "will" if an offer was intended, and a reasonable person hearing those words would believe his assent to it would constitute a binding legal agreement. Roxanne also used the word "interested," which connotes exactly that -- that Roxanne was interested but was not committed to selling her car. A reasonable person hearing the vague subject term "right" price would have no manner of determining what price was intended. Hence, no offer was intended and Roxanne's statement was simply an invitation for an offer.

A conclusory answer would be: **"An offeree in Arnold's shoes would not consider Roxanne's words to be an offer because Roxanne stated that she "might be interested in selling her car for the right price." Roxanne used language which indicated her uncertainty to make an offer. Thus, there is no offer."**

The first answer tells you <u>why</u> a particular result is reached while the second answer fails miserably. The issue addressed by the answer is what a reasonable person would think, hearing Roxanne's statement.

The first answer explains why the statement made by Roxanne is too uncertain and vague to constitute an "offer." Roxanne's statement is dissected word by word, phrase by phrase and the author explains <u>why</u> each word or phrase either supports or disproves the assertion made. The second answer, by contrast, reiterates Roxanne's statement, and reaches the conclusion that the statement is too uncertain, but fails to explain <u>why</u> that is so.

The key word to those who would be conclusory is the word "BECAUSE." As demonstrated in the following example, using the word "because" will force you to explain yourself. If you are writing a conclusory answer, employ the following method:

X's statement did not constitute an offer BECAUSE:

(1) BECAUSE

(2) BECAUSE
(3) BECAUSE

This method of writing will force you to explain your reasoning, thereby avoiding a conclusory answer. Your instructor will grade you primarily on application, not your ability to regurgitate the facts or the law. Application is what you get credit for in law school, and in real life.

Because application is so important, the "application" section of each model examination in this book is set forth in bold type.

(6) REACH A CONCLUSION

As a problem solver, you must reach a conclusion. Ironically, at least on a law school essay examinations, it usually does not matter what conclusion is reached. What is important is you ability to apply the law to the facts and the legal reasoning supporting your conclusion. Unlike mathematics, where one plus one always equals two, you will find that the answer to a legal question is sometimes "gray." It is your ability to distinguish arguments on both sides and raise all appropriate legal arguments that counts, not the ultimate conclusion.

Also, in reaching a conclusion, always conclude your analysis one way or another; do not be wishy-washy! While an issue may be a "close call" requiring discussion of both sides, do not fall victim to perpetual uncertainty. Try to avoid the use of adjectives such as "probably" or "maybe." Remember, you are solving a problem, not creating one.

Now that we have reviewed each step in the examination taking process, let's recap each step:

Six Steps of Exam Taking

(1) **READ THE QUESTION** - Read the question carefully for content and determine what facts are relevant to solving the problem.

(2) **VISUALIZE THE PROBLEM** - See the fact pattern come to life and commit these facts to memory.

(3) **DETERMINE WHAT QUESTIONS ARE PRESENTED, APPLY THE PROBLEM SOLVING APPROACH AND CREATE AN OUTLINE** - Determine what particular issues are presented by the problem, apply your problem solving approach (or LAW CHART) and organize your analysis (e.g., outlining).

(4) **MAKE A QUICK JUDGMENT CALL AS TO HOW MUCH TIME TO SPEND DISCUSSING EACH ISSUE** - Divide the number of issues by the available time according to the relative importance of each issue.

(5) **WRITE OUT YOUR ANSWER** - We will focus on basic I-R-A-C to express your answer.

(6) **REACH A CONCLUSION, MOVE ON TO THE NEXT PROBLEM/ISSUE** - Always conclude one way or another; don't be wishy-washy! Also, once you have completed the problem, move on to the next issue or problem once your allotted time is up.

Follow these six steps religiously and relentlessly in solving every law school exam regardless of whether the problem calls for a multiple choice, essay or short answer. Commit these essential steps to memory until each step becomes second nature to you.

Law Charts

Part III

Torts

Criminal Law

Contracts & Contract Remedies

Civil Procedure

Real Property

TORTS LAW CHART

I. What causes of action exist & are the elements met? Intentional torts, negligence, strict liability, products liability, defamation, or miscellaneous torts?

II. What defenses apply?

III. Do any general considerations exist?

I. INTENTIONAL TORTS:

Intentional conduct by D against P.

ISSUE #1: PRIMA FACIE CASE?

BAF IT TC

BATTERY
ASSAULT
FALSE imprisonment
INTENTIONAL infliction emotional distress
TRESPASS to land
TRESPASS to chattels
CONVERSION

BATTERY -

(1) an affirmative act - voluntary act; absence of mistake, coercion, duress?

(2) w/ intent to touch another - actual intent or intent to a substantial certainty?

(3) resulting in actual harmful or offensive touching of P. Harmful or offensive to the reasonable person? (Exception: Eggshell theory) & actual contact with P?

ASSAULT -

(1) an affirmative act (same as above);

(2) w/intent to place P in apprehension;

Did D actually intend to cause P's apprehension?

(3) of an immediate -here and now!

(4) harmful or offensive touching.

Reasonable apprehension? D's apparent ability sufficient

FALSE IMPRISONMENT-

(1) an act/omission which causes P's confinement to particular area;

(2) w/ intent to confine someone, resulting in;

(3) actual confinement of P (P could not escape by reasonable means);

(4) either awareness of the confinement or injury resulting therefrom.

INTENTIONAL INFLICTION OF EMOTIONAL DISTRESS -

(1) an extreme & outrageous conduct;

(2) w/ intent (purposeful or knowing) to cause severe emotional distress or recklessness w/ regard to such injuries (no transferred intent);

(3) resulting in severe emotional distress (but no actual injury).

TRESPASS TO LAND -

(1) an affirmative intentional act;

(2) which invades the P's possessory interest (actual injury not required);

(3) in land.

TRESPASS TO CHATTELS -

(1) affirmative intentional act;

(2) which interferes w/ P's possessory interest;

(3) in movable personal property;

(4) resulting in injury;

(5) measure of damage: depends on nature of trespass.

CONVERSION -

(1) Act/omission;

(2) w/ intent to assert control over a chattel;
(3) which in fact belongs to P;
(4) resulting in substantial injury to the chattel;
(5) measure of damages; full/fair value of property.

DEFENSES TO INTENTIONAL TORTS
ISSUE #2: DO ANY DEFENSES APPLY

COPS NA

CONSENT
defense of **OTHERS**
defense of **PROPERTY**
SELF-DEFENSE
NECESSITY
ARREST

CONSENT -

(1) Actual consent? (What did P say?)
(2) Apparent consent? (What did P do?)
(3) Implied consent? (Does the law imply consent?)
(4) Informed consent? (What was P told?)
(5) Did D's acts exceed scope of P's consent? (Did D go too far?)
(6) Does P have capacity to consent? (P drunk, minor or crazy?)
(7) Did P consent to criminal act? (Tort please!)
(8) Was consent vitiated by fraud /duress? (P pressured or lied to?)

Defense of OTHERS -

(1) MAJ - D stands in the shoes of the protected party - Was protected party entitled to use same amount of force?
(2) MINORITY - protects actor's reasonable mistake: What amount of force did D believe was reasonable?

Defense of PROPERTY-

(1) Intrusion by other party not privileged;
(2) Actor reasonably believes force necessary to prevent intrusion;
(3) Demand made that intruder stop unless futile;
(4) Force will not cause serious harm.

RECAPTURE OF PROPERTY:

(1) D entitled to immediate possession;
(2) Demand for return made and ignored or futile;
(3) D in fresh pursuit of tortfeasor;
(4) Recapture from dispossessor/3rd party having knowledge.

SHOPKEEPER'S PRIVILEGE:

(1) reasonable grounds for suspicion:
(2) detention for reasonable period;
(3) reasonable non-deadly force;
(4) detention itself reasonable.

PRIVILEGE TO RECLAIM PROPERTY ON ANOTHER'S LAND:

(1) demand for permission to enter made unless futile or emergency circumstances;
(2) entry made in reasonable time and manner.

PRIVILEGE TO RECLAIM LAND:

(1) Self-help not privileged, since other alternatives available (i.e. ouster).

SELF-DEFENSE -

(1) D reasonably believes she is in danger from P;
(2) force used reasonably appears necessary to prevent harm (obj. test);
(3) no deadly force unless danger of death or great bodily injury;
(4) MAJ - no duty to retreat;
(5) No defense for aggressor unless she withdraws.

NECESSITY -

(1) Public Purpose? No liability if to avoid public disaster;
(2) Private purpose? Liable for actual damage;
(3) Abate nuisance - if D owns land affected by actual nuisance, has made immediate demand nuisance be abated and reasonable force is used.

ARREST -

(1) w/ warrant -
(a) if warrant is fair and properly executed.
(2) warrantless-
(a) Felonies (officer can arrest if probable cause exists);
(b) Misdemeanors (if breach of peace and committed in arrestor's presence).

II. NEGLIGENCE:

Careless conduct by D against P. "Breach of duty of due care which is the actual & proximate cause of P's injuries."

ISSUE #1: PRIMA FACIE CASE?
ISSUE #2: APPLICABLE DEFENSES?

(1) DUTY?

Cardozo -(MAJ) Duty owed only to foreseeable P or person in zone of danger.

Andrews -(MIN) Duty owed to all members of society.

Any special duty issue?

COLA APE

duty to **CONTROL** third persons
duty to **OWNER** of land
duty to **LESSEE**/vendee
duty to **AUTO** driver
duty to **AID** others
PRENATAL injuries
negligent **EMOTIONAL** distress

Duty to CONTROL third persons.

RULE: Where D who has actual ability & authority to control 3rd person, duty owed if:
(1) D holds public premises open to public;
(2) D is liable as a parent for negligently failing to control child.

Duty to OWNER of land.

RULE: D's duty depends on character of land & P's status:
(1) Where P outside D's land, no duty of care where injuries caused by natural conditions;
(2) If artificial condition abuts D's land, D has duty to inspect and maintain in safe condition (i.e. excavation ditch);
(3) If D knows or should know of P's presence on land, then duty to warn against artificial condition or dangerous activities;
(4) D liable under attractive nuisance doctrine if D knows/should know that children will trespass and that condition is dangerous to children, children would not realize risk and danger to children outweighs D's burden of eliminating danger;
(5) If P is gratuitous licensee (i.e. comes onto land for own purposes w/D's consent) D has duty to warn re: nonobvious dangers;
(6) If P is an invitee (business visitor) D has duty to warn re: nonobvious dangers, to inspect, and make any dangerous conditions safe.
(7) If public entrants (e.g. firemen, police) enter during regular hours, they are treated as invitees.

> Many cts. reject common law rules and apply reasonable person standard.

Duty to LESSEE/Vendee.

(1) where P outside land, D's duty limited to conditions involving unreasonable risk of harm until transferee has chance to discover/fix condition;
(2) No duty after transfer of possession unless otherwise agreed, but must warn of unreasonable obvious dangers;
(3) (MAJ) D owes no duty to 3rd persons coming on land w/ vendee's/lessee's consent; (MIN) same duty as owed to vendee/lessee.

Duty to AUTO Driver.

D, driver of car, owes duty to P, her passenger,
(1) If passenger paid $ as invitee;
(2) If no $ paid, then passenger is a guest & D must warn of non-obvious defects in car and drive carefully;
(3) Guest statutes under modern law impose liability of driver to guest only where negligence is wanton or gross.

Duty to AID others.

(1) Innkeeper's duty to guest;
(2) Common carrier to customer;
(3) Jailer to prisoner in peril;
(4) If D caused P's peril's or injuries; one who undertakes to aid another must exercise due care. (Rescuer doctrine)

PRENATAL Injuries.

RULE: (MAJ) Duty of care towards viable fetus, while (MIN) extends to nonviable fetus; cts. split over whether wrongful death action exists if fetus stillborn.

Negligent EMOTIONAL distress.

Duty of due care not to subject others to emotional distress which could foreseeably cause them physical injury. No duty towards 3rd persons' distress resulting from fear for another's safety unless 3rd party in zone of danger, 3rd party is a close relative of injured person, & D had knowledge of 3rd party's presence & relationship to injured party.

(2) WHAT IS THE STANDARD OF CARE?

Duty to act as a REASONABLE PERSON would have acted in he same or similar circumstances.

EXCEPTION: Those with special knowledge/disability (e.g. professionals, handicapped, children) held to a like standard. Custom does not establish standard of care, but may be evidence of negligence. Apply standard of care set forth in civil statute, but if criminal, only if statute defines required conduct. Legislature intended to protect class from harm and P is a member of class.

(3) DID THE DEFENDANT BREACH THE STANDARD OF CARE?

(How did D actually act?)

D breaches standard of care that exposes other to unreasonable risk of harm.

Violation of statute: (MAJ) Conclusive presumption of negligence(negligence per se);
(MIN) Rebuttable presumption of negligence.

Res Ipsa **TIP**

(1) **Type** of accident does not occur unless s omeone negligent;
(2) D has exclusive control over **Instrumentality**;
(3) **P** not contributorily negligent.

Effect: (MAJ) inference of negligence; (MIN) rebuttable presumption of negligence.

(4) CAUSATION (Who's fault?)

Cause-in-fact: Was D's conduct a cause of P's injury?
Test: "But for" rule; Substantial Factor Rule.

Proximate cause: Was D's conduct the legal cause of P's injuries?
Test: Direct cause? (no intervening cause) or indirect (intervening cause) cause case, then apply applicable test:

Direct:

(1) Polemis (D is always liable!);
(2) Wagon Mound Modern Trend (D liable for reasonably foreseeable caused consequences);
(3) Restatement (D liable unless highly extraordinary that D's act caused P's injury);
(4) Eggshell Theory (Take your P as you find her).

Indirect:

(1) Dependent (D liable if foreseeable);
(2) Independent (D not liable if unforeseeable);
(3) If reasonable person would not foresee, but intervening cause causes a foreseeable result, D liable unless criminal act, reckless 3rd party takes over or lapse of time after D's conduct.

(5) DAMAGES - proof of actual damages required

Past damages: Medical expenses, lost earnings & pain & suffering.
Future damages: Future medical bills, lost earnings, future pain & suffering.
Caveat: D must mitigate damages & no attorney fees are recoverable.

(6) DEFENSES TO NEGLIGENCE

Contributory Negligence:

If P caused injury & was negligent herself, no recovery, but Last Clear Chance Doctrine allows P to recover if D could have avoided accident but didn't.

Comparative Negligence:
MAJ rejects absolute bar and compares relative negligence of P/D; Pure (P can always recover); 50% (P loses if fault equal to D); 50% or less (P loses if negligence greater than D).

Assumption of the Risk:
If P expressly/impliedly consented to harm, recovery barred if P recognized/understood danger and voluntarily chose to encounter it.

III. STRICT LIABILITY:

Inherently dangerous conduct by D against P "Liability imposed for a breach of an absolute duty to make safe which is the actual and proximate cause of P's injuries."

(1) ANIMALS:
Domestic animal (D must know propensity);
Wild animal(strictly liable for harm)

(2) ABNORMALLY DANGEROUS ACTIVITIES: **VLECS**
(a) **Value** of activity to community;
(b) **Location** of activity;
(c) Risk cannot be **Eliminated** by due care;
(d) Activity is not a matter of **Common** usage;
(e) probability of **Serious** Harm to others.

(3) CAUSATION:
(MAJ) same rules as negligence;
(MIN) not even act of God excuses liability.

(4) DEFENSES:
Assumption of risk but not contributory negligence unless P knew of danger and negligently caused miscarrying activity. Some states apply comparative negligence.

IV. PRODUCTS LIABILITY

PRIMA FACIE CASE:

ME SIN

MISREPRESENTATION (Restatement 402b)
breach of **EXPRESS** warranty
STRICT products liability
IMPLIED warranty
NEGLIGENCE

(1) MISREPRESENTATION UNDER RESTATEMENT 402B:

M-R. M-I-C
(a) **Misrepresentation** of a material fact;
(b) P must **Rely** on the representation in using product;
(c) Representation must be **Made** by D or fairly chargeable against him;
(d) Must be **Intended**/expected to reach a class of which P is a member;
(e) D must be a **Commercial** supplier of chattels.
(f) Damages awarded for personal injury/property loss.

Defenses: Contributory negligence not a defense, but assumption of risk and misuse are.

(2) BREACH OF EXPRESS WARRANTY UNDER UCC 2-313:

Same as above except any seller is liable, but
(a) P, cohabitant and guests can recover for personal injuries;
(b) Extends to anyone who could be expected to be personally injured by goods;
(c) Personal injury, property damage, economic losses recoverable;
(d) Entity can sue.

Defenses: Same as above, but failure to give notice and inadequate warning is also a defense.

(3A) STRICT PRODUCTS LIABILITY (RESTMT 402A)

CUDIFFE

(a) D **Caused** product to be placed on market;
(b) At time D put product on market it contained an **Unreasonably Dangerous Defect;**
(c) P hurt while using product in **Intended** and **Foreseeable** manner;
(d) D **Engaged** in business of selling/supplying product.

(3B) FEASIBLE ALTERNATIVE TEST:

DOC BAT

(a) **Danger** imposed;
(b) **Obviousness** of danger;
(c) **Cost** of improved design/practicality;
(d) **Benefit** of product;
(e) **Alternative** design;
(f) **Technology**.

DEFENSES:

Contributory negligence not a defense but assumption of risk, misuse of product,
not following instructions are:

State of Art Defense?
(a) Did safer mechanism exist?
(b) Why didn't D use it?
(c) Did others use it?
(d) Would use of it at that time adversely affect benefit of product?
(e) Feasibility/scientific knowledge/practicality.

(4) BREACH OF IMPLIED WARRANTIES:

(a) Warranty of merchantability guarantees that goods are fit for ordinary purposes that goods are used where D is a merchant of such goods;
(b) Warranty of fitness for a particular purpose arises if seller recommends particular product after told by buyer of particular needs regardless of whether D is merchant.
(c) Damages: same as in express warranty

Defenses: Assumption of risk, misuses of product, failure to follow directions, failure to complain to seller w/i reasonable time

(5) NEGLIGENCE:

(a) Same analysis as negligence

V. DEFAMATION

Publication to 3rd person by D defaming P, capable of being understood by 3rd persons in defamatory sense, causing damage to P's reputation. Defamation can be slander (oral) or libel (written).

PRIMA FACIE CASE:

(1) Was the matter defamatory?
(TRAD TEST) Exposes P to public hatred, contempt, ridicule;
(RESTMT 2) Adversely affects P's reputation.
If not defamatory on its face, P must explain why.
(2) Did D publish the defamation, intentionally or negligently to a 3rd person?
(Uniform Single Publication Rule-single edition of paper, magazine or book is one publication.)
(3) Was the defamatory matter subjectively understood by at least one third person to be of and concerning P or an exclusive group P is part of?
(4) Causation same as negligence.
(5) Did P suffer damage? If defamation slander or oral then special pecuniary damages required unless slander per se:

BODU
BUSINESS criminal OFFENSE DISEASE UNCHASTITY

If defamation libel or written, then general damages presumed.

DEFENSES TO DEFAMATION:

(1) Absolute privilege?

(a) Truth;

(b) Judicial (must be related)/Legislative Proceeding (Absolutely privileged)/Made to Official(must be related to duty);

(c) Between Husband & Wife;

(d) Made during political broadcast?

(e) Consent?

(2) Qualified privilege (abuse it, lose it)

(a) First Amendment privilege; For public figure, i.e. famous person or voluntary publicity seeker, P must prove constitutional malice(knowledge of falsity or reckless disregard) against media or non-media D; for private person, P must prove negligence and actual damages.

(b) Opinion?

(c) Protection of private interest if reasonable belief that important interest threatened, relevant to protected interest, person hearing stmt. can protect interest, relationship between D & person published to;

(d) Public interest where stmt made to protect legitimate public interest;

(e) Published as report of public proceeding.

(3) Retraction: full/fair retraction will mitigate damages or negate malice but follow retraction statute.

VI. MISCELLANEOUS TORTS:

A. INVASION OF PRIVACY: Four torts:

(1) Intrusion - highly offensive/outrageous intrusion relating to private facts;

(2) Public disclosure of offensive private facts;

(3) Placing P in false light in public eye;

(4) Appropriation of P's name or likeness for commercial advantage.

Defenses: Consent or Newsworthy, but not truth, inadvertence, good faith or lack of malice, 1st Amendment (only in false light or disclosure).

B. NUISANCE:

Public: Unreasonable interference with public interest in use of land that offends public's sense of value.

Private: Unreasonable interference with individual's use of land.

Test: Weigh and balance harm w/ utility of D's conduct.

Defense: Did P come to the nuisance?

C. HARM TO P'S BUSINESS RELATIONS:

Three torts:

(1) injurious falsehood, including disparagement (Publication of false assertion of fact injuring P's economic interest w/ improper intent that is the cause of special damages;

(2) interference w/K (Act by D w/knowledge of K for purpose of interfering w/K right of P);

(3) interference w/ economic advantage: (same as (2) but no K required.)

D. MISREPRESENTATION:

Intentional misrepresentation and negligent misrepresentation:

Misrepresentation of past or present material fact (made intentionally or negligently) and D intends that P will rely on statement, P justifiably relied on statement and was damaged by such reliance.

E. MALICIOUS PROSECUTION; WRONGFUL CIVIL PROCEEDINGS:

Initiation of criminal/civil proceeding w/o probable cause w/malicious intent which terminated in favor of D resulting in actual damage; ABUSE OF PROCESS: D's misuse of legal process for ulterior purpose causing actual injury.

VII. GENERAL CONSIDERATIONS:

A. VICARIOUS LIABILITY:

(1) Parent-child where parent entrusts child w/ dangerous instrumentality, child acting for parent, parent knows and approves of wrongdoing OR fails to exercise reasonable control;

(2) Ownership of vehicle - liable if negligent entrustment to another, if car used in family affair, and owner consent statutes;
(3) Respondeat-superior -master liable for all torts committed by servants w/i course of employment;
(4) Joint enterprise -those who act in concert are liable if committed w/i scope of enterprise.
(5) Dram Shop Acts: Alcohol seller liable for drunk who injures another.
(6) Independent Contractor: Principal is liable if contractor engaged in inherently dangerous activity since the duty is non-delegable.

B. IMMUNITY:

(1) Governmental (liable for ministerial functions);
(2) Charitable immunity (MAJ abolished);
(3) Inter-family immunities (MAJ denied recovery for inter- spousal & parent-child torts, but MIN contra).

C. RECOVERY FOR INJURY TO ANOTHER:

(1) Spouse can recover for loss of services/consortium; injuries to members of family;
(2) While common law actions did not survive death except where personal property involved, statutes allow survival of tort actions after injured's death;
(3) Wrongful death - not at common law but allowed under statute;
(4) Wrongful life (no cause of action)/wrongful birth (yes).

D. MULTIPLE DEFENDANT PROBLEMS:

Ds may be held jointly and/or severally liable for P's injuries:

(1) Several liability - individual liability allowed when logical basis exists for distributing damages among Ds;
(2) Joint liability - each D liable for entire judgement when logical division of damages impossible; some states hold that liability is proportionate to D's fault where D is judged to be less at fault than P or where non-economic damages are at issue.
(3) Satisfaction - full acceptance by P of compensation;
(4) Release - P surrenders claim against party;
(5) Indemnity - D who pays claim may recover from another.
(6) Contribution - all parties are liable.

E. STATUTE OF LIMITATIONS -

Runs from time of injury, not time of D's tortious act or omission.
Medical malpractice - runs from time of discovery.
Modern trend: in all cases, statute begins to run from time of discovery.

CRIMINAL LAW CHART

I. What crimes were committed? (SAC BIMARK PURE CF & HOMICIDE)
II. Are there any defenses that apply? (I DEMAND (my) POPS)

I. IDENTIFY CRIME COMMITTED:

SAC BIMARK ALBERT PURE CF!!
(SEE BELOW)

SOLICITATION:

Inciting another to commit any felony or misdemeanor involving breach of the peace.

Actus reus: instigation or origination of criminal scheme;
Mens rea: specific intent to incite another to commit a crime.
General considerations:
- Vicarious liability (accomplice liability if one solicited either attempts/perpetrates crime);
- Merger (solicitation merges into liability solicitor incurs as conspirator/accomplice);
- Withdrawal (solicitor who withdraws remains guilty of solicitation but avoids accomplice liability).

ATTEMPT:

An act in the direction of perpetrating an intended crime.
Actus reus: Act in the zone of perpetration;
Mens rea: Specific intent to perform or cause an act which, if accomplished, would be the target crime.
General considerations:
- Merger (attempt merges into consummated target offense); withdrawal (MAJ - D's abandonment of plan does not excuse liability; MIN - absolves D if she voluntarily, permanently and successfully abandons criminal project);
- Impossibility (legal impossibility precludes attempt liability, while factual impossibility does not);
- Mistake of fact (no defense).

CONSPIRACY:

A combination or agreement for an unlawful purpose.
Actus reus: Mere act of 2 or more persons combining or joining together to achieve an unlawful goal (MAJ. requires overt act);
Mens rea: actual intent to combine + specific intent to achieve unlawful goal.
General considerations:
- No merger;
- Withdrawal (no defense unless conspirator withdraws before commission of overt act);
- Vicarious liability (Under Pinkerton rule, conspirator liable for any criminal act of co-conspirators in furtherance of conspiracy);
- Wharton's Rule (It takes two to tango: crimes which require two parties cannot be prosecuted as conspiracies);
- Impossibility (Where conspiratorial objective legal, no conspiracy);
- Chain theory: (D's liability extends to acts of any co-conspirator)
- Wheel Theory: (no liability where other people independent conspire w/ confederate).

BATTERY:

Intentional or criminally negligent application of unlawful force to the person of another.
Actus reus: slightest touching;
Mens rea: actual either to contact V or being criminally negligent.

FALSE IMPRISONMENT:

Intentional use of force to confine the person of another.
Actus reus: force and confinement;
Mens rea: actual intent to exert force and achieve confinement.

MAYHEM:

Maiming or disfiguring another w/malice.
Actus reus: causing bodily injury which permanently maims or disfigures another;
Mens rea: presence of actual intent or wanton conduct.

ASSAULT:

"Attempted" battery rule: Act of perpetration
Actus reus: with specific intent of committing an act which would be a battery
Mens rea: (MIN) requires present ability to injure V.
- "Intentional Inducement of Fear" Rule: Menacing act or

gesture with specific intent to produce in another a fear of imminent battery (Mens rea).
General Consideration: Aggravated assault occurs where deadly weapon use or D acts with the intent to murder, rape or maim. No crime of attempted assault.

RAPE:
Sexual intercourse w/ female not his wife when he knows or should know it is w/o consent.
Actus reus: slightest penetration of vaginal area w/o consent;
Mens rea: actual intent to have intercourse or criminal negligence. Statutory rape imposes strict liability if the prosecutrix is under the stated age regardless of consent.

KIDNAPPING:
False imprisonment accompanied by asportation of the V.
Actus reus: false imprisonment coupled with coerced movement of V;
Mens rea: actual intent to asport and confine another.

ARSON:
Malicious burning of the dwelling of another.
Actus reus: any act which causes another's dwelling to burn;
Mens rea: intent that burning take place.

LARCENY:
Trespassory taking & carrying away of another's personal property w/ intent to deprive him/her of it permanently.

BURGLARY:
Trespassory breaking & entering of dwelling house of another at night w/ specific intent to commit a felony or larceny therein.
Actus reus: Any slight physical intrusion into a dwelling house w/o consent;
Mens rea: Specific intent to commit a felony or larceny.

EXTORTION:
Use of threats of future harm w/ specific intent to induce another to relinquish property.

ROBBERY:
Larceny from the person or presence of another by the use of force or intimidation upon him/her.

LARCENY BY TRICK:
The use of fraud to procure a temporary delivery of mere possession of another's property w/ intent to deprive him/her of it permanently.

FALSE PRETENSES:
fraudulent misrepresentation of past or present fact which causes the V to pass title to personal property made w/ specific intent to defraud.

UTTERING:
Offering as genuine an instrument known to be false with intent to defraud.

RECEIVING STOLEN PROPERTY:
Receiving of property knowing it to be stolen w/ specific intent to deprive the owner thereof.

EMBEZZLEMENT:
Conversion of personal property of another by a person in lawful possession (as a result of fiduciary relationship).

LARCENY BY CONVERSION:
Conversion of personal property by a person in lawful possession w/ specific intent to defraud.

FORGERY:
Making of a false writing having apparent legal significance w/ intent to defraud.

II. IDENTIFY APPLICABLE DEFENSES

I DEMAND (my) POPS!!

(SEE BELOW)

INSANITY:

Where mental illness has certain prescribed effects on one's mind, acts otherwise criminal are excused.
Rules:
- M'Naghten Rule: (disease of mind causes a defect of reason such that D lacks ability at time of his actions to know WRONGFULNESS of actions & nature/quality of act);

- Irresistible Impulse: Mental disease makes D incapable of controlling his conduct;
- Durham Test: Crime was the product of mental disease or defect;
- ALI Substantial Capacity Test: Mental disease causes to D lack substantial capacity to appreciate criminality of conduct or conform conduct to requirements of law;
- Diminished Responsibility: Mental illness short of insanity may be asserted in homicide case/specific intent crimes to mitigate culpability/reduce charge.

DRUNKENNESS:

- Involuntary intoxication: defense applies where substance taken because of force, mistake, fraud or medical prescription.
- Voluntary intoxication: applies only to specific intent crimes.

ENTRAPMENT:

One may excuse his/her admitted performance of illegal act (other than one involving serious injury) by showing that s/he did it at the instigation of law enforcement agent.

- MAJ. & FED Rule (focuses D's subjective disposition to commit the crime) v.
- MINORITY Rule (objective effect of police activity on reasonable law abiding person)

MISTAKE:

An honest mistake which negates a mental state w/ respect to any material element of an offense is a defense.

- Mistakes of fact: look to reasonableness of mistake/type of intent required;
- Mistake of law: not a defense unless government has not publicized law or knowledge of law is a material element of offense.

AGE:

- Any person 14 years old and older is criminally responsible;
- those under age 14 are presumed incapable of realizing moral wrongfulness of acts;
- if D under age 7, the presumption is not rebuttable.

NECESSITY:

Conduct which would otherwise constitute an offense is justifiable where physical forces of nature make this necessary to avoid a greater evil.

DURESS:

One may excuse an actus reus (not involving violence to another) performed or caused by showing s/he acted under a threat from another to imminently inflict death or serious bodily harm upon.

(MY)

PREVENTION OF A CRIME:

One is justified in using amount of non-deadly force which reasonably appears necessary to prevent a misdemeanor or felony constituting a breach of the peace, and deadly force may be used to prevent a dangerous felony.

DEFENSE OF OTHERS:

- MAJ holds that D may use the same force in defending another as the person being protected is privileged to use,
- while MIN holds that D may use such force which he reasonably believes is necessary.

PROPERTY DEFENSE:

One is justified in using that amount of non-deadly force which is reasonably necessary to prevent imminent trespass to his/her real or personal property; deadly force not justified unless to prevent intrusion into home.

SELF-DEFENSE:

Innocent person justified in using non-deadly force which seems reasonably necessary to prevent physical attack; deadly force may be used only in response to deadly force. MAJ: imposes no duty to retreat while MIN does unless at home.

CRIMINAL HOMICIDE:

Killing of a human being by another + criminal intent.

(A) Elements of homicide:

Killing of: any voluntary act/omission that causes death.

a human being: baby is human being when it is born alive, i.e., circulation independent of mother; death occurs when there is a permanent cessation of heartbeat/respiration or brain death.

by: Apply torts proximate cause rules; death must occur within 1 year of criminal act (some states extend to 3 years).

another: suicide is not homicide
with criminal intent: D's state of mind determines crime as set forth below.

(B) Common Law Murder:

Homicide committed with malice aforethought:
Criminal homicide +

- actual intent to kill;
- actual intent to inflict grave bodily injury;
- wantonness;
- state of mind one is in while committing inherently dangerous felony - Felony Murder Rule (FMR).

Felony Murder Rule Checklist:

(1) Did an UNINTENDED death occur during crime? (FMR applies to unintentional killings)
(2) Was the crime a FMR FELONY?
(Applies to inherently dangerous felonies: burglary, arson, rape, robbery, kidnapping, sodomy)
(3) Does the MERGER doctrine apply?
(Is purpose of felony underlying FMR totally independent of homicide)
(4) Are all the ELEMENTS of the underlying felony present?
(5) Did killing occur during PERPETRATION of the felony?
(Perpetration ends when felon has escaped by reaching place of seeming safety)
(6) Was the killing a FORESEEABLE result of the felony?
(7) Was the killing act PERFORMED by one of the felons?
CL: Killing could be committed by co-felon, V, police officer or bystander; CA/NY require killing committed by accused/co-felon.
(8) Was the victim an INNOCENT person?
CL: FMR applied to killing of any person, even co-felon. REDLINE (Pa. case): FMR does not apply where felon justifiably shot by police officer; CA and NY require V to be "innocent party" before FMR applies.

(C) Statutory Categories of Murder

- First degree murder: Intentional criminal homicide w/ malice aforethought, premeditation & deliberation; includes felony murders committed during inherently dangerous felonies (burg, arson, rape, robbery, kidnapping, sodomy); any murder committed by means of poison, torture, ambush, bomb.

- Second degree murder: Intentional criminal homicides with malice aforethought but w/o premeditation and deliberation. Includes wanton and depraved heart murders, FMR murders not named above. Residual category which includes all murders which are not first degree.

(D) Manslaughter

- Voluntary manslaughter: an intentional criminal homicide committed w/o malice, i.e. w/ mitigating factors, such as imperfect self-defense, unreasonable mistake of fact, coercion, voluntary intoxication, mental disease, anger, heat of passion (reasonable provocation + inadequate cooling time).

- Involuntary manslaughter: an unintentional homicide committed w/o malice; an intent to inflict non-serious bodily harm or state of mind one is in when s/he is acting in a way that creates grossly negligent risk of death or great bodily injury. Misdemeanor manslaughter rule: accidental killing while engaged in a non-dangerous felony or misdemeanor, that is malum in se, commits involuntary manslaughter.

(E) Defenses to Homicide

COA SIN - CRIME prevention, defense of OTHERS, AGE, SELF-defense, INSANITY and NECESSITY.

CONTRACTS LAW CHART

Preliminary Issue: Does Common law or U.C.C Apply? (U.C.C. Provisions apply to sales of goods, and certain transactions between merchants; Common law applies to all other transactions.)

I. Is there a legal relationship between the parties?
II. If so, do any defenses bar the contract?
III. Are there any conditions which must be fulfilled before the duty to perform arises, and if so, have the conditions been satisfied or excused?
IV. Has the duty to perform been discharged?
V. Has the duty to perform been breached?
VI. Are there any third party beneficiaries, assignment & delegation issues?
VII. What is the remedy for breach? (<u>See</u> Contract Remedies.)

I. CONTRACT FORMATION:

Is there a legal relationship between the parties?

(Offer + Acceptance + Consideration - Defenses)

A. INVITATION FOR AN OFFER -

No legal binding effect

B. OFFER -

Requirements:

• Intent to K - Would reasonable offeree think his/her acceptance would create a contract? TEST: Analyze words used & surrounding circumstances.

• Content - Offer must be certain and definite as to parties, price, subject matter, time, place: quantity (cannot be implied); but output Ks are usually enforceable.

UCC - reasonable price & time for performance may be implied if consistent w/ parties' intent (UCC §2-305; § 2-309).

• Communication - Would reasonable offeree consider it to be a communication?

Termination of an Offer:

If there is an offer, was it terminated before valid acceptance?

• Revocation allowed unless:

• option K supported by consideration;

• reasonable detrimental reliance by offeree;

• UCC firm offer: signed written offer to buy/sell goods that expressly states it will remain open is irrevocable for period stated or reasonable time, but not more than 90 days. (UCC §2-205)

• part performance of unilateral K;

• Rejection by offeree;

• Operation of law: if K illegal, subject matter destroyed, insanity/death of offeror if K not executed; lapse of reasonable time;

• Indirect revocation: unaccepted offer terminates when offeree learns of acts of offeror inconsistent with offer.

C.ACCEPTANCE -

Requirements:
Knowledge of the offer;
Communicated to offeror;
Unequivocal -

> but grumbling acceptance valid;
> silence is not unless previous dealings, intent to K exists, or benefits taken;

• UCC § 2-207 exception: Unless offer makes clear that no change is allowed, modifications viewed as proposals for additions to K, and K deemed accepted; proposal is part of K if: offeror is merchant and does not object, proposal is not inconsistent with K and does not materially alter the K.

Accepted by Offer's terms:

UCC: offer may be accepted by any "medium reasonable in the circumstances" (UCC §2-206).

Unilateral: K must be accepted by performance;

> Notice of performance not required unless requested;

> Under MAJ, bilateral K arises when performance begins.

Bilateral: K must be accepted with a promise & must notify offeror of acceptance. UCC allows acceptance by either performing act or by a timely promise to do so (UCC §2-206(2)).

> Note that general Kors use of sub-Kors bid in its primary bid is not acceptance of the bid.

> MAIL BOX RULE: Where offer expressly authorizes acceptance by mail, acceptance effective upon dispatch while revocation/rejection effective upon receipt. If mode of acceptance used is not authorized, then effective upon receipt.

D. CONSIDERATION -

Requirement:

(Bargained for benefit + legal value) + (Bargained for detriment + legal value) OR unbargained for detriment reasonably incurred (promissory estoppel).

Consideration not required where:

- promise to pay barred legal obligation;
- promise to perform voidable preexisting duty;
- promise to pay for past services where promisee expects payment;
- promise to modify pre-existing K in good faith if both parties agree (UCC §2-209);
- promisor's full performance of illusory K.

> Beware of gifts, past and moral consideration, pre-existing duty to perform, illusory promises.

II. DEFENSES TO K:

If so, do any defenses bar the K?

IF (I) C SCUM

ILLEGAL
FRAUD
(I)
CONSENT, lack of
STATUTE of frauds
CAPACITY
UNCONSCIONABLE K
MISTAKE

ILLEGAL:

- parties in pari delicto (void) but where one party is innocent and K involves a malum prohibitum act, relief in quasi-K is available.

FRAUD:

- in inducement: V realizes that bargain made but consents w/ false impressions given by other party (voidable);
- in execution: V doesn't know K was even made (void).

(I)

CONSENT, LACK OF -

- Duress, coercion: voidable but economic duress not enough unless promisee created situation or actively sought to aggravate situation.

SATUTE OF FRAUDS -

The following Ks must be in writing which contains parties, subject matter, terms & conditions of K, consideration & signature of party to be charged:

> guaranty Ks unless for promisor's benefit;
> Ks for an interest in land;
> K for sale of goods over $500 unless goods already delivered/accepted, pymt. already received/accepted, goods specially manufactured and production begun;
> intangible rights over $5000;
> Ks that cannot be performed w/i 1 year;
> prenuptial Ks;
> written confirmation sent by 1 merchant serves to bind both unless merchant who receives it dispatches written objection w/i 10 days from receipt;
> if injustice would result;
> if part or full performance rendered by one party;
> under (MAJ) K which violates SoF is voidable; (MIN) void.

Contracts not within the statute of frauds include those for specially manufactured goods, goods partially paid for or partially accepted or land sale contracts where party paid all or part of the sales price, where party in possession of property or where valuable improvement was added.

CAPACITY:

> minors: voidable except quasi-K recovery allowed for necessaries;
> mental: voidable if one unable to understand nature and consequences of K, but quasi-K for necessaries (K void if entered into after party judged insane).

UNCONSCIONABLE K:

> where K is one-sided;
> gross disparity between the parties;
> against public policy;
> court can refuse to enforce K in whole/part or may blue pencil (strike unconscionable terms). (UCC §2-302)

MISTAKE:

Mutual: No K if error is grave/material and K executory (Ct. less likely to hold no K if K executed).
Unilateral: Ct. will enforce where non-mistaken party in GOOD FAITH formed commercially reasonable expectation on terms of bargain; if BAD FAITH, then no K!
Transmission error by intermediary: No K if non-mistaken party acts in bad faith.

PAROL EVIDENCE RULE: where parties have reduced their agreement to a final integration, parol evidence is not admissible to vary terms.

TEST:

Is extrinsic (oral or written) evidence as to content of K admissible?
(1) Is there a final writing (intent)?
(2) If so, is the proffered evidence parol? (prior extrinsic evidence)
(3) If so, what is the impact of the parol evidence? If it contradicts, varies or adds to integrated writing it is inadmissible unless it is offered to:

> clarify ambiguous terms;
> show defense to K formation;
> show existence of condition;
> show no final integration;
> show consistent collateral subordinate K that normally would not be included in integrated writing.

UCC: consistent additional terms can be shown by oral evidence unless K has iron clad merger clause or ct. finds the K was intended to be a final & exclusive agreement (UCC §2-202).

III. PERFORMANCE OF K:

Are there any conditions which must be fulfilled before duty to perform arises AND if so, have the conditions been satisfied or excused?

IDENTIFY AND CATEGORIZE CONDITION:

Express condition:

- Does the contract provide for a condition or promise?
- Which party is making the provision?
- if it is the party to perform act, then promise, if it is the party not to perform act, then condition;
- LOOK TO intent of parties (controlling), action of parties, circumstances of case;
- express language ("provided that" "if" "unless" "subject to", terms, subject matter);
- tendency for cts. to find promise, since condition creates harsh forfeiture.
- If ct. finds promise, then failure to perform is a breach.
- What type of express condition?
- Condition precedent: A contingency (other than time) which must occur before present K duty matures. Until condition is satisfied or excused, the promisor has no duty to perform K duties. (e.g. "Performance required if Y earns $ this year.")
- Condition concurrent: A contingency which must be satisfied at the same time that performance is rendered. This condition makes K performances mutually dependent, and there is no duty to perform by either party until satisfied or excused (by simultaneous performance). (e.g. "I agree to give X my car when he gives me $5000.")
- Condition subsequent: A contingency which extinguishes a previously matured (i.e. absolute) duty. Unless the condition ripens, the promisor must perform duty; if condition occurs, then further performance on duty is discharged. (e.g. "I agree to give X $5 a month unless he dates Y.")
- Effect of classifying conditions: The above classifications of a condition will determine whether P-promisee or D-promisor must prove the occurrence or non-occurrence of the condition:

π's Burden: Because P-promisee must show that D-promisor had a present matured duty in order to prove breach, must plead and prove that all conditions precedent or concurrent were satisfied or excused. General allegations are sufficient; D must then specifically plead conditions not satisfied or excused.

D's Burden: D must specifically plead (& prove) existence and ripening of any conditions subsequent discharging his duty.

STRICT COMPLIANCE REQUIRED.

Implied conditions:

- Will the court imply a condition?
- Ct. will imply conditions factually inferable from K as necessary or as matters of good faith and cooperation.
- Test: would a reasonable person believe that parties contracted with the implied understanding that certain facts would exist?

STRICT COMPLIANCE REQUIRED.

Constructive conditions:

- Are any conditions created by operation of law?
- Constructive condition concurrent: each party's performance is a condition precedent to the other's performance. Simultaneous tender of performance is required.
- Constructive condition precedent: one party's performance is a condition precedent to the other's performance where one party's performance is required before the other's or one party's performance is due in stages and other party's obligation can be performed instantly.

SUBSTANTIAL COMPLIANCE REQUIRED.

HAVE THE CONDITIONS BEEN EXCUSED?

PAWDIE

PREVENTION of performance
ANTICIPATORY repudiation
WAIVER
DISABLEMENT
IMPOSSIBILITY
ESTOPPEL

PREVENTION OF PERFORMANCE:

Did promisee intentionally or negligently hinder satisfaction of condition upon which his duties depends?

ANTICIPATORY REPUDIATION:

Did promisee expressly repudiate her intention to perform her K obligations? If so, promisor may treat reputation as a present material breach, excusing all conditions and giving promisor an immediate action on the K.

TEST: Would a reasonable person consider the statement as a present, absolute & unequivocal renunciation of the obligation?

If so, promisor can (1) reject repudiation, telling promisee he still expects performance; (2) treat the anticipatory repudiation as a present breach & sue. (UCC §2-610)

Adequate Assurances of Performance Doctrine: Under UCC & ML, stmts. or acts falling short of disablement or repudiation which raise a reasonable doubt as to promisee's ability or willingness to perform can be dealt w/ by: (1) promisor makes written demand upon promisee for adequate assurance of performance; (2) while waiting, promisor may suspend performance of his own K duties; (3) failure of promisee to respond w/i a reasonable period, not over 30 days, may be treated as repudiation & a present material breach.

WAIVER:

Did promisor knowingly accept defective performance?

If so, this extinguishes non-breacher's right to suspend performance and sue for breach of K. She must perform. If promisee whose duties are conditional tenders his counterperformance knowing that the condition has not been satisfied, the condition is held to be excused by waiver.

DISABLEMENT:

Voluntary disablement is the implied repudiation of a K duty by conduct of promisee prior to the time for performance which manifests intention not to perform. Effect: puts promisee in present material breach.

IMPOSSIBILITY:

Objective impossibility (no one could perform) excuses performance but subjective impossibility (party cannot perform) does not.

ESTOPPEL:

Estoppel occurs when the promisee, by words or conduct prior to the time for satisfying a condition, leads the promisor to believe that he will not insist on satisfaction.

IV. HAS THE DUTY TO PERFORM BEEN DISCHARGED?

IF SIC

IMPOSSIBILITY
FRUSTRATION of purpose
SUBSEQUENT agreement of parties
IMPRACTICALITY
CONDITION subsequent

IMPOSSIBILITY:

Supervening illegality, death or destruction of subject matter of K discharges duty to perform. Objective = discharge; subjective = no discharge, rather breach.

(Destruction Rules & Risk Allocation) C/L - risk of loss on buyer when legal title passes.

UCC - Destruction of specific goods w/o fault of either party discharges both parties. Risk transfers when:

(1) if delivery to specific location not required, then when seller gives to carrier;

(2) if specific location required, when carrier gives goods to buyer;

(3) if no shipment, when seller gives to buyer-merchant, if buyer not a merchant, upon tender of delivery. FOB (free on board): risk passes to buyer upon tender of delivery of name/location; FAS (free along side): seller at own risk until goods alongside vessel; CIF (cost of goods, insurance, freight): risk passes to buyer at pt. of shipment.

Construction K - K duty not discharged if structure destroyed.

UNIFORM ACT: Risk on seller unless buyer has title/possession at time of loss.

FRUSTRATION OF PURPOSE:

Unforeseeable supervening act frustrating or destroying known K purpose.

SUBSEQUENT AGREEMENT OF PARTIES:

> mutual rescission - "let's call it off" UCC requires writing (UCC §2-209);
> subsequent modification;
> novation: mutual agreement to substitute new party in K;
> UCC good faith modification;
> substitute K that discharges old K;
> accord & satisfaction or account stated "alright, let's settle this";
> unilateral discharge by obligee - "you don't have to do it".

IMPRACTICALITY:

Performance excused if more expensive/difficult to render performance then when K was made. Requires unforeseeable circumstance; impractical w/ respect to original K consideration, obligor did not assume risk. UCC - liberal, no foreseeability required.

CONDITION SUBSEQUENT:

Occurrence releases D.

V. IF THERE IS A BREACH, WHAT EFFECT?

Material: aggrieved party gets all foreseeable damages of breach, can rescind K and may thus be suspended from duty, but has duty to mitigate damages.
Minor: aggrieved party must perform but can recover damages for immaterial breach.

VI. THIRD PARTY BENEFICIARIES, ASSIGNMENT & DELEGATION

• DELEGATION

> Identify the issue:
"This is a delegation K because the promisor has delegated his duty to perform to another."

> Label the players:
Delegator = person who makes the delegation.
Delegatee = person to whom delegation made.
Obligee = person to whom performance is due.

> Is this a delegable duty?
Delegation proper only where the obligation is an ordinary commercial obligation and the delegatee is a person of the same reputation/competence as delegator.

> What is the effect?
"If delegatee performs obligation, then the delegator's obligation to obligee is satisfied. Obligee must accept performance of delegatee."

> If delegatee does not perform:
Delegator is liable secondarily to obligee; delegatee is liable to delegator; delegatee is liable to obligee only if obligee is a 3rd party beneficiary.

• ASSIGNMENTS:

> Identify issue:
"This is an assignment K because (assignor) assigned her right to receive performance from (obligor) to (assignee)."

> Label the players:
Assignor: person who makes assignment.
Assignee: person who receives the assignment.
Obligor: person who owes performance to assignor.

> Is it a valid assignment? (three part test)
Did assignor Intend to assign to assignee?
Does the assignment Increase the obligor's duty, e.g. personal service (If so, obligee can refuse to recognize assignment.)

Did the assignee give the obligor notice of the assignment?

> What is the effect of the assignment?
Once obligor receives notice, he must render performance to the assignee.

> If the obligor breaches:
assignee (stepping in assignor's shoes) can sue obligor (subject to any defenses or set offs the obligor would have had against the assignor) and can sue assignor for breach of implied warranty.

> Rescission/revocation of assignment:
Generally, underlying K cannot be modified to the prejudice of the assignee. Assignments for consideration are irrevocable, and gratuitous oral assignments are revocable unless assignee detrimentally relies, receives performance from obligor, and there is a written assignment or token chose delivered to assignee. U.C.C. allows good faith modification.

• THIRD PARTY BENEFICIARIES

> Identify issue:
"This is a third party beneficiary K because (promisor) entered the K with (promisee) for (3rd party)'s benefit."

> Label the players:
Promisor: person who promises to perform.
Promisee: person to whom performance owed.
3rd Party Beneficiary: intended beneficiary of K.

> Is it a valid third-party beneficiary K?
Did the parties intend that 3rd party beneficiary benefit from the K?

> Effect?
3rd party beneficiary has a direct, personal action to remedy breach of promised performance.

3rd party beneficiary can sue promisor, subject to any defenses promisor may have asserted against promisee. But promisor cannot assert promisee's defenses against beneficiary.

3rd party beneficiary has no rights against promisee. Promisee may sue promisor.

CONTRACT REMEDIES LAW CHART

I. What damages are recoverable and what limitations apply?
Common law v. U.C.C.? What is the measure of damages?
II. Is restitution, rescission or reformation available?
III. Can specific performance be obtained?
IV. Land sale, construction and personal service contracts.

I. DAMAGES

A. Standard Measure:

Market Price - Contract Price

B. Consequential Damages:

Damages arising from breach as a result of special needs or position of the buyer may be recovered if:

1. Damages naturally arose from breach;

2. Damages were reasonably w/i the contemplation of both parties at the time the K was entered into. (Did breaching party have knowledge of special circumstances giving rise to breach?) (Hadley v. Baxendale)

C. Incidental Damages:

may recover reasonable costs of reselling or repurchasing goods & shipping, storing or inspecting goods if such costs are reasonable.

D. Nominal Damages:

Where there has clearly been a breach, but there is no proof of actual damage, π is entitled only to nominal damages.

E. Punitive Damages:

NEVER available unless breach of K is malicious or intentionally harmful. Watch out for: BAD FAITH BREACH OF INSURANCE, breach by Employer or when breaching party is in a fiduciary relationship.

F. Limitations on Damages:

1. FORESEEABLE: Consequential damages must be foreseeable under (Hadley v. Baxendale)
2. UNAVOIDABLE: Damages must be unavoidable (duty to mitigate).
3. CAUSAL: Damages must be caused by breach.
4. CERTAIN: Damages must be established w/ certainty.

G. Liquidated Damages Clause:

Parties may fix a sum certain in the event of a breach if:

- damages difficult to determine,
- stipulated figure represents a reasonable forecast of fair compensation for breach and
- LDC cannot be a penalty.

H. UCC:

1. Seller's Remedies:

a. Before Buyer's Acceptance, Seller may:

- withhold goods or stop goods in transit;
- resell to another in good faith & recover difference in price;
- sue for the K price if $ damages are inadequate (no resale price);
- recover K price - market price (if no difference, measure is net profit lost -expenses saved).

b. After Buyer's Acceptance, Seller may:

- Sue for the K Price;
- Reclaim goods if seller learns that buyer is insolvent he can reclaim w/i 10 days of buyer's receipt of goods but 10 day limitation does not apply if buyer gave seller a written misrepresentation of solvency w/i 3 months before delivery.

2. Buyer's Remedies:

a. Before Buyer's Acceptance, Buyer may:

- Demand goods if money damages are inadequate;
- Cancel the K and purchase from another, and recover damages;

• Withhold amount equal to his damages (notice to seller required);
• Claim goods by tendering balance due where seller is insolvent & buyer has paid part of purchase price and
• withhold nonconforming goods as security for damages.

b. After Buyer's Acceptance, Buyer may:
• Accept non-conforming goods at K price but recover consequential/incidental damages;
• Revoke K if there is a substantial breach and where acceptance of goods is induced by reasonable expectation of prompt cure which did not occur OR a latent (undetectable) defect.

c. Buyer accepts by:
• telling seller goods are acceptable;
• failing to reject w/i reasonable time;
• doing any act inconsistent w/ seller's ownership of goods. (If goods are nonconforming buyer can reject or accept in whole or in part.)

3. UCC Duties:

a. Aggrieved party must NOTIFY breacher of breach following PROMPT INSPECTION of goods.

b. If time for performance has not yet passed, seller has chance to CURE if he had reasonable grounds to believe his tender would be acceptable.

c. Buyer must mitigate damages by either following seller's instructions re: non-conforming goods or by making a REASONABLE EFFORT to market goods for sellers account if the goods are PERISHABLE or WILL GO DOWN IN VALUE QUICKLY. Buyer can keep proceeds from sale and apply such proceeds against his damages.

II. RESTITUTION, RECISISION OR REFORMATION AVAILABLE?

RESTITUTION-QUASI K:

Action for unjust benefit received pursuant to unenforceable K available where: Mistake, Fraud, Material Breach, Illegal, Statute of Fraud (SoF) Violation, Impossibility (K rate is maximum recovery), Incapacity, Frustration of purpose.

RESCISSION/CANCELLATION OF K:

"I want out!!" Same grounds as above but equitable defenses apply! π Must elect - can't affirm K and later seek rescission.

REFORMATION:

Reformation of K allowed only where there is a prior valid unambiguous K between the parties & the writing fails to conform thereto as a result of MISTAKE of law or fact or FRAUD.

Defenses: Parol Evidence Rule is not a defense; SoF is not a defense under MAJ, but MIN denies reformation to enlarge land grant; Failure to read is NOT a defense.

III. SPECIFIC PERFORMANCE

REQUIREMENTS

A. Inadequacy of Legal Remedy:

*Damages Speculative/ too small;
*Multiplicity of suits;
*Irreparable Injury;
*Unique Chattel/ Land sale K.

B. Definite and Certain Terms:

The parties must have entered into a K which is sufficiently definite & certain that the court can determine what it must order each party to do.

C. Feasibility:

Specific performance (S/P) not granted where enforcement is unreasonably difficult or where court supervision is required over

a lengthy period.
*Personal Service K: S/P never allowed;
*Land sale K: Historically, if land located outside of jurisdiction, no, but under M/L, yes if court has personal jurisdiction over the parties;
*Construction Ks: generally yes, even though supervision problems exist.

D. Mutuality:

Traditionally specific performance was granted only if D could have obtained like relief had π breached the K (e.g. Could D have obtained specific performance from π at the time K entered into?). Today, most courts reject this view, requiring instead mutuality of PERFORMANCE - court must be satisfied that it can secure π's counter performance under the K.

E. Defenses:

SoF, Laches, Unclean Hands, OR Hardship. (Inadequacy of consideration which is either: (1) Grossly inadequate or (2) coupled with unconscionable K or sharp practices. Adequacy of consideration is tested at date K entered into.)

IV. LAND-SALE, CONSTRUCTION and PERSONAL SERVICE KS

LAND-SALE KS

A. Death of Seller:
Upon death of seller who entered executory land K, title to land passes to beneficiary as personal property, & buyer may seek S/P by joining administrators of seller's estate & heirs.

B. Death of Buyer:
Upon death of buyer, her interest in land passes as real property, & seller may seek S/P by joining administrator & heirs.

C. Risk of Loss due to accident/destruction:
MAJ & C/L: Buyer is regarded as owner in equity from the time K entered into and bears risk of loss. Seller retains legal title subject to the right to convey.

MIN, CA & Uniform Vendor & Purchaser Risk Act: Passes to buyer when he has possession.

D. Buyer's Remedies for Breach of Executory K:
Out of pocket or benefit of Bargain + consequences for delay; S/P w/ abatement; restitution.

E. After Conveyance:
Damages for Breach of covenant; restitution for overpayment.

F. Defaulting Seller can get S/P w/ abatement if breach immaterial.

G. Seller's remedies for buyer's breach of executory K: Market value - K price on date of performance + consequential damages; S/P; Rescission & restitution (must restore any partial payment - damages); Quiet title action.

H. After conveyance: Damages (action at law for the price) & foreclosure of grantor's lien. No S/P or Quasi-K.

I. Defaulting Buyer can get restitution - seller's damage.

J. Fraudulent Seller? Tort = K price - actual value + Punitives; K= Expected value of land - actual value - no Punitives.

CONSTRUCTION KS

A. Builder's Remedies:
1. Before Performance: Builder's lost profits.
2. After Full Performance: Action for the Price or restitution in Quasi K for value of services.
3. After Partial Performance; K price - cost of completion (to builder).

B. Defaulting Builder: May obtain restitution for work performed - owner's damages.

C. Owner's Remedies:
1. If builder abandons after part performance: cost of completion + consequential damages.
2. If builder breaches after substantial performance: Cost of repair or replacement or diminution in value.
3. Restitution/Specific Performance usually denied.

PERSONAL SERVICE KS

S/P never allowed! 13th Amendment involuntary servitude; supervision problems; freedom of association; mutuality.

A. Employer's remedies: Cost of replacing employee's services - mitigation; rescission + restitution if wages advanced.

B. Employee's Remedies: Can sue for K price and has duty to mitigate, but need not TAKE substantially different or inferior employment (or in foreign locale) (Parker v. 20th Century Fox). Restitution allowed where part performance rendered.

> Court will imply negative covenant not to compete where employee breaches and:

1. Legal remedies are inadequate;
2. Employee is a unique service provider;
3. Least drastic means are employed. D only prohibited from that type of work - limited to the geographic zone of competition for a reasonable period of time;
4. In CA, negative covenant enforceable only if services are unique & salary is $6K or more.

1. Watch out for unconscionable Ks amounting to illegal restraint of trade; Blue Pencil rule, and Equitable Defenses apply.

CIVIL PROCEDURE LAW CHART

I. Does the court have personal jurisdiction over the defendant, subject matter jurisdiction over the action and are notice and venue requirements met?
II. Are there any pleadings issues raised?
III. Are the claims/parties properly joined for trial? (Joinder of claims/parties; class action; intervention; interpleader; impleader)
IV. Discovery issues
V. Pretrial Conference
VI. Trial (Right to a jury trial; jury selection; verdicts)
VII. Trial and Post-Trial Motions
VIII. Final Judgment: Res Judicata; Collateral Estoppel; Full Faith & Credit

I. JURISDICTION, NOTICE & VENUE

Before a court may properly hear a case, it must have personal jurisdiction over the parties, subject matter jurisdiction over the cause of action & notice & venue requirements must be met.

PERSONAL JURISDICTION:

(Same test in Federal & State cts)

(1) In personam: gives the ct power over D, enforceable in other states.

(2) In rem: gives the ct power over property located in the state.

(3) Quasi-in rem: gives the ct power to determine the rights of particular persons respecting specific property w/i the ct's control. Minimum contacts are required if the dispute does not involve the attached property.

TRADITIONAL TESTS: Most states allow personal jurisdiction in four situations:

(1) D'S PRESENCE in the state at the time of personal service, (Pennoyer v. Neff), but transient presence w/o more is not enough (Shaffer v. Heitner);
(2) DOMICILE in the forum state (Milliken);
(3) EXPRESS CONSENT to jurisdiction (e.g. by voluntarily appearing, by agreeing under K);
(4) IMPLIED CONSENT (e.g. statutorily conferred, driving car into state, engaging in heavily regulated business) (Hess v. Pawloski);
(5) WAIVER OF JURISDICTIONAL OBJECTIONS (failure to assert jurisdictional defenses in answer or pre-answer motion).

MODERN TEST: "D must have certain minimum contacts w/ the forum state such that maintenance of the suit does not offend traditional notions of fair play and substantial justice." (International Shoe)

CAPFI BLIMFEW

(SEE BELOW)

(1) What is the statutory authority?
Long Arm Statute (some states, including CA): assertion of jurisdiction is proper on any bases not inconsistent with U.S. Constitution; other states have statutes that specify when personal jurisdiction is allowed.
(2) Sufficient Minimum Contacts?

Cause of Action -
Where did cause of action arise?

Activities - Scrutinize these activities in forum state: Quality & nature, systematic v. sporadic, direct v. indirect; dangerous activity?

Purposeful availment - Has D purposefully availed itself of the benefits and protections of forum's laws? (Hanson v. Deckla)

Foreseeability - Could D foresee or expect to defend in the forum state? (WW Volkswagen)

Initiate - Did D initiate contact with forum state?

(3) Fair Play & Substantial Justice:

Burden of Parties - If juris. is asserted what would be the burden on the parties (Economic & time burdens; relative burdens on π & D).

Law - What forum's law will be applied to this case?

Interest of state - in providing a forum for its residents' and protecting health & safety concerns.

Multiplicity of suits - CoA result in total resolution of suit?

Forum - Alternative forum available? Fair & convenient?

Evidence - Where is the bulk of the evidence?

Witnesses - Where are the witnesses & are they available for trial?

DEFENSES: (Challenging personal jurisdiction)

(1) **Special appearance** - where D appears specially to challenge jurisdiction w/o waiving it. If D loses he can appeal or fight the case on its merits, but he cannot w/draw, take a default judgment and collaterally attack the jurisdiction of the ct in a later suit.

(2) **General appearance** - where D appears in ct, waiving all jurisdictional objections.

(3) **No appearance** - where D allows entry of default against him and in the second proceeding to enforce the judgement challenges the jurisdiction of the first ct. While collateral attack permits D to avoid the cost of defending in a distant forum, if his attack fails, he is bound and cannot fight judgment on the merits of the case.

(4) **Limited appearance** - in quasi-in-rem cases, D's liability is limited by the property attached by π. Some cts allow D to make a limited appearance to defend the case on its merits, binding only the property if he loses. Other cts hold that by defending, D is subject to personal juris. & can be held liable for entire judgment.

CHOICE OF LAW?

(What law applies to the case?)

State Law in Fed Ct: Under Erie doctrine fed cts must apply state statutes in case law to non-federal causes and defenses (e.g. state claims) but may apply FED PROCEDURAL RULES, even if those rules would affect the outcome of litigation. If there is a question as to whether conflict is substantive or procedural use BYRD balancing test: (1) How strong is state interest? (2) Federal interest? (3) Different results? (4) Forum shopping? (5) Impact on federalism?

Fed Common Law in Fed Ct: applies to interpretation of federal constitution, statutes, rules whether the case is in federal or state ct & applies where there is fed power over the substance of the action even if no statute has been enacted.

Fed law in state court: state cts must apply fed substantive law & cannot apply procedural rules if these would interfere with the proper application of fed laws.

Fed review of state ct decisions involving fed law: USSC can review any state ct decision involving fed law, provided all state remedies are exhausted.

SUBJECT MATTER JURISDICTION (SMJ)

SMJ IN STATE CT IS STATUTORY.
FEDERAL CT REQUIRES EITHER:

(1) FEDERAL QUESTION - Is a federal question embedded in the cause of action? The fed cts have original jurisdiction of all civil actions arising out of the constitution, laws or treaties of U.S.

(2) DIVERSITY -

(a) Diversity of citizenship (domiciles of all π's must differ from all Ds) OR

* Diversity is determined at time action commenced.
* Corp is a citizen of place of incorp. and principal place of business. Look to domicile & intention to remain.
* Partnership/association are treated as individuals.
* Class actions - only citizenship of named representatives in class considered.
* Representative actions - rep's citizenship considered, not person represented.

(b) Amount in Controversy (more than $75,000 PER π except Federal Interpleader Act more than $500).

* Good faith required.
* A single π may AGGREGATE all claims against a single D. But two or more π, even in a class action suit, cannot aggregate their claims. Each π's claim must exceed $75,000. Nor may a π aggregate claims against multiple Ds.

(3) PENDENT or "SUPPLEMENTAL" jurisdiction - state claim may be joined w/ a substantial federal claim if both claims derive from a common nucleus of operative fact.

> A pendent party claim (e.g. a claim by a party as to whom the only claim asserted does not meet fed. SMJ) may be heard by the ct if it is transactionally related to a claim over which there is juris. and that claim is not based solely on diversity of juris.

(4) ANCILLARY or "SUPPLEMENTAL" jurisdiction - If ct has juris. over principal claim, it can hear ancillary matters (counter claims) if fed claim is substantial and fed & state claim arise from the same transaction or occurrence (STO).

(5) REMOVAL - D may remove case from state to fed ct if there is a fed question OR diversity juris. existed when action filed AND juris. was proper in state ct. where action was brought. If a separate or independent claim is joined with nonremoval claim, the entire case may be removed or remanded.

NOTICE: must be reasonably calculated to appraise interested parties that the action is pending. In personam: personal service is required but mail & publication allowed where practical (TEST: reasonable diligence.) In rem: at least mail. FED: Rule 4.

VENUE: determines which of the courts having SMJ the case may be tried.

Diversity cases: Venue is proper where any D resides if all Ds reside in same state OR where a substantial part of acts took place OR where all Ds are subject to PJ when case commenced.

Fed Question cases: Venue is proper where any D resides so long as all Ds reside in same state OR where substantial part of acts took place OR if requirement met, then in district where any D may be found.

* If Ds reside in different judicial districts in one state, venue is proper in either.
* Corporation - where corp licensed to do business or where it is doing business.
* Action removed from state ct goes directly to fed ct of district in which state action was pending.
* LOCAL ACTION RULE: where action involves title to or injury to real property, action must be tried in forum where property is located. Not applicable to transitory actions (e.g. nuisance; specific performance of land K).

Transfer: Ct can transfer case where venue is improper ONLY to a ct where the action might have originally been brought, and where personal jurisdiction and venue are proper. Test: Interest of justice.

II. PLEADING:
Two types - fact and notice.

FACT: requires statement of facts setting forth CoA or defense in ordinary and concise language.

NOTICE: short and plain statement of the claim showing that pleader is entitled to relief.

> Pleadings must be made in good faith and certified and signed by an attorney.

COMPLAINT: π must be a real party in interest, have capacity & standing to sue; must set forth at least one CoA, special damages, prayer for relief, SMJ in fed ct.

CHALLENGING THE COMPLAINT:

JT PPICSS D

(SEE BELOW)

Lack of **Jurisdiction** over subject matter* or person;
Motion to **Transfer** for improper venue;
Insufficiency of **Process**;
Judgment on the **Pleadings**;
Failure to join an **Indispensable** party*;
Failure to state a **Claim**;
Motion for **Summary** judgment where no triable issue of material fact exists as a matter of law;
Motion to **Strike** irrelevant, impertinent, scandalous allegations;
Motion for more **Definite** statement.
* = These motions cannot be waived.

ANSWER: D may deny π's allegations by asserting general, specific, qualified, denial based on info/belief. Defective denials are deemed admissions. D may also assert affirmative defenses & counterclaims.

AMENDMENT: Pleadings can usually be amended once & amendment is liberally allowed if no prejudice.

*Relation Back Doctrine: If amended complaint arose out of same transaction or occurrence as original complaint it relates back to the filing date of original claim & any statute of limitation (SOL) problem is barred.

*New claim may be added if same transaction or occurrence (STO).

*New parties may be added if given strict or implied notice of action & new parties knew or should have known suit would be brought but for mistake concerning identity of true party. A "mistake" occurs where misnomer, excusable neglect, where D misled π, or where there is an identity of interest between D & π.

VARIANCE: Where unpleaded issues arise at trial, amendment allowed if no surprise or prejudice would result.

III. JOINDER OF PARTIES & CLAIMS

PARTIES:

(1) Permissive - party which has some interest in CoA & joinder is convenient may be joined if claim arises out of STO & common ?s of fact or law exist and all juris. req. met.

(2) Necessary - available party whose joinder is desirable to enable ct to grant complete relief or would avoid risk that party would be impaired in her ability to protect interests SHALL be joined if available (provided that SMJ/Venue not destroyed). TEST: Identical facts & law.

(3) Indispensable - unavailable party whose joinder is necessary to render an effective judgment, & ct has no SMJ w/o party. TEST: interest of π v D's interest; interest of unnamed parties; judicial economy; adequacy of judgment in party's absence.

CLAIMS:

By π - may join all claims he has v. D regardless of nature of claim or relief sought. However, in code juris., joinder restricted to claims similar in type arising out of STO.

By D - Permissive - counterclaims permitted (but in fed ct, counter claim must be supported by independent SMJ).
Compulsory - if counterclaim STO as π's claim, failure to raise it bars it!
Cross-claim - if STO, D can sue Co-D.

CENCTAB
(SEE BELOW)

CLASS ACTION - "All together now!" Certification requirements:

Roughly definable **Class** of which π is a member
Judicial **Economy** served
Potential Ps too **Numerous** for joinder
Claims have **Common** legal theory or arise out of STO
Claim of named π must be **Typical** of the class
Named parties must **Adequately** represent class
Action must fall within one of three categories of
Fed Rule **23(b)**

(b1): individual suits would result in conflicting adjudications or would hurt interest of non-parties;
(b2) injunctive/declaratory relief necessarily applies to entire class (civil rts, employment discrim. or environmental cases)
(b3) on balance, class suit is fairest & most efficient way to adjudicate controversy. Common ?s must predominate over individual ?s.

> Notice requirements: In (b1) & (b2) suits notification to class members of suit is not mandatory but ct has discretion; in (b3) suit relief is limited to those class members actually notified who did not opt out of suit. π must pay for notice. Mail is required if address is known or ascertainable; if not, publication will suffice.

INTERVENTION - "Let me in!" Intervenor permitted on its own motion to join action:

Broad Rule: Intervention allowed if intervenor has interest in decision;

Strict Rule (CA): Intervenor must have direct interest in success of party before
the court.

Fed Rule:
*Permissive Intervenor: must have conditional statutory right or question of fact or law common to claim + SMJ & venue met.
*Intervenor As of Right: allowed where unconditional statutory rt OR intervenor must have interest in property or transactions which are the subject of litigation, intervenor's interest will be impaired, is not adequately represented by existing party; ancillary or supplemental juris. will be used, no independent SMJ required, except in diversity cases.

INTERPLEADER - "You split it up!"

General rule - stakeholder is facing adverse, competing & overlapping claims; " (not D) stakeholder must be disinterested in outcome of suit; stakeholder not independently liable to either claimant on other claims.

Federal rule - stakeholder facing adverse, competing, overlapping claims, multiple claims or vexatious litigation; ct. must have PJ over Ds:

* FEDERAL INTERPLEADER ACT - debt deposited w/ ct.; minimal diversity required (one claimant must differ from others) & $500 in controversy; nationwide service of process + venue proper where claimant resides; easy to obtain state ct. injunctions.

*RULE 22 debt not deposited w/ ct; Federal question or total diversity with more than $75,000 required; regular service of process and venue required; hard to get injunctions v. state ct.

IMPLEADER: D can implead non-party whom D might be entitled to indemnification from. Ancillary juris. applies.

IV. DISCOVERY

DISCOVERY DEVICES:

DADIES

DEPOSITIONS (written or oral)
ADMISSIONS of facts
DOCUMENTS & other items (if good cause)
INTERROGATORIES
EXAMINATION (mental or physical)
SUBPOENA (duces tecum)

Scope/Limitations:
*Discovery must be relevant;
*Privileged matters are not discoverable;
*Attorney work product normally not discoverable unless substantial need, unavailability and prejudice shown.
*Oppressive discovery may be curtailed by protective orders.

RULE 26 Discovery requires disclosure of witness information, tangible evidence, damage computations, insurance agreements, expert W testimony and W list.
Sanctions for Non-Compliance: Contempt, pleadings stricken, default, adverse finding of fact, costs.

V. THE PRETRIAL CONFERENCE:

Trial judge may order parties to appear for a pretrial conference to familiarize the litigants & the ct. w/ the issues involved, determine the possibility of a settlement & reduce the danger of surprise at trial.

VI. TRIAL:

A. ADJUDICATIONS WITHOUT TRIAL:

(1) Motions to dismiss JTPPICS;
(2) Voluntary dismissal;
(3) Involuntary dismissal;
(4) Default.

B. RIGHT TO A JURY TRIAL:

"7th Am. in suits at CL, rt. of jury trial shall be preserved." TEST: Is there a rt to a jury trial as to a particular issue?
*Determine what the CoA are & whether as a tactical concern; does π/D want a jury trial on each issue?
*Determine whether CoA is being brought in st. or fed. ct.

If state ct., then 7th Am is not applicable. However, most states have a provision similar to 7th Am & this determines the relation back date.

If fed ct., then jury trials are favored. In diversity cases, rt. to jury trial is determined by federal standards.

*Determine whether there was a rt. to jury trial in 1791 (relation back date for federal constitution); if in state ct., and the state constitution has a similar provision then use the date when the state constitution took effect as the relation back date. If the answer is clearly yes or no then follow. If it is unclear (e.g. no such cause of action existed back in 1791), then look to the following factors:

DETERMINE NATURE OF ACTION BY ANALOGY: draw an analogy to a similar CoA that existed in 1791, and see whether a jury trial was provided for that CoA (i.e. "discrimination" claim, which did not exist in 1791 might be analogized to intentional infliction of emotional distress, which did exist in 1791 and is a LEGAL cause of action; thus, jury trial allowed.

DETERMINE WHAT THE REMEDY FOR THE CAUSE OF ACTION IS: Actions at law include suits for money damages and recovery of real and personal property; actions in equity include specific performance, reformation or cancellation of an instrument, injunctive relief, trust administration and control of fiduciaries, and family status (e.g. divorce). However, remedy for CoA is not determinative.

DETERMINE WHETHER THE "GIST" OF THE ISSUE IS LEGAL OR EQUITABLE: The nature of the claim is not determined by how the cause of action is framed, or by semantics, but depends on the nature of the underlying issue (e.g. an action for an "accounting" may be legal or equitable depending on the nature of the action).

DETERMINE WHAT THE PRACTICAL ABILITIES AND LIMITATION OF THE JURY ARE: (e.g. jury trial may be inappropriate where highly complex litigation is involved).

*If there are both equitable and legal claims the trial judge must usually try the legal claims first, so as to preserve the rt. of jury trial as to those claims. Only if the party asserting the equitable claims would be irreparably harmed by having these claims

delayed until after the legal claims are heard, will the equitable claims be heard first.
*Determine whether π waived the right to a jury trial by failing to make a timely demand.

C. JURY SELECTION:

Due process insures that method used to select a jury be fair and impartial, and equal protection demands that the jury be a cross-section of the community, and that there is no systematic discrimination against any group. Attorney may question a juror concerning possible bias and may challenge juror for cause or exercise a peremptory challenge.

D. JURY VERDICTS:

General verdict, special verdict, or general verdict w/ interrogatories.

VII. TRIAL AND POST-TRIAL MOTIONS:

A. NONSUIT:

Motion is granted after π presents her case and fails to show a rt. to relief.

B. MOTION FOR JUDGMENT AS A MATTER OF LAW:

Motion is granted if there is no evidence on which the jury could find for non-moving party.

C. RENEWED MOTION FOR JUDGMENT AS A MATTER OF LAW:

Motion is granted after verdict if there is no evidence on which the jury could find for non-moving party. Court must find that as a matter of law, jury's use of the evidence was unreasonable. Under the MAJ view, this motion can only be made if directed verdict motion was made.

(1) Evidence is considered in the light most favorable to party against whom relief is sought;
(2) Evidence must be such that reasonable persons cannot differ as to which party can prevail;
(3) Court is not weighing evidence.

D. MOTION FOR NEW TRIAL:

Motion is granted if court feels injustice has occurred & can grant modification of the verdict in whole or in part. Ct. may conditionally grant a new trial:

(1) Remittitur - π agrees to LESSER damages or court will grant a new trial;
(2) Additur - D agrees to greater damages or court will grant a new trial. (NOT ALLOWED IN FED!)

E. MOTION FOR RELIEF FROM JUDGMENT:

Grounds for reopening case in ct's discretion after judgment. Mistake, inadvertence, surprise, excusable neglect, newly discovered evidence or fraud.

VIII. FINAL JUDGMENT:

Party has a right to one appeal from a final judgment (e.g. one which is determinative of the entire case in all respects) unless waived.

A. Effect of Final Judgment on Future cases:

"Res judicata & Collateral estoppel prevent relitigation of same CoA between same parties or same issue in different CoA between same parties to promote judicial economy."

RES JUDICATA: "We already decided that cause of action!"

TEST:
(1) Same **Primary** rights involved?
(2) Same **Evidence**?
(3) Same **Transaction** or occurrence?
(4) **Judgment** on the merits?

COLLATERAL ESTOPPEL (CE): "We already decided that issue!" Prevents relitigation of fact issue previously decided.

TEST:
Issue **Necessary** to first action?
Identical issues?
Actually **Litigated**?
"Who can use it?" D can always use as a shield, since CE is to protect D but π cannot use as sword, unless π could not have joined earlier action, it was not foreseeable at time of first suit that other suits might arise; judgment asserted by π consistent w/ prior Js; full and fair adjudication.

WHO'S BOUND: "Does it apply to me?"
RJ and CE apply to parties, privies, non-parties but mutuality (i.e. opportunity & incentive to litigate issue) was once required, and now non-party can use judgment defensively against someone who was party to first action.

FULL FAITH AND CREDIT CLAUSE:
The Full Faith and Credit Clause requires that public acts, records and judicial proceedings of sister states are honored. While this clause only applies to states, Fed statute compels recognition of Fed ct judgments. Only applies to final judgments, i.e. judgments on "merits" involving substance of π's claim (not jurisdiction, venue, capacity to sue, misjoinder or dismissal w/o prejudice) and default and consent judgments and judgments not subject to collateral attack. Recognition of foreign judgments is voluntary unless required by treaty.

REAL PROPERTY LAW CHART

I . A. IDENTIFY THE TYPE OF OWNERSHIP INTEREST: PRESENTLY OWNED OR POSSESSED (ownership in "fee," leasehold, joint interest), FUTURE INTERESTS, INCORPOREAL INTERESTS, RIGHTS IN LAND, FIXTURES, ADVERSE POSSESSION)
B. WHAT CHARACTERISTICS ARE INHERENT IN SUCH OWNERSHIP AND WHAT RIGHTS AND DUTIES ARISE FROM SUCH OWNERSHIP?
II. ARE THERE ANY LIMITATIONS ON SUCH OWNERSHIP? (PUBLIC LAND & USE CONTROL)
III. LAND SALE CONTRACTS ISSUES

I. IDENTIFY THE TYPE OF OWNERSHIP INTEREST AND THE CHARACTERISTICS INHERENT IN SUCH OWNERSHIP, AND THE RIGHTS AND DUTIES WHICH ARISE FROM SUCH OWNERSHIP?

A. PRESENTLY OWNED/ POSSESSED LAND

1. PRESENTLY OWNED LAND ("Freehold")

* **FEE SIMPLE ABSOLUTE**- complete ownership of land:
C/L: "Fred & his heirs"
M/L: "from Fred to Barney."

* **FEE TAIL** - land which passes by descent only to lineal descendants:
C/L: "Fred to Barney & the heirs of his body."
M/L: abolished; a fee simple absolute results.

* **LIFE ESTATE** - lifetime ownership of land:
> Simple Life Estate: "Fred to Barney for life."
measured by the life of the grantee; Fred has a reversion.

> Pur Autre Vie - measured by the life of another: "Fred to Barney during Betty's life."

> Under C/L, if Barney died before Betty, no one owned the land, but under M/L, the land goes to Barney's heirs.

> Curtesy: Under C/L, husband received life estate in all of wife's property upon her death; M/L has abolished curtesy in favor of intestate succession.

> Dower: Under C/L, W received life estate in 1/3rd of husband's property accumulated during marriage; M/L has abolished dower in favor of intestate succession.

* **FEE SIMPLE DEFEASIBLE** - land is subject to the possibility of being taken away.
> Fee Simple Determinable on a Special Limitation - Estate automatically reverts to grantor upon occurrence of contingency: "to Barney so long as/while/during/ until/unless/ (Condition occurs)"
> Fee Simple Defeasible Subject to a Condition Subsequent - Estate is subject to grantor's right of re-entry upon occurrence of contingency - "to Barney upon condition that/provided that/but if used for any other purpose than X"

2. LEASEHOLD LAND ("Non-Freehold")

* **TENANCY FOR YEARS:** "July 1999 until February 2000." Estate for a fixed period of time which automatically terminates by terms of lease, leaving a reversion in (L)andlord.

* **PERIODIC TENANCY** - "Month to month." Estate for a year or lesser stated period which automatically renews itself at the end

or lesser stated period which automatically renews itself at the end of each period; may be terminated upon proper notice - CA: 30 days notice; C/L: 6 months notice required for year to year lease & one month notice for month to month lease; reversion in L.

* **TENANCY AT WILL:** "Either party may terminate." Estate may be terminated by L or T at will; C/L requires no notice, but M/L requires reasonable notice.

* **TENANCY AT SUFFERANCE:** Estate where T stays after expiration of leasehold; no notice is required; L may retake possession & sue for damages or hold T to a periodic tenancy for up to one year.

* **NO LEASE AGREEMENT:** Generally, a tenancy at will is created which may transmute into a periodic tenancy if periodic rent is paid by T. Termination under C/L requires no notice, but some states, including CA, require 30 days notice.

TENANT'S RIGHTS AND DUTIES:

T has a duty to pay rent

Defenses to non-payment of rent

> purpose of leasing property becomes IMPOSSIBLE

> lease involves an ILLEGAL purpose

> leasehold is taken by EMINENT DOMAIN (amount or rent excused is proportionate to the extent of the taking)

> L's BREACH OF implied covenant of QUIET ENJOYMENT;

ISSUE: Has L substantially interfered w/ T's beneficial enjoyment of the land?

RULE OF EVICTION: ACTUAL eviction occurs when L deprives T of possession of leasehold; PARTIAL eviction occurs when T is deprived of part of the leased premises; CONSTRUCTIVE eviction occurs when L's conduct substantially interferes with T's enjoyment of the leasehold, where L has a duty to act or where the condition is w/i L's control.

EFFECT: T must vacate premises w/i a reasonable time of the breach & sue for damages.

> breach of other lease covenants (e.g. "to keep the plumbing in good order") are generally held to be independent of each other, & breach by one party does NOT excuse performance of the other. Under the MIN view, such breach constitutes constructive eviction.

> L's BREACH OF the implied covenant of HABITABILITY: a covenant of habitability is implied in every residential lease and requires the lease premises to be fit for living purposes (look to housing codes/standards or danger to T's health or safety). If L breaches, T can vacate & sue for damages; T can stay & not pay rent until premises are habitable; T can repair & deduct; T can pay fair market value of rent; L cannot retaliate.

> Retaliatory eviction defense: T may inform authorities of L's wrongdoing, and L cannot retaliate by eviction; there is a presumption that attempted eviction and/or rent increases w/i short period of the reported violation are improperly motivated.

> Destruction of the premises is not a defense at C/L, but M/L excuses rent where destruction is complete; if destruction is partial, then rent excused pro rata to the extent structure is destroyed.

T has duty to avoid waste & must pay for resulting damages: three types of waste:

> Voluntary waste: T's negligent/intentional conduct causes damage to property.

> Permissible waste: T's omission to act causes damage to property.

> Amelioratory waste: T's conduct substantially alters the lease premises.

> Modern law allows beneficial structural changes where long term leases are involved.

LANDLORD'S RIGHTS & DUTIES

> L may evict T for non-payment of rent, but cannot employ self-help, in lieu of an unlawful detainer action.

> If T abandons premises, L has no duty to mitigate and still can collect rent.

> If T surrenders premises, and L accepts, either by acts or by express agreement, then T's liability to pay rent ceases.

> L does not have to refund T's advance rental payment if T defaults, but must refund security deposit, less actual damage, to T at end of lease.

> L has duty to maintain common areas under his control (e.g. driveways, common hallways).

> L is responsible for injuries caused by hidden defects on leased property which he knows or should know about, but which a reasonable inspection by T would not reveal.

> If L agrees to repair, he will be liable for injury to a foreseeable P.

> L has a duty to make the premises comply w/ all housing, building, safety, and health codes in accordance w/ the implied covenant of habitability.

> Assignment & sublease of a leasehold: T may assign or sublease her leasehold interest, unless agreement provides otherwise. Assignment occurs when T transfers the entire interest; assignee remains primarily liable for rent, but assignor-T is also liable; sublease occurs when T transfers less than the entire interest in the lease; T remains liable for rent, and sublessee is liable to T.

> When L convenants against assignments or subletting, while such provisions are strictly construed by the courts, such agreements are generally voidable at L's election, unless L consents to an assignment by the T.

3. CONCURRENTLY OWNED ESTATES

* JOINT TENANCY: "Fred & Bambam as joint tenants." Each tenant owns an undivided fraction of the whole, subject to the right of survivorship, e.g. the survivor takes all.

The "Four Unities" are required:

> Time: all interests must vests together;
> Title: created by the same instrument;
> Interest: each party owns an equal share;
> Possession: equal rights to possession of land.
> Joint Tenancy may be severed.

* TENANCY BY THE ENTIRETY: "Fred & Wilma as husband & wife, w/right of survivorship." Estate owned by husband and wife which is subject to the right of survivorship. The "Four Unities" are required and the interest is not severable, except upon: divorce/death, joint conveyance by H & W to 3rd party; conveyance by one spouse to the other; execution by creditor against both H & W; mutual agreement of spouses.

* TENANCY IN COMMON: (Statutorily preferred) "Barney & Betty, as tenants in common." Each tenant owns an undivided fractional part of the whole; the shares need not be equal; freely alienable by intervivos & testamentary transfer, passes by succession & is subject to claims by T's creditors.

CO-TENANTS' RIGHTS AND DUTIES

> Right to demand partition (physical division of property);
> Right to possess all parts of the property;
> Right of co-T in possession to retain profits from her use without sharing. NOTE: in some juris., co-T in possession must

account to co-Ts not in possession for rent received from third parties; however, in these juris. the co-T must always account if profits are received from an activity that substantially reduces the value of land;
> Co-T in possession cannot compel other co-Ts to contribute to cost of improvements; however, Co-T may compel contributions for preservation of property costs;
> Each co-T must pay taxes & interests on mortgages;
> Co-Ts are in a fiduciary relationship with one another.

B. FUTURE INTERESTS

1. GRANTOR'S INTERESTS:

* REVERSION: The estate remaining when an estate less than a fee simple absolute is granted: "Morticia to Gomez for life."

* POSSIBILITY OF REVERTER: The reversion to the grantor when the contingency set forth in the fee simple determinable on a special limitation occurs: "Morticia to Uncle Fester so long as Uncle Fester grows corn."

* RIGHT OF RE-ENTRY: The right of re-entry in the grantor when the contingency mentioned in the fee simple defeasible subject to a condition subsequent occurs: "Morticia to Cousin I.t. provided that Cousin I.t. grows corn."

2. GRANTEE'S INTERESTS:

* REMAINDERS: future interest created in one other than the grantor upon end of a prior estate. Remainder must be expressly created and are alienable, devisable & inheritable. Four types:

> Vested Remainder: A remainder to an ascertained & existing person, becoming possessory whenever the preceding estate comes to an end: "Mo for life, remainder to Curly and his heirs."

> Vested Remainder Subject to Complete Divestment - A remainder to an ascertained & existing person, subject to a condition subsequent: "To Mo for life, remainder to Larry & his heirs, but if Larry dies w/o a child, then to Curly and his heirs."

> Vested Remainder Subject to Open - A remainder to a group of persons at least one of whom is ascertained and in existence: "To Mo for life, remainder to Mo's child & their heirs."

> Contingent Remainders - remainders created in favor of an unborn ascertainable person OR subject to a condition precedent: "to Mo for life, remainder to Curly & his heirs if Curly attains 21."

* EXECUTORY INTERESTS: future estate in a party other than the grantor which becomes possessory only by taking the estate away from the grantee of a vested remainder or a defeasible fee. These interests are freely alienable, devisable and descendible and are indestructible. Two types:

> Springing Interest - divests the grantor of his estate: "Mo to Curly for life, then 10 years after Curly's death to Larry." or "to Curly and his heirs one year from today" or "to Mo for life remainder to Curly and his heirs one year after Mo's death."

> Shifting - divests a third person of his estate: "To Curley for life, remainder to Mo & his heirs, but if Mo fails to attain 21, to Larry and his heirs" OR "To Curley & his heirs, but if Curley dies without children, then to Larry and his heirs."

> Contingent remainders and executory interests are subject to RaP.

THE FOUR FUTURE INTEREST RULES

DOCTRINE OF MERGER: if one person owns two successive (e.g. present & future) estates, they merge: "Gilligan to Skipper for life, remainder to Ginger & her heirs." If Ginger conveys her remainder to Skipper, the estates merge & Skipper has a fee simple absolute.

THE RULE IN SHELLY'S CASE: (Abolished in most states) If a grant creates a freehold in the grantee and creates a remainder in the grantee's heirs, the grantee receives a fee simple: "Gilligan to Skipper for life, remainder to Skipper's heirs." Skipper has a fee simple.

THE DOCTRINE OF WORTHIER TITLE: The grantor cannot give a remainder to her own heirs: "Eddie to Beaver for life, remainder to Eddie's heirs," is a void conveyance and & Eddie's heirs take a reversion by descent.

THE RULE AGAINST PERPETUITIES (RaP): An interest is void if there is any possibility that it may vest more than 21 years after some life in being at the creation of the interest. Analysis:

1. Is an executory interest or a contingent remainder at issue?
2. Will the interest be owned by an EXISTING, ASCERTAINED PERSON AND NOT BE SUBJECT TO A CONDITION PRECEDENT, w/i 21 years after some life in being?
    a. Look at the date the instrument is created;
    b. Determine who "the life in being" is;
    c. Add 21 years;
    d. Ask, will the interest vest or fail.

"Beaver to Eddie for life, remainder to Eddie's children who attain the age of 22" violates RaP. Assuming that the instrument takes effect at Beaver's death, the "life in being" would be Eddie's. Since a child could be born after Eddie's death, and that child's interest will not vest or fail within 21 years, the entire interest is void.

e. Do any exceptions apply? The Rule does not apply to gifts from one charity to another and does not apply to vested remainders & reversions.

C. INCORPOREAL OR "USE" RIGHTS IN LAND

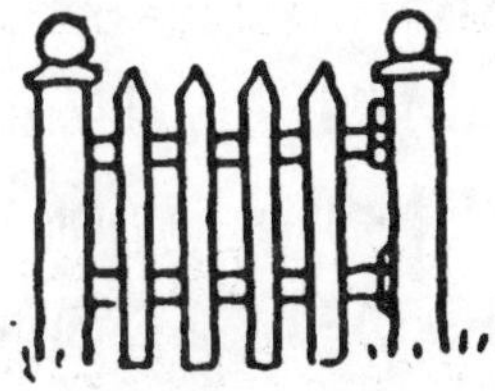

* EASEMENTS:

create a right in the easement holder to go onto land in possession of another and use it. Easements are either appurtenant or gross (attached or not attached to land) and are either affirmative or negative in nature:

> Easement in Appurtenant: creation of easement is attached to a piece of land & benefits the owner of such land in his use & enjoyment thereof (e.g. right of way easement). Requires for its existence two pieces of land owned by two different persons:
Dominant tenement: land whose owner is benefitted by easement.
Servient tenement: land whose owner is burdened by easement.

Conveyance of dominant estate transfers ownership of easement as well.

> Easement in Gross: creation of easement unrelated to land owned by easement holder (e.g. easement giving holder the right to take gravel from land). Conveyance of a commercial dominant estate transfers ownership of easement in gross as well, but not where non-commercial estates are conveyed.

> Affirmative Easement: entitles holder of benefit to make affirmative use of servient estate (rt. of way, laying utility lines, draining water, etc.)

> Negative Easement: prevents owner from servient estate from uses that would otherwise be lawful. Five types: Air, Light, Lateral support, Subjacent support, Artificial stream control.

EASEMENTS ARE CREATED BY:

GREEN DIP

implied **GRANT**
implied **RESERVATION**
EXPRESS grant or reservation
ESTOPPEL
NECESSITY
DEDICATION
(I)
PRESCRIPTION

Implied Grant:

created in favor of the grantee on severance of land which was formerly owned as a whole. During time of common ownership, owner must have used the easement for the same purpose during common ownership (called a quasi-easement). This quasi-easement becomes an implied easement when the dominant tenement is conveyed. The existence of the quasi-easement must be: (1) apparent from a reasonable inspection of the land; (2) used continuously; (3) reasonably necessary to the use of the dominant tenement.

Implied Reservation:

created in favor of the grantor on severance of a common ownership. Same requires as in easement by implied grant, but STRICT NECESSITY is required.

Express grant or reservation:

created by written grant or by reserving its use in a written conveyance.

Estoppel:

created where the intention to create an easement exists, but is invalid for non-compliance w/ Statute of Frauds. Requires detrimental reliance by easement holder, that is $ spent on reliance of easement.

Necessity:

easement creates where dominant & servient tenement were at one time under common ownership; strict necessity required (substantial impracticality to own land w/o easement); terminates when necessity ceases.

Dedication:

created in favor of public use; can be created formally by deed or other means manifesting an intent to dedicate to public and actual public use.

Prescription:

created through adverse possession. Hostile, Adverse, Notorious, Open, Actual, Continuous, Exclusive, 20 yr. statutory period at C/L; periods of adverse use by different users may be tacked together.

RIGHTS & DUTIES OF EASEMENT HOLDERS

> Location of easement cannot be changed except by mutual agreement. When the grant is general in nature, the servient tenement may determine the exact location of the easement, which must be reasonably convenient to the easement holder.

RIGHTS AND DUTIES OF EASEMENT OWNER

> the easement holder may only use the easement for those activities reasonably contemplated at the creation of the easement;

> where the scope of the easement's use is not specified, a reasonable scope will be implied;

> while the scope of use may change with the times, change from family use to commercial use overburdens the easement;

> easement owner has both the right & duty to make repairs on the easement, but cannot substantially change the nature of an easement in the name of repairs;

RIGHTS AND DUTIES OF SERVIENT TENEMENT HOLDER

> servient tenement holder may make nay use of his property which does not interfere with the easement holder's rights & has no duty to maintain easement.

EASEMENTS TERMINATE UPON:

ABUSE - servient landowner may receive injunction & damages;
TERMS OF AGREEMENT - when a stated contingency occurs;
AGREEMENT - by written release;
MERGER - of the dominant & servient estates;
ENDING OF NECESSITY;
ABANDONMENT - manifested by extended non-use;
CHANGED CIRCUMSTANCES - e.g. destruction of servient estate;
ESTOPPEL - where holder represents intent to abandon &

servient tenement so relies.

* **COVENANTS:** agreement between two parties regarding land; may be either affirmative or negative (as in easements).

* **EQUITABLE SERVITUDES:** an agreement between two parties not to do something re: land use.

* **IMPLIED RECIPROCAL SERVITUDE:** where a common plan exists, where one lot is restricted, a similar restriction is implied on the remaining land.

* **PROFITS:** creates the right to take something from the land of another (sand, gravel, wood); necessarily includes an easement for access to material subject to the profit.
Two types:

Profit in Appurtenant: creation of profit is attached to a certain dominant tract. May be exclusive or non-exclusive.

Profit in Gross: creation of profit unrelated to any land owned by the profit holder. Profit is assignable but is not divisible where non-exclusive.

* **LICENSE:** Personal privilege to use land granted by a land owner to another. A license is not an interest in land and may be created orally. Only the intention to create an easement is required to create a license, and licenses are revocable at the will of the licensor, but the following exceptions apply:

(1) where a property interest is involved (i.e. licensor consents to the placing of licensee's personal property on the land), license is irrevocable so long as the "interest" lasts; (2) where license is executed (e.g. license detrimentally relies on license) there is a split in authority; some cts. hold license irrevocable while others hold contra (3) once a license is revoked, a licensee is allowed reasonable time to remove any property.

7. DOES THE EASEMENT, COVENANT, PROFIT OR EQUITABLE SERVITUDE RUN WITH THE LAND?

Some interests, e.g. covenants, easements, profits, etc. are considered personal (i.e. not concerning the land), while others are said to "run with the land," permitting a successive owner of the property to enforce the interest. Analyze as follows:

STEP ONE: Does the covenant involve a benefit and/or burden?
(1) a "benefit" is an agreement which enhances value of land
(2) a "burden" is an agreement which makes land less valuable
STEP TWO: Does the interest "touch and concern" the land? (Does it affect the quality or value of the property?)
STEP THREE: Did the original parties INTEND that the interest would run with the land and that successive owners would be bound by the interest?
STEP FOUR: Determine what type of non-possessory interest is at issue (i.e. easement, profit, covenant or equitable servitude), and determine whether additional elements are met:

For a burden to run, NOTICE to the party to be bound is required; notice may be constructive (through operation of recording acts) actual or inquiry.
For a covenant or agreement to run (as opposed to easements, profitsor equitable servitudes):
a BURDEN requires horizontal privity, e.g. privity of estate between original contracting parties or where both parties hold interests in the same piece of land & the covenant touches and concerns those interest; AND vertical privity, where covenant accompanies a conveyance of land interest.
a BENEFIT requires vertical privity.

Exceptions: A negative equitable servitude runs with the land where there is a common plan & notice, either actual, constructive or inquiry notice; a license does not run with land unless estoppel or it is coupled w/ an interest on the land.

8. RIGHTS IN LAND: PARTY WALLS & RIGHTS TO NATURAL RESOURCES, FIXTURES

* PARTY WALLS: if the wall is built on the property of one party, the other adjoining owner is granted an appurtenant easement to use that wall for support; if the wall is on the property of both, each owner owns that part of the all which rests on his land. A promise

to maintain or pay for the wall runs with the land.

* RIGHT TO LATERAL & SUBJACENT SUPPORT OF LAND: ownership of land carries w/ it the absolute right to have land supported in its natural state by adjoining land (lateral support) as well as the right to underground support (subjacent support). Landowner who causes damages to buildings on adjoining lands is liable only if the land would have collapsed in its natural state OR where landowner is negligent.

* RIGHTS TO WATER: rights to water depend on the character of the water:

> Watercourses (streams, rivers & lakes): "RIPARIAN" SYSTEM gives owners who's land touches the water the right to use water w/ the land, and forbid owners from altering the natural flow of the watercourse. Under the "PRIOR APPROPRIATION" SYSTEM, the first party to use the water gets it regardless of whether the party owns the land. Under M/L, state licensing applies.

> Ground water: C/L allowed absolute ownership by owner of overlying land for any purpose; M/L allows the same right, but water may only be used for the overlying land.

> Surface water (rainfall, seepage): C/L permits landowner to make any use of his land, regardless on the effect on the flow of surface water, while M/L holds that owner of lower land must receive surface water in its natural flow from higher land, and cannot block drainage.

* FIXTURES: A fixture is a chattel which is regarded as part of real property & which passes with the property to which it is annexed. How to determine whether a chattel is a fixture:

> Intention of the parties;
> degree of actual physical annexation;
> extreme weight of chattel;
> ease of removal w/o damage to property;
> whether the article is peculiarly adapted to the realty (e.g. windows, shades, etc.)
> whether article is essential to building's use;
> local customary items (e.g. furnaces, hot water heater)
> trade fixtures of tenant where landowner defaults belong to tenant and not mortgagee.

9. ADVERSE POSSESSION

Defined: Title to real property and easements may be acquired by adverse possession. The statute of limitations begins to run when claimant goes adversely into possession of true owner's land.

Requirements:

HA NO ACE

HOSTILE - intent to claim land
ADVERSE - in derogation of true owner's rights
NOTORIOUS
OPEN sufficiently apparent to put owner on notice.
ACTUAL
CONTINUOUS
EXCLUSIVE

Tacking: There need not be continuous possession by the same person. Adverse possessor can tack on to his own possession the periods of adverse possession of his predecessors.

Tolling Due to Disability of True Owner: Statute of limitations does not begin to run if true owner is under some disability to sue when cause of action first accrued (e.g. minority, imprisonment, insanity). However, "tacking" of the disabilities is not allowed, since only the disability for the owner existing at he time cause of action arose is considered.

II. ARE THERE ANY LIMITATIONS ON SUCH OWNERSHIP? (PUBLIC LAND & USE CONTROL)

Power of Eminent Domain:

The power of government to take private property for public purposes.

Limitations on Power: 5th Amd requires both due process & just compensation prior to taking. Cts will generally not ask whether the taking will achieve an intended public purpose (i.e. govt. can take land for urban renewal projects, even though the land will be sold to private developers for private use). The ct will determine what constitutes "just compensation," which is the fair market value of the property. Where the govt. does not take all the land, the owner may receive severance damages, reflecting the decrease in the value of the owner's remaining land. Where the value of the remaining land is increased by the taking, fed. law sets off the increase against the FMV of the taken land.

Remedy of Inverse Condemnation: Severe land use restrictions may constitute a taking and entitle the landowner to relief or payment of just compensation.

Zoning Power:

The power of government to divide land into districts where certain uses of land are permitted or prohibited, generally through local zoning ordinances. The purpose of zoning is to segregate incompatible uses & protect established uses from economic loss new uses might impose.

Limitations on Power: Equal Protection clause protects against spot zoning, and requires comprehensive planning. If the land use regulation destroys the land's economic value, it is considered an exercise of eminent domain. There is no clear test as to what constitutes a taking, giving rise to eminent domain, but look to reasonableness of the taking, and weigh public/ private interests involved.

Exceptions to Zoning Ordinances:

(1) Amendment of ordinance by local legislature;
(2) Issuance of conditional use permits, provided specified conditions exist;
(3) Granting of a zoning variance, where unnecessary hardship is shown, provided ordinance precludes any reasonable use of the land & the public will not suffer substantial detriment from the variance;
(4) Contract zoning, which allows the city to contract with developers to rezone land if land developed in a certain way;
(5) Floating zones allow landowners to replace existing zoning restrictions w/ uses permitted under specified circumstances;
(6) Planned unit development (PUD) allows developer to vary residential spaces & uses on tract for appropriate commercial & business uses in order to make housing developments more self-sufficient.

III. LAND SALE Ks & DEEDS

Land Sale Ks:

Requirements:

(1) Must be in writing & signed by seller (but part performance will take it out of SoF);

(2) Must contain essential terms including description of property, identification of parties, price, manner of payment, etc. (Parol admissible to resolve LATENT ambiguities but NOT essential terms);

(3) Subject to implied covenant of marketability: requires title to be reasonably free from doubt which a well-informed reasonable prudent buyer would be willing to accept (zoning restrictions not included); Buyer must wait & see if seller's title is marketable - if closing occurs, K & deed merge & seller's liability on covenant ceases;

Risk of loss prior to closing: equitable conversion places risk of loss of subject matter of land K on buyer (MAJ) - Uniform Act places risk on seller unless buyer has possession or title.

(4) Transfer of land title generally requires a deed.

Deed Requirements:

(a) Must be in writing & signed by grantor;

(b) Must identify parties;

(c) Must show intention to transfer an interest;

(d) Must contain description of land conveyed.

> Rules of Construction: Where the description is inconsistent or conflicting, the methods of description are given the following priority: natural monuments, artificial monuments, courses, distances, name, quantity.

(e) Must be delivered: requires objective manifestation of grantor's intent that the instrument of conveyance take immediate effect. If grantor fails to deliver deed during his lifetime, title does not pass to the intended grantee.
If grantor retains control over deed, there is no delivery.

Presumptions:
If grantee has the deed there is a rebuttable presumption that it has been delivered;
If grantor has the deed, then contra presumption.

Acknowledgement & recording of a deed creates a presumption that deed has been delivered.

Dating of the deed is irrelevant, but if delivery is established then there is a presumption that the deed was delivered on that date.

Conditional Delivery:
Delivery may be subject to a condition precedent.
If grantor conditions on death, grantor has L/E & grantee has vested remainder.
Grantor may deliver a deed in escrow to a third person with instructions that the deed be delivered to the grantee when the condition occurs. The date that title passes relates back to the time deed is delivered to escrow holder.
Grantor can recover deed from escrow agent prior to condition precedent unless there is a written K.

(f) Deed must be accepted by grantee. Some states presume acceptance, while others presume acceptance if grantee has knowledge of the deed.

COVENANTS OF TITLE

5 covenants found in general warranty deed:
(1) Covenant of seisin: grantor promises he has the estate he is conveying;
(2) Covenant of right to convey: grantor promises he has authority to make the grant;
(3) Covenant against encumbrances: grantor promises there exist no physical or title encumbrances;
(4) Covenant for quiet enjoyment: grantor promises that grantee's possession won' be disturbed by another party's claim;
(5) Covenant of warranty: grantor agrees to defend against reasonable claims of title by third party;
(6) Covenant of further assurances (not one of the usual covenants): grantor promises to perform acts reasonably necessary to perfect title conveyed.

Breach of Covenant:
If (1), (2) & (3) are breached, if at all, at the time of conveyance, and generally do not run w/ the land (i.e. remote grantees cannot sue on the covenant). With respect to (3), most states find breach even if grantee knew of encumbrance, but others find no breach where grantee knew (including constructive knowledge) of the encumbrance(i.e. obvious easement).

(4), (5), & (6) are not breached until someone interferes w/ the possession of the grantor; these covenants run w/ the land (i.e. remote grantee can sue at the time his possession is disturbed). The grantor must have notice of the claim to be liable, and need not defend against wrongful claims. Remote grantee may sue anyone up the line, but her recovery is limited extent of $ received by grantor, while other jurisdictions limit recovery to the lesser of what she paid or what grantor received.

ESTOPPEL BY DEED

Applies where deed conveys a particular estate; N/A to quitclaims. If grantor conveys land he does not own, but later acquires it, land goes to grantee.

There is a split in authority as to what happens to land if grantor later conveys to a BFP subsequent to conveying to grantee. Under the majority rule, the grantor is personally estopped from claiming he did not later acquire title for grantee, and thus BFP will take. Under minority rule, title passes to original grantee by operation of law, and thus takes to the exclusion of any BFPs.

RECORDING ACT

Purpose: The recording acts are based on C/L priority favoring BFP for value w/o notice w/ legal interest in land, over prior equitable interests, where grantor conveyed the same property twice. Applies to any conveyance, transfer or mortgage of real property, leases over one year, but not interests created by implication or operation of law.

How grantee records:
* Grantee records her deed in the county in which the property is located;
* The deed is copied & indexed; There are 2 types of indexes: Grantor-Grantee Index (& Grantee-Grantor Index) , an alphabetical index listed under the last name of the grantor (or grantee); Tract Index, an index by lot & block number
* Acknowledgement or witnesses may be required in some states;
* Deed must comply w/ necessary formalities, or it does not give constructive notice to BFP; however in most states it is sufficient if subsequent taker has actual notice;
* Failure to record does not affect rights of grantor & grantee; only relates to the rights of subsequent purchasers.

How to Conduct a Title Search:
*Tract Index: the title searcher will find all conveyances on one page, but must also examine other public records.
*Grantor-Grantee Index: The searcher begins with the name of the grantor, and checks to see if grantor has already conveyed property to another; the searcher then follows the same procedure for the predecessors of the grantor until he reaches the root of title. Other public records must also be checked.

> The courts are split as to whether an error in indexing will result in a deed being held not to be recorded.

> In most states, a deed which is outside the chain of title (i.e. deed would not be discovered in a reasonable title search) is deemed not recorded.

Three Major Types of Recording Acts:

* Notice Statute: The last BFP has priority (e.g. "No conveyance shall be good against any subsequent BFP unless the same be recorded").

* Race-Notice Statute: First BFP to record wins (e.g. "Every conveyance which shall not be recorded is void as against any subsequent BFP whose interest shall be first duly recorded").

* Race Statute: (very common) the first person to record wins irrespective of notice.

Who is protected by the Recording Act?
* General Rule: Only BFPs protected under "notice" and "race-notice" statutes. BFP means person must be a "purchaser," "w/out notice" & pay a "valuable consideration." (must be more than nominal, but need not be FMV — if interest taken to settle pre-existing debt, then req. not met).
* Purchaser: buyers are always protected.
*Mortgagees: most statutes protect mortgagees.
* Creditors: general creditors normally not protected by recording acts; but creditors who become purchasers by buying at a judicial sale are protected. Some statutes protect creditors against subsequent (but not prior unrecorded) purchasers.
* Person who buys from Heir: is protected against prior unrecorded conveyances of the ancestor.
* Person who takes from a BFP: will prevail against any interests which the transferor BFP would have prevailed against, even if BFP's transferee has actual notice of a prior unrecorded conveyance. However, if transferee previously held title, then this rule does not apply, since transferee could simply wash title through BFP to be protected.

MORTGAGES

Defined: Landowner (mortgagor) borrows money and gives mortgage on land to secure promise to repay; lender (mortgagee) has right to satisfy debt out of land if loan not repaid. The transaction normally includes both a promissory note & mortgage.
Effect of Mortgage on Mortgagee- Mortgagor rights: In majority of state, mortgagee has lien, while in other states mortgagee has title. Treatment of parties is identical in both:
* Mortgagor is entitled to possession until foreclosure;
* Foreclosure is by judicial sale;
* Mortgagor has statutory right to redeem;

* Deficiency judgement possible where proceeds of the sale are less than debt, if statutes permit.

Sale of Mortgaged Property:
* Sale to BFP cuts off mortgagee's interests (but mortgages are usually recorded so no BFP);
* Grantee who takes "subject to mortgage" is not personally liable on the mortgage note, but the mortgage is satisfied out of land as between mortgagor and grantee;
* Grantee who assumes mortgage is personally liable on mortgage debt, as is original mortgagor on promissory note, absent novation;
* If deed is silent, transfer is treated as "subject to mortgage" if purchase price reflects existence of mortgage debt.

Ten Rules to Write By

How To Answer a Torts Problem

Intentional Torts
Negligence
Defamation
Strict Liability
Products Liability

How To Answer a Criminal Law Problem

Crimes
Homicide

How To Answer a Contracts Problem

Contract Formation
Defenses to a Contract
Conditions
Excuse of Conditions
Discharge of Duty to Perform
Breach and Remedies

How To Answer a Civil Procedure Problem

Jurisdiction, Notice & Venue
Joinder
Pleadings
Demand For a Jury Trial

How To Answer a Real Property Problem

Identifying the Interest & Its Characteristics
Rule Against Perpetuities
Landlord & Tenant Problems
Rights in Land
Adverse Possession

"Now which shell is the law under?"

Congratulations! If you have made it this far, and soaked in even a fraction of the material covered in the text, you have soared light years ahead of your classmates who have not read this book. If you feel a bit overwhelmed, please do not panic; had I known even a third of the information in this book before taking my first law school examination, I would have been blessed. Remember that the information in this book is the result of years and years of research, study, and experience.

In this section, you will learn how to write essay examinations in each first-year subject. If you are thinking to yourself, that you thought you just learned how to answer law school exam questions, you would be half right. There is a world of difference between knowing how to solve a legal problem, using the six steps of exam taking, and actually writing out the answer on a blank piece of paper.

The purpose of this section is to show you how to write, structure and organize your analysis. Each model answer follows the I-R-A-C structure and demonstrates how to write a logical, well reasoned, "lawyer-like" analysis. I-R-A-C is simply a logical, organized method by which to write your exam answer. While you will and should develop your unique writing style, keep in mind always that the basic structure and organization of your answer should necessarily include the basic components of the I-R-A-C format. If you are not a prolific writer, then use I-R-A-C, which forces you to include each essential component in your analysis and gives you a system to follow in analyzing exam problems. You will find that as your flair for exam writing improves, your writing style will evolve, becoming more concise and compact. However, a good legal analysis always includes each element of I-R-A-C.

While the I-R-A-C writing style recommended in this book is a universally accepted method of writing examinations, if there is a conflict in what is suggested here and what your professor desires, follow your instructor's preference. For example, a good legal analysis always includes the statement of the rule. If your professor tells you, "Do not, and I repeat, do not, state any of the rules of law on the examination, just write out the application," then do exactly that.

After reading and applying the strategies and concepts in this section, you will know how to write a legal analysis. But do not stop there. You should apply your newfound knowledge to give your professor exactly what he or she wants. Talk to your professor or to students who have aced the professor's class, and discover exactly what the professor wants to see. Armed with this knowledge, you will know how to modify your exam writing style to meet the individual expectations of each professor.

Of course, unless you understand the law conceptually, you will be unable to solve an exam problem. That is why you must read the cases, brief the cases, struggle with the principles of law in class, discuss the law with your classmates and professors, keep a running outline of class materials and develop a problem-solving approach. Each of these challenges will contribute substantially to your understanding of the law. Without understanding what the word "intent" means, for example, it is impossible to determine whether the intent requirement is met in a battery problem. You cannot solve a problem with a tool you do not know how to use.

This does not mean that you should wait to understand every piece of law before attempting to take examinations. The process of taking examinations and solving exam problems will assist you in understanding the law, and how the law applies to new factual situations.

Ten Rules to Write By

As we tackle each first year subject head on, notice the similarities in how each model answer is structured and written, regardless of the subject matter analyzed. Every analysis of each legal question contains a statement of the issue, the rule, application of the facts to the law, and conclusion. Also, the following rules of thumb should be observed in writing all examinations.

1. Grammar Is Everything

You must know how to write well in order to succeed on law school examinations and in your legal career. If grammar is not one of your strong suits, then take a refresher course or buy a good book on basic grammar and essay writing. Your professors will expect perfect grammar and syntax and will not take the time to teach you how to write in class.

There is absolutely no room for sentence fragments, parallel structure problems, misspellings, slang or colloquialisms and other grammatical errors. You are expected to communicate your reasoning in a clear, concise, and grammatically correct fashion. You will be penalized dearly for failing to do so.

I repeat, if writing and grammar are a problem, then deal with it now. Learning proper grammar is an investment that will pay off tenfold over the years to come.

2. Write Neatly

Nothing offends a professor's good graces and patience more than horrendous handwriting. If you ever attempted to read someone else's illegible chicken scratches, you will agree with the age old caveat: THOU SHALL WRITE LEGIBLY. The importance of writing legibly cannot be stressed enough. What professor enjoys the mental chore of deciphering strange characters in order to discover what the writer is attempting to convey? Even worse, many professors understandably will not take the time to figure out what you are trying to say. If penmanship is not one of your strong points, then learn how to type or write legibly. The key to improving your handwriting is no different than what is taught in grade school: practice.

3. Always Use Headings

Unless your instructor specifically tells you otherwise, always use headings. A heading is a label or a flag that tells your professor exactly what issue or element of law you are discussing. Headings force you to compartmentalize, i.e., separate each discussion of the law.

For example, in writing a torts problem involving issues of battery, assault, and negligence, your headings might appear as follows:

I. Bart v. Homer

A. Intentional Torts
- **1. Battery**
  - **Defenses to Battery**
- **2. Assault**
  - **Defenses to Assault**

B. Negligence
- **1. Duty**
- **2. Standard of Care**
- **3. Breach of Standard of Care**
- **4. Causation**
  - **a. Actual or legal cause**
  - **b. Proximate case**
- **5. Damages**
- **6. Defenses to Negligence**

a. Contributory/comparative negligence
b. Last Clear Chance Doctrine

In a contracts problem, where the question is whether there is a legal relationship between the parties, your headings might read:

<u>Letter of January 5th</u>

<u>Invitation for An Offer</u>
<u>Offer</u>
<u>Termination of the Offer</u>
<u>Acceptance</u>
<u>Consideration</u>

In a criminal law problem, where the issue is what crimes were committed and what defenses may apply, your headings might read:

<u>People v. Felon B. Goode</u>

1. **<u>Crimes</u>**
   Robbery
   Extortion
   Larceny
   Forgery

2. **<u>Defenses to Crimes</u>**
   Duress
   Crime Prevention

These examples illustrate the value of using headings. Headings immediately focus your instructor on the issues which you are analyzing, and in turn make it easier for your professor to grade your examination.

Remember that your examination will be one of hundreds, and whatever you can do to make your examination less painful to grade will be sincerely appreciated by your instructor. After grading thousands of examinations, I can attest to the mundane nature of this process. Grading an essay examination is a subjective process which is invariably affected by factors such as when your examination is graded, the quality of the exam read before and after your examination is read, and other factors beyond your control. Instead of worrying or complaining about things which you are unable to control, do everything you can to insure that your examination will be easy on your professor's mind and eyes.

In organizing your examination, begin by stating the parties. For example, in a torts problem involving multiple parties, separate each party and each cause of action, and organize your analysis according to what party did what to whom. In a criminal law problem, organize the problem according to the parties who are charged with crimes. Therefore, your answer should generally begin with a statement of who the parties are, i.e., Fred v. Wilma or People v. Pebbles.

The next set of headings depends on the type of problem you are solving. The headings for a "burglary" problem might be "burglary" or "elements of a burglary" followed by "defenses to a burglary." More detailed headings might recite each element of the burglary, i.e., "specific intent," etc.

As your ability to write a clear concise legal analysis improves, you may find it unnecessary to use headings. But as a beginner, headings will help focus your analysis on the appropriate issues, and segregate your analysis of each issue.

4. Know What You Are Going to Write Before Writing It

Good legal writing is rarely the result of a stream of consciousness. Rather, it is imperative that the writer know what he or she is trying to say before writing it so that important issues are not glossed over or missed altogether.

Before writing out your examination answer, it is suggested that you outline your answer. Unless you have a photographic memory and can outline and compartmentalize in your mind the discussion of numerous issues, the facts of the case, the issues presented, the rules of law, your application and conclusions, you should outline your answer. Naturally, the amount of information included in your outline will depend on your individual ability to organize your answer. One person might write out a detailed outline using an I-R-A-C format, while another might jot down simple key phrases and words.

However, do not become carried away with creating the perfect outline to an exam answer. In most cases, you will not be asked to submit your outline and will not receive credit for writing an outline.

Here is an example of an outline of the David and Mattie "burglary" example:

People v. Gifford Gangster

I. Burglary

State the general burglary rule and issue
1. Trespassory - w/o true owner's consent; here premises leased to David & Mattie, who did not consent to Gifford's entry
2. Breaking - GG uses glasscutter to cut hole in window
3. Entering - slightest entry sufficient - iron hand used to enter premises; iron hand actually penetrates structure.
4. Dwelling house - C/L required that the structure be a residence - here David occasionally slept in offices
5. Of Another - office leased to David and Mattie
6. At the nighttime - abolished under modern law
7. With the specific intent to commit larceny or felony - GG intended to steal Maria's file at time of entry

Another student's outline might contain more or less detail. The above outline merely recites the elements to be discussed and the relevant facts to be used in solving the issue. The outline is used to organize the exam writer's thoughts and assists the writer in deciding exactly what she is going to write before writing it.

An outline is like a map: it is a plan or strategy which you will use and refer to in writing out your answer. As a result of the above outline, the writer knows exactly what elements will be analyzed, what facts will be applied to the law, and in what order the analysis will proceed. Writing an exam answer is much easier when you know exactly what to write.

5. Use Simple Language and Vocabulary

Your professor is conducting neither a spelling bee or a vocabulary test. Clarity of expression is everything. Use simple sentences to illustrate whatever point you are making. Your objective is not to make the analysis more complicated than it is, but to simplify it through step by step, logical reasoning. In order to convey your reasoning, simple language such as "Bart saw Spot bite Lisa before and therefore should have been aware of Spot's propensity to bite people," is more than sufficient.

Do not attempt to write a Court of Appeal opinion. I recall once reading a sentence in an opinion that was forty-five words long. It was the sentence that wouldn't die! Do not write paragraphs or sentences which run on forever. Generally, each paragraph should not contain more than four to seven sentences. If you are writing more than seven sentences per paragraph, chances are that you are either repeating yourself or not compartmentalizing each component of your analysis. Economy of words is always the rule.

6. Write Professionally

While attorneys are sometimes described as "frustrated actors," when writing your examination, do not exude the wit or prose of a comedian or Oscar-winning scriptwriter. While your professor may possess a sense a humor, your exam must not. A law school examination is not a place for pretentious contentions: "the plaintiff is a lying scuzz-bucket!", or jovial jokes "assuming that D doesn't stand for dummy;" or arrogant proclamations: "obviously the law is in error and anyone who cannot see the same has the mind of a gnat."

The law examination is not a creative writing piece nor is it a place to express your great sense of humor or take poetic license. Legal writing requires a largely objective, analytical, point by point, well-organized analysis of a legal problem or issue.

Avoid using the first person to express your views. Instead of writing, "I think that the plaintiff has proven a case for intentional infliction of emotional distress," write "Plaintiff has proven a case for intentional infliction of emotional distress." Do not personalize your views by stating "I believe . . ." or "My contention is . . ." State your arguments using the named party who will ultimately make such an argument, i.e., "Plaintiff argues . . ." "Defendant maintains . . ." etc. Always write in the third person.

Never use contractions in your exam answer. Legal writing is formal writing and should be devoid of slang words, clichés and other informal language.

This is by no means an attempt to teach proper composition. This book is not intended to be a comprehensive grammar primer. If you have problems in writing in a lawyer-like fashion, closely study the model examinations that follow.

7. Argue Both Sides of an Issue Where Appropriate

Just as there are two sides to every story, there are usually two or more arguments that can be made in response to a legal issue. When do you argue both sides of an issue? The answer is, whenever it is appropriate. Some issues require you to do so, while others do not. There are major issues, minor issues and non-existent issues. The only way you will know when to argue both sides, or even when to discuss an issue at all, is by making your own judgment calls as to when it is appropriate.

In your legal career, you will be called on to make numerous judgment calls in deciding when to argue a point and when the point is best conceded or glossed over. On law school examinations, some issues are more important than others, and require a more in-depth discussion. For example, in a burglary problem, the major issue presented by a particular fact pattern might be whether the defendant had specific intent while a minor issue might be whether the defendant committed a trespass. For example:

Freddie Fox forcibly entered Fannie Fox's house without Fannie's consent in order to propose marriage. Fannie Fox was not home, so Freddie took some chocolate chip cookies. Is Freddie guilty of burglary?

This burglary problem requires an analysis of each element of a burglary. In this example, however, the element of "trespass" is not a major issue. Because the problem plainly states that Freddie did not have Fannie Fox's consent, a great deal of discussion of this issue is not warranted. A major issue, which requires a discussion of both sides, is the issue of specific intent. Your answer on the issue of specific intent might be:

The issue is whether Freddie Fox had the specific intent to commit a burglary. A burglary requires that the defendant have the specific intent to commit a felony or larceny at the time of the entry. Freddie would argue that he did not have the intent to commit a theft of the cookies at the time that he entered Fannie's home. He would claim that he only intended to propose marriage, which was the purpose of his entry. However, it could be argued that a person does not forcibly break into another's home to propose marriage, and that Freddie's asserted reason for entering Fannie's home is not worthy of belief. If it could be proven that Freddie harbored the intent to commit a felony or theft at the time he entered Fannie's house, this element would be met. However, if Freddie did intend to propose only marriage, no burglary is proven.

Although both sides are discussed in the above example, a conclusion is reached, and the reader is not left "hanging." Discuss both sides, but reach a conclusion one way or the other. Do not be wishy-washy unless the issue is truly one incapable of resolution. Also, each argument is explored and articulated. The more effective argument is framed first, followed by the less effective argument.

Let's analyze the minor issue of "trespass":

The issue is whether Freddie Fox committed a trespassory entry. Burglary requires that the defendant enter without the true owner's consent. Freddie entered Fannie's home without her knowledge or consent. Therefore, this element is met.

The fact pattern practically hands you the trespass element on a silver platter by telling you that Freddie did not have Fannie's consent. However, a comprehensive analysis of the elements of burglary would include a discussion of whether the trespass element was met. While there is no need to discuss both sides as with the discussion of specific intent, the issue is still a minor issue that should be addressed.

An example of a non-issue is whether Freddie ate the chocolate cookies, or how Fannie determined that the cookies were missing. A non-issue is one which is not raised by the fact pattern and need not be discussed in relation to solving the problem. It is unnecessary to answer non-issues, as you will have plenty of real issues to discuss.

The key to arguing both sides is putting yourself in the shoes of the party making the argument. In your career, you will be required to understand your opponent's arguments and contentions better than your own; whether it be the point of view of the plaintiff, defendant, prosecution, defense, appellant or appellee, judge or juror, a good lawyer considers and studies all possible perspectives that may have some bearing upon the issue at hand. A good problem solver is one who understands and anticipates the concerns and arguments of all interested parties.

8. Use Common Sense

In solving exam problems, use common sense. All too often, in the flurry of rules, law and logic, common sense is left standing outside the door. You may begin to feel like a robot, processing a fact pattern. But do not forget that your professor is really testing your ability to use common sense to solve pseudo-real life problems, similar to the type of problems and cases you will later face in your career. Application is not a mere recitation of the relevant facts in response to an issue; the essential link is what you really think about how the law should be applied to a particular situation. Law school examinations test you on how you think, not your ability to regurgitate the law and facts.

9. Manage Your Time

Because most law school examinations must be completed within a finite time period, usually from one to three hours, time is of the essence as law school examinations are concerned. In real life you will generally be afforded sufficient time to research the law, but in law school you must learn how to solve problems quickly and efficiently.

The only cure for the lack of speed is practice and absolute awareness of the time constraints you will be subject to. The student is well advised to time herself during each practice examination in order to monitor the speed with which the problems are completed. Speed will come with time. Initially, take whatever time is necessary to thoroughly analyze a problem; however, as you take more and more practice examinations, concern yourself with the element of time.

The objective is to get past that finish line. An incomplete examination will result in an incomplete grade. Always keep that finish line in mind when taking any examination.

As you begin taking examinations, you will find it necessary to allocate the available time to each of the six exam-taking steps. For example, if you have one hour to solve a problem, you might apportion 10-15 minutes to read and visualize the problem, 10 minutes to decide what issues are presented and to outline an answer, and the remaining 35-40 minutes to write out your answer. As you become more and more experienced at exam writing, you will be able to "size up" an exam question, and determine what issues are more deserving than others and how much time to spend on each of the various issues before you.

The classic first year horror story is that of the student who is given a two part exam to complete in one hour, and writes a beautiful, textbook answer to part one, but because of the time constraints, never even reads the second part of the problem and sadly fails the examination. This is not a situation in which you wish to be in.

10. Do Not Panic

From time to time, in writing examinations, you may experience writer's block, or even worse, your mind may go blank. This is not unusual, and happens to the best legal minds. The lesson to learn, however, is not to panic.

When experiencing writer's block, close your eyes for a moment and take a deep breath. Clear your mind and then set upon the problem before you.

Conclusion

This selection of exam writing tips may seem overwhelming. Rather than attempting to master these tips overnight, take each tip one at a time, and master that tip before moving onto the next. For example, if the first tip on your list is "neatness," then spend a week or two writing meticulous exam answers and improving your handwriting. After your handwriting is satisfactory, then tackle the use of headings. As your skills as a problem solver progress, you will be pleasantly surprised at the speed with which you are able to incorporate these concepts into your exam writing.

How to Answer a Torts Problem

As stated in the introductory section, the law of torts concerns a private wrong. A typical torts exam problem involves a fact pattern in which two or more parties commit wrongs against one another. You will be required to sort through the facts and figure out what causes of action exist and what defenses and general considerations apply.

In solving an exam problem, begin with the "big picture." What this means is that you begin with the big questions and work your way down to the more detailed questions. In torts, the three major issues are:

(1) What **theory** of tort liability? Intentional tort, negligence, strict liability, etc?

(2) What **defenses** apply?

(3) Do any **general considerations** apply?

These are the questions you will ask when confronted with any torts problem.

Intentional Torts

CAPTAIN'S LOG, today's date: Imagine that you are in a spacecraft traveling in the great void of space. As you whisk along at warp speed, you approach the Torts galaxy. Within this galaxy, there are three universes: intentional torts, negligence and strict liability.

First stop, the universe of intentional torts. In this universe there are seven planets, one for each of the seven intentional torts. When you enter this universe, you must ask yourself seven questions. Is there a battery? Is there an assault? Is there false imprisonment? Intentional infliction of emotional distress? Trespass to land? Trespass to chattels? Conversion?

Once you have determined what planet you are on, you must then decide what moons revolve around the planet. For each intentional tort, different defenses may apply. For battery: self-defense, defense of others, defense of property, privilege of arrest, and consent may apply. For trespass to land: the defense of necessity and defense of property may apply.

Now back to the real world.

Assume that the issue is whether or not a battery was committed. What questions will you ask? How will you solve this problem? The answer is "with my Torts *Law Chart*." As you have already learned, a problem-solving approach is a tool that can be used to solve any problem in a particular area of law. Let's look at the problem-solving approach taken from the Torts *Law Chart*:

Problem-solving Approach for Battery

Issue to Be Solved: DID D COMMIT A BATTERY?

What's the Rule: **A BATTERY IS AN AFFIRMATIVE ACT WITH THE INTENT TO TOUCH ANOTHER RESULTING IN ACTUAL HARMFUL OR OFFENSIVE CONTACT.**

What **Elements** Must Be Proven?

(1) Is there an **affirmative act**?
• An affirmative act is one which the actor performs voluntarily.

(2) Did the defendant **intend** for the contact to occur?
• The actor must actually intend to inflict the harmful or offensive contact or be substantially certain that such contact would occur.

(3) Was there **actual contact** between plaintiff and defendant?
• Battery requires actual contact between D and P or something closely connected to P.

(4) Was the contact **harmful or offensive** to a reasonable person?
• Battery requires that the contact be harmful or offensive to a reasonable person under same or similar circumstances.
• EXCEPTION: Unless the defendant knew of the P's special sensitivity.

This is one possible approach to solving a battery problem. This approach sets forth the issues that must be answered whenever a battery problem is presented. First, an affirmative act must be proven. An affirmative act means that the act performed by the party being sued was voluntary, on his or her own accord, and not as the result of coercion, duress, or accident. Secondly, there must be the intent to touch another. As you will learn in the famous case of Garratt v. Dailey, which involved an incident where a young boy pulled a chair out from under a woman, causing her to fall, intent is met where the defendant actually intends to make contact OR where the defendant should have been substantially certain that contact would occur. Thirdly, there must be actual contact between the plaintiff and defendant OR something closely connected to defendant's person. Fourthly, the contact must be harmful or offensive to the reasonable person.

Now, instead of focusing on the "law" of what a battery is, focus instead on the fact that a battery is simply a checklist of various circumstances that must exist before a battery is proven. Understanding that the law of torts involves an analysis of whether the elements of a cause of action are met is fundamental to the law of torts.

The same is true for each of the intentional torts, negligence, and all other causes of action in tort law. While the requirements of each tort will vary, the "checklist" approach is the same for all torts. In order to ascertain whether a cause of action exists, you must determine if each element is proven. For example, the law of defamation concerns itself with situations when one "defames" or publicly ridicules another. As with battery, there are certain requirements that must be met before plaintiff has proven a case of defamation against the defendant.

Read through the above problem-solving approach several times to insure that you understand the law that will be applied in the examples that follow. We will spend a great deal of time in the realm of battery in order to demonstrate how to write a successful exam answer.

Now let's apply our torts problem-solving approach to a simple single-issue fact pattern:

Intentional Torts Example #1: Student v. Lee

At a martial arts demonstration, Bruce Lee delivered a stunning front kick to a kicking bag, which was held by Student. Student suffered severe injuries as a result of Lee's forceful kick. Please discuss Lee's liability for battery.

Now assuming that you have gone through the Six Steps of Exam Taking, that is, reading, visualizing, determining what questions are presented and applying the problem-solving approach, the final question is "what do I write and how do I write it?"

You will be expected to write a well-organized, structured answer that comprehensively covers each issue raised in a neat and understandable format. You are asked to identify each issue and recite the relevant laws. Finally, you are required to present a well-reasoned analysis explaining each conclusion reached. Sound simple? Actually, it really is.

The writing style and structure employed in each of the examples in this book follows the basic I-R-A-C format. Though the I-R-A-C format of writing is neither exciting nor especially creative, it works and will serve you well if you have difficulty organizing your analysis.

The basic I-R-A-C format you would use to solve a battery problem as follows:

The issue is whether ______ is liable to ________ for battery.

A battery is an affirmative act with the intent to touch another resulting in harmful or offensive contact.

The first issue is whether there was an affirmative act. An affirmative act is one which the D performs voluntarily. (APPLICATION) Therefore, this requirement is met/not met.

The second issue is whether D intended to make contact with P. The actor must actually intend to inflict the harmful or offensive contact or must be substantially certain that such contact would occur. (APPLICATION) Therefore, this element is met/not met.

The third issue is whether there was harmful and offensive contact between P and D. Battery requires actual contact with the person or something closely connected to the person. Such contact may be direct or indirect. (APPLICATION) In addition, the contact must be harmful or offensive to the reasonable person. (APPLICATION) Thus, the harmful and offensive contact requirement is met/not met.

In conclusion, D is liable/not liable for battery as against P.

The above I-R-A-C format covers each issue comprehensively and separately, one at a time. Each discussion of each element of battery contains a statement of the issue to be solved and the rule of law to be applied, followed by an analysis that explains and leads up to the conclusion.

Crutches are used to hold each paragraph together, i.e., "the first issue . . ." These "crutches" are often unnecessary surplusage, and you may find that your analysis will stand without them. However, crutches often assist the exam writer in starting off a paragraph or in structuring an analysis. Crutches also may help you overcome writer's block.

You will find that a good part of your examination will be prewritten or preordained before you even walk into the examination room. That is because the issues you will ask and the rules of law that you apply are constants and do not change. Only the application of those rules change with each new fact pattern.

Let's look at one possible exam answer to Student v. Lee, following the above I-R-A-C format. As you read through this example, focus on the application, which is set apart in **bold** type.

Model Answer: <u>**Student v. Lee**</u>

A. <u>Battery</u>

The issue here is whether Lee is liable to Student for battery.

A battery is an affirmative act with the intent to touch another resulting in actual harmful or offensive contact.

The first issue is whether Bruce committed an affirmative act. An affirmative act is one which the actor performs voluntarily. **It can be inferred from the fact that since Lee was performing a martial arts demonstration when he kicked Student, he acted on his own accord, as opposed to accidentally or mistakenly. There is no evidence that Bruce's act of kicking was coerced or involuntarily induced.** Therefore, this requirement is met.

The second issue is whether Bruce intended to make contact with Student. The actor must actually intend to inflict the harmful or offensive contact or must be substantially certain that such contact would occur. **It can be reasonably inferred from Bruce's act of kicking Student during the course of a martial arts demonstration that Bruce actually intended to make contact with the kick bag. Student held the bag for the express purpose of aiding Bruce in the demonstration, and Bruce "delivered" the kick, with knowledge of his act. However, if it is shown that Bruce is an expert martial artist, Student's claim that Bruce intended the contact would be bolstered, as an expert would presumably know what he or she was doing.**

If actual intent is not proven, in the alternative, the substantial certainty element would be met. **A reasonable person would be substantially certain that if one kicks a bag held by a person, contact would occur with that person. Therefore, Bruce knew to a substantial certainty that he would make contact with Student when he kicked the bag.** Thus, the intent element is met.

The third issue is whether there was harmful and offensive contact between Bruce and student. Battery requires actual contact with the person or something closely connected to the person. Such contact may be direct or indirect. **While there was no direct physical contact between Bruce's person and that of Student, there was indirect contact because Student was holding the bag that Lee kicked. Therefore, actual contact occurred because the bag was "closely connected" to Student.** Thus, this element is met.

The contact must also be harmful or offensive to the reasonable person. **Any reasonable person would consider being kicked both harmful and offensive**. Thus, the harmful and offensive contact requirement is met.

In conclusion, Bruce is liable for battery as against Student.

While the above "model answer" is only one possible answer to the problem, let's compare the model answer to other answers which "miss the boat" completely:

COMPARE: **CONCLUSORY ANALYSIS**

Bruce's act constituted a battery. A battery is an affirmative act with the intent to touch another, resulting in harmful and offensive contact. Bruce acted on own accord in kicking the bag held by Student. He also intended to kick the bag when he kicked it. Also, he caused contact with student that was harmful and offensive to him when he kicked the bag.

COMPARE: **DISORGANIZED ANALYSIS**

The kicking of the bag was a battery against Student. There was contact with student, and Bruce intended that such contact occur. That contact was harmful and offensive because Student was injured, although the rule of battery does not require actual injury. Bruce's act could have also constituted an assault. Thus, Bruce is liable for battery.

COMPARE: **FAILURE TO STATE THE LAW**

Bruce is liable for battery. First, the act of kicking was voluntary to demonstrate his technique. Secondly, he intended to make contact with the bag, since he performed the kick for the purpose of demonstrating how to deliver a kick. Finally, he made contact with Student by kicking the bag, and anyone would find being at the receiving end of a kick harmful and offensive.

COMPARE: **WISHY-WASHY ANSWER**

Bruce might be liable for battery. While the act of kicking would normally be a voluntary act, it cannot be determined if Bruce acted on his own or whether some other force caused him to kick Student. Bruce's intent is not clear, as he said nothing before kicking student. Lastly, some people would find holding a kicking bag enjoyable while others would not. Thus, it cannot be decided whether Bruce is liable for a battery.

COMPARE: **WEIRD, FLAKEY, HALLUCINATORY ANSWER**

Bruce would not be liable for battery. On the issue of intent, Bruce did not have the intent to make contact with Student. In martial arts, Students have to follow the teachings and instructions of their masters. Because Student

was a student of Bruce's, it is unlikely that Bruce wanted to hurt Student. Student probably paid Bruce to learn martial arts, and Bruce would not wish to hurt "the goose that laid the golden egg." Thus, Bruce did not commit battery.

COMPARE: **BUT DOES THE ANSWER HAVE TO BE SO LONG?!**
The short answer is, of course not! The above analysis simply takes each issue, point by point, issue by issue, rule by rule, application by application, etc. However, an answer could be drafted which contains the I-R-A-C substance in short form, as is demonstrated in the following example. However, heed this WARNING: If you are not a prolific writer, stick to an I-R-A-C format until you become better versed in expressing each of the I-R-A-C elements.

Example:

Battery is an affirmative act with the intent to touch another resulting in harmful or offensive touching.

The element of an affirmative act is met because Bruce's kick was performed voluntarily to demonstrate a martial arts technique and not the result of duress, accident or mistake. The intent requirement is also met because Bruce actually intended to make contact with the bag, as he acted with the knowledge and purpose of demonstrating a kick to the bag. Notwithstanding actual intent, a reasonable person kicking a bag would be substantially certain that contact would occur with the person holding the bag. The harmful and offensive contact requirement is met because anyone would consider being kicked to be harmful and offensive, and there was actual contact between Bruce and the bag, which was closely connected to Student's person.

Thus, Bruce is liable to Student for battery.

Although the analysis in the above example is shorter and less verbose, each sentence contains a statement of the issue, rule and application, compacted into a single, flowing sentence. The shorter version contains the same reasoning as the strict I-R-A-C example but gets there faster. Again, do not attempt to write in this fashion until after you have mastered the basic I-R-A-C writing style.

Before moving on to bigger and more complex problems, let's take a moment to analyze two additional battery problems using the basic I-R-A-C format. Notice how the structure of each battery analysis is identical to that employed in Student v. Lee. In the model answers following each question, the application is set forth in **bold** type:

Intentional Torts Example #2: Peg v. Marcie

Peg had just received a mink coat from her husband Al when she saw Marcie and Steve. Peg said, "Ah, Marcie, you'll never guess where I got this mink coat." Marcie replied, "Woolworth's" and spit on Peg's jacket. Did Marcie commit battery?

Model Answer: Peg v. Marcie

The issue here is **whether Marcie committed a battery when she spit on Peg's jacket**. A battery is an affirmative act with the intent to touch another resulting in harmful or offensive contact.

An affirmative act is one which the actor performs voluntarily. **Generally speaking, spitting is a voluntary act unless done accidentally, such as, during an involuntary spasm. Here, since there are no facts indicating that Marcie spit because of some involuntary force, it can be inferred from the circumstances that she acted of her own accord and spit out of spite**. Thus, this requirement is met.

The intent element is fulfilled where the defendant actually intends contact or should have been substantially certain such contact would occur.

It can be argued that Marcie actually intended to spit on Peg's jacket. Her expression "Woolworth" was made in response to Peg's rather gloating and arrogant statement, "You'll never guess where I got this mink coat." Given the relationship between Peg and Marcie – apparently not a friendly one, one could infer that Marcie knew exactly what she was doing when she spit on Peg's jacket, that is, ruining and causing damage to the subject matter of the insults.

Further, given that the two were in earshot of one another, Marcie should have been substantially certain that expectorate expelled from her mouth at that short of a distance would strike someone.

Thus, the intent requirement is met.

Finally, battery requires that there be actual contact between plaintiff and defendant, and that such contact be harmful and offensive to the reasonable person. **Anyone would find being spit at to be harmful and offensive, and here the actual contact requirement is met since Marcie's spit, an instrumentality of her person, made contact with something closely connected to Peg, the coat.** Thus, this requirement is met.

Therefore, Marcie is liable to Peg for battery.

Intentional Torts Example #3: **Harriett v. Fritz Kafka**

Fritz was playing frisbee at Golden Gate Park when he saw Harriett Hotpants, who had recently jilted him for another man. He took his frisbee and threw it at Harriett, intending to miss her by a few inches, as he was still madly in love with her. Unfortunately, Fritz had a poor aim and the frisbee hit Harriett in the neck, causing her great pain.

Model Answer: **Harriett v. Fritz**

The issue is whether Fritz's act of hitting Harriett with the frisbee constitutes a battery. A battery is an affirmative act with the intent to touch another resulting in harmful or offensive touching.

An affirmative act is one which the actor performs voluntarily. **Here Fritz was engaged in playing frisbee at the park and threw the frisbee in Harriett's direction to gain her attention, and did so of his own accord, not as the result of any accident, coercion or involuntary force. In addition, the act of throwing a frisbee requires use of motor skills,** i.e., **flick of the wrist, which involves volitional force.** Therefore this requirement is met.

Intent requires that the actor actually intend contact or be substantially certain such contact would occur. **Here Fritz did not intend contact, but "intend(ed) to miss her by a few inches"; therefore, actual intent is not present. However, Fritz, having "poor aim," should have been substantially certain contact would occur, since anyone who is not an expert in frisbee throwing would know that a spinning object thrown in another's person's direction would likely make contact with that person.** Therefore, intent is met.

Here there was actual contact between an instrumentality of Fritz, i.e., **the frisbee, and Harriett's neck,** and therefore the actual contact requirement is met.

Finally, **any reasonable person non-consensually struck by a frisbee, causing her great pain, would find such contact harmful and offensive,** and therefore this requirement is met.

Based on the above, Fritz is liable to Harriett for battery.

Notice how each model answer follows an identical pattern. Each element of a battery is taken one at a time, issue by issue, and the basic I-R-A-C structure is employed. This basic I-R-A-C structure is the foundation of all exam writing.

Before reading on, you should write and re-write your answer to these single-issue battery problems until you are able to write out your analysis with ease. As you build a strong foundation beginning with these simple problems, you will see that the same basic principles and writing style apply equally to complex multi-issue and multi-party problems.

Next, let's take another battery problem, this time adding an issue as to whether any defenses apply. In this example, we will use the defense of property as an example. First, a review of the requirements of the defense:

DEFENSE OF PROPERTY

WHAT'S THE RULE:
One may use reasonable force to prevent the commission of a tort against his property IF:

- A request to desist precedes the use of force, unless the request would be futile or dangerous.
- Use of force was reasonable and did not cause death or serious bodily injury.

Read the examination question carefully, and follow the six steps of exam taking:

Intentional Torts Example #4: **Bennie v. Frankie**

Frankie was walking out of the Hard Rock Cafe when he saw Bennie Burglar smashing the window of Frankie's new Porsche with a hammer. When he approached Bennie, he said, "Stop that, what are you doing?" to which Bennie replied, "I was trying to kill a mosquito that was on the window." Frankie replied "Well, I'm gonna smash a mosquito too," at which point he took the hammer and smashed Bennie's skull to smitherines.

Model Answer: **Bennie v. Frankie**

A. Battery

The issue is whether Frankie is liable to Bennie for battery.

A battery is an affirmative act with the intent to touch another resulting in harmful or offensive contact.

Frankie's act of taking the hammer and smashing Bennie's skull would no doubt be found to be affirmative. An affirmative act is one which the actor performs voluntarily. **There is no indication that Frankie acted out of duress or**

coercion, or that he acted involuntarily. To the contrary, Frankie acted on his own accord in order to protect his property, therefore, this requirement is met.

Second, the actor must actually intend the harmful or offensive contact or must be substantially certain that such contact would occur. **Here it would appear that Frankie actually intended to hit Bennie. He walked out of the restaurant and observed Bennie smashing his car window, giving him a motive to strike Bennie. The strongest evidence of Frankie's intent was his statement, "Well, I'm gonna smash a mosquito too." Immediately after making this threatening statement, Frankie struck Bennie with the hammer, therefore acting in accordance with his expressed intent. These statements speak for themselves,** and the intent requirement would be met. Notwithstanding actual intent, **Frankie should have at least been substantially certain that contact would occur when he swung the hammer at Frankie, as any reasonable person would be**.

Finally, there must be actual contact and such contact must be harmful or offensive to the reasonable person. **The actual contact requirement would be met because the hammer held by Frankie made actual contact with Bennie's skull. As to the "harmful and offensive" element, anyone who was hit in the head with a hammer would find it harmful as well as offensive**.

Therefore, Frankie is liable for battery.

B. <u>Defenses to Battery</u>

In defense of battery, Frankie would argue that the defense of property applies, excusing him of liability for battery.

Under this defense, a person may use reasonable force to prevent the commission of a tort against his or her property. However, such use of reasonable force must be preceded by a request to desist unless circumstances make it clear that the request would be futile or dangerous, AND the use of force must be reasonable (<u>i.e.</u>, not force which will cause death or serious bodily harm).

Applying the first prong, Frankie expressly told Bennie to stop hitting his car with a hammer when he said, "Stop that, what are you doing?" There is no indication whether Bennie did, in fact, stop hitting Frankie's windshield upon Frankie's request, but if he did, then Frankie's action would be unwarranted, since he would not be acting to <u>prevent</u> a tort. If Bennie did not stop upon Frankie's request, then this element would be met.

The second prong, however, would not be met. Here Frankie sought to protect his property by taking a hammer and smashing Bennie's skull. Reasonable force

is reasonable under the circumstances when it cannot cause death or bodily harm. The force used here was unreasonable, to an extreme, under the circumstances given. It is not reasonable for one to hit another with a hammer in the head with such force to shatter the skull because that person broke a car window.

Furthermore, the force used here could easily cause death, and no doubt would cause bodily harm, as it did here.

Therefore, because the second prong is not met, the defense of property does not apply, and Frankie would not be excused of liability for battery.

* * *

Note how the defense of property issue is structured and organized in the same fashion as the discussion of battery. The I-R-A-C structure is applied in the same fashion as in the discussion of battery.

Having analyzed four battery problems, we will now analyze a somewhat more complex problem, using the same characters and events used in the first "Bruce Lee" example. In the model answer that follows, a point by point, sentence by sentence narrative is offered, explaining the purpose of each sentence and the significance of each statement made:

Intentional Torts Example #5: **Louie Lawstudent v. Lee**

On October 25, Jocko College of the Law sponsored a martial arts demonstration featuring the great martial arts master, Bruce Lee. One week before the demonstration, Jocko advertised the event as follows:

TO ALL STUDENTS AND FACULTY: MEET THE GREAT BRUCE LEE IN PERSON! ONE OF OUR HONORABLE STUDENT BODY WILL BE CHOSEN TO MEET MR. LEE FACE TO FACE ON OCTOBER 25TH IN THE RING. ALL INTERESTED PERSONS PLEASE APPLY IN THE STUDENT INFORMATION CENTER.

Of the many students at Jocko, only Louie Lawstudent applied. Louie awoke bright and early on October 25 and went to the school auditorium where the demonstration was to be held. As soon as Louie entered the room, he was approached by Dean Jimmy who said, "Congratulations, my son, you have won the contest!" With that, he had Louie sign a form that read as follows:

I HEREBY GIVE UP ALL MY RIGHTS AGAINST JOCKO COLLEGE OF THE

LAW FOR ANY INJURY OCCURRING AS A RESULT OF MY PARTICIPATION IN THE GUNG FU MATCH HELD ON OCTOBER 33. SIGNED, LOUIE LAWSTUDENT.

Then Louie was taken to the front of the room and handed a kicking bag. Louie could hear students in the background singing, "Louie, Louie." From nowhere, Bruce Lee ran towards Louie and demonstrated a flying jump kick to the kicking bag. Louie, who had never even held a kick bag before, flew nearly one hundred feet before coming to a stop on his head.

Dean Jimmy ran to Louie's aid and said, smiling, "Well, you sure got to meet Bruce face to face."

Louie suffered four broken ribs and two chipped teeth. As a result of the latter, Louie could not brush his teeth for four weeks and lost the love of his sweetheart, Crest Scope.

Louie has come to your office for consolation and advice. As a result of his injuries, he was unable to take his midterms. He tells you that he is not interested in pursuing his case against Jocko Law School because of his status as a student there, but seeks to sue Bruce Lee for battery.

Please discuss Bruce's liability to Louie for battery.

MODEL ANSWER AND POINT BY POINT ANALYSIS
LOUIE LAWSTUDENT v. BRUCE LEE

In studying this model examination, note that the text of the answer is in **bold type**, and the narrative is in regular type.

Louie Lawstudent v. Bruce Lee (State the title of the case)

The issue here is whether Bruce Lee (D) is liable to Louie Lawstudent (P) for battery, and if so, whether any defenses may apply. (Begin by stating the general issue. The issue to be addressed by the student is stated clearly and concisely. The student is saying, "Hey look, I'm gonna see first whether a cause of action for battery exists, and then I'm gonna see whether any defenses exist!" The instructor immediately can see where the student's analysis is going.)

Battery

A battery is an affirmative act with the intent to touch another resulting in actual harmful or offensive contact. (Observe that each element of a battery is contained in the rule of law. In turn, each element found within the battery rule will open doors to other information you have learned. For example, when you see the words "affirmative act," you think, BINGO, the defendant must commit a voluntary act. When you see the phrase "with the intent to touch another," within the battery definition, you are reminded of the rule that the defendant must actually intend contact or at least be substantially certain contact would occur.)

First, D must do some voluntary act which causes the offensive or harmful touching. (Begin your discussion with the first element of battery by stating the sub-rule for the affirmative act element. This sentence serves to inform your professor that you know the issue and the rule of law. This is the "I" and "R" of I-R-A-C) **Bruce's act of performing a flying jump kick, thereby making contact with the bag held by Louie, would constitute an affirmative act because the act was done voluntarily. The act was performed in order to demonstrate a martial arts technique and was performed consciously by Bruce.** (After stating the issue and the rule, you must "apply" the facts to the rule. Many students make the mistake of merely citing the relevant fact and the issue to be addressed by writing "The affirmative act requirement is met here as Bruce kicked the bag voluntarily." While this sentence recites the relevant fact and shoves it together with the rule, it fails to address <u>why</u> the act is voluntary. Here the model answer takes the analysis one step further and tells the grader WHY: "The act was performed in order to demonstrate a martial arts technique and was performed consciously by Bruce." In other words, Bruce is consciously attempting to demonstrate how to deliver a kick. Although this reasoning may strike you as being as obvious as the nose on your face, you must explain <u>how</u> and <u>why</u> you reached a particular conclusion. That is the essence of application.) **Therefore, this element is met.** (Always state your conclusion)

Second, the intent requirement is met where D intends to inflict the offensive touching or acts in a manner that is substantially certain to cause the touching. <u>Garratt v. Dailey</u>. (Here again the rule is recited, which serves the dual purpose of informing your professor what question you are answering and demonstrating that you can cite the applicable rule. This is the "I" and "R" of I-R-A-C. Also note that the case of <u>Garratt v. Dailey</u> is cited; most professors will not expect you to cite cases, but if you do cite a case, make sure that it stands for whatever proposition you are making. Generally, it does not hurt to cite a case, but it will hurt you if you cite it incorrectly.)

Actual intent is met where the actor subjectively intends that contact would occur. (The rule of actual intent tells the grader what issue you are analyzing and the rule of actual intent.) **Here the act of kicking was performed during the course of a martial arts demonstration in which Bruce was exhibiting his martial arts skills. Thus, Bruce had knowledge of the act and acted with the purpose of demonstrating a technique. Given Bruce's expertise, it is unlikely that he kicked the bag accidentally or unintentionally. From this, it**

can be inferred that Bruce actually intended to make contact with Louie. (This is application! This discussion explains that because the act was performed at a demonstration where Bruce of exhibiting martial arts skills, and **because** Bruce was an experienced practitioner, and **because** his act of kicking was not accidental or intentional, he must have actually intended contact with the bag. **Bruce can possibly argue that he intended to make contact with the bag, but not with Louie, but given that Louie was holding the bag, Bruce would likely lose.** (Recognize opposing arguments and deal with them appropriately, explaining why they are valid or invalid)

Intent is also met where a reasonable person performing such an act should be substantially certain that contact would result. (Be comprehensive in your analysis – do not stop with your discussion of actual intent; you must discuss the issue of substantial certainty. If you were arguing this case to a jury, you would argue both!) **A reasonable person delivering a forceful kick to a bag held by another would be substantially certain that contact with the person holding the bag would occur. Here again Bruce's expertise would be a relevant factor, since he was aware of his strength and the effect of the application of his kick to the bag on Louie.** (Be creative with the facts. The facts tell you that Bruce is a gung fu expert, and so it is fair to assume that he was aware of this strength and how the force used would impact upon Louie. It is not enough to say that Bruce was substantially certain contact would occur to Louie; you must state WHY) **Hence, the intent requirement is met.** (Again the conclusion is stated.)

Third, the act must result in actual harmful or offensive touching. (Again you begin your discussion of the third element of battery by stating the issue and rule. Note that this element breaks into two sub-issues: (1) actual contact; (2) harmful or offensive contact to the reasonable person. The application addresses both issues separately). **The issue is whether there was actual contact between P and D.** (State the issue to be solved) **Battery requires actual contact with the plaintiff or with something closely connected to plaintiff's person.** (State the rule of actual contact) **Bruce's contact with the kicking bag fulfills the "actual contact" requirement because the kicking bag was closely connected to Louie.** (Apply the rule to the facts) **Under <u>Fischer v. Carrousel</u>, Bruce needed only to make actual contact with the bag.** (Case citation) **Finally, a reasonable person would find being at the receiving end of a forceful kick quite offensive, as well as harmful, as Louie did.** (This one sentence incorporates the issue, and rule <u>e.g.</u> harmful & offensive to the reasonable person, and the application as well.) **Thus this element is met.** (Conclusion)

Therefore Bruce would be liable to Louie for a battery. (Don't forget to state the overall conclusion after you have analyzed each element)

II. <u>Defenses to Battery</u> (This heading tells the grader you are now analyzing the defenses to a battery)

Bruce would respond to the battery charge by arguing that Louie consented to the battery. In most jurisdictions, consent is a complete defense to a battery. (Look familiar? Like the introduction to the battery analysis above, begin by telling the your professor what issue you intend to address)

The first issue is whether Louie actually consented to the battery. (State the issue) **Actual consent is found where the plaintiff expressly agrees to the tort.** (Now the rule) **Louie made no statements suggesting that he agreed to hold the bag for Bruce. The only arguable statement that could be imputed to Louie is the waiver of liability form signed by Louie, wherein Louie gave up all his rights against Jocko College for injury resulting in his "participation" in the gung fu match. Therefore, Louie did not give up any rights as against Bruce. Furthermore, the language contained in the form mentions nothing about holding a bag for Bruce. By agreeing to participate in the demonstration, Louie did not specifically agree to be the subject of a martial art technique.** (Now hit 'em with the application - did Louie expressly consent to battery by signing the waiver form?) **Therefore, the waiver form alone does not constitute an express consent to being subject to Bruce's kick or a waiver of liability as against Bruce.** (Conclusion)

The second issue is whether Louie consented to the battery by his conduct. (Issue) **Implied consent is found when the plaintiff engages in conduct which would lead a reasonable person to infer consent.** (The Rule!) **Here Louie applied to meet Bruce "face-to-face" in the ring at the school and signed a vague waiver form and held a kicking bag. His act of holding the bag would not cause a reasonable person to believe that Louie knew what would follow. A reasonable person would not think that by holding a bag, he or she would be subject to a forceful kick a few seconds later.** (A-P-P-L-I-C-A-T-I-O-N!!) **Bruce could argue that any reasonable person who went to a gung fu demonstration and was handed a bag used for the purpose of kicking, would know that he or she would be used as target practice. But because most spectators would not consent to injury, this argument is weak, and Louie would prevail.** (Always consider opposing arguments)

The <u>implied</u> <u>consent</u> doctrine has no application here.
(By pointing out that you considered the implied consent doctrine, you are telling your professor that you know the law and are carefully considering each issue to determine whether it may apply; while you would not lose any points by <u>not</u> including this information, it certainly will not hurt!)

The next issue is whether Louie's consent was informed. (Issue) **Even where a plaintiff consents, such consent must be informed.** (State the rule: Is this deja vu or what?) **Here, Louie was not given any information as to what he was in**

for. In fact, misinformation was given here. First, the advertisement distributed by the school stated that a student would meet Bruce Lee face to face. By "face to face" most people would conclude that they would meet Bruce, not be kicked by him. The waiver form was also misleading in that it merely stated that Louie would waive rights for injuries resulting from his "participation" in the martial arts match. The word "participation" is extremely broad and would not lead one to believe he might be injured as a result. Also, the waiver form stated the wrong date, October 33. There are 31 days in the month of October, not 33. (Explain why the waiver form did or did not provide Louie with the information necessary to validly consent) **This blatant misinformation should negate any consent.**

Even if Louie consented to holding the bag, Bruce's act of kicking the bag exceeded the scope of Louie's consent. (This sentence states the rule and the issue: did Bruce's act exceed the scope of Louie's consent?) **Louie's consent to hold the bag simply does not mean that he agreed to be kicked. Louie was not forewarned that the bag he held would be kicked by Bruce. Hence, if it is determined that Louie consented to hold the bag, that consent will be vitiated because Bruce exceeded the scope of Louie's consent.**

If Louie was somehow incapable of consenting, i.e., he was drunk or was a child, then consent would not be found. (Again, this is a non-issue, since you are not given any facts indicating Louie's age or sobriety, however, you gain brownie points by telling your instructor, briefly, that you considered these non-issues; but you would not be penalized for not including this sentence)

Under the majority rule, consent to a criminal act is valid unless the crime involves a breach of the peace. Bruce's act could be considered tantamount to the crime of battery, and hence, under the majority rule, consent would be invalid, because battery is a violent crime that constitutes a breach of the peace. Under the minority rule, a plaintiff may never consent to a criminal act. The same conclusion would result under the minority rule, because Louie could not consent to battery, a criminal act. (Here is an example of a discussion of both a majority and minority rule; when you are taught both the majority and minority rule, your instructor will expect you to discuss both and apply both to the set of facts before you. Here each rule is stated in I-R-A-C format and the facts are applied to each.) **Therefore, under either rule, the defense would not apply.**

Finally, Louie could argue that any consent was vitiated by fraud, due to the misrepresentations made by the school, as discussed above. (Where your analysis would be repetitive, do not hesitate to refer to previous discussions of the law or application.) **Fraud would destroy consent, since the misrepresentations concerned the very nature of the contact between Louie**

and Bruce, an essential matter. Thus, fraud would bar the defense of consent.

Therefore, because there was no actual or apparent consent, and any consent was uninformed, Bruce's consent defense will fail. (Conclude one way other the other!)

Thus, Bruce should be held liable for battery against Louie. (State the overall conclusion)

The next exercise breaks down the exam writing process even further. Instead of showing you the finished product, you are given an assembly line approach, by which you watch each issue evolve from its very inception. We shall dissect this analysis into its fundamental parts, that is, the issue, rule, relevant facts considered, application and conclusion. Put on your seat belts and enjoy the ride:

Battery Example #6: **Marvin v. Stu Pid**

Lois Law Student, who was extremely depressed and distraught over her mid-term grades, decided to drown her sorrows in a few martinis at a local pub. Lois had also recently broken up with her fiance, Stu Pid, who incessantly teased her about not making the Law School Lame Journal, of which he was the editor.

When Lois entered the bar, she ordered two martinis, which she quickly drained. There, she met Marvin Marvelous, a well-known attorney. Marvin explained to her that she need not be so distraught over "that idiot Stu" and her mid-term grades. Marvin also told her that he too, had flunked two mid-terms in law school but had triumphed on his final exams. Marvin reached over and grasped Lois' hand in an attempt to offer her support in her time of sorrow, carefully removing his thick glasses. For the first time in weeks, Lois felt a new, fresh perspective on her legal studies that would truly change her life, and hopefully, her grades.

At that very moment, Stu entered the bar and ordered a beer. Seeing Lois at the end

of the bar, hand in hand with Marvin, Stu flew into a rage. As soon as the beer was served, he slid his mug down the bar, causing it to collide with Lois' martini glass, which was positioned a few inches in front of her. The martini glass shattered, and a splinter of glass entered Marvin's eye. Stu laughed and yelled, "See, that's what you get for moving in on my territory, bud." Marvin later went blind in one eye and emerged from thirty hours of surgery with a glass eye.

Marvin now wishes to sue Stu for battery. After he learned of the suit against him, Stu apologized to Marvin, stating, "Sorry about the beer, bud. It was an accident." Please advise Marvin of his rights.

After carefully reading the fact pattern, and following the six steps of exam taking, the following structure would be used to I-R-A-C your answer in any battery problem:

1. Introduction

State General Issue to be Solved: ______________________________

State General Rule: ______________________________

Sub-Issue #1: Affirmative Act?

State Sub-Rule: ______________________________

State Relevant Fact: ______________________________

Application: ______________________________

Conclusion: ______________________________

Sub-Issue #2: Intent?

State Sub-Rule: ______________________________

State Relevant Fact: ______________________________

Application: ______________________________

____

Conclusion: ______________________________

Sub-Issue #3: Actual Contact?

State Sub-Rule: ______________________________

State Relevant Fact: ______________________________

Application: ______________________________

Conclusion: ______________________________

Sub-Issue #4: Harmful or Offensive?

State Sub-Rule: ______________________________

State Relevant Fact: ______________________________

Application: ______________________________

Conclusion: ______________________________

Overall Conclusion: ______________________________

Let's look at the bits and pieces forming the foundation of your answer:

1. Introduction

State General Issue to be Solved: Did Stu (D) commit a battery against Marvin(P)?

State General Rule: A battery is an affirmative act with the intent to touch another resulting in actual harmful or offensive contact.

Sub-Issue #1: Affirmative Act?

State Sub-Rule: An affirmative act is one which the actor performs voluntarily.

State Relevant Fact: Seeing Lois at the end of the bar, hand in hand with Marvin, Stu flew into a rage. As soon as the beer was served, **he slid his mug down the bar**, causing it to collide with Lois' martini glass, which had been positioned a few inches in front of her.

Application: There are no facts indicating that Stu's act of sliding his mug down the bar toward Marvin and Lois was anything but voluntary. There is no evidence that his act was coerced or involuntary. To the contrary, Marvin acted out of anger and jealousness and of his own accord and desire.

Conclusion: Therefore the act was voluntary.

Sub-Issue #2: Intent?

State Sub-Rule: The actor must actually intend to make contact or be substantially certain such contact would occur.

State Relevant Fact: **Seeing Lois at the end of the bar, hand in hand with Marvin, Stu flew into a rage. As soon as the beer was served, he slid his mug down the bar, causing it to collide with Lois' martini glass, which had been positioned a few inches in front of her. The martini glass shattered, and a splinter of glass entered Marvin's eye. Stu laughed and yelled, "See, that's what you get for moving in on my territory, bud." Marvin later went blind in one eye and emerged from thirty hours of surgery with a glass eye.**

After he learned of the suit against him, Stu apologized to Marvin, stating, "Sorry about the beer, bud. It was an accident."

Application: Actual Intent - While no one can read another's mind, here Stu's actual intent is evidenced by what he saw and said. Stu saw his ex-girlfriend and Marvin holding hands and became jealous and angry. After making those observations, he slid his beer mug down the bar in the direction of the couple. From this action one could infer that he intended to make contact with Marvin, as he clearly had a motive and reason to do what he did. Furthermore, Stu expressly stated, "See, that's what you get for moving in on my territory, bud," which would appear to be a threat expressing his intent to harm Marvin. Stu's statement following his act would indicate that he intended the result, that is, contact with Marvin. Regarding Stu's belated apology expressing that the incident was an accident, this is more inclined to be interpreted as a self-serving statement bearing little on the issue of intent.

On the other hand, Stu could argue that he only intended to make contact with Lois' martini glass, not Marvin, and that any such contact was merely accidental. However, considering the fragile nature of martini glasses, it should have been at least foreseeable that the glass would shatter and cause contact with a nearby patron.

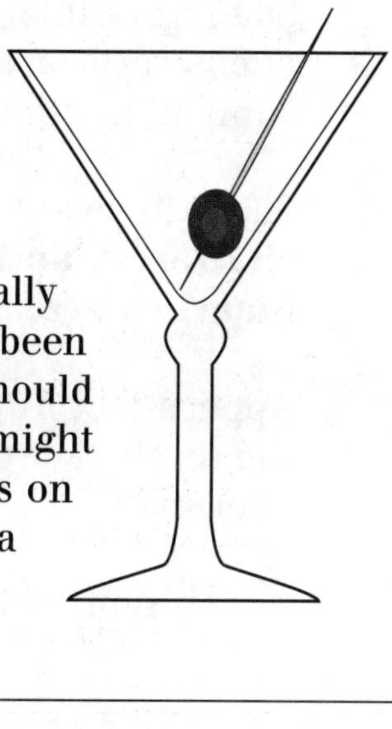

Substantial Certainty: Notwithstanding whether Stu actually intended to make contact with Marvin, he should have been substantially certain that such contact would occur. Stu should have known that his act of sliding a beer mug down the bar might cause the beer mug to collide with another or another glass on the bar, thereby causing injury to someone. This act, at a minimum, was extremely reckless, and any reasonable person would know that contact would likely occur.

Conclusion: Therefore, the intent element is met.

Sub-Issue #3: Actual Contact?
State Sub-Rule: Battery requires actual contact with the person or something closely connected to the person.

State Relevant Fact: **He slid his mug down the bar, causing it to collide with Lois' martini glass, which was positioned a few inches in front of her. The martini glass shattered, and a splinter of glass entered Marvin's eye.**

Application: Here there was no actual contact between Stu and Marvin, as at no time did the two men physically touch each other. However, Marvin could argue that the beer mug, which made contact with the martini glass in front of Lois, was a mere extension of Stu's person. Stu should not escape liability for battery because Stu himself did not touch Marvin, but used an instrumentality instead. Marvin could then argue that the martini glass was an item closely connected to him in that it was a few inches from Lois, next to whom he was sitting.

On the other hand, Stu could argue that there was no actual contact and that the martini glass could not be characterized as a mere extension of Marvin. In the case of Fischer v. Carrousel, a plate held by the plaintiff was ruled to be an extension of his person. Stu would argue that this case is distinguishable in that here Marvin was not holding the martini glass.

Conclusion: This element is met, because Stu in effect used the beer mug as an extension of his person to touch Marvin.

Sub-Issue #4: Harmful or Offensive?

State Sub-Rule: Battery requires that the contact be harmful or offensive to a reasonable person under same or similar circumstances.

State Relevant Fact: **The martini glass shattered, and a splinter of glass entered Marvin's eye.**

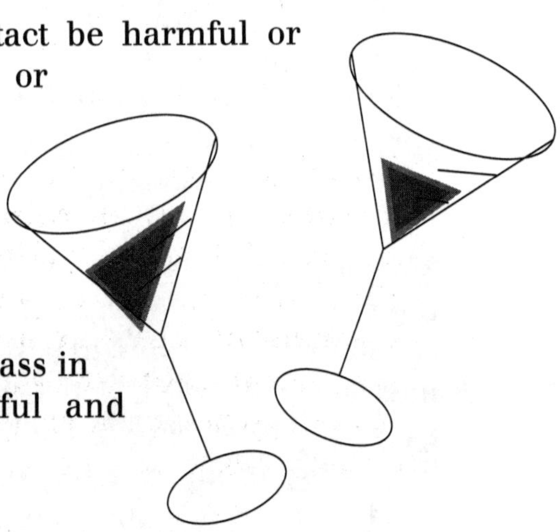

Application: Anyone struck with a splinter of glass in the eyeball would find such contact harmful and offensive.

Conclusion: This element is met.

Overall Conclusion: A cause of action exists against Stu.

The examples analyzed thus far have ranged from single-issue problems to multi-issue problems involving battery and the applicable defenses. The next example presents a multi-party question that raises multiple parties, multiple torts and a discussion of the general principles of vicarious liability. A multi-party question is one in which there are more than two parties. Multi-party questions are typical of Torts final examinations. The key to organizing multi-party questions is separating your discussion of the liability of each party. For example, if the problem reads: "A hit B who hit C who hit D. Please discuss the liability of all parties," you would organize your answer by the parties:

<u>B v. A</u>
- Battery
- Defenses to Battery

<u>C v. B</u>
- Battery
- Defenses to Battery

<u>D v. C</u>
- Battery
- Defenses to Battery

Each discussion of tort liability follows the parties who are involved in that particular tort. Your discussion in each section is limited to the tort liability of the parties stated in each heading. For example, under <u>B v. A</u>, you would discuss only those facts relevant to the tort liability of B, the plaintiff, against A, the defendant. In addition to organizing your discussion of each party's liability, you must also sort through the facts and determine which facts are relevant to solving which causes of action between which parties. Before confusing you any further, let's take a prime example of a multi-issue problem:

Intentional Torts Example #7: **<u>Frank, Dennis & Conco</u>**

A storage shed on the suburban yard of Construction Co. (Conco) caught fire on a Sunday morning. Dennis, Conco's draftsman at its downtown office, happened to be bicycling by on a personal errand. He broke into the yard office through a closed window and notified the local volunteer fire department. Then he located ignition keys and moved eight pieces of heavy equipment onto an adjacent field. The heavy equipment consisted of trucks and bulldozers, which were threatened with imminent destruction but were not damaged.

Unknown to Dennis, the adjacent field belonged to a wholesale florist,

Frank. Although the field appeared to be vacant and unused, Frank had planted it with valuable tulip bulbs. Bulbs valued at $9,000 were destroyed under the weight of the heavy equipment.

After fire fighters extinguished the fire, Frank asked Dennis to come to his office to discuss the damage. Dennis agreed. As soon as Dennis entered the office, Frank told Dennis, in the presence of four of Frank's employees, that Dennis would have to remain at the office until he summoned the president of Conco and the president had arrived at the office. When the president arrived an hour later, Frank told Dennis he could leave, and Dennis left.

1) What are Frank's rights against Dennis and against Conco? Discuss.

2) What are Dennis' rights against Frank? Discuss.

After reading the question and the interrogatories carefully, you must then re-read the facts and determine which facts are relevant to solving which causes of action. Your headings should be "Frank v. Dennis" "Frank v. Conco" and "Dennis v. Frank" representing each of parties involved in this problem. You are required to determine which causes of action in tort law exist for each party stated. In essence, a multi-party problem is like solving "mini-problems" within one fact pattern.

You must then decide which facts are relevant to solving which problems. For example, under Frank v. Dennis, the relevant facts are those which address any tortious conduct suffered by Frank, and committed by Dennis. Thus, the relevant facts are:

A storage shed on the suburban yard of Construction Co. (Conco) caught fire on a Sunday morning. Dennis, Conco's draftman at its downtown office, happened to be bicycling by on a personal errand. He broke into the yard office through a closed window and notified the local volunteer fire department. Then he located ignition keys and moved eight pieces of heavy equipment onto an adjacent field. The heavy equipment consisted of trucks and bulldozers, which were threatened with imminent destruction but were not damaged.

Unknown to Dennis, the adjacent field belonged to a wholesale florist, Frank. Although the field appeared to be vacant and unused, Frank had planted it with valuable tulip bulbs. Bulbs valued at $9,000 were destroyed under the weight of the heavy equipment.

These are the facts which describe what Dennis did to Frank. Thus you must cull through these facts to determine what intentional torts may have been committed. Battery? No. Assault? No! False Imprisonment? NOOOO! Intentional Infliction of Emotional Distress? NNNNOOOOO! Trespass to Land? BINGO!!!!!

Likewise, you would run through the defenses to intentional torts and determine if any defenses apply. Consent? No. Defense of Others? No! Defense of Property? NOOOOO! Necessity! ANOTHER BINGO! After analyzing Frank v. Dennis, and the torts of trespass to land and necessity, you would move onto the next heading, Frank v. Conco, and discuss the doctrine of vicarious liability, since Conco's liability depends on whether Dennis committed the tort within the scope of his employment. The relevant facts are:

A storage shed on the suburban yard of Construction Co. (Conco) caught fire on a Sunday morning. Dennis, Conco's draftsman at its downtown office, happened to be bicycling by on a personal errand. He broke into the yard office through a closed window and notified the local volunteer fire department. He next located ignition keys and moved eight pieces of heavy equipment onto an adjacent field. The heavy equipment consisted of trucks and bulldozers, which were threatened with imminent destruction but were not damaged.

After analyzing Conco's liability to Frank, you would turn the tables and determine which facts were relevant to determining Frank's tort liability to Dennis, Dennis v. Frank:

After fire fighters extinguished the fire, Frank asked Dennis to come to his office to discuss the damage. Dennis agreed. As soon as Dennis entered the office, Frank told Dennis, in the presence of four of Frank's employees, that Dennis would have to remain at the office until he summoned the president of Conco and the president had arrived at the office. When the president arrived an hour later, Frank told Dennis he could leave, and Dennis left.

You would scrutinize the above facts and analyze Frank's tort liability for false imprisonment, and then discuss the defense of consent. Each party's liability is discussed and analyzed separately, as is demonstrated in the following model answer:

1. Frank v. Dennis

Trespass to Land

The issue is whether Frank may sue Dennis for trespass to land. Trespass to land is defined as an affirmative intentional act which invades the plaintiff's possessory interest in land. **Dennis committed an intentional act by driving the heavy equipment onto Frank's land in order to avoid property damage to the equipment. Dennis' act invaded Frank's possessory interest as the land was owned by Frank, and finally, the subject of the tort was land.** Thus, all elements are met and Dennis is liable for trespass.

Defense of Necessity

Dennis will raise the defense of private necessity. Where a defendant commits a tort to avoid private property damage, as opposed to a public purpose, the defendant is liable only for actual damage to that property. **Because Dennis acted to save the heavy equipment of his employer Conco from fire damage, he will be held liable only for the amount of actual damage caused by the trespass.**

Frank v. Conco

Trespass to Land - Vicarious Liability

Conco's liability for trespass will depend on whether the doctrine of *respondeat superior* applies. An employer is liable for all torts committed by servants within the course of employment. **Dennis was employed by Conco at the time he committed the tort. However, Dennis was employed as a draftsman, not a security guard or fireman, and thus Dennis was not acting within the scope of his employment position when he committed the tort. Furthermore, Dennis was involved in a personal errand at the time the tort was committed, and was not working Sunday morning. Therefore he was not working within the course of his employment. Frank, however, could argue that an employee who observes damage to his employer's property would normally act to salvage such property, and therefore Conco is liable for Dennis' acts.** However, given the circumstances in this case, Frank will not prevail.

2. Dennis v. Frank

False Imprisonment

The issue is whether Frank is liable to Dennis for the tort of false imprisonment. False imprisonment is defined as an act or omission with intent to confine someone resulting in actual confinement of plaintiff. Actual awareness of the confinement or injury resulting therefrom is also required. **Here Frank committed an intentional**

act resulting in confinement when he told Dennis he would have to remain in the office, a "bounded" area. Frank clearly intended to confine Dennis by his statement stating the same, and the presence of Frank's four employees suggest that Dennis was not free to leave the office. Dennis was subjected to "actual confinement" for one hour until Conco's president arrived. Finally, although Dennis suffered no actual injury, Dennis was no doubt aware of his confinement, as he was conscious during the confinement. Therefore, Frank is liable for false imprisonment.

<u>Defenses of Consent</u>

Frank may raise the defense of consent. A defendant is not liable for a tort where the plaintiff consents to the commission of the tort, either expressly or through his conduct. **While Dennis initially "agreed" to entering Frank's office, such consent was vitiated because Frank did not tell Dennis he would have to remain in the office until after Dennis had entered the office. Therefore, Dennis' consent was not informed, and even if it was, the scope of Dennis' consent was clearly exceeded.** Thus, consent would not bar Dennis' recovery for false imprisonment.

* * *

The purpose of the preceding section is not to analyze battery problems for you, but to show you the PROCESS of how to solve an examination. Each example, beginning with <u>Student v. Lee</u> to <u>Louie Law Student v. Bruce Lee</u> and beyond, takes you from the simple to the not-so-simple process of using I-R-A-C to solve a variety of exam problems. The key is that regardless of the complexity of the problem and number of issues presented, the same I-R-A-C technique is employed consistently again and again, to achieve a successful analysis. While reading each of the above examples, focus on the PROCESS of solving an exam problem. Notice how each answer, regardless of the subject matter analyzed, is remarkably similar. Study the format of the basic essay answer, <u>i.e.</u>, "The issue presented is . . ." "The rule is . . ." and see how every exam answer follows the same format.

Build a strong foundation early on by learning how to apply I-R-A-C to simple problems. The best way to use this section is to write and re-write, and re-re-write, if necessary, each of the questions in this section until you have written "the perfect" examination. Begin with <u>Student v. Lee</u>, and write and re-write your answer until you have mastered the single-issue problem. Once you have attained that level of competency, move on to <u>Peg v. Marcie</u>. Again write and re-write your answer until it is right. Then move onto the next example.

Repeating the same question again and again may not be the most exciting exercise, but it will focus your efforts on the PROCESS involved in problem-solving, without having to search for the applicable law and becoming accustomed to new and different fact patterns. It will also force you to constructively criticize and re-evaluate your work, which is what a lawyer does every day. Only in this way will you truly learn how to write a winning exam answer.

2. Negligence

Negligence may strike you as a new and different animal than the intentional torts, but it is the same dog, same fleas, and same type of I-R-A-C analysis that must be followed in writing out a negligence analysis. While the tools are different, the basic I-R-A-C principle remains the same.

Like battery, and all other torts for that matter, negligence is made up of various elements a plaintiff must prove before he/she will prevail. The issue in a negligence problem is whether the plaintiff has proved a case of negligence, and if so, what defenses apply.

One element is that of "**duty**." In order for a defendant to be liable for negligence, plaintiff must prove that defendant owed plaintiff a legal duty to exercise due care. There are two theories of duty. One is a minority view, which holds that every human being owes a duty to every other human being in the world, and therefore there is always a duty. This is the rule embraced by the dissenting Judge Andrews in the famous Palsgraf case. However, the majority rule fashioned by Judge Cardozo in the same case is that a duty is owed only to a foreseeable plaintiff or a plaintiff in the geographic zone of danger created by the defendant's negligence.

Another element is that of **standard of care**. In order to determine whether someone is negligent, you would ascertain how a reasonable person would act under the circumstances. Of course, there would be exceptions to this standard, especially where professionals or children were concerned, because they would understandably be held to a greater or lesser standard than that of a reasonable person.

Once the standard of care is established, then you look to the defendant's actual conduct and determine whether the defendant failed to meet or "breached" the standard of care.

The next issue is **causation**. In order to hold a defendant liable for negligence, defendant's act must be the cause of the plaintiff's injury. There are two types of causation, both of which must be met in a negligence suit: actual cause and legal cause. In order to be an actual cause, "but for" the defendant's act the injury to the plaintiff would not have occurred. In other words, defendant's act must have been one of the causes in the chain of causation. If, say, there were five or six events which led up to plaintiff's injury, then defendant's conduct would have to be one of the links in that "chain" of causation. Proximate cause, by contrast, asks if defendant's conduct was the "legal" cause of plaintiff's injury. Legal cause presents an issue when more than one possible cause contributed to the plaintiff's injuries. The legal cause inquiry largely turns on whether plaintiff's injury was foreseeable to defendant when defendant committed the act.

Once causation is determined, the final requirement of a prima facie case of negligence is whether plaintiff sustained actual injury, which is an essential requirement in every negligence suit.

Then, as with battery, the issue of defenses is raised. There are four principal defenses to a negligence action: contributory negligence, comparative negligence, assumption of the risk and the last clear chance doctrine.

While this skeleton of the law of negligence will be filled out in greater detail with other rules and exceptions awaiting you in the universe of negligence, this narrative will give you a general idea of what a negligence analysis involves.

As with battery, much of your negligence analysis is preordained before you even know the facts of the problem you are solving, as demonstrated by in the following example:

<u>Negligence</u>

The issue here is whether plaintiff ____________ has a cause of action for negligence against defendant __________. Negligence is defined as a breach of duty of due care that is the actual and proximate cause of plaintiff's injuries.

The first issue is that of duty. Under the majority <u>Cardozo</u> rule, duty of care is owed only to a foreseeable plaintiff or a person in the zone of danger. (APPLICATION) Thus, duty under the <u>Cardozo</u> rule is met/not met. Under the <u>Andrews</u> and minority view, a duty is owed to all. (APPLICATION) **Thus, under this standard, a duty exists/does not exist.**

The second issue is that of the applicable standard of care. The defendant owes plaintiff a duty to act as a reasonable person would have acted in the same or similar circumstances. (APPLICATION).

The third issue concerns breach. A defendant breaches the standard of care by conduct that exposes other to an unreasonable risk of harm. (APPLICATION) Therefore defendant breached/did not breach its duty to plaintiff.

The fourth issue is causation. The defendant's conduct must be the actual and legal cause of plaintiff's injuries. (APPLICATION OF "BUT-FOR" AND PROXIMATE CAUSE RULES)

The final requirement is actual injury. (APPLICATION)

In conclusion, plaintiff has proven/has not proven a prima facie case of negligence.

Defenses to Negligence

Contributory Negligence

The defense of contributory negligence can be raised by the defendant. Contributory negligence is defined as conduct by the plaintiff that is a contributing cause to his or her injuries and falls below the standard of care to which he is required to conform for his own protection. If met, this defense effectively bars plaintiff's recovery. However, in the majority of states, the comparative negligence doctrine will be applied, requiring the court or jury to fix a certain percentage reflecting the degree of contributory negligence. (APPLICATION) Therefore, the defense of contributory negligence does/does not bar plaintiff's recovery.

Assumption of the risk

Defendant could also claim that plaintiff assumed the risk. If the plaintiff expressly or impliedly consented to the harm, recognized and understood the danger and voluntarily chose to encounter it, recovery is barred. (APPLICATION) Therefore, the defense of assumption of the risk bars/does not bar plaintiff's recovery.

So, without further adieu, let's beam down to the planet surface and meet a negligence problem, again beginning with a simple fact pattern:

Negligence Example #1:
Paula Painless v. Carl Careless

Carl Careless, a clerk at the local grocery store, ate a banana on his break and dropped the skin onto the floor, causing shopper Paula Painless, who was skateboarding down the aisle, to fall and break her hip. Is Carl liable for negligence?

Model Answer: **Paula Painless v. Carl Careless**

The issue here is whether plaintiff Paula has a cause of action for negligence against defendant Carl. Negligence is defined as a breach of duty of due care that is the actual and proximate cause of plaintiff's injuries.

The first issue is that of duty. Under the majority Cardozo rule, duty of care is owed only to a foreseeable plaintiff or a person in the zone of danger. **Here it was foreseeable that a customer of the grocery store might be injured by an employee's negligence. Because Paula Painless was a shopper in the store, she was a foreseeable plaintiff.** Paul was also in the zone of danger created by Carl's act of leaving the banana peel in the aisle. Thus, duty under the Cardozo rule is met. Under the Andrews minority view, **a duty is owed to all, and therefore a duty would be owed to Paula.** Thus, under this standard, a duty exists.

The second issue is that of the applicable standard of care. The defendant owes plaintiff a duty to act as a reasonable person would have acted in the same or similar circumstances. **A reasonable person in Carl's shoes would know that a banana peel left on the floor constituted both a health and safety hazard. A reasonable person would also know that a banana peel is slippery, and if left unattended, could cause a person to fall. Thus, a reasonable person would not leave a banana peel on the floor.**

The third issue concerns breach. A defendant breaches the standard of care by conduct that exposes others to an unreasonable risk of harm. **Carl failed to adhere to a reasonable standard of care by dropping the banana peel on the floor.** Therefore, defendant breached his duty to plaintiff.

The fourth issue is causation. The defendant's conduct must be the actual and legal cause of plaintiff's injuries. **"But for" Carl's act of discarding the banana peel on the floor, Paula would not have been injured. Thus, Carl's act is the actual cause of Paula's injury. Carl's act is also the legal cause of her injuries, as there are no intervening causes between Carl's act of discarding the peel and Paula's injury. Carl's act, therefore, was a direct cause of Paula's injury, and, therefore, the proximate cause of the same.**

The final requirement is actual injury. **Because Paula suffered a broken hip,** this requirement is met.

In conclusion, Paula has proven a prima case of negligence.

Defenses to Negligence

Contributory Negligence

The defense of contributory negligence could be raised by the defendant. Contributory negligence is defined as conduct by the plaintiff that is a contributing cause to his or her injuries and that falls below the standard of care to which he is required to conform for his own protection. If met, this defense effectively bars plaintiff's recovery, although in the majority of states, the comparative negligence doctrine will be applied, requiring the court or jury to fix a certain percentage that reflects the degree of contributory negligence.

Paula's act of riding a skateboard at the time she was injured contributed to her injuries, because she may have avoided the banana peel altogether had she been walking instead of skating. Because a reasonable person would not skateboard down the aisle at the local market, Paula's actions failed to conform to the standard of care necessary to insure her own safety. Thus, in a contributory negligence state, Paula's cause of action would be completely barred. However, in a comparative negligence state, Paula's recovery would be reduced in proportion to the degree of her negligence. Thus, Paula's recovery would not be barred, but would be limited to that amount actually attributable to Carl's negligence.

<u>Assumption of the risk</u>

Defendant could also claim that plaintiff assumed the risk. If the plaintiff expressly or impliedly consents to the harm, recovery is barred if the plaintiff recognized and understood the danger and voluntarily chose to encounter it. **Here Paula, by entering the store and skating down the aisle, did not assume the risk that she would encounter a banana peel on the floor. Therefore, it cannot be said that Paula subjectively understood the danger of injury she risked by entering the store. Furthermore, by engaging in skateboarding, Paula may have voluntarily chose to partake in a dangerous sport, but not to slip on a banana peel on the floor. Therefore, the defense of assumption of the risk does not bar plaintiff's recovery.**

* * *

See how simple and straightforward the basic I-R-A-C writing structure is? Once you master the basic I-R-A-C structure, you will find that applying I-R-A-C to more complicated problems is a piece of cake. So instead of talking about it, let's move onto the next step in the universe of negligence. Ready for a curve ball?

Negligence Example #2: **<u>Freya Fan v. Dodgers</u>**

Plaintiff Freya Fan attended a baseball game at Dodger Stadium. She occupied a seat on the first base side in an unscreened area. During the course of the game she was struck by a batted ball. She subsequently instituted a personal injury action, alleging that defendant was negligent in failing to protect her against such an occurrence.

Plaintiff and her husband had occupied the identical seats on a previous occasion; thus she knew before entering the stadium that her seat was located in an unprotected area. Plaintiff did not request a seat in a protected area of the ballpark. During the first inning of the game, a foul ball struck and injured her. She received treatment at the ballpark's first aid station and returned to her seat until she left the stadium. However, after leaving the stadium, she complained of constant headaches, which she had not experienced prior to the injury.

Plaintiff, a self-described "ardent Dodger rooter," had been following the team since she attended a game at Ebbets Field, when the baseball club was still the Brooklyn Dodgers. In addition to her previous visits to major league games, she had watched baseball on television since 1959. Moreover, plaintiff attended her two sons' little league games and had seen home movies of every game in which they played. In her deposition, plaintiff admitted that she had witnessed baseballs hit into the stands and was "generally familiar" with the game; however, in a subsequent declaration, she denied that she "understood the game of baseball" and the danger to which spectators are subject.

Dodger Stadium is a multi-level facility which seats 56,000 patrons. Since its opening in 1962, a protective screen measuring 75 feet by 25 feet has been in place behind home plate. This screen protects approximately 2,000 field seats and an additional 1,000 loge seats. Additionally, of the 53,000 unscreened seats, there are approximately 20,000 seats on the reserved level pavilions where the chances of being struck by a batted or thrown ball are extremely remote.

In their declarations, two veteran Dodgers' employees in charge of ticket sales stated that as far as they were aware, no spectator had ever requested seats in the screened area for reasons of protection. They further declared that if a patron were to request a seat in a protected area, every effort would be made to accommodate him.

The backside of each ticket issued by the Dodgers reads: "The holder assumes all risk and danger incidental to the Game of Baseball, whether occurring prior to, during, or subsequent to, the actual playing of the game, including specifically (but not exclusively) the danger of being injured by thrown bats and thrown or batted balls, and agrees that the Participating Clubs, their Agents and Players, are not liable for injuries resulting from such causes."

Defendant Dodgers have moved for a summary judgment based on the foregoing facts. Please determine the merits of the motion.

MODEL ANSWER: <u>Plaintiff Freya Fan v. Dodgers</u>

The issue here is whether plaintiff Fan has a cause of action for negligence against the Dodgers. Negligence is defined as a breach of duty of due care that is the actual and proximate cause of plaintiff's injuries.

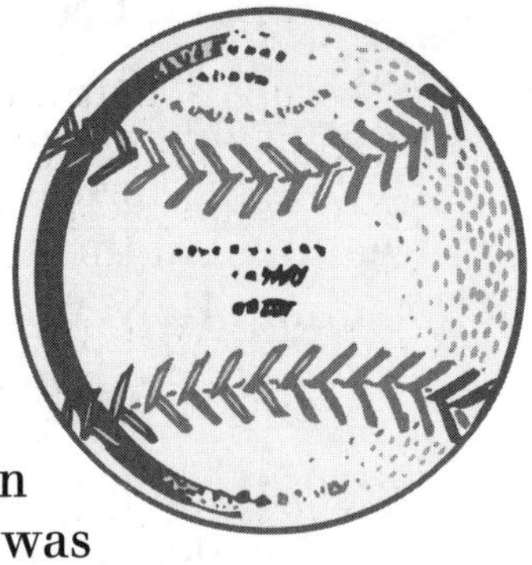

The first issue is that of duty. Under the majority Cardozo rule, duty of care is owed only to a foreseeable plaintiff or a person in the zone of danger. Here Fan is a foreseeable plaintiff as the Dodgers could foresee that a patron might be injured by negligence resulting from activities of the Dodgers. Fan was also within the zone of danger created by the activity involved - baseball. Here Fan was seated in Dodger Stadium and was within an area where she was exposed to possible danger from being struck by a batted ball. Thus, duty under the Cardozo rule is met. Under the Andrews and minority rule, a duty is owed to all members of society. Under this rule, the duty element would likewise be met, because the Dodgers owed a duty to any member of society, including Fan.

The Dodgers would also owe Fan a special duty as an owner and occupier of land. Fan would be afforded the status of an invitee, since she paid to enter the land to observe the baseball game. Thus the Dodgers owed a duty to inspect the premises for any dangerous conditions and to warn of any obvious dangers.

The second issue is that of the applicable standard of care. The Dodgers owe plaintiff Fan a duty to act as a reasonable person acted in the same or similar circumstances. A reasonable person would act in a manner consistent with consumer and public safety and would take necessary precautions to protect others from unreasonable harm. A reasonable person also knows that a baseball, when struck, is liable to fall anywhere, and in the case of a foul ball, on a patron. A reasonable person would also know that in every baseball game, batted balls fall towards the audience and would know the danger involved in the game of baseball. However, taken to its logical extreme, safety concerns would require that every person watching a baseball game would have to be completely protected by a screen or cage of some sort. While observing a baseball game, the consumer may find it unappealing to be in caged quarters and might protest the loss of an opportunity to catch a batted ball. In addition, some might argue that the excitement of the game would be lessened by extreme protectionism, and that in order to balance the two competing interests, both options should be available to the consumer, either to sit in a protected or an unprotected area. Based on the facts presented, it is likely that the court will agree.

The third issue concerns breach. A defendant breaches the standard of care by conduct that exposes others to an unreasonable risk of harm. The Dodgers would argue that they acted reasonably in providing a safe environment for patrons, because, as noted above, they provided both protected and unprotected areas from which a patron could view the game. Nearly one half the seats provided safety for the patrons. In addition, the backside warning on the tickets specifically stated that the patron assumes the risk, and one would have to assume that the ticket holder read the ticket, or at least was familiar with the risk he or she was assuming by attending a baseball game and sitting in an open, unprotected section of the ballpark. The Dodgers also had provisions to meet any requests by patrons to sit in a protected area. Considering the competing interests noted above, the Dodgers acted reasonably. Hence, there is no breach, as the Dodgers acted reasonably in providing a safe environment for patrons and warned patrons seated in unprotected areas of the danger created by batted balls.

Fan could argue that the entire ballpark should be protected from batted balls, but such a result would not be welcomed by baseball fans, as patrons should have the freedom to sit in uncaged areas if they wish to assume such a risk. Thus, Fan's argument would propose an unreasonable alternative.

There is no question that the batted ball and the unprotected area, together, were the but-for cause of plaintiff's injuries and were the proximate or legal cause of plaintiff's injuries, because there are no superseding causes, and the ball was directly responsible for plaintiff's injuries.

Finally, Fan suffered injuries.

In conclusion, plaintiff Fan cannot prove a prima facie case of negligence; therefore Dodgers' motion for summary judgment should be granted.

Defenses to Negligence

Contributory Negligence

The defense of contributory negligence could be raised by the Dodgers. Contributory negligence is defined as conduct by the plaintiff that is a contributing cause to his or her injuries and which falls below the standard of care to which he is required to conform for his own protection. If met, this defense effectively bars plaintiff's recovery, although in the majority of states, including California, the comparative negligence doctrine will be applied, requiring the court or jury to fix a certain percentage reflecting the degree of contributory negligence.

Here Fan could have chosen to sit in one of the 3,000 seats located behind a protected screen, where she could be completely safe from batted balls. Likewise, she could have sat in one of the 20,000 seats where the chances of being struck by a batted or thrown ball are extremely remote.

Also, it is clear that Fan was familiar with the game of baseball. She was not a first-time observer, as she and her husband had attended previous games in the same seats and in the same stadium. She was aware before attending the game that her seat was located in an unprotected area. She had followed the game for nearly 30 years and was quite aware of the risk involved in sitting in an unprotected area, as anyone who watched a few games of baseball would have seen a batted foul ball hit into the stands.

Thus, even if a cause of action for negligence was sustained, she was contributorily negligent in failing to take precautions to avoid the very injury she sustained.

Assumption of the Risk

The Dodgers would also argue that Fan assumed the risk. If the plaintiff expressly or impliedly consents to the harm, recovery is barred if the plaintiff recognized and understood the danger and voluntarily chose to encounter it. Fan had occupied the same seats on a previous occasion and was aware her seat was in an unprotected area. Furthermore, as discussed above, Fan was extremely familiar with the game of baseball, having attended games and observed televised games and home movies. Although Fan denies understanding the game, because balls are struck into the stands quite frequently during a baseball game, Fan at least understood that she could be struck by a batted ball. Thus, this defense would bar Fan's action for negligence.

* * *

Next, let's get out of the batting cage and go for it! The next problem appeared on the California Bar Examination, one of the most difficult bar examinations in the nation. This problem is a negligence problem involving multi-parties and issues.

Negligence Example #3: **Pat v. Transit and Dr. Ard**

Transit operates buses in a city. One morning, Driver, a Transit driver, awoke with a bad cold. He consulted the yellow pages of the telephone directory and called Doctor Ard, a physician listed under the category, "Physicians & Surgeons - M.D. - Eye, Ear, Nose & Throat." Driver told Doctor Ard that he had a bad cold and was scheduled to report for work at noon that day. Doctor Ard listened to Driver describe his symptoms, said he could not give Driver an appointment, and told him to buy a bottle of "Pyrib" at a drug store and to use its contents as directed on the label. Pyrib is a cold remedy antihistamine prepared and marketed by Drugco. Driver obtained the Pyrib from a drug store, took the first dosage called for on the label and reported for work at noon.

At 1:30 p.m. that day, while driving his bus, Driver felt drowsy. However, he continued driving and shortly thereafter, fell asleep. The bus jumped a curb and hit a pole. Pat, a paying passenger on the bus, was injured.

Pyrib is known to cause drowsiness and sleep in about 20% of the persons who take it. Dr. Ard did not warn Driver that the medication prescribed might cause drowsiness and sleep and the label on the bottle did not contain any such warning.

1) What are Pat's rights against Transit? Discuss.

2) What are Pat's rights against Doctor Ard? Discuss.

Model Answer: **<u>Pat v. Transit and Dr. Ard</u>**

I. <u>Pat v. Transit</u>

The issue is whether Driver was negligent, and if so, whether Transit is vicariously liable for such negligence on a respondeat-superior theory.

Negligence is defined as the breach of a duty of due care, which is the actual and proximate cause of P's injuries.

The first issue is whether Driver owed a duty to Pat. Under the <u>Cardozo</u> majority view, a duty is owed only to a foreseeable plaintiff or a plaintiff in the zone of danger. Pat was a foreseeable P, as Driver should have foreseen injury to a passenger on his bus due to his inability to drive the bus safely. Pat was also in the zone of danger, as she was a passenger in the bus driven by Driver. Under the <u>Andrews</u> minority rule, which holds that a duty is owed to all, Pat was owed a duty of due care. Finally, under the special duty owed by a common carrier to a passenger, duty will be imposed regardless of foreseeability.

The second issue is what standard of care applies. A defendant owes a duty to act as a reasonable person would have acted in the same or similar circumstances. A driver of a public transportation vehicle owes his or her passengers a duty to employ reasonable care in driving the vehicle to insure that no injury or damage occurs to the passenger, and to drive the vehicle in a safe and prudent fashion.

The third issue is whether Driver breached that standard of care. Driver was aware that he was ill, and a reasonable person should know that illness may affect a person's ability to drive safely. Driver also consumed cold antihistamine, and again a reasonable person should know that cold medicines may make one drowsy and unable to operate a vehicle safely. Furthermore, prior to the accident, Driver felt drowsy. At this point, he should have known that his ability to drive was impaired and that his passengers might be in danger. Hence, driver breached the applicable standard of care.

The fourth issue is that of causation. Driver's act was the cause-in-fact of Pat's injuries. But for driver's falling asleep at the wheel, Pat would not have been injured. Driver's act was also the proximate cause of Pat's injuries, because no intervening causes occurred between Driver's act of falling asleep and the accident causing Pat's injuries. Thus, both elements are met.

The final issue is that of damages. In a negligence action, plaintiff must suffer actual injuries. Here this element is met because Pat was injured.

There is no indication that the defenses of contributory or comparative negligence would bar Pat's recovery, or that she knowingly assumed the risk of Driver's negligence. Therefore, Driver would be liable to Pat on a negligence theory.

Transit's liability, once again, depends on whether Driver was acting within the scope of his employment. Driver was employed as a bus driver and was working in the course of his employment at the time the tort was committed. Therefore, Transit would be vicariously liable to Pat for Driver's negligence.

2) Pat v. Doctor Ard

The issue is whether Doctor Ard is liable to Pat for negligence, as defined in section one, supra.

The first issue is that of duty. Pat was a foreseeable P, because Doctor Ard was told by Driver that he was scheduled to work that day, and the Doctor should have foreseen that incorrect advice to a patient might result in a patient injuring another. Under the minority Andrews rule, Dr. Ard owed a duty to all persons, including Pat.

The second issue is standard of care. Dr. Ard, a health professional with special training and knowledge, would be held to the same standard that a reasonably prudent practitioner would possess. While a reasonable medical practitioner might instruct a patient over the phone to take cold medication to combat a common cold, a reasonable medical doctor would not fail to inform the patient of possible side-effects of the drug. Here, there was a 20% probability that Driver might be affected by drowsiness and sleep, and a reasonable practitioner would have advised Driver of the same. Thus, the third issue would be resolved against Dr. Ard, as he breached the applicable standard of care.

The fourth issue is that of causation. Dr. Ard's conduct was a cause-in-fact of Pat's injuries, because "but for" Dr. Ard's failure to advise Driver of the side effects of Pyrib, Pat would not have been injured. If advised properly, Driver would not have reported to work, or in the alternative, would not have taken the Pyrib before going to work. Dr. Ard may argue successfully, however, that his conduct was not the legal or proximate cause of Pat's injury, if he could prove that the accident was not caused by the side-effects of Pyrib, and that some other cause was responsible for causing Driver to fall asleep. However, because no intervening causes occurred, Dr. Ard will not prevail, and his conduct will be held to be the actual and legal cause of Pat's injuries.

Finally, as noted above, Pat suffered actual damage; therefore, this requirement is met.

There is no indication that Pat was contributorily or comparatively negligent or that she assumed the risk of Dr. Ard's negligence. Therefore, no defenses would bar Pat's cause of action.

* * *

Once again, you have traveled light years into the universe of Torts, so take a moment and pat yourself on the back. Negligence appears on most final torts examinations around the country, so your time, energy and enthusiasm are being well invested.

3. Defamation

Imagine that you are one of the participants in a game show called, "Defamation." In order to win the game, you must answer a series of questions, which leads up to the final million-dollar question, "Is there a cause of action for defamation?" As with intentional torts or negligence, the series of questions put to you are the "issues" or "checklist" of the tort in question: defamation. Ready to play?

The first question you must answer is whether the statement made was defamatory. Tick, tick, tick, tick. Two tests commonly used are the traditional test and the Restatement 2nd. The traditional test holds that a statement is defamatory if it exposes the plaintiff to public hatred, contempt or ridicule. By contrast, under the Restatement 2nd, a statement is defamatory when it adversely affects the plaintiff's reputation.

The second question is whether the defendant published or announced the statement to a third party. The next question is whether a third party subjectively understood the statement. The fourth question involves causation, and the last question is whether damages were suffered. The issue of damages then branches off into two sub-questions, that is, whether the defamation was slander, (i.e., oral) or libel, (i.e., written). The answer to these questions will determine whether the plaintiff must prove special pecuniary damages or whether damages will be presumed.

Finally, the defenses to defamation must be considered. A defense may give the defendant an absolute or qualified (or partial) defense to defamation. For example, "truth" of the defamatory statement is a complete defense, while the First Amendment right to free speech is a qualified privilege or defense, which may be lost if abused.

Like your checklist for negligence, a cause of action for defamation is made up of various elements that must be met. Let's try a defamation question on for size:

Defamation Example: Darrow v. Simon

On May 1st, the case of People v. Mo was scheduled for trial before the Superior Court. Mr. Mo was charged with five counts of attempted murder against Mr. Curley, the alleged victim, and two counts of misdemeanor assault with a deadly weapon. Mr. Mo was represented by Clarisa Darrow, a famous trial attorney who had won nearly one half of the 200 cases she had tried over the past 20 years. In the community Ms. Darrow had an impeccable reputation as a trial lawyer and had maintained a successful law practice. The State was represented by Sara Simon of the District Attorney's Office.

Following selection of the jury panel, which took nearly three days, the case was called to trial. The first witness, Mr. Larry, did not appear for the trial. Ms. Simon moved for a continuance, but could not provide the court with a served subpoena; therefore, she was forced to dismiss the case on her own motion. As the jury was leaving the courtroom, Ms. Simon screamed: "You got to my witness, didn't you!" The statement was heard by five members of the jury, the court reporter, Ms. Darrow and her client, Mr. Mo and a room full of spectators who had come to see Ms. Darrow in court. Unbeknownst to either Ms. Simon or Ms. Darrow, Mr. Larry, the witness, was out of the country on vacation. When Ms. Simon learned of this two weeks later, she called Ms. Darrow on the telephone and apologized. However, by this time, Ms. Darrow had lost all of her clients because of Simon's statement, which was published in a legal periodical, the Daily Recorder.

Under state law, it is a felony for a person to obstruct justice by preventing attendance of witnesses at a criminal proceeding.

Ms. Darrow thought it wise to hire counsel to determine whether she might have a legal cause of action against Ms. Simon and the District Attorney's

Office. Your employer, Victoria Sifuentes, has hired you to write a memorandum evaluating Darrow's chances of prevailing against Ms. Simon. Please advise her accordingly.

MODEL ANSWER: Darrow v. Simon

The issue is whether Ms. Darrow has a cause of action for defamation against Ms. Simon. Defamation is defined as a publication to a third person by a defendant, defaming plaintiff, capable of being understood by third persons in a defamatory sense, causing damage to plaintiff's reputation.

The first issue is whether the statement was in fact defamatory. Under the traditional test, a defamatory statement is one exposing the plaintiff to public hatred, contempt or ridicule. Under this rule, Simon's statement, "You got to my witness, didn't you," impliedly accused Darrow of somehow tampering with the lawful process of a court proceeding. Certainly, anyone accused of bribing or interfering with public justice would be subject to public dishonor and ridicule, because the statement implied that Darrow acted in an illegal or unethical manner. Thus, the traditional test is met.

Under the Restatement 2nd test, the statement must adversely affect the plaintiff's reputation. Here, Simon's statement suggested that Darrow was dishonest and untrustworthy because she had committed an act that prevented the witness from appearing and testifying. Because honesty is a characteristic valued and expected in an attorney, Simon's statement adversely affected Darrow's "impeccable" reputation accrued over the past 20 years. Thus, the Restatement 2nd test is met.

Second, the defendant must publish the defamatory statement either intentionally or negligently to a third party. This element is met because Simon made the statement intentionally in the presence of five members of the jury, the court reporter, Ms. Darrow's client, Mr. Mo, court spectators and the readers of the Daily Recorder.

Third, the defamatory matter must be subjectively understood by at least one third person to be of and concerning the plaintiff. In this case, the statement was directed toward Ms. Darrow. Ms. Simon expressly used the word "you" in referring to Ms. Darrow. Therefore, it is likely that each of the third parties listed above understood the statement as referring to Ms. Darrow. Furthermore, Darrow was involved in a trial with Ms. Simon, and the third parties, including the court personnel, client, and spectators, were aware of the proceedings and the significance of the statement as it related to Ms. Darrow. Thus, this element is met.

Fourth, plaintiff's injury must be caused by defendant's statement. Here, but for Simon's statement, Darrow's reputation would not have been injured. Additionally, no intervening causes occurred so as to break the chain of causation between Simon's statement and the resulting injury to Darrow's practice. Thus, Simon's statement was the actual and proximate cause of Darrow's injuries.

Finally, defendant must suffer damages. If the defamation is slanderous or oral, then the defendant must show special pecuniary damages unless it qualifies as slander per se. Slander per se exists where the defamatory statement concerns defendant's business, an accusation of crime committed by the defendant, or a disease or unchastity attributed to the defendant.

In this case, Simon's statement affected Ms. Darrow's business and her practice of law. Certainly, an accusation relating to an attorney's veracity and ethics affects an attorney's business, because of the public trust and honesty expected of an attorney. Because Simon's statement directly concerned Darrow's business practices, it would qualify as slander per se.

As a separate ground, Simon's statement also accused Darrow of committing a crime. Simon accused Darrow of getting to her witness, implying that Darrow committed some act that prevented her witness from testifying, thereby obstructing justice. Because obstruction of justice is a crime in California, Simon's statement qualifies as slander per se.

Simon's statement also constituted libel, because it was published in the <u>Daily Recorder</u> newspaper. Where defamation is written or libelous, then general damages are presumed. Thus, because Simon's statement was published in the newspaper, Darrow need not prove special damages.

Therefore, Darrow would prevail against Simon because each element of a defamation action is met.

<u>Defenses</u>

<u>Truth</u>

Simon will be unable to claim truth as a defense. Truth is an absolute defense to defamation. Here the witness, Mr. Larry, did not appear because he was out of the country on vacation. Unless Simon could prove that Darrow was responsible for Mr. Larry's non-appearance at trial and that she somehow committed witness tampering, this defense would be rejected.

<u>Judicial Proceeding</u>

Simon will claim that the statement was privileged because it was made during a judicial proceeding. Statements made in a judicial proceeding are privileged only if related to those proceedings. Simon will argue that the statement referred to the fact that her witness did not appear at a judicial proceeding and involved a statement made in connection with that proceeding. The proceeding involved a lawsuit between Mo and Curley, and the first witness failed to appear even though he had been subpoenaed to appear. Simon might claim that she was simply informing the spectators, jurors and client <u>why</u> witness Larry was not present.

However, Simon's statement was made after the case was dismissed. No court proceedings were in progress at the time the statement was made, and the jury had been dismissed. Thus, Simon's statement was gratuitous and not necessary to further the representation of her client or her responsibilities or obligations as an attorney. Thus, this defense is not meritorious.

<u>First Amendment Privilege</u>

Simon may claim a First Amendment qualified privilege. For a public figure, which includes a famous person or voluntary publicity seeker, the plaintiff must prove constitutional malice. Constitutional malice requires knowledge of falsity or reckless disregard. It is unlikely that Darrow will be considered a public figure, even though she is a famous trial attorney and has maintained a successful law practice for twenty years. There is no indication that she sought publicity, and instead it appears that her notoriety is due to her position as a trial attorney. While she is known as an attorney, she cannot be said to be a famous individual like a politician or actor, who might expect public scrutiny and criticism. If the court so found, as a private person Darrow need only prove negligence and actual damages.

Regardless of what standard is employed, Simon's statements were not only negligently made, as she could have determined from a reasonable inquiry the whereabouts of Mr. Larry, but her statements also satisfied the standard of constitutional malice. While she was unaware that her statements were false, there is no indication that she made any attempt to determine the truth of the accusation she made against Darrow. Simon had no facts giving her a basis to believe that Darrow was responsible for Mr. Larry's failure to appear as subpoenaed. Thus, at a minimum, at least recklessness is shown. In her defense, Simon could argue that she acted out of anger and that she had no means of determining where Mr. Larry was at the time the statement was made.

However, it is likely that the court will find that Simon acted with the requisite intent and reject any First Amendment privilege.

<u>Opinion</u>

Simon might also claim that her statement was merely an opinion. An opinion is a judgment or belief and may be subject to a qualified privilege if not abused. This argument might be valid if the statement were more tentative. However, Simon plainly stated that Darrow had gotten to her witness. Therefore, her statement was not an opinion, but an assertion that Darrow had committed wrongdoing.

Public Proceeding

As to the publication of Simon's statement in the Daily Recorder, Simon might claim that the statements were published as a report of a public proceeding. Reports of a public proceeding are subject to a qualified privilege. Here, a criminal trial is a public proceeding. However, because the proceedings had ended, this defense would not apply. Simon was not furthering any purpose of the proceeding, nor was she explaining the nature of the proceedings when she made the statement concerning Darrow. Moreover, the applicability of this defense would not effect her liability for making the initial statement, as Simon was not reporting any public proceeding at the time she made the statement. Therefore, this defense would be rejected.

Effect of Apology

Simon might claim that she retracted the statement. However, her apology to Darrow two weeks after the incident would probably not qualify as a retraction, because it was not published to anyone except Darrow and was public in nature. A retraction is defined as a public acknowledgment of wrongdoing. Therefore, Darrow's damages will not be mitigated by Simon's apology.

Darrow v. District Attorney's Office

The issue is whether Simon's employer, the District Attorney's Office, should be liable for the torts of its employee, Ms. Simon. Under the doctrine of respondeat-superior, an employer is liable for all torts committed by its employees within the course of employment. Because Simon was at work and involved in carrying out her responsibilities as a prosecutor at the time she made the statement concerning Darrow, the statement was made during the course of her employment. Therefore, the District Attorney's Office is vicariously liable for defamation.

* * *

In the example above, notice how each element of defamation is dealt with, one at a time. Again, the checklist approach mirrors the approaches in the previous examples. The basic issues in a defamation action are: (1) How harmful was the statement? (2) Did D say it to someone else? (3) Did that someone else understand the statement concerned P? (4) Did D's statement cause P's injury (5) Was there damage to P? Whenever you are faced with a defamation question, these questions must be asked.

The checklist approach forces you to be meticulous and comprehensive in your discussion of the issues. Imagine being on an Easter egg hunt. You walk into a big back yard and see a garden, a planter box and lawn area. How would you go about searching for eggs? You might begin methodically, taking each square foot one at a time, or you could run about aimlessly, hoping to spot some eggs. While the latter method is much more fun, the more comprehensive you are in your search, the more likely it is that you will not miss any eggs.

On a law school examination, you cannot afford to overlook any issues. In the above example, if you did not apply a checklist approach to the defenses, chances are you will have missed at least one of the applicable defenses. If you were able to instantly "spot the issues" and determine that the applicable defenses were truth, judicial proceedings, opinion evidence, public proceeding, and First Amendment, then more power to you. On the other hand, if you missed one of these essential issues, follow a checklist so you do not overlook important issues. Using the checklist approach, you would ask: ABSOLUTE PRIVILEGE? Is truth a defense? What about judicial or legislative proceedings? Husband and wife communications? Political broadcast? Consent? You would then turn to the QUALIFIED PRIVILEGES, including the First Amendment privilege, opinion, protection of a private or public interest and a report of a public proceeding.

After mentally reciting this checklist of defenses, your mind should ring with a resounding "BINGO!!!" when each applicable defense is discovered. With each issue or Easter egg uncovered, you will be able to determine which issues require discussion in a given problem.

Let's regress for a moment and take a problem which again stresses the basics of I-R-A-C. Besides, after all this hard work, we deserve a breather!

Strict Liability

This problem involves the theory of strict liability for domestic and wild animals, specifically a dog. Strict liability refers to the imposition of tort liability regardless of the presence of any mental intent; that is, liability based on solely on the commission of an act, regardless of whether the actor acted intentionally or negligently:

Strict Liability Example: Peebles v. Barney

Fred the mailman was walking Barney's pitbull Dino one Saturday morning. When Peebles tried to pet Dino, Dino bit Peebles. Is Barney liable to Peebles for her injury?

Now let's take a look at an I-R-A-C answer to this problem. There are two issues here. The first is whether a pitbull is a wild or domestic animal, and secondly, what standard of knowledge applies to each. To recap the rules involving the liability of an owner of an animal, if the animal is "wild," then the owner is strictly liable for any damage; on the other hand, if the animal is "domestic," the owner is liable only if she is aware of the animal's propensity to cause the harm.

The issue is whether Barney is liable to Peebles for Dino's act of biting her. The owner of a wild animal is strictly liable for any harm caused. The owner of a domestic animal is not liable for any harm caused unless he or she knew of the animal's propensity to injure another.

Barney's liability would turn on whether a pitbull would be considered a "wild" or "domestic" animal. Barney would argue that a domestic animal should include any animal commonly kept as a house pet, such as dogs, cats, hamsters, and birds. Barney would contrast such pets with "wild" animals, such as tigers, lions and the like. Peebles would argue that because pitbulls are dangerous animals which are known to have a propensity to commit violence, they should be characterized as "wild" animals, and Barney should be strictly liable.

Because pitbulls are dogs, it is likely that Dino will be considered a domestic animal. Thus, Barney would be liable only if he had knowledge that the pitbull had a dangerous propensity. On this issue Peebles will prevail, since it is common knowledge that pitbulls are dangerous animals who often bite and injure others. Even if Dino had never bitten anyone before, Barney should have known of the dangerous reputation and character of pitbulls. Thus, Barney is liable to Peebles.

Products Liability

Before moving onto the exciting world of criminal law, let's tackle a Products Liability Problem.

The area of Products Liability is really made up of five separate torts, each of which is comprised of certain elements that must be met before a cause of action is said to exist. In answering a products liability problem, address each theory of liability separately; use headings if it will help you to compartmentalize your discussion of each tort:

Products Liability Example: Sammy Skinny v. Macho Man

Macho Man, a world heavyweight champion wrestler, designed a new exercise device known as the "Flexer." The "Flexer"is a device that is made up of two handles which are pulled in opposite directions and held together by springs and coils. Macho Man appeared in a local ad promoting the device and guaranteed that the product would "safely and painlessly transform a wimp into a Macho man." Sammy Skinny saw the advertisement and immediately purchased a "Flexer." However, the "Flexer" purchased by Skinny was defective, containing a broken spring that caused the device to recoil dangerously. After using the device for only a few minutes, following the exercises demonstrated by Macho Man in the instruction booklet, Skinny suffered injuries requiring hospitalization.

Model Answer: Sammy Skinny vs. Macho Man

Misrepresentation

The issue is whether Skinny may sue for misrepresentation under the Restatement 2d. The first element is that there must be a misrepresentation of a material fact. Here Macho Man represented that the product was safe when in fact it was not. Secondly, the plaintiff must rely upon the representation in using the product. Here Skinny heard Macho Man's representation that the item was safe and painless and presumably relied upon the statement in purchasing the device. Thus, this element is met. Thirdly, the representation must be made by the defendant or fairly chargeable against him. Macho Man himself made the statement, and thus this element is met. Fourthly, the representation must be intended and expected to reach a class of which plaintiff is a member. Because the ad was broadcasted to the public, and Skinny is a member of the public, this element is met. Finally, the defendant must be a commercial supplier of chattels. Because Macho Man is in the business of supplying exercise equipment, this element is met.

Breach of Express Warranty

Skinny may also sue for breach of express warranty under U.C.C. 2-313. Where the elements of a misrepresentation action are met, an action may be brought under contract law. U.C.C. 2- 313 extends liability to any seller and extends protection to anyone who could be expected to be personally injured by the goods.

Strict Products Liability

The issue is whether Skinny may recover from Macho Man based on a strict products liability theory under Restatement 402A. First, the defendant must cause the product to be placed on the market. Macho Man was in the business of selling the "Flexer," and, therefore, caused the item to be placed on the market. Second, at the time the defendant put the product on the market, the product contained an unreasonably dangerous defect. The "Flexer" was defective because it contained a broken spring. The defective "Flexer" could be compared to a product not containing the defect, thereby proving that the product purchased by Skinny was defective. The broken spring caused the device to recoil dangerously and posed an unreasonable danger to whoever used the device. Thus, this element is met. Third, the plaintiff must be hurt while using the device in an intended and foreseeable manner. Here Skinny was using the product in accordance with the instructions accompanying the device, and therefore, was using the device in its intended manner. The manner in which Skinny used the product was foreseeable to Macho Man, as he himself demonstrated how to use the device in the manual. The final element is that the defendant must be engaged in the business of selling and supplying the product, and this element is met because Macho Man is in the business of selling exercise devices.

Therefore, Skinny would prevail on a strict products liability action under Restatement 402A.

Breach of Implied Warranties

The issue is whether Skinny may sue for breach of implied warranties. The warranty of merchantability guarantees that goods are fit for the ordinary purposes for which goods are used, where the defendant is a merchant of such goods. Because Macho Man is a merchant of exercise equipment, the warranty of merchantability applies, thereby guaranteeing that the "Flexer" is fit for the uses for which it was designed. Because the "Flexer" purchased by Skinny was not fit for use as an exercise device due to the broken spring, Skinny will prevail on this theory.

Negligence

The issue is whether Skinny will prevail on a negligence action against Macho Man. Negligence is defined as the breach of duty of due care that is the actual and proximate cause of plaintiff's injuries.

The first issue is that of duty. Under the Cardozo rule, a duty is owed to a foreseeable plaintiff. Because Macho Man advertised to the public, it was foreseeable that a member of that public who responded to the ad would be injured by a defective device. Thus, under the Cardozo rule, duty is met. Under the Andrews rule, a duty is owed to all. Under this rule, because Skinny is a human being, a duty exists.

The second issue is the applicable standard of care. A manufacturer would exercise due care in inspecting its products to insure that its products did not contain unreasonably dangerous defects. The third issue of breach must be resolved against Macho Man, because Macho Man breached the standard of care by failing to properly inspect the "Flexer" and to detect the broken spring.

The fourth issue is causation. But for Macho Man's failure to discover the defect in the "Flexer" device, Skinny would not have been injured. Hence, Macho Man's omissions were a cause-in- fact of Skinny's injuries. Because no intervening circumstances occurred, and Skinny was injured a direct result of Macho's failure to inspect, Macho Man's omission was the legal or proximate cause of Skinny's injuries.

Finally, the fifth element of negligence is met since Skinny suffered actual injuries.

As you can see, a products liability analysis involves a five-level analysis of each of the possible causes of action. In addition, you must discuss any applicable defenses as well.

Now, let's move on to the area of criminal law...

How to Answer a Criminal Law Problem

CRIMES

The law of crimes begins with a laundry list of various types of criminal conduct which are generally referred to as "crimes." In reality, each state's legislature has determined what conduct is illegal and has drafted Codes and laws to reflect the conduct which has been defined as criminal. Hence, criminal law will vary from state to state. Also, the federal system has its own criminal laws and its own system to enforce those laws. Thus, the two sources of criminal law are the state and federal laws.

You will not learn each and every criminal statute during your first year of law school. For example, in your state, it may be a crime to smoke a cigarette in a state owned building or to walk your dog without a leash; it is extremely unlikely that your professor will take the time to cover such specific and trivial crimes. Instead, you will learn the most common crimes found in the majority of jurisdictions.

These crimes are generally placed in four categories: the inchoate or planning crimes of solicitation, attempt and conspiracy; crimes against the person, including battery, false imprisonment, mayhem, assault, rape, robbery, kidnaping and homicide; crimes against property, usually encompassing arson, larceny or theft, burglary, extortion, larceny by trick, false pretenses, uttering, receiving stolen property, embezzlement, larceny by conversion, and forgery. While your professor may cover a few additional crimes during your first year, these crimes represent the basic crimes taught throughout the country.

As stated in the introductory section, each crime is made up of two basic components: **mens rea** and **actus reus**.

First, mens rea, or intent is required. Remember that the criminal laws punish the mind as well as the conduct involved. Thus, an alleged shoplifter is not guilty of larceny or theft if she leaves the store without paying for the broach in her pocket <u>without</u> the intent to steal it. She is not guilty because she does not possess the necessary intent to steal the item.

There are two categories of criminal intent. The first type of mens rea is known as general intent. **General intent** requires only that the actor intend to commit the act. A crime which requires only general intent is known as a general intent crime. Battery is a general intent crime, because it requires only that the actor intend to make contact with the victim. Thus, a defendant who commits a battery must only intend that he makes contact with the victim, and not with any special or specific intent in mind.

The second type of intent is **specific intent**. Specific intent requires that in addition to having general intent, the defendant acts with a special intent unique to the crime charged. For example, as we have already learned, burglary requires specific intent. In order to be found guilty of burglary, the defendant must actually intend to commit a felony or larceny within the building before entering the building. Burglary is thus a specific intent crime.

In addition to the categorization of a crime as requiring "specific" or "general" intent, there are different states of minds with which a crime may be committed, such as criminal negligence, intentional and malicious knowledge, wantonness and strict liability. Each state of mind represents a different mens rea and is defined in the glossary.

The second component of a crime is the act known as the "actus reus." The act in the shoplifting example above is the taking and carrying away of another's property. Thus, the actor must take property belonging to another and transport that property before the actus reus component of larceny is met. In the burglary example, the act is the trespassory breaking and entering into a structure. Thus, like mens rea, the actus reus required is unique to each crime.

The *Law Chart* on Criminal Law lists each crime by area, beginning with the inchoate crimes and ending with homicide. Each crime listed in the approach has its unique mens rea and actus reus clearly delineated in a checklist format. These "elements" are the questions you will answer in determining whether that particular crime has been committed.

When solving a criminal law exam problem, the first issue will always be, "Did the defendant commit a crime?" You then turn to your laundry list of crimes and determine which specific crimes may have been committed in much the same way. You will examine the facts to determine if each element of the crime has been committed by the defendant. Once you have analyzed each crime, you turn to the issue of defenses. As you can see, the analysis involved is quite similar to the intentional torts approach.

We will begin with the inchoate or "planning" crimes. These crimes, by definition, involve the planning of crime. For example, solicitation occurs when one solicits criminal conduct. The actus reus is the instigation or origination of a criminal scheme, while the mens rea requires the specific intent to incite another to commit a crime.

Each inchoate crime has certain general principles of law which must be considered in analyzing an inchoate crime. For example, a solicitor is vicariously guilty for the crime committed by the person solicited. A second general principle of consideration is that solicitation merges, or is "eaten up" when the defendant is convicted of conspiracy or the crime intended. Another general consideration is that the solicitor may withdraw by unequivocally stating his or her intention to do so, and is still guilty of solicitation, but not guilty of whatever crimes are committed by the person solicited.

Let's take an example:

Crimes Example #1: <u>People v. Dickie the Detective</u>

Dickie the Detective approached Sally Streetwalker and said, "How about sex for money, honey?" Sally kicked Dickie in the shins and walked to another

corner. Is Dickie the Detective guilty of solicitation?

Model Answer: People v. Dickie or State v. Dickie

Solicitation

The issue is whether Dickie is guilty of solicitation. Solicitation is defined as inciting another to commit any felony or misdemeanor involving breach of the peace.

The actus reus requires the defendant to instigate or originate a criminal scheme. Here, assuming that prostitution is prohibited in State X, Dickie made a statement which solicited a criminal scheme, involving the exchange of sex for money. In this statement, Dickie requested that Sally participate in a criminal act. Therefore, the actus reus requirement is met.

The mens rea requires the specific intent to incite another to commit a crime. If Dickie was a police officer and approached Sally only with the intention of arresting her for criminal conduct, Dickie would not have the required specific intent because he did not intend to incite Sally to commit the act requested. However, on the other hand, Dickie's statement was explicit, and expressly requested that Sally participate in a violation of law. Thus, in the absence of proof that Dickie did not actually intend to solicit a crime, this mens rea requirement would be met.

Thus, because both the mens rea and actus reus are met, Dickie is guilty of solicitation.

Note the use of headings in this example. Depending on the custom of your state, criminal actions will usually be entitled, "People of the State of X vs. Defendant" or "State X vs. Defendant" or "Commonwealth vs. Defendant." You should first identify the cause of action you are addressing by stating the parties involved, usually the state or the government and the defendant. You should then identify the crime which you are analyzing. While this may appear unnecessary in a problem involving a single crime, in analyzing a fact pattern for multiple crimes, use of headings will assist you in compartmentalizing your discussion of each crime.

Next, compare the writing style and format of the solicitation answer to what you have already seen in the area of Torts. Yes, it is your old friend and ally, "I-R-A-C." Think of a super hero named "I-R-A-C" man or "I-R-A-C" woman. This superhuman being flies to the rescue, whenever disorganization and poor writing reeks havoc on your examination answer. You should call on the "IRAC" Super hero on each examination, regardless of whether the subject matter is Torts or Criminal Law or Property.

Also notice that your discussion of the mens rea and actus reus are compartmentalized, that is, discussed separately. It is often helpful to place your discussion of each "issue" into separate paragraphs, so that your thoughts will not run together. By your writing short and concise paragraphs, your analysis will be better communicated to the reader. In the example above, each issue is addressed separately. The actus reus discussion focuses on the act committed by Dickie, which in this case was the statement suggesting that the crime of prostitution be committed. The mens rea analysis focuses on Dickie's specific intent to commit the crime suggested.

Now, let's move onto a more difficult problem, again using inchoate crimes as an example, involving multiple crimes and parties:

Criminal Law Example #2: Prosecution vs. Motley & Crew

Motley, who was short of funds, approached Crew and said, "Let's rob a bank." Crew agreed and Motley bought a ladder and rope which were to be used in committing the robbery. Motley subsequently lost interest and did not participate in the bank robbery which Crew committed alone. Please discuss the criminal liability of all parties.

Model Answer: People v. Motley

Solicitation

The issue is whether Motley is guilty of solicitation. Solicitation is defined as inciting another to commit any felony or misdemeanor involving breach of the peace. The actus reus is the instigation or origination of a criminal scheme. Here Motley approached Crew and suggested that they commit a bank robbery, and thus this element is met. The mens rea requires the specific intent to incite another to commit a crime. Motley acted with the intent to incite and involve Crew in a crime, and thus had the specific intent to commit solicitation. Further, Motley made an express statement which directly suggested that they commit robbery and is evidence of his intent. Thus, Motley is guilty of solicitation.

Motley, as a solicitor, would also be vicariously liable for the crime committed by Crew. Under this doctrine, the solicitor is liable as an accomplice if the person solicited either attempts or perpetrates a crime. Thus, Motley would be vicariously liable as an accomplice for the robbery committed by Crew.

Solicitation merges into the liability the solicitor incurs as a conspirator and accomplice. Thus, if Motley is convicted of conspiracy, as discussed below, the crime of solicitation will "merge" into the crime of conspiracy. Likewise if, Motley is convicted of robbery as an aider and abettor, his liability for solicitation merges into the offense of robbery.

Motley may contend that he withdrew from the criminal scheme, and if he unequivocally communicated this fact to Crew, Motley would not be liable for crimes committed by Crew. However, Motley remains guilty of the crime of solicitation.

<u>Attempt</u>

The issue is whether Motley is guilty of attempted robbery. An attempt is an act in the direction of perpetrating an intended crime, such as robbery. The actus reus requires an act in the zone of perpetration. Here Motley secured a rope and ladder which, according to his plan, was to be used in a bank robbery. Both of these acts went beyond mere preparation and involved the securing of the actual instrumentalities used to commit the crime. Thus, because both acts were within the zone of perpetration of the crime of robbery, the actus reus requirement is met. The mens rea requires the specific intent to perform or cause an act which, if accomplished, would be the target offense of robbery. Here, Motley approached Crew and suggested, by words, that they commit a robbery. This statement is sufficient evidence of his intention to commit a robbery at the time it was made. As with solicitation, Motley's liability for attempted robbery would merge into the crime of robbery.

The majority view holds that the defendant's abandonment of a plan does not excuse liability. Under this view, Motley's failure to carry out his scheme would not excuse his liability for attempted robbery. Under the minority view, Motley would be excused only if he permanently and successfully abandoned the criminal project. Thus, under this rule, Motley would not be guilty of attempted robbery if he in fact completely abandoned the criminal enterprise.

<u>Conspiracy</u>

The issue is whether Motley is guilty of conspiracy. Conspiracy is defined as a combination or agreement for an unlawful purpose. The actus reus requires the act of two or more persons combining or joining together to achieve an unlawful goal. This element is met because Crew and Motley agreed to join together to commit a bank robbery. However, under the minority view, an overt act is required in addition to the act of combining. Because Motley committed two overt acts in preparation of the robbery by securing the rope and ladder, the minority view requirement would be fulfilled. Thus, under either rule the actus rea requirement is met.

The mens rea requires an actual intent to combine and the specific intent to achieve an unlawful goal. First, Motley and Crew specifically agreed to work together, and thus Motley had the actual intent to combine. Furthermore, Motley specifically intended to achieve the goal of committing a robbery.

Thus, Motley is guilty of conspiracy to commit robbery.

Motley's conviction of conspiracy does not merge into any other offenses.

Motley cannot claim that he withdrew from the conspiracy unless he withdrew prior to the commission of an overt act. Motley committed two overt acts, securing the rope and ladder, before deciding to abandon his criminal scheme. Thus, he failed to withdraw and remains guilty of conspiracy.

Under the Pinkerton rule, a conspirator is liable for any criminal act committed by a co-conspirator in furtherance of the conspiracy. Thus, Motley is guilty of the robbery committed by Crew, since the robbery was committed in furtherance of the agreement between Motley and Crew to commit bank robbery.

Therefore, Motley is guilty not only of conspiracy, but also of robbery.

* * *

As you read this model answer, notice the consistency with which the basic I-R-A-C formula is applied to each crime. Each crime, while containing different elements to be analyzed, is organized in the same fashion. First, the general definition of the crime is given, taken straight from the *Law Chart* on Criminal Law in this book. Next, the actus reus rule is stated and applied to the facts of the problem. Then the mens rea requirement is stated and analyzed. A conclusion is given, and finally, the "general considerations" are discussed, one at a time.

This point by point, issue by issue, analysis may seem painstaking, but it captures the essence of a good legal analysis by presenting a well-organized, comprehensive discussion of the issues. If you were sitting in the defendant's chair, charged with a crime, is that not what you would expect of your lawyer?

Naturally, you would be appalled if your lawyer said, "Well, I'll just cover the elements in a haphazard fashion. I don't have time to cover each general consideration, so I'll just roll them into one." Such an analysis might resemble the following:

People v. Crew

Crew is guilty of conspiracy to commit robbery and robbery. Conspiracy is defined as an agreement to commit a crime. Because he committed a robbery suggested by Crew, this crime was committed. Since Crew also did

the robbery, even though Motley did not, Crew is guilty of robbery. Crew would also be liable for the acts of Motley, such as Motley's acts of obtaining the rope and ladder.

Not only is this analysis completely disorganized, but it fails to state the issues, rules or application. If you find yourself writing such mish-mash, do not hesitate! Call 1-800-GET-IRAC to the rescue!

We will now move to the area of defenses. In most jurisdictions, the following defenses will either excuse or mitigate criminal conduct: insanity, drunkenness or intoxication, entrapment, mistake, age, necessity, duress, prevention of a crime, defense of others, defense of property and self-defense.

Consider the following exam problem involving the defense of "Entrapment":

Crimes Example #3: People v. Do-Wrong

Officer Do-Right approached Defendant Do-Wrong, a drug dealer, and asked Do-Wrong to purchase an ounce of cocaine. Do-Right told Do-Wrong that he was a drug addict who was in desperate need of the drug.

Model Answer: People v. Do-Wrong

Defense of Entrapment

The issue is whether Defendant Do-Wrong could raise the defense of entrapment to sale of a controlled substance. The defense of entrapment excuses the commission of a crime if the defendant committed the act at the instigation of law enforcement.

Under the majority rule, the defendant's subjective disposition to commit the crime is considered in determining whether he was entrapped to commit the charged crime. Here, because Do-Wrong was a drug dealer, he was predisposed to sell narcotics and therefore cannot raise the defense of entrapment. While Do-Right may have enticed Do-Wrong to sell narcotics on this one occasion, the defendant was previously involved in drug dealing and therefore was predisposed to commit a crime.

The minority view focuses on the objective effect of the police activity on a reasonable law-abiding person. Under this view, entrapment would not apply because a reasonable law- abiding person asked to supply Do-Right with an ounce of cocaine would not be enticed to commit a crime. In fact, a reasonable law-abiding person would probably walk away. Do-Wrong might argue forcefully that a reasonable law-abiding person would respond to Do-Right's sympathetic and desperate requests for drugs to supply his habit, but because a reasonable law-abiding citizen would not respond by supplying drugs, and since Do-Right's actions did not rise to the level of instigating criminal conduct, the defense of entrapment does not apply.

Always discuss the majority and minority rules where appropriate. When your professor takes the time to explain the minority rule, you will be expected to know that rule and to apply it on the examination.

Before moving to the area of homicide, let's take a criminal law exam problem involving both crimes and defenses:

Crimes Example #4: Prosecution v. Sammy Slick

Sammy Slick, who had a history of mental illness and alcoholism, approached Violet Victim and asked her if she was registered to vote. Violet said she was not and agreed to sign what she believed to be a voter's registration form. Unbeknownst to Violet she had, in fact, signed a form bequeathing all of her worldly possessions to Sammy. Sammy then physically forced Violet onto a public bus and accompanied Violet to a bank, where he forced her to withdraw all of her savings and give Sammy a cashier's check in Violet's name. Violet signed her name only after Sammy threatened to "get her" if she did not do so. Sammy took the cashier's check and presented it to the bank clerk and signed the name "V. Victim." The bank clerk, however, refused to cash the check after reading the inscription, "This is a bank robbery, give me all you money," on the back of the check, which Violet had written in order to draw attention to Sammy; Sammy, in anger, dropped a lit cigarette in a nearby trash can, causing a small fire, saying, "I hope this stinkin' bank burns to the ground!"

What crimes is Sammy guilty of, and what defenses apply?

Model Answer: People v. Sammy Slick

The issue is what crimes may Sammy Slick be convicted of, and what defenses, if any, may apply.

False Pretenses

(STATE THE GENERAL ISSUE) The issue is whether Sammy is guilty of false pretenses. (STATE THE RULE) False pretense is defined as a fraudulent misrepresentation of past or present fact which causes the victim to pass title to personal property made with the specific intent to defraud. (APPLICATION) Here Sammy asked Violet to sign a voter's registration form, which, in fact, was a document bequeathing Violet's belongings to Sammy. Thus, Sammy committed the actus reus by misrepresenting the true nature of the form he induced Violet to sign, thereby causing Violet to pass title to her life savings to Sammy. Therefore, the actus reus is met. The mens rea requires the specific intent to defraud. Here Sammy presumably knew the form he induced Violet to sign was not a voter's registration form, and Sammy acted with the purpose of causing Violet to pass title of her life savings to him. Because Sammy intended to defraud Violet, the mens rea is met.

(CONCLUSION) Thus Sammy is guilty of false pretenses.

False Imprisonment

The issue is whether Sammy is guilty of false imprisonment. False imprisonment is the intentional use of force to confine the person of another. The actus reus requires both force and confinement. Sammy forced Violet to get into the bus, and accompany him to bank; thus, Violet was confined within the bus and the bank due to physical force employed by Sammy. Thus, the actus reus is met. The mens rea requires actual intent to exert force and achieve confinement. Here Sammy acted with the purpose of causing Violet to transfer her savings to him, and thereby acted intentionally to confine Violet. Thus, the mens rea is met.

Therefore, Sammy is guilty of false imprisonment.

Kidnaping

The next issue is whether Sammy is guilty of kidnaping. Kidnaping is defined as false imprisonment accompanied by asportation of the victim. The actus reus requires false imprisonment, as analyzed above, and coerced movement of the victim. Because Sammy used physical force to cause Violet to accompany him, which resulted in actual movement or asportation of Violet's person from one location to another, the actus reus is met. The mens rea requires actual intent to move and confine another. Because Sammy acted intentionally with the purpose of transporting Violet to secure her savings, the mens rea requirement is met.

Burglary

The issue is whether Sammy is guilty of burglary. Burglary, at common law, is the trespassory breaking and entering of the dwelling house of another at night with the specific intent to commit a felony or larceny therein. Under modern law, a burglary may be committed against a non-residential structure such as a bank at any hour of the day, even if no actual breaking occurred. Thus, under modern statutes, both the actus reus and mens rea are met because Sammy entered the bank with the intention of committing a larceny of Violet's savings therein.

Therefore, Sammy is guilty of burglary. However, because no dwelling house was involved, most states provide a lesser penalty.

Extortion

The issue is whether Sammy is guilty of extortion. Extortion is defined as the use of threats of future harm with specific intent to induce another to relinquish property. The actus reus is met because Sammy threatened to "get" Violet if she did not withdraw her savings in the form of a cashier's check and give the check to Sammy. Sammy's threat that he would "get her" if she did not relinquish her savings and the cashier check is a threat of future harm. Given that Sammy had forced Violet to accompany him to the bank, Sammy's threat was real and not imagined. The mens rea requires the specific intent to induce another to relinquish property. Sammy acted with the purpose of causing Violet to pass her savings onto him, and therefore possessed the necessary specific intent. Sammy's intent is also evidenced by his later of act of attempting to pass the check and receive the proceeds.

Therefore, Sammy is guilty of extortion.

<u>Receiving Stolen Property</u>

The issue is whether Sammy is guilty of receiving stolen property. Receiving stolen property is defined as the receiving of property, knowing it to be stolen with the specific intent to deprive the owner thereof. The actus reus is met because Sammy received the cashier check from Violet, and was aware that the funds were the subject of a theft perpetrated by Sammy. The mens rea is met because Sammy acted with the intent of depriving Violet of her savings. Thus, Sammy is guilty of receiving stolen property.

<u>Uttering</u>

The issue is whether Sammy is guilty of uttering. Uttering is defined as offering as genuine, an instrument known to be false with the intent to defraud. The actus reus was committed when Sammy presented the cashier's check to the bank teller after having signed the name "V. Victim," on the check. The mens rea is also met. Sammy knew that his name was not V. Victim and therefore knew that the instrument was false. Furthermore, Sammy possessed the specific intent to defraud the bank teller by misrepresenting his identity in order to cash the check.

Thus, Sammy is guilty of uttering.

<u>Forgery</u>

The issue is whether Sammy is guilty of forgery. Forgery is the making of a false writing having apparent legal significance with intent to defraud. Sammy committed the actus reus by signing the name of "V. Victim" to a cashier's check in Violet's name. Sammy also possessed the mens rea, because he intended to defraud the bank into cashing the check, and he signed the check for that purpose.

Therefore, Sammy is guilty of forgery.

<u>Robbery</u>

The issue is whether Sammy is guilty of robbery of the bank and Violet. Robbery is defined as larceny from the person or presence of another by the use of force or intimidation upon him or her. Because Sammy did not commit a trespassory taking and carrying away of any property of the bank, he could not be convicted of bank robbery.

However, Sammy might be found guilty of attempted robbery. An attempt is an act in the direction of perpetrating an intended crime. The actus reus requires an act in the zone of perpetration. Sammy's act of presenting the bank teller with a demand for money would qualify as an act which went beyond mere preparation and involved perpetration of the robbery. The mens rea, however, requires the specific intent to commit a robbery. Thus, unless Sammy knew that Violet had written the inscription on the check, or intended to use force to commit a larceny from the bank teller, he would not be guilty of attempted robbery.

Sammy would be guilty of robbery of Violet. Sammy used physical force and the threat of harm to cause Violet to pass a cashier check to Sammy, fulfilling the actus reus requirement. Sammy also acted with the specific intent to deprive Violet of her savings. Therefore, Sammy is guilty of robbery of Violet.

Arson

The issue is whether Sammy is guilty of arson. Arson, at common law, is the malicious burning of the dwelling house of another. Under modern law, the actus reus is met where the defendant commits any act which causes the burning of any structure. Although Sammy's act of throwing a cigarette into a trash can cause a fire, there is no evidence of damage to the structure, and therefore the actus reus is not met. The mens rea requires that the defendant intend that the burning take place; the best evidence of Sammy's intent is his statement, "I hope this stinkin' bank burns to the ground," which was made in anger, after the bank teller refused to cash a check presented by Sammy. Sammy acted purposefully and maliciously in throwing the cigarette in the trash can, and therefore the mens rea requirement is met. However, because there was no damage to the structure, Sammy is not guilty of arson.

Sammy, however, could be convicted of attempted arson. Sammy committed an act in the zone of perpetration by throwing the cigarette in the trash can. This act went far beyond mere preparation and was the act necessary to start a fire. As stated above, because Sammy possessed the mens rea, he may be convicted of attempted arson.

Defenses to Crime

Insanity

The issue is whether insanity would bar Sammy's guilt of any of the above crimes.

Under the M'Naghten Rule, a defendant who lacks the ability at the time of his actions to know the wrongfulness of actions and nature and quality of his act is not guilty of the crime. Thus, only if Sammy's mental illness prohibited him from knowing the wrongfulness of his acts and nature and quality of the act would his crimes be excused. Under the Irresistible Impulse rule, if a defendant is incapable of controlling her conduct, she is properly acquitted of the crimes charged. If Sammy were unable to control his behavior, the defense of insanity would bar his liability. Under the American Law Institute test, the insanity defense applies if the defendant lacks the substantial capacity to appreciate the criminality of his conduct or conform to the requirements of law. If Sammy was unable to form the capacity to understand the wrongfulness of his acts or to follow the law, he would be acquitted of all charges by reason of insanity.

The doctrine of diminished responsibility holds that mental illness short of insanity may be asserted in specific intent crimes. Thus, Sammy may raise his mental illness as a defense if it interfered in his ability to form the specific intent to commit a specific intent crime. This defense would apply to the crimes of kidnaping, burglary, extortion, robbery, false pretenses, uttering, and receiving stolen property.

Intoxication or Drunkenness

Sammy could raise his alcoholism as a possible defense. Voluntary intoxication is a defense to specific intent crimes, where alcohol consumption affects the defendant's capacity to form the necessary specific intent. Thus, if Sammy's alcohol problem interfered with his ability to form the specific intent to commit any of the specific intent crimes charged such that he was unable to form the necessary intent, he would be acquitted on this basis.

* * *

WHEW!!! How's that for a humdinger? Now you can see why a problem-solving approach is a must in solving exam problems. A student who employs a checklist is not bound to miss important issues. In the above examples, the crimes of false imprisonment, burglary, extortion and receiving stolen property could have easily been overlooked. The only way to insure against this is to use a checklist approach.

HOMICIDE

The law of homicide presents a good example of a complex legal analysis involving multiple issues, crimes and defenses. Although homicide may, at first glance, appear to be much more complicated than burglary or assault, remember that it's the same old I-R-A-C analysis which will serve you faithfully again and again.

Homicide, like other crimes, involves the two components of mens rea and actus reus. The actus reus is "criminal homicide." Criminal homicide is defined as the killing of a human being by another. As set forth in the *Law Chart* for Criminal Law, your actus reus checklist includes: (1) killing of (2) a human being (3) by (4) another. Each of these four elements must be fulfilled before the actus reus of a "criminal homicide" is proven.

The mens rea component involves an analysis of the defendant's state of mind at the time the homicide occurs. First, under old common law, four states of mind sufficed to prove murder: actual intent to kill, actual intent to inflict great bodily injury, wantonness and felony murder. The presence of any of these states of mind coupled with criminal homicide, constituted murder. Thus, in solving a homicide problem, first analyze the fact pattern to determine if the defendant is guilty of common law murder.

Under modern law, murder is divided into degrees. Thus, after determining whether the defendant is guilty of common law murder, at some point in your analysis you would turn to the question of how modern law would classify the criminal homicide. A first degree murder is an intentional killing with malice aforethought and with premeditation and deliberation. A second degree murder, by contrast, is also an intentional killing with malice aforethought, but without premeditation and deliberation.

After discussing modern law classifications of murder, you would consider manslaughter. Voluntary manslaughter is an intentional killing committed without malice. Thus, voluntary manslaughter applies where the defendant kills intentionally, but some mitigating factor reduces the killing from murder to manslaughter. Common factors which operate to reduce a murder to manslaughter include: heat of passion, imperfect self-defense (i.e., where the actor has good faith but unreasonable belief in the need to defend himself), mental disease, coercion, voluntary intoxication and anger. Involuntary manslaughter is an unintentional killing committed without malice, and is limited to situations where the killing is unintended, or where it occurs during the course of a misdemeanor, i.e., the misdemeanor manslaughter rule.

Finally, after discussing both murder and manslaughter, you would then turn to the issue of defenses to homicide, which include self-defense, defense of others, crime prevention, age, insanity and necessity.

Enough said! Time now for an example, right out of annals of the California Bar Examination:

Homicide Example #1: People v. Doug

Doug was watching television in his ground floor apartment. When outside noise made it difficult to hear the sound, he looked out and saw a party in progress on the lawn. Doug yelled at the party-goers to be quiet and threw an empty bottle at them. The bottle hit a woman on the leg. Her boyfriend, Tom, ran to Doug's apartment, broke down the door, and he approached Doug shaking his fist. Doug, who had been drinking heavily, reached into a drawer, removed a pistol and immediately shot and killed Tom.

MODEL ANSWER: People v. Doug

I. Doug's Liability for Homicide

(STATE THE GENERAL ISSUE) The issue is of which crimes will Doug be convicted.

(STATE THE FIRST SUB-ISSUE: DID DOUG COMMIT HOMICIDE?) Criminal homicide is defined as a killing of a human being by another with criminal intent. Doug caused the death of Tom by shooting him and, therefore, committed homicide. Doug's intent or mens rea, however, will determine his liability for murder, manslaughter or justifiable homicide.

Common Law Murder

(STATE RULE) Common law murder is homicide committed with malice aforethought. Malice aforethought requires actual intent to kill, an intent to inflict grave bodily injury, wantonness or conduct falling within the felony murder rule. **(APPLY RULE)** Here Doug's intent to kill Tom may be inferred from his act of purposely picking up his gun and shooting Tom. **(CONCLUSION)** Therefore, Doug could be found guilty of common law murder.

Modern law categorizes murder as first or second degree. **(STATE FIRST DEGREE MURDER RULE)** First degree murder requires premeditation and deliberation. **(APPLY RULE: DID DOUG ACT WITH PREMEDITATION/DELIBERATION?)** Here the evidence will probably not support a finding of either premeditation or deliberation, because Doug acted quickly and rashly in shooting Tom. Doug did not plan the killing of Tom, but he shot Tom in response to Tom's act of breaking down Doug's door. Doug did not carefully weigh any alternatives to killing Tom, but acted "immediately." **(CONCLUSION)** Thus, Doug should not be convicted of first degree murder.

(STATE SECOND DEGREE MURDER RULE) Second degree murder is an intentional killing with malice aforethought but without premeditation or deliberation. **(APPLY THE RULE: DID DOUG ACT W/ INTENT/MALICE?)** Here

Doug's act was intentional, as he shot Tom in order to defend himself. Doug also acted with malice, as he intended to shoot Tom, thereby intending at least to seriously injure Tom. **(STATE CONCLUSION)** Thus, in the absence of mitigating or excusing factors, Doug is guilty of second degree murder.

Manslaughter

(STATE GENERAL ISSUE) Manslaughter is divided into two types: voluntary and involuntary.

Voluntary Manslaughter

(STATE VOLUNTARY MANSLAUGHTER RULE) Voluntary manslaughter is the intentional killing of another human being with some mitigating circumstance, such as alcohol intoxication, reasonable provocation or imperfect self-defense.

(APPLY RULE: ALCOHOL INTOXICATION?) Doug may argue that alcohol intoxication affected his ability to form malice aforethought and reduces the charge from murder to manslaughter. Doug was "drinking heavily" at the time he shot Tom, and thus may have been unable to form malice aforethought or the specific intent to kill.

(STATE AND APPLY RULE: HEAT OF PASSION KILLING?) Doug may also argue that he acted in the heat of passion. However, in order to reduce murder to manslaughter, the provocation must be such that a reasonable person would kill and insufficient cooling time exists. While Doug did not have adequate time to calm down, a reasonable person would probably not kill a person who threatened non-deadly force. If Doug could raise a reasonable doubt in proving that a reasonable person would fear for his life and act in a similar fashion, he could be convicted only of manslaughter.

Involuntary Manslaughter

(STATE INVOLUNTARY MANSLAUGHTER RULE) Involuntary manslaughter is the unintentional killing of another or a killing which occurs during the course of an inherently dangerous misdemeanor (the misdemeanor manslaughter rule). **(APPLICATION)** Because Doug intended to kill Tom, which can be inferred of Doug's action of reaching into a drawer, removing a pistol and then shooting Doug, he could not be properly convicted of involuntary manslaughter. **(CONCLUSION)**

Defenses to Criminal Homicide

(STATE ISSUE) Doug would claim self-defense. **(STATE RULE)** An innocent person is justified in using deadly force in response to deadly force. **(APPLICATION)**

Arguably Doug is an aggressor, as he threw a bottle at a woman party-goer, but he took no actions toward Tom and was therefore entitled to protect himself against Tom. Tom not only confronted Doug but broke down Doug's door, and he approached Doug, shaking his fists. A reasonable person in Doug's position might believe that Tom would fight with Doug, but would not fear death. Thus, because Tom did not threaten the use of deadly force, Doug was not entitled to use deadly force. **(CONCLUSION)** Therefore, self-defense does not excuse Doug's liability for homicide.

(BROWNIE POINT) However, such a situation may reduce the crime of murder to manslaughter, if the trier of fact found that Doug had a good faith unreasonable belief in the need to defend himself.

As you can see in the model answer, a homicide analysis requires a careful point-by-point discussion of each tier within the crime of homicide, from common law murder, to the statutory degrees of homicide, to voluntary manslaughter and then the defenses. The key to understanding the law of homicide is that it is the state of mind of the accused that determines the crimes which the accused may be convicted. Again, the basic I-R-A-C format is employed, and headings are used to identify the issues analyzed.

A popular test area within the area of homicide is the felony murder rule. The felony murder rule is a judicially created rule which allows a finding of malice aforethought when, during the course of a dangerous felony, an accidental or unintended killing occurs. Hence, when a pedestrian is accidentally killed during the course of a getaway following a bank robbery, the participants are guilty of murder, not involuntary manslaughter.

As set forth in the Law Charts for Criminal Law, the felony murder rule applies only in certain circumstances, and, as with other areas of law, you must run through a checklist of issues to determine whether the rule applies. Let's do exactly that in the following example:

Homicide Example #2: <u>The Felony Murder Rule & Moral and Hardy-Up</u>

Moral and Hardy-up decided to rob a bank. During the course of the bank robbery, Moral was shot by a bank guard. Is Hardy-up guilty of murder?

Model Answer:

The issue is whether the felony murder rule applies. Under the felony murder rule, malice aforethought is implied if the homicide occurs during the course of an inherently dangerous felony.

First, the killing must be unintentional. Although the killing was committed by a bank guard, Hardy-up did not intend his partner's death, and therefore the killing was unintended by Hardy- up. **Second**, the crime must be an inherently dangerous felony; because robbery is included in the list of inherently dangerous felonies, this requirement is met. **Third**, the purpose of the felony must be totally independent of the homicide. Because Moral's death was not a planned circumstance of robbery, this requirement is met. **Fourth**, all of the elements of the underlying felony must be present. Because Hardy-up perpetrated a bank robbery, presumably all elements of a robbery are met.

Fifth, the killing must occur during the perpetration of the felony. Perpetration ends when the felon has escaped by reaching a place of apparent safety. Here the killing occurred while Hardy-up and Moral were committing the robbery; hence, this requirement is met. **Next**, the killing must be a foreseeable result of the felony. Anyone committing a bank robbery should be well aware that such a dangerous activity involves the probability that someone will be injured. Thus, this requirement is met. Therefore, the felony rule applies, and Hardy-Up is guilty of murder.

Under common law, the killing could be committed by a felon, the victim, a police officer or bystander. However, in New York and California, the killing must be committed by either the accused or the co-felon. Under the latter rule, Hardy-up would be not guilty of murder.

Under common law, the felony murder rule applied to the killing of any person, including a co-felon. However, under the <u>Redline</u> case, followed in Pennsylvania, the felony murder rule does not apply where a felon is justifiably shot by a police officer. <u>Redline</u> would probably extend liability to a shooting of a co-felon by a bank guard, since the bank guard is acting in a law enforcement capacity, and thus Hardy-up would be not guilty under the <u>Redline</u> case. Both California and New York, by contrast, require the victim to be an innocent party before the felony murder rule applies. Under this view, Hardy-up would be not guilty of murder, because Moral was a co-felon who participated in the robbery and therefore was not an innocent party.

* * *

The checklist approach, along with I-R-A-C, makes even an eight-part analysis easy. Note the continued use of "**crutches**," which hold the analysis together and assist the writer in comprehensively covering each issue.

Homicide Example #3: People v. Uhura, Spock & Chapel

On the set of "Star Trek 10" Captain Kirk, attempting to scare Uhura, grabbed Uhura and placed a "Spock hold" grip on her. Uhura, believing that Kirk's act was part of the script, stabbed Kirk with the "prop knife" that had been supplied by Scotty. Scotty, who hated "Bones," knew from reading the script that the "prop" knife was to be used to stab Bones. Scotty was deeply in love with Nurse Chapel, who was having an affair with the good doctor "Bones," and switched the real knife with the prop knife in order to get even. Unbeknownst to Uhura, the knife was razor sharp and Kirk was seriously injured. Kirk was hospitalized for fifteen months due to the knife wounds. The wounds were quite serious, and Kirk developed gangrene within five months of the stabbing. While at the hospital recovering from his wounds, Kirk was visited by Spock, who brought Kirk a TV dinner laced with arsenic. Spock stated to Kirk: "Captain, enjoy this meal, because it may be your last." Kirk replied: "Thank you, my good friend, and as you know, if I do not survive, you will be captain." Spock replied, "Kirk, live long and prosper."

Kirk put a spoonful of the salisbury steak from the TV dinner in his mouth, but died of gangrene before he could digest the food, fifteen months after he had been stabbed by Uhura. Nurse Chapel, who had been assigned to care for Kirk's injuries, saw that Kirk had died, and ate the TV dinner since Kirk had no need for it. Nurse Chapel became ill and began hallucinating. Thinking that Scotty was a Klingon, she shot him with her phaser, killing Scotty.

Please discuss the criminal liability for murder of all parties.

MODEL ANSWER:

I. People v. Uhura

The issue is whether Uhura committed a criminal homicide against Kirk when she stabbed him with the knife, and if so, whether that homicide would be a murder or manslaughter.

A. Criminal Homicide

A criminal homicide is the killing of a human being with criminal intent. A criminal homicide is the actus reus of a murder or manslaughter crime.

1. "Killing" requirement

The "killing" requirement is met when the defendant commits any voluntary act or omission which causes death. Here Uhura's act of stabbing Kirk was voluntary because she grabbed the knife consciously and stabbed Kirk, believing that the script required her to do so. The stabbing was not the product of an accident or uncontrollable impulse and hence was voluntary.

2. "Human being" requirement

Kirk is presumably a human being and this requirement is met.

3. "By"

The killing must be proximately caused by the voluntary act of another. Here the issue is whether Uhura's act of stabbing Kirk was the proximate cause of Kirk's eventual death. Kirk died of gangrene, but not from the stab wounds. The facts do not indicate whether Kirk contracted gangrene as a result of the knife wounds, only that Kirk developed gangrene within five months of the stabbing.

Uhura would argue that Kirk developed gangrene independent of the stabbing and that the two events were unrelated. Uhura would thus argue that the gangrene was a superseding cause which broke the chain of causation. The prosecutor would argue the contrary, that the gangrene was a direct result of Uhura's stabbing, and that Kirk would not have contracted gangrene but for the stabbing, and that it was quite foreseeable that one stabbed with a knife would foresee her victim contracting gangrene as a result thereof. Under this reasoning, the stabbing would be a dependent intervening cause; that is, the stabbing not only indirectly caused Kirk's death, but also generated the direct cause.

The court, however, will likely find that the stabbing was an independent intervening cause; that is, while the stabbing was indirectly responsible for causing Kirk's death, the gangrene developed independent of the stabbing. First, gangrene does not necessarily develop in all stabbings, and if the trier of fact so found, this factor supports Uhura's position. Secondly, stab wounds do not ordinarily take fifteen months to heal, and the gangrene eventually caused Kirk's death, not the stab wounds.

If the court so found, then Uhura's act would not be proximate unless Uhura should have or did foresee its occurrence, or intended to cause death in much the way it happened. Clearly Uhura, by her act and with her intent of fulfilling the script requirements, could not foresee Kirk's death. She at no time intended to cause any injury to Kirk, as she believed that the knife was a "prop" knife. She therefore could not foresee any injury or disease that Kirk would suffer as a result of the stabbing. Uhura is not responsible for Kirk's death if the stabbing was an independent intervening cause of Kirk's death.

Also, Uhura's liability may be precluded by the one-year rule, which holds that every direct cause that produces death within one year of its occurrence is proximate. Here there was a fifteen-month lapse of time between the stabbing and Kirk's death. Therefore, even if the stabbing is considered to be a direct cause of Kirk's death, Uhura could not be held liable due to the lapse of time. However, it should be noted that some jurisdictions have extended this rule to encompass three years, and if Uhura was tried in such a jurisdiction, she could not escape liability on this basis.

4. "Another" requirement

Here Kirk was stabbed by Uhura and not by himself, and therefore this requirement is met.

B. Mens Rea Requirement

Criminal homicide may be committed with either subjective intent (i.e., purpose or knowledge that death will result) or general intent (i.e., wanton reckless disregard for the possibility of death or culpable negligence in regard to death); the state of mind of the defendant (mens rea) will determine the crime.

Here the only evidence which exists as to Uhura's state of mind is that she believed she was acting. This is somewhat questionable because the facts also state that Scotty knew from the script that the knife was meant for Bones, not Kirk, and presumably both Scotty and Uhura read the same script. In any event, if Uhura in fact believed that she was only acting, and that she was using a prop knife when she stabbed Kirk, her state of mind cannot be found to be criminal. She had no reason to believe that Kirk would die of her actions, because the facts explicitly state that Uhura was unaware of the authenticity of the knife. Neither can her acts be characterized as culpable negligence nor wanton, unless she had some reason to believe that the knife she stabbed Kirk with was in fact real.

In conclusion, Uhura would not be guilty of murder or even manslaughter because of the lack of proximate cause and mens rea stated above.

C. Applicable Defenses

Self-Defense

First, Uhura would raise self defense to the charge of murder. Kirk had placed a spock hold on her with the purpose of scaring her, and she could have reasonably believed her life was in danger. This would depend on the consequences of a "Spock hold," which is not apparent from the facts. If the "Spock hold" was deadly, then it could be said that she acted reasonably in fear of her life because deadly force, such as attacking one with a knife, is only justified when the defender is being attacked with deadly force. If it was a mere tap on the shoulder, then another finding might result.

Even if Uhura's belief was not reasonable, any evidence that she acted out of fear might mitigate a murder charge to voluntary manslaughter.

Mistake

Uhura would claim mistake as a defense. This defense applies where an honest mistake negates the mental state with respect to any material element of murder, which in this case would be intent. Because murder is a specific intent crime, Uhura's mistake would be a complete defense, regardless of the reasonableness of her belief. If a reasonable person had realized the knife was real, she could still succeed in claiming mistake. However, for general intent homicide (i.e., involuntary manslaughter) the mistake must be reasonable, that is, a reasonable person in her shoes would have made such a mistake. This determination depends on what the knife itself looked like. For example, if the real knife was a samurai sword and the fake knife a pen knife, the reasonableness of her error might be suspect.

Thus, even if Uhura was found to have committed murder, either self defense or mistake would bar her liability.

2. People v. Spock

Spock would be not guilty of murder, but may be guilty of attempted murder.

While Spock obviously had the intent to kill Kirk, as he presumably knew the food served was laced with arsenic (i.e., acted with "malice aforethought" by using poison), arsenic poisoning was not the cause of Kirk's death. The arsenic played absolutely no role in Kirk's death, being neither the "but for" nor "proximate" cause of his death. Kirk died as a result of gangrene. Therefore, Spock is not guilty of murder.

An attempt is an act in the direction of perpetrating an intended crime. As discussed above, Spock had the specific intent to kill Kirk, and therefore had the specific intent to commit the target offense of murder. Spock also committed an act in the zone of preparation by handing Kirk the TV dinner laced with arsenic. This act went beyond mere preparation and completed the crime of attempted murder.

3. People v. Nurse Chapel

Nurse Chapel is guilty of murder. She committed a criminal homicide by shooting and killing Scotty. In the absence of mitigating circumstances reducing the killing to manslaughter, Chapel is guilty of at least second degree murder. However, Chapel would use the defense of involuntary intoxication. That defense provides that where a person kills another through force, mistake, fraud or medical prescription, a drug has temporarily affected one's mind, his or her causing of an actus reus will be excused as it would be had mental illness affected her mind.

Here Nurse Chapel unknowingly ate the arsenic laced food intended for Kirk and suffered delusions which caused her believe she was shooting a Klingon, not Scotty. The drug was presumably the only reason why she shot Scotty, and therefore her liability for Scotty's death would be excused.

* * *

If you have made it this far, and absorbed even a fraction of the information in this book, you have soared light years ahead of your brethren. A word for the weary: remember to take breathers in your study schedule. All too often, law students become victims of burn out, reading page after page, studying hour after hour, analyzing case after case. Do not let this happen to you as a law student or lawyer.

I am not condemming hard work and discipline. These two traits are necessary ingredients of a great lawyer. But do not fall into the well of neurotic law students who feel that they must study more than they breathe air. As you plan your daily study plans, schedule in quality recreation time. Quality recreation time means exactly that – go out and do something which is great fun and non-law related. Of course, if your idea of a good time is watching a law television show or reading advance sheets in the law school library, then so be it. But if you get a kick out of roller skating, bowling, golf, bungee cord jumping or some other activity, then make time to do whatever it is you enjoy.

Quality time also means guilt-free time. Do not feel guilty when you are doing something other than studying. Every skilled problem solver knows the value of taking time away from the project before him or her, in order to gain a new and fresh perspective. Therefore, if you have hammered away at the rock of "conditions" in contracts or the Rule Against Perpetuities in property law, and cannot seem to even chip away at the subject matter, give it a rest, do something fun or crazy and come back to it later, your enthusiasm renewed and attitude fresh, like a sculptor with a sledgehammer.

How to Answer a Contracts Problem

A contracts law professor who will remain nameless once imparted the most important rule of contracts law: "If, for some reason on a contracts exam, you cannot recall the rule of law, just make up a rule that is reasonable – chance are, you're probably right." While at first glance, these words might seem to spark anarchy and lawlessness, the professor's advice is right on, especially in the area of contracts. It is important to keep in mind that all rules of law were created by human beings, who tried, for better or worse, to apply common sense and public policy to create various rules of law which apply to a plethora of different situations.

The law of contracts, to a large degree, is based on common sense. Because the law of contracts attempts to regulate business transactions between people, common sense rules more often than not. While the terms may often sound foreign and the reasoning complex, when you distill contracts down to their basic essentials, you will find that the rules attempt to spell out how reasonable persons should deal with one another.

For example, if your friend asked you out to the movies this weekend, how would you know if your friend was serious or not? You might consider the language employed by your friend when he or she posed the proposition. Indeed, there is a world of difference between, "Let's go to the movies tonight, okay?" and "Perhaps we'll do something tomorrow, like a movie, I don't really know if I'm free." Why is there a difference? The first proposition clearly shows a commitment to go to the movies, and specifically requests a response, while the second proposition indicates a reluctance to commit to anything, much less to see a movie. The point is that you would undoubtably consider the words used in communicating a proposition or invitation extended to you.

You might also consider whether the <u>terms</u> of the proposition were included: "Let's go to the eight o'clock showing of Germinator Part IV at the Coronet Theater on Friday night. I'll treat and you buy the popcorn and candy." While most people would not speak with such specificity, this statement sets forth the subject matter (movie), the title of the movie, the theater, the time the movie is shown and the terms of the engagement. After hearing the above statement, most people would conclude that the person making the statement was extremely serious about going to the movie because of the specificity included in the body of the statement.

Finally, you would consider whether the statement was communicated to anyone. If that statement was made in a letter which was never sent, for example, it would be impossible to determine if the author of the letter ever intended to propose attending a movie to anyone.

The law of contracts begins with the concept of a legal or contractual relationship. The first step in this legal relationship is that of the offer. The person making the offer is the offeror. The person to whom the offer is made is the offeree. The offeror in the above example would be the individual who made the initial proposition, and the offeree would be the person to whom the proposition was made. The issue or question to be resolved is whether an offer was in fact made.

As set forth in the Contracts Solving Approach, an offer requires that three elements be met: (1) there must be an **intention** to contract; (2) the offer must be **certain** and **definite** as to its terms, including parties, price, subject matter, time, place and quantity; (3) the offer must be **communicated** to the offeree.

The first element of intent is determined by examining the words used in the offer. The issue is whether or not a reasonable person, hearing those words, would conclude that an offer was intended. Rather than to lobotomize the offeror in order to determine his or her subjective thoughts, the law instead looks to what a reasonable person would conclude from hearing whatever the offeror said. In that way, an objective test is employed in determining whether the law will recognize a statement as a valid offer or not. Make sense? You bet. Common sense.

The second element or component of an offer is certainty and definiteness of terms. Just as the proposition to attend the movies sets forth the specific terms, a legally valid offer must also set forth the specifics of the offer, such as the parties to the offer (the offeror and offeree), price, subject matter, time and place for performance, and quantity, which cannot be implied except in the case of output contracts, where a party contracts to sell or manufacture all of the requirements of the other, i.e., "I agree to make X enough dolls as X requires." In applying this element, you must look again to the language of the offer to determine if each of the specific terms are stated.

The third and final element of an offer is that it must be communicated to the offeree. Again, the law requires an objective manifestation of the offer, in order to determine whether it was actually communicated to the offeree.

While different law professors may use different terms to state the above elements (for example, some professors use the word "promise" in lieu of "intention"), these three elements will be found in varying order in every analysis of an offer.

Once an offer is found, the next issue or question is whether any act of the offeror or offeree "terminated" or killed the offer. In other words, an offer does not exist forever, and can be terminated by revocation, rejection or operation of law. Revocation occurs when the offeror withdraws the offer for any reason whatsoever, "The offer's withdrawn!" Rejection occurs when the offeree – the person to whom the offer was made – expressly or impliedly rejects the offer. An offer may also be terminated by operation of law, that is, if the contract is illegal, or the subject matter of the contract is destroyed, if the offeror dies or becomes insane, or if a reasonable amount of time lapses after the offer is made.

If the offer has not been terminated, then the next issue is that of acceptance. The four requirements of acceptance are set forth in the *Law Charts* for Contracts, and should be "applied" in a similar fashion to the "elements" of an offer.

If an acceptance is found, then it must be determined whether "consideration" exists. Consideration requires that both the offeror and offeree suffer a legal detriment and obtain a legal benefit. At the risk of simplifying consideration, it requires that each party give something up to obtain a benefit.

If an offer, acceptance and consideration are found to exist, you have a LEGAL RELATIONSHIP!

Yes, it's that time again. Let's begin with a simple, one sentence, example of an offer exam problem:

CONTRACTS FORMATION

Example #1: Betty v. Boop

Betty told Boop, "Perhaps, I might be interested in selling my little cat Felix for 25 cents."

Before solving this little problem, let's look at the structure of the answer:

The issue is whether __________ statement constitutes a valid offer. An offer is a proposal manifesting a present intention to contract which creates a power of acceptance in the offeree. An offer must manifest (1) a present intention to contract; (2) impart certainty and definiteness of terms; and (3) form a communication to the offeree.

The first issue is whether there is a present intention to contract. The proposal must indicate more than an intention to negotiate or solicit an offer. (APPLICATION) Therefore, this element is met/not met.

The second element of an offer is that the parties must agree as to parties, subject matter, time for performance, price and quantity. (APPLICATION) Thus, this element is met/unmet.

The final element is that the offer must be communicated to the offeree. (APPLICATION) Therefore this element is met/not met.

Based on the foregoing, __________ statement constituted/did not constitute an offer.

Note the similarities in the structure of this model answer and the I-R-A-C structures in Torts and Criminal Law. Yes, it's your old friend, I-R-A-C Super hero, to the rescue. This is, of course, only one example of a possible I-R-A-C model answer. You should, as always, tailor an approach specific to your professor's teaching style and curriculum.

In solving the above problem, the issue is whether Betty's statement constitutes a valid offer. Thus, the issue of offer focuses exclusively upon Betty's statement to Boop:

Model Answer: <u>Betty & Boop</u>

The issue is whether Betty's statement constitutes a valid offer. An offer is a proposal manifesting a present intention to contract, which creates a power of acceptance in the offeree. An offer must manifest (1) a present intention to contract; (2) impart certainty and definiteness of terms; and (3) form a communication to the offeree.

The first issue is whether there is a present intention to contract. The proposal must indicate more than an intention to negotiate or solicit an offer. Here Betty stated only that she "might be interested" in selling Felix. The word "interested" connotes at best that Betty is considering or pondering the sale of her cat, but is not yet committed to selling Felix. Betty used the word "might," which indicates uncertainty, and suggests that she had not yet decided whether she would sell Felix. Betty could have used the words "will" or "shall," which would indicate a commitment to sell Felix, but she did not. Betty also prefaced the statement that she might be interested in selling Felix with the word "perhaps." The word "perhaps" indicates indecision and a lack of commitment. Therefore, because a reasonable person hearing Betty's statement would conclude that an offer was not intended, this element is not met.

The second element of an offer is that the parties must agree as to parties, subject matter, time for performance, price and quantity. Here the parties are clear, Betty and Boop, the subject matter is Felix, the cat, the price is stated as twenty-five cents, and the quantity is one cat. Although the time for performance is unstated, the court could imply a reasonable time for performance. Thus, this element is met.

The final element is that the offer must be communicated to the offeree. Here the statement was verbally communicated to Boop. Therefore, this element is met.

Based on the foregoing, Betty's statement did not constitute an offer because there was no present intention to contract.

COMPARE: **CONCLUSORY ANALYSIS**

Betty's statement did not constitute an offer. Betty's statement did not state a present intention to contract, although it was sufficiently certain as to the parties, subject matter, time for performance and price, and Boop clearly understood the offer. Hence, I would conclude that there was no offer.

COMPARE: **DISORGANIZED ANALYSIS**

Betty's statement constituted an offer. Her statement was sufficiently certain, since it mentioned the price of 25 cents, and included the subject matter and parties. The elements of certainty are therefore met, and further indicate a present intention to contract on Betty's part. The price, however, was stated as 25 cents, and therefore that factor would weigh in favor of an offer. Hence, the elements of an offer are met.

* * *

The conclusory analysis fails to explain <u>why</u> and <u>how</u> each conclusion is reached. Instead of explaining WHY a reasonable person hearing Betty's statement would conclude that no offer was intended, the conclusory analysis merely concludes that no offer was intended. The language of Betty's statement is not analyzed, and the writer instead assumes that the reader understands how and why a particular conclusion is reached. Stay away from a conclusory answer like the plague!

The disorganized analysis fails to separate and compartmentalize the discussion of each issue. Instead, the elements or components of an offer run together, thrust together like pieces of a collage which do not fit. The result is a confusing, almost nonsensical answer, which tells the reader absolutely nothing about why or how a particular conclusion was reached, because it is impossible to separate each element of the analysis.

Again, the key to avoiding a conclusory analysis is to ALWAYS EXPLAIN WHY a particular conclusion is reached, and the key to organization is to take each issue, one at a time, just as you did in analyzing Torts and Criminal Law.

A recurring question in the area of contracts law is, "How do I organize a contracts problem?" Do I organize the problem by legal concept, that is, offer, acceptance, consideration, defenses to a contract, etc., or do I organize by some other method? For the answer to this question, it is suggested that you ask your professor to see what he or she prefers. If your instructor voices no preference, then it is recommended that you organize your answer by legal transaction. By definition, a contracts problem must be analyzed in this fashion. It is quite impossible, for example, to analyze for acceptance before you have determined if an offer exists. Let's take an example:

Contracts Formation Example #2: <u>Moby v. Ahab</u>

Ahab sent Moby a letter asking seventy-five cents for a filet-o-fish sandwich. Moby agreed to Ahab's terms by telegram.

In the above example, you would not begin by analyzing whether Moby had validly accepted Ahab's offer. You would first begin by determining whether Ahab had made a valid offer to Moby. After determining that issue, you would then move to the issue of acceptance. Thus you would organize the problem by legal transaction, as follows:

<u>Moby v. Ahab</u>

<u>Ahab's letter to Moby</u>

Valid offer?
- Present intention to contract
- Certainty & definiteness of terms
- Communicated to Moby?

<u>Moby's telegram to Ahab</u>

Valid acceptance?
- Knowledge of offer?
- Communicated to offeror?
- Unequivocal?
- Accepted by Offer's terms

Another way of organizing the problem, which might be preferred or favored by your professor, is by legal concept:

<u>Offer</u>

- Present intention to contract
- Certainty & definiteness of terms
- Communicated to Moby?

<u>Acceptance</u>

- Knowledge of offer?
- Communicated to offeror?
- Unequivocal?
- Accepted by Offer's terms

Regardless of which method of organization you choose, it is important to find a structure which works for you. The need for such a structure will become more and more evident as the problems become more complex and difficult. Let's add a few facts to the Ahab-Moby problem:

Ahab sent Moby a letter asking seventy-five cents for a filet-o-fish sandwich. Moby agreed to Ahab's terms by telegram, but said he would pay only 50 cents. Ahab immediately wired Moby, "no problem with your terms." After Moby sent the telegram, he learned from King Burger that Ahab had sold the filet-o-fish sandwich to Dick, and he bought a filet-o-fish from Carl Junior. Moby then telephoned Ahab and told him that the deal was off. Ahab sued Moby for breach of contract.

While the overall issue is whether Ahab has a cause of action in contract against Moby, how would you organize your answer? If you organize the problem by legal concept, i.e., offer, acceptance, it may appear a bit confusing. However, if you organize the problem chronologically by legal transaction, your job is made much easier:

Ahab's letter to Moby

Moby's telegram to Ahab

Ahab's wire to Moby

Moby's telephone call to Ahab

Once you have determined the transactions you are required to analyze, then you need only determine the **legal effect** of each transaction, applying your problem-solving approach:

Ahab's letter to Moby

Offer?

Moby's telegram to Ahab

Acceptance or Counteroffer?

Ahab's wire to Moby

Valid Acceptance?

Moby's telephone call to Ahab

Revocation?

Whatever format you decide upon, try it out and make sure it works before stepping into the exam room. As you become more familiar with the structure of contracts problems, the style best suited to your analysis will become evident.

Let's take on a contracts formation problem involving multiple agreements between two parties:

Contracts Formation Problem # 3: Peter v. Darby

Darby placed an ad in the newspaper on August 1 stating: "Interested in selling my residence Amberacre. Will consider $50,000 if payment not contingent on waiting for mortgage arrangements. Also have fifty acres prime farm land adjacent to Amberacre and will sell for a fair price."

Peter wrote Darby on August 3: "No mortgage needed, I'll pay you $50,000 for Amberacre."

Peter telegrammed Darby on August 4: "Will pay $500 per acre for twenty-five acres of farmland adjacent to Amberacre."

Having received both Peter's letter and telegram, Darby wrote Peter on August 8, "I will sell you my farmland, but only if you buy all fifty acres and pay $600 per acre."

On August 9 at 9:00 a.m., Peter mailed Darby a certified check for $50,000, with the notation, "payment for Amberacre" inscribed on it. At noon Peter received Darby's letter regarding the farmland. On August 10, Peter mailed a $30,000 certified check to Darby with "payment for farmland" inscribed on it.

On the morning of August 11, Peter received a telegram from Darby stating, "Have sold Amberacre, to Tom for Sixty Thousand Dollars; returning your $50,000 check by mail." Peter immediately telegrammed back: "Forget about the farmland, I don't want it without Amberacre, and I'm suing you because you broke our contract re: Amberacre." Darby received the telegram that evening.

On August 12, Peter received the $50,000 check in the mail. Darby received the $30,000 check, cashed it and wrote Peter, "You can pick up the deed to the farmland or I'll mail it to you, please advise."

Peter sued Darby for:

(a) Breaching the Amberacre contract. What result?

(b) Returning of the $30,000. What result?

This problem demonstrates the importance of organizing the facts before analyzing the problem. Begin by following the *six steps of exam taking* ; however, because the facts of the Amberacre and farmland contracts are intermeshed with one another, first separate and organize each fact according to the contract to which it relates. Let's look at the facts relevant to solving the Amberacre Contract:

<u>Peter v. Darby</u>: Breach of the Amberacre Contract.

<u>Date</u>

August 1 = **AD IN THE NEWSPAPER**: Darby is "interested" in selling Amberacre; will "consider $50,000 if payment not contingent on waiting for mortgage arrangement"

August 3 = **LETTER FROM PETER**: no mortgage needed - $50,000 is offered

August 9 = **CERTIFIED CHECK FOR $50,000 MAILED BY PETER**

August 11 = **PETER RECEIVED TELEGRAM FROM DARBY**: informing Peter that Darby sold Amberacre to Tom for $60,000; returning your $50,000 check by mail

August 12 = **PETER RECEIVED $50,000 CHECK IN MAIL**

When the transactions relating to the Amberacre contract are placed in chronological order, the chain of events become apparent. Now, your task is to determine whether there is a legal relationship between Peter and Darby, giving rise to a cause of action for breach of the Amberacre contract. In the following model answer, the answer is organized by transaction.

<u>Peter v. Darby</u>: Breach of the Amberacre contract

The issue is whether there is a legal relationship between Peter and Darby for the sale of Amberacre, and if so, whether Peter may recover for breach of contract. A legal relationship requires an offer, acceptance and consideration.

<u>August 1: Ad in the Newspaper</u>

An offer requires (1) intent to contract; (2) essential terms, and (3) communication to the offeree. Applying the first element, a reasonable person reading Darby's ad in the newspaper would not believe his or her acceptance would create a contract. Darby specifically stated that he was "interested" in selling Amberacre. The word "interested" connotes that Darby was seeking offers on the property, not that he was in fact offering Amberacre for sale. Furthermore, Darby stated in the ad that he would "consider" $50,000 as a purchase price, and a reasonable person would conclude that Darby was merely suggesting an amount he might accept. Had Darby intended to offer Amberacre for sale, he would have used language which unequivocally stated his intention to do so. Thus, there was **no intention to contract**.

Applying the second element, the **parties** would be Darby and the general public to which the ad was addressed. The **subject matter** was land specifically Amberacre, but it is unclear whether the dimensions of Amberacre were ascertainable, since no legal description of the parcel of land was included in the ad. The **price** was uncertain, because Darby merely suggested a price he would consider but not necessarily accept. The **time and place for performance** were not stated but could be implied. Therefore, the essential terms were not present.

The third element is not met because the statement contained in the ad was **communicated** only to the general public, not to any specific individual.

However, because there was **no intention** to contract, and the essential terms did not appear in the ad, Darby's ad constituted an **invitation for an offer**, having no legal binding effect.

<u>August 3: Letter from Peter</u>

The letter from Peter constituted an **offer**. First, Peter clearly intended to make an offer by the language contained in the letter. Peter wrote Darby, "I'll pay you $50,000 for Amberacre," thereby communicating his desire to purchase the property for a definite sum. Peter's use of command language, "I'll pay you," indicates that his desire to purchase Amberacre was clear and unequivocal. Peter's letter also contained all the **essential terms**: **Parties** (Darby and Peter), **price** ($50,000), **subject matter** (Amberacre) and **time and place for performance**, which could be implied by the court. Finally, Peter's offer was **communicated** to Darby by letter.

Hence, Peter's letter constituted an **offer** for the purchase of Amberacre, creating the power of acceptance in Darby.

<u>August 9: Check for $50,000</u>

The mailing of the check was without legal significance because Darby had **not accepted** Peter's offer.

August 11: Darby's telegram

The issue is whether Darby's telegram **terminated the offer. An offer may be terminated when the offeree rejects the offer.** Here Darby's telegram informed Peter that Darby had sold Amberacre to Tom, and that Darby was returning Peter's check in the mail. Thus, Darby's telegram informed Peter that he was selling to another, and that Peter's offer was rejected. Thus, the offer was **terminated**.

In conclusion, because Darby never accepted Peter's offer, there was **no legal relationship** between Darby and Peter for the purchase of Amberacre. Peter's suit for breach of contract for Amberacre will fail.

Defenses

Statute of Frauds

However, even assuming that there was a legal relationship between Darby and Peter, **the Statute of Frauds would bar the contract. The Statute of Frauds requires that a contract for the sale of land be in writing and signed by the party to be charged.** The party to be charged in this case is Darby. Because Darby did not sign any document, the contract is void.

* * *

Note that the rules of law are stated only once. If you have already stated a rule, and the same rule is raised later in your discussion, refer the reader back to the original definition by using supra or see above. It is unnecessary to repeat the definition of "offer" each time the issue is raised. Also, the manner of organization and the use of headings in their example inform the reader of which transaction is being analyzed. By organizing this problem by transaction, in chronological order, and explaining the legal significance of each transaction, the problem is simplified and easier to understand.

Let's solve the second part of this problem.

(b) Return of the $30,000: the Farmland Contract

August 1 = **DARBY'S AD IN NEWSPAPER**

August 4 = **TELEGRAM FROM PETER**

August 8 = **DARBY'S LETTER**

August 9 = **PETER RECEIVES DARBY'S LETTER**

August 10 = **$30,000 CHECK MAILED BY PETER**

August 11 = **TELEGRAM FROM PETER ATTEMPTING TO CALL OFF DEAL**

The issue is whether there is a **legal relationship** between Darby and Peter for the sale of the farmland.

August 1: Newspaper ad

The elements of an offer are defined above. The language in the newspaper ad concerning the farmland was too uncertain to constitute an offer. Darby only asserts that he owns 50 acres of farm land. Darby did not include a legal description of the farmland, and therefore it is unclear what parcel of land he was offering to sell. Darby also said that he "will sell" the land for a "fair price." A reasonable person hearing this language would be unable to determine what a "fair price" is since the value of such land may be subjective in nature. Therefore, there was **no intention to contract**.

While the **parties** (Darby and the public reading the ad) are ascertainable, because the essential term of **price** was not included in the newspaper ad, the content required in an offer was not present. Furthermore, for the same reasons stated above, the **subject matter**, "farmland," was too vague and could not be determined with specificity. Therefore, this element is not met.

Finally, the ad was "**communicated**" only to the general public and not to a specific offeree and thus this element is not met. Because of the lack of a price term and subject matter, the ad was an invitation for an offer, giving rise to **no legal effect**.

August 4: Telegram from Peter

Peter's letter constituted an **offer**. First, Peter stated that he "will pay" for the land, indicating unequivocal commitment to purchase the land. Secondly, Peter included the price he was willing to pay, $500 per acre. Peter also stated the quantity of 25 acres. A reasonable person reading Peter's letter would conclude that an **offer was intended**.

The **essential terms** are likewise contained in Peter's letter: **parties** (Darby and Peter), **price** ($500 per acre), **quantity** (25 acres), **subject matter** (farmland adjacent to Amberacre) and a reasonable **time and place for performance** may be implied.

However, Peter could argue that because no legal description was included, the description "farmland adjacent to Amberacre" was too vague, and therefore the offer would fail for want of the **subject matter** of the agreement. Peter could argue that there were more than one parcel of land adjacent to Amberacre which could be the subject of the agreement. However, if Darby only owned one parcel of land containing fifty acres, then Peter's argument would likely fail.

Finally, the offer was **communicated** to Darby by telegram.

Thus, Peter's telegram constituted a **valid offer**.

<u>August 10: Darby's Letter on August 8</u>

The issue is whether Darby's letter on August 8 constituted an **acceptance** or a **counteroffer. A statement which materially alters the terms of an offer is a counteroffer and not an acceptance.** Here, Darby's letter materially altered Peter's initial offer because Darby offered to sell the land only if Peter purchased a greater number of acres at a greater price. Hence, Peter's offer was impliedly rejected, and a **counteroffer was made** by Darby.

<u>August 10: Mailing of the $30,000 Certified Check</u>

The issue is whether Peter's act of mailing Darby the $30,000 check constituted an **acceptance. Acceptance requires an unequivocal act by the offeree with knowledge of the offer, accepted by the offer's terms.** Here Peter responded to Darby's counteroffer for a $30,000 sale (50 acres X $600 per acre). Peter's act of tendering a check for the amount anticipated by Darby's counteroffer was an unequivocal act expressing Peter's intent to accept Darby's counteroffer. Peter also inscribed on the check "payment for farmland" further evidencing his intent. Peter also had knowledge of Darby's counteroffer and accepted Darby's counteroffer by its terms. Therefore, Peter **accepted Darby's counteroffer.**

An acceptance is effective upon dispatch. Thus, a legal relationship was formed for valuable consideration (<u>i.e.</u>, land for money) upon dispatch of the check on August 10th.

<u>August 11 Peter's Telegram</u>

Peter's telegram, attempting to call off the transaction on August 11, was ineffective, because Darby's counteroffer had already been accepted by Peter on August 10.

* * *

Compare the organization of the "farmland" analysis with that of the "Amberacre" discussion, and note the similarities.

All right. Maybe you are tiring of the same old I-R-A-C. Besides, is not variety the spice of life? Why is it that there are over 63 different flavors of ice cream world wide? How about a writing style that's a little more daring, flashy and dangerous? Here is an example of a blue ribbon answer which does not follow the traditional I-R-A-C structure:

Contracts Formation Example #4: Darian v. Gekko

Stockbroker Gekko wired Darian, a customer: "I can get you 1000 shares of Trump stock at 50. Love you, G.G." Gekko's wire was received on September 10, at 10:00 a.m. At 12:00 p.m., Darian called Gekko and said, "Give me all your stock, Love, Pooh-pooh." However, by this time, Trump stock had jumped ten points and Gekko could not secure the stock at 50. Gekko wired Darian: "Stock prices jumped, honey. Bought 1000 shares at 60." Darian received the wire at 1:00 p.m., and she wrote Gekko by letter, "Your deal is satisfactory – hold my shares, love-buckets, and charge them to my account." Darian's letter, which was sent on September 11, at 9:00 a.m., did not arrive in Gekko's office until two days later, on September 13, at 9:00 a.m. Because Gekko had not heard from Darian, he sold the shares to Bud. Is Darian entitled to damages?

Darian v. Gekko

Darian's action for damages against Gekko may be maintained only if there is a **legal relationship** between the parties.

September 10, 10:00 a.m.: Gekko's Wire

Gekko's wire to Darian received at 10:00 a.m. on the 10th of September constituted an offer. **In order to constitute an offer, the offeror's communication must (1) manifest a present intention to contract; (2) be certain and definite as to all essential terms; (3) be communicated to the offeree.**

(1) Manifestation of a Present Intention to Contract

The query here is whether a **reasonable person** in Darian's shoes would conclude from Gekko's communication that his or her acceptance would create a contract. Here, the words used strongly suggest that an offer was made, since Gekko specifically informed Darian that he could purchase 1000 shares of a specific type of stock at a specific price. There being no objective indicia of any contrary expressed intention by Gekko (i.e., words made in jest, reservations), the communication was serious enough to warrant a reasonable person in believing that his or her acceptance was invited and would create a contract.

(2) Certainty and Definiteness of Terms

The contract must be of sufficient, **certain** and **definite** as to its essential terms: parties, price, subject matter, quantity and time for performance. Gekko's communication was explicit as to the parties (Darian and Gekko), price (50), subject matter (Trump stock) and quantity (1000 shares). While no time for performance was stated, it can be reasonably implied that due to the highly volatile nature of the stock market that the transaction was to be performed immediately.

(3) Communicated to the Offeree

The wire was received by Darian and hence was "**communicated**" to the offeree.

Hence, Gekko's wire of the 10th constituted a **valid offer**, creating the power of acceptance in Darian.

September 10th - 12:00 pm: Darian's telephone call

Darian's act of calling Gekko constituted a **valid acceptance**, since Darian accepted the offer with **knowledge** of the offer, Darian's acceptance was **unequivocal** and **unqualified** and was communicated by telephone to Gekko, and it was accepted **by the terms** of Gekko's offer. As to this latter point, Darian can successfully argue that the telephone was a valid mode of acceptance under the circumstances, since the offer did not expressly require any particular mode of communication.

However, Darian's acceptance was untimely. An offer lapses, by operation of law, after a **reasonable time**. The computation of a reasonable time begins from the date the offer is received by the offeree. Here Darian allowed two hours from the time of receipt to elapse before accepting. Given the volatile nature of the subject matter – stock shares – Darian had reason to know that the availability and purchase price of the stock was subject to immediate change and that a timely acceptance was required. While a "reasonable time" is a question of fact, Darian's delay in accepting was unreasonable. Hence, the offer was terminated and Darian had no power of acceptance.

If the court finds to the contrary, a binding contract would be formed, because, as discussed above, the other criteria of acceptance strongly suggest that Darian's acceptance was valid. Further, here there is no problem as to **consideration**, since each party incurred a **legal detriment** (Gekko's act of giving up stock; Darian's payment for the stock) and received a **legal benefit** (Darian's receipt of stock; Gekko's receipt of Darian's payment).

<u>September 10th, 1:00 p.m. - Gekko's second wire to Darian</u>

Gekko's subsequent wire to Darian informing Darian that he purchased 1000 shares at 60 constituted a **counter offer** or **new offer**, since as noted above, Gekko's original offer had lapsed. Gekko's new offer carried the same objective indicia of seriousness as did the initial offer, was similarly definite and certain as to all essential terms, with the exception of time for performance, and was communicated to Darian. As discussed above, the court would imply a time for performance and hence Gekko's communication would be deemed a **valid offer**.

<u>September 11th, 9:00 a.m. - Darian's letter to Gekko</u>

Darian's letter to Gekko, posted on the 11th of September at 9:00 a.m., did not constitute a **valid acceptance**. The issue here is whether the **mode of acceptance** was proper. Darian's offer was communicated by way of wire. The rule is that unless the offer provides otherwise, the offeree can communicate her acceptance of the offer by any reasonable means, under all the circumstances. Under these facts, acceptance by letter is not a reasonable means of acceptance due to the highly unstable nature of the subject matter, stock. While the offer did not specify the precise mode of acceptance, a letter would require a substantial amount of time to reach Gekko, as compared to a wire. Hence, there was **no contract** between Darian and Gekko; Darian is not entitled to damages.

Gekko could therefore properly sell the stock to Bud.

However, this is arguably a close question and should it be determined that the mail was a reasonable mode of acceptance, then Darian's communication would constitute an acceptance, effective as of the date of dispatch – 9:00 a.m. on September 11. The communication was accepted by Darian with knowledge of the offer, was unequivocal and unqualified in its wording ("Your deal is <u>satisfactory</u>"), was communicated to the offeror and was accepted by the terms of the offer (bilateral contract requiring a <u>promise</u> by Darian in order to accept, which is what Darian tendered).

Finally, there is no problem as to consideration for the same reasons as stated above.

Thus, should this latter view be adopted by the court, Darian could recover damages against Gekko for breach.

* * *

Ah, a blue ribbon exam is like sweet music to the ears. The purpose of showing you a "9.9999" examination is to show you what you are striving for. Now do not immediately abandon I-R-A-C for what may appear to be an entirely new animal. Your writing style will evolve on its own with time. For the time being, stick to the basic I-R-A-C format, which is the basic foundation for all legal writing, including the style employed in the above example.

The above example differs from the basic I-R-A-C format only in writing style. The application is intermeshed like fine prose, and each argument is treated like a rare wine. But the basic arguments and issues addressed are no different from what would be found in any answer which follows basic I-R-A-C.

Note how the above example takes great pains to discuss both sides of an argument where appropriate. As discussed in the Fannie Fox example, both sides of a particular issue must be argued where there is a real question presented. For example, there is no real question that the offers were "communicated" to the offeree; thus it would be inappropriate to discuss both sides because no issue is presented on this element of an offer. By contrast, there is a real issue as to what constitutes a reasonable means of acceptance; hence, a discussion of both sides is required. Use common sense in determining what a minor issue is and what a major issue is. If there is no real issue involved, do not beat it to death; dispose of the issue in a few quick sentences and move on. Save your enthusiasm for a real issue, which will require a careful, in-depth analysis.

Also, quickly review the Darian v. Gekko model answer and observe the use of **bold type** to emphasize those key words which are crucial to the analysis. By underlining, highlighting or otherwise emphasizing certain key words on your examination, you assist the grader in focusing in key phrases and issues in your analysis.

Do not be discouraged if you find this problem or others in this book extremely difficult, or at first glance, even impossible. Rome was not created in a day. Good lawyering is truly an ongoing process; some skills, such as jury selection or cross-examination skills, or good brief writing, take many years to develop. Remember, take exam writing one step at a time; begin at the beginning, with the simplest, one-sentence problems, and move one step forward to the next level of difficulty. Make sure that you have mastered the task at hand before moving onto the next problem. Only in this way will you master the exam writing process.

Now for something different, and a little wild and crazy! We will now put on our rubber gloves and operate on a somewhat difficult contracts problem, dissecting each paragraph, each sentence, each word, section by section, phrase by phrase, taking great pains to explain how the problem is analyzed and the purpose of each sentence in the model answer. In this way, we will re-create "Frankenstein's monster" by demonstrating how an exam answer is put together, from "scratch" so to speak:

Contracts Formation Example #5: Tenant v. Shore & Cliff

On Thursday, May 14, Tenant received the following letter from Shore: "Dear Tenant, I will let you have my "Shore House" for this June-through-August season, same terms under which you occupied it last year. Please reply in a week." Tenant noticed Shore's letter was postmarked May 11.

Earlier in May, Tenant had made inquiry at "The Cliffs," a mountain resort owned by Cliff. In Cliff's absence, Joe, one of Cliff's caretakers, had shown Tenant two available houses, "Hi-Vu" and "Lo-Vu," owned by Cliff, which Joe stated were listed for rent at $6,000 and $3,000 respectively, for one season.

On May 15, Tenant received a letter from Cliff which read, "This confirms statements by Joe. You may have Hi-Vu at $6,000, or Lo-Vu at $3,000, for the season June through August, all services included, payable in equal monthly installments.

On May 17, Tenant wrote to Cliff as follows, "I think your prices are high. Will you take $5,000 for Hi-Vu? If not, then I'll have to settle for Lo-Vu, and I agree to pay the $3,000 you ask, only I hope you may be willing to consider some concession if I pay the whole $3,000 in advance.

On May 17, Tenant learned that Shore had sold Shore House to Jones for Jones' immediate occupancy.

On May 18, Cliff received Tenant's letter and Cliff immediately telegraphed Tenant, "No change in prices. See my letter of the 16th." Tenant received Cliff's telegram the same day, May 18. Later that day Tenant also received Cliff's letter of May 16, which read, "Our deal is off." Tenant immediately wrote Shore, "I'll take Shore House per your letter of the 11th."

The normal course of post between Tenant and Shore and Tenant and Cliff was one day.

What rights, if any, does Tenant have against Shore and against Cliff? Discuss.

Again, you must separate and strain out those facts which are relevant to solving each problem before you. After going through the *z*, you would first determine which facts are relevant to solving <u>Tenant v. Shore</u>:

On Thursday, May 14, Tenant received the following letter from Shore: "Dear Tenant, I will let you have my "Shore House" for this June-through-August season, same terms under which you occupied it last year. Please reply in a week." Tenant noticed Shore's letter was postmarked May 11.

On May 17, Tenant learned that Shore had sold Shore House to Jones for Jones' immediate occupancy.

Tenant immediately wrote Shore, "I'll take Shore House per your letter of the 11th."

The normal course of post between Tenant and Shore and Tenant and Cliff was one day.

These are the only facts with which you must concern yourself in solving Tenant v. Shore. In writing your answer, you could choose to organize your answer by transaction. In this problem, there are two transactions: (1) Shore's Letter to Tenant on May 14th and (2) Tenant's Letter to Shore on May 18th. Your headings might appear as follows:

Tenant v. Shore

(1) Shore's Letter to Tenant on May 14

(2) Tenant's Letter to Shore on May 18

The overall issue is whether there is a legal relationship between Tenant and Shore for the rental of Shore House. Begin by telling your professor exactly that:

Tenant v. Shore

The issue is whether there is a legal relationship between Tenant and Shore for the rental of Shore House.

Next, state the general rule:

Tenant v. Shore

The issue is whether there is a legal relationship between Tenant and Shore for the rental of Shore House. A legal relationship requires offer, acceptance and consideration.

Having set forth the general issue and rule, you then evaluate the first transaction, that is Shore's letter to Tenant and determine whether the Shore's letter was an offer or an invitation to an offer. But before getting to the meat and potatoes, i.e., "application," you "set up" the problem by telling your professor what issue you are solving, and the rule of law analyzed:

(1) Shore's Letter to Tenant on May 14

The issue is whether Shore's Letter to Tenant on May 14 constituted a valid offer. In order to constitute an offer, the offeror's communication must (1) manifest a present intention to contract; (2) be certain and definite as to all essential terms; (3) be communicated to the offeree.

Now we are ready for APPLICATION. AS ALWAYS, TAKE EACH OF THE THREE ISSUES ONE AT A TIME. Let's start with "present intention to contract." The issue is what a reasonable person hearing the words contained in Shore's letter would think. In other words, you must slip on the shoes of the hypothetical "reasonable person" and ask yourself, "Hm, would a reasonable person think that Shore was making a serious offer, after hearing those words?" You must evaluate and analyze the words contained in Shore's letter, and explain **WHY** those words demand a particular result. Before writing out the answer, let's look at the issues presented by Shore's letter:

"DEAR TENANT, I WILL LET YOU HAVE MY "SHORE HOUSE" FOR THIS JUNE THROUGH AUGUST SEASON, SAME TERMS UNDER WHICH YOU OCCUPIED IT LAST YEAR. PLEASE REPLY IN A WEEK."

What does this language say about whether Shore was serious or not in making an offer to Tenant? First of all, he uses the phrase, "I WILL LET YOU HAVE" the rental property. What significance are these words? Shore does not say, "I am considering renting Shore House," or "I might let you rent Shore House," or other language which would indicate indecision or lack of commitment. Shore instead uses words which reek of commitment and decision. What else does Shore say? Shore specifies the property, the season it is available, and makes reference to the terms of a prior agreement between Shore and Tenant. Finally, Shore requests a reply within a week's time. Why would Shore request a reply unless he was making an offer?

One possible model answer might appear as follows:

(1) Shore's Letter to Tenant on May 14

The issue is whether Shore's Letter to Tenant on May 14 constituted a valid offer. In order to constitute an offer, the offeror's communication must (1) manifest a present intention to contract; (2) be certain and definite as to all essential terms; (3) be communicated to the offeree.

Present intention to contract requires that a reasonable person in the offeree's shoes conclude that his or her acceptance would create a contract.

Shore used language in his letter which unequivocally informed Tenant that he could rent Shore House. Shore used the command, "I will let you have," leaving little doubt that Shore wanted to rent Shore House to Tenant. These words indicate Shore's commitment to offer the rental property to Tenant. Shore also appraised Tenant of the availability of the rental and made reference to prior dealings, from which a price and other terms could be ascertained. Shore also requested a reply in a week, from which it could be inferred that Shore requested an acceptance. Thus, Shore's letter constituted an offer.

The first sentence states the "present intention" rule; the second sentence only states a conclusion, that the language used by Shore in the letter clearly told Tenant he could rent Shore House; without more, this sentence leaves the analysis entirely conclusory. The third, fourth, fourth, fifth and sixth sentences are the meat and potatoes of the analysis. This is APPLICATION. Application explains why and how the conclusion framed in the second sentence is arrived at.

In essence, there are three reasons supporting the conclusion reached. The first is that the language "I WILL LET YOU HAVE," is command language, which suggests no ambivalence in Shore's decision to offer Shore House to Tenant for rental. The second reason is the specificity of terms included in the letter – the months when the rental was available, that the prior terms were to be applied to the offered rental, and the subject matter of the rental. This is a completely different issue than "certainty and definiteness of terms," because here you are concerned only with what impression a reasonable person would have hearing the words of Shore's letter. Thus, you must compartmentalize or separate your discussion of certainty and definiteness of terms until later. Confine your discussion only to the fact that the inclusion of certain terms indicates the offeror's seriousness, and leave it at that. The third reason is that Shore requested a reply in a week. These three facts are discussed, and it is explained why these facts demand the result reached. The seventh and final sentence merely states the conclusion reached.

Now, onto the next issue:

(1) <u>Shore's Letter to Tenant on May 14</u>

The issue is whether Shore's Letter to Tenant on May 14 constituted a valid offer. In order to constitute an offer, the offeror's communication must (1) manifest a present intention to contract; (2) be certain and definite as to all essential terms; (3) be communicated to the offeree.

Present intention to contract requires that a reasonable person in the offeree's shoes conclude that his or her acceptance would create a contract. Shore used language in his letter which unequivocally informed Tenant that he could rent Shore House. Shore used the command, "I will let you have," leaving little doubt that Shore wanted to rent Shore House to Tenant. These words indicate commitment to offer the rental property to Tenant. Shore appraised Tenant of the availability of the rental and made reference to prior dealings, from which a price and other terms could be ascertained. Shore also requested a reply in a week, from which it could be inferred that Shore requested an acceptance. Thus, Shore's letter constituted an offer.

The contract must be sufficiently certain and definite as to its essential terms: parties, price, subject matter, quantity and time for performance. The parties are Shore and Tenant. Shore's communication stated no price, but price and other terms such as security deposits could easily be determined by Shore's reference to the prior agreement between Shore and Tenant. The subject matter was "Shore House," and rental period or quantity, was June-through-August. No time for performance was stated, but Tenant's response was requested within a week, and the court would imply a reasonable time thereafter. Thus, this element is met.

* * *

Again, the rule of law is stated first. The rule of law is concise and does not waste a breath on unnecessary words or phrases. The second, third, fourth and fifth sentences address each essential term and explain the significance of the inclusion of the term in Shore's letter. The final sentence again states the conclusion.

Let's add the final issue of "communication" and then the overall conclusion, and put it all together:

<u>Tenant v. Shore</u>

The issue is whether there is a legal relationship between Tenant and Shore for the rental of Shore House. A legal relationship requires offer, acceptance and consideration.

(1) <u>Shore's Letter to Tenant on May 14</u>

The issue is whether Shore's Letter to Tenant on May 14 constituted a valid offer. In order to constitute an offer, the offeror's communication must (1) manifest a present intention to contract; (2) be certain and definite as to all essential terms; (3) be communicated to the offeree.

Present intention to contract requires that a reasonable person in the offeree's shoes conclude that his or her acceptance would create a contract. Shore used language in his letter which unequivocally informed Tenant that he could rent Shore House. Shore used the command, "I will let you have," leaving little doubt that Shore wanted to rent Shore House to Tenant. These words indicate commitment to offer the rental property to Tenant. Shore appraised tenant of availability of the rental and made reference to prior dealings, from which a price and other terms could be ascertained. Shore also requested a reply in a week, from which it could be inferred that Shore requested an acceptance. Thus, Shore's letter constituted an offer.

The contract must be sufficient certain and definite as to its essential terms: parties, price, subject matter, quantity and time for performance. The parties are Shore and Tenant. Shore's communication stated no price, but price and other terms such as security deposits could be easily determined by Shore's reference to the prior agreement between Shore and Tenant. The subject matter was "Shore House," and rental period or quantity was June through August. No time for performance was stated, but Tenant's response was requested within a week, and the court would imply a reasonable time thereafter. Thus, this element is met.

The letter was received by Tenant on May 14 and hence was "communicated" to the offeree.

Hence, Shore's letter constituted a valid offer, creating the power of acceptance in Tenant.

* * *

Instead of creating a monster, we have created a logical, well-organized analysis of <u>Tenant v. Shore</u>. Remember that it is not the ultimate conclusion that counts, but how you get there. Now let's move onto the issue of whether Tenant's letter constituted a valid acceptance:

(2) <u>Tenant's Letter to Shore on May 18</u>

The issue is what legal effect Tenant's letter of May 18 had, if any. Since you have already determined that Shore's letter constituted an offer, the next question on your Contracts *Law Charts* checklist is whether the offer was terminated. If the offer was not terminated by revocation, rejection or operation of law, then it may be accepted by the offeree. The facts which are relevant to solving this issue are:

On May 17, Tenant learned that Shore had sold Shore House to Jones for Jones' immediate occupancy.

Tenant immediately wrote Shore, "I'll take Shore House per your letter of the 11th."

The normal course of post between Tenant and Shore and Tenant and Cliff was one day.

Are there any facts which suggest that the offer was directly or indirectly revoked? You bet! As set forth in your Contracts *Law Charts* , indirect revocation occurs when the offeree learns of acts of the offeror which are inconsistent with the offer. This issue is obviously raised by the fact that on "May 17, Tenant learned that Shore had sold Shore House to Jones for Jones' immediate occupancy." Application requires that you explain why this fact demonstrates or fails to demonstrate that an indirect revocation occurred.

The issue is whether Shore's offer was indirectly revoked. An unaccepted offer terminates when the offeree learns of acts of the offeror inconsistent with the offer. Here Tenant learned that Shore had sold Shore House to Jones for Jones' immediate occupancy on May 17. Thus, Tenant learned that Shore had sold the very property which was the subject of the offer to another. This act was entirely inconsistent with the offer, and Tenant learned of these facts prior to his acceptance. Therefore, Shore's offer was revoked, and Tenant's power of acceptance extinguished.

Although Shore requested a reply within one week, Shore made no promise to keep the offer open until that time. Therefore, Tenant's attempted acceptance on May 18 was without legal effect, and he has no rights against Shore.

Again, begin by informing the reader of the issue you are analyzing. The first sentence clearly tells the reader that the question to be addressed is whether Shore's offer was indirectly revoked. The second sentence states the rule, straight out of the Contracts *Law Chart.* The third sentence merely restates the fact that Tenant learned of Shore's sale to Jones, but the fourth and fifth sentences apply the "indirect revocation" rule to facts and explain that the rule applies because Tenant learned of Shore's act of selling the property, and that act was inconsistent with the offer to rent the same property to Tenant. The sixth sentence states the conclusion.

The second paragraph merely explains the effect of the indirect revocation on Tenant's purported acceptance of Shore's May 11 offer. It is also explained that Shore's earlier request for a reply in a week does not preclude Shore from withdrawing the offer.

Let's move to the second part of the problem. Here are the facts relevant to solving

<u>Tenant v. Cliff</u>:

Earlier in May, Tenant had made inquiry at "The Cliffs," a mountain resort owned by Cliff. In Cliff's absence, Joe, one of Cliff's caretakers, had shown Tenant two available houses, "Hi-Vu" and "Lo-Vu," owned by Cliff, which Joe stated were listed for rent at $6,000 and $3,000 respectively, for one season.

On May 15, Tenant received a letter from Cliff which read, "This confirms

statements by Joe. You may have Hi-Vu at $6,000, or Lo-Vu at $3,000, for the season June through August, all services included, payable in equal monthly installments.

On May 17, Tenant wrote to Cliff as follows, "I think your prices are high. Will you take $5,000 for Hi-Vu? If not, then I'll have to settle for Lo-Vu, and I agree to pay the $3,000 you ask, only I hope you may be willing to consider some concession if I pay the whole $3,000 in advance.

On May 18, Cliff received Tenant's letter and Cliff immediately telegraphed Tenant, "No change in prices. See my letter of the 16th." Tenant received Cliff's telegram the same day, May 18. Later that day Tenant also received Cliff's letter of May 16, which read, "Our deal is off."

The normal course of post between Tenant and Shore and Tenant and Cliff was one day.

How do we begin? The same way we began our analysis of <u>Tenant v. Shore</u>. Because this is a contracts formation problem, we look to the transactions we must analyze:

Early May: <u>Joe's Statements to Tenant</u>

May 15: <u>Cliff's Letter</u>

May 17: <u>Tenant's Letter to Cliff</u>

May 18: <u>Cliff's Telephone Call to Tenant</u>
May 18: <u>Tenant Receives Cliff's Letter of May 16</u>

The first issue in a contracts formation problem is: "Is there a valid offer?" Therefore, the first question to be solved is whether Joe's statements to Tenant constitute an offer.

Early May: <u>Joe's Statements to Tenant</u>

The issue is whether Joe's statements to Tenant constituted an offer. Joe only stated that two homes were available for $6,000 and $3,000. Hence Joe expressed no present intention to contract, nor did he state any specific terms. Thus, there is no offer at this point.

Notice that the rule of an offer is not restated. You might ask, "why isn't it?" It is because you have already stated the rule once. Unless your professor tells you otherwise, it is generally unnecessary to restate a rule already stated in the same answer. As noted earlier, if you are concerned about being penalized for failing to state the rule, you can always write, "<u>See</u> rule above," or "<u>See</u> <u>supra</u>," to inform your instructor that you have already cited the rule once.

The second and third sentences raise two points: the content of Joe's statement, and why Joe's statements do not give rise to a present intention to contract. Note how the application really cuts directly into the heart of the issue, makes the necessary points and reaches a swift conclusion. This is not an issue that requires two or three paragraphs of discussion, since it is rather clear that Joe's statements did not constitute an offer of any sort. Save yourself for other issues requiring more time, attention and analysis. Speaking of the devil, here comes a more spicy issue:

May 15: Cliff's Letter

The issue is whether Cliff's letter of May 15 constituted a valid offer. (See definition of offer, above) Cliff's letter expressed a present intention to contract because Cliff stated that Tenant could have Hi-Vu at $6,000 and Lo-Vu at $3,000, for June-through-August, all services included, payable in equal monthly installments. Cliff's statement unequivocally offered the rental of either property to Tenant according to the terms stated and requested his acceptance. Cliff's statement also included price ($6000 & $3000), subject matter (Hi-Vu & Lo-Vu), method of payment (monthly installments), collateral services and time for performance. Finally, Cliff's statement was communicated to Tenant. Therefore, Cliff's statement is a valid offer.

Again, this is not a humongous major issue, but make sure to dot your "i's" and cross your "t's". Cover each and every element of an offer, even though it may seem fairly obvious that Cliff's letter constituted an offer. Each element is dealt with quickly, but care should be taken to explain why each element is met. Now, finally, we have a major issue to contend with:

May 17: Tenant's Letter to Cliff

The issue is whether Tenant's Letter to Cliff constituted an acceptance. An acceptance must be unequivocal, communicated to the offeror, accepted by the offer's terms and made with knowledge of the offer. Two days after receiving Cliff's letter, Tenant agreed to pay the $3,000 Cliff requested for Lo-Vu; his acceptance was unequivocal by his use of the word agree. While Tenant's acceptance is clouded by Tenant's statement that Cliff's prices were "high" and his counteroffer of $5,000 for Hi-Vu, these wishful remarks do not convert Tenant's acceptance of Cliff's offer to rent Lo-Vu into a counteroffer or rejection. However, somewhat troublesome is the phrase following Tenant's acceptance of Lo-Vu: "only I hope you may be willing to consider some concession if I pay the whole $3,000 in advance." This is arguably not a counteroffer, however, since Tenant only "hoped" that Cliff would consider some reduction in the price, and would be more akin to a "grumbling offer."

Tenant had knowledge of the offer, since he received Cliff's letter, and the acceptance was thereafter communicated to Cliff by letter.

The mailbox rule provides that where the offer authorizes mail as a mode of acceptance, an acceptance is effective upon dispatch. Under this rule, Tenant accepted Cliff's offer as of May 17.

The first paragraph states the issue and rule of acceptance, and then cuts to the heart of the issue: Was Tenant's acceptance unequivocal, and was the offer accepted by its terms? These two issues require the bulk of the discussion and application.

The second paragraph quickly addresses the two remaining elements of acceptance.

The final paragraph states the effective date of the offer. This is raised as an issue, since Cliff attempts to revoke the offer later in the fact pattern.

May 18: <u>Cliff's Telephone Call to Tenant</u>
May 18: <u>Tenant Receives Cliff's Letter of May 16</u>

Cliff's attempted revocation received by Tenant on May 18 (Cliff's Letter of May 16) is of no consequence, since Cliff could not revoke the offer once Tenant accepted it on May 17. A revocation is effective when received, and Tenant did not receive it until May 18, and hence the revocation is without legal effect.

This paragraph begins by stating a conclusion, which is fine, just so it is explained why that conclusion is supported by the facts. The rule of revocation is stated in the second sentence and is applied in the third sentence, which also contains the conclusion that the revocation is without legal effect. Notice that each component of I-R-A-C is contained in this paragraph, irrespective of the order in which they are stated.

Before leaving this question, do not forget to address the issue of consideration and reach an overall conclusion.

There is no consideration problem here, since the promises to rent/lease Cliffhouse are clearly supported by mutual legal detriment (lodging) and legal benefit (rent money).

Thus, should Cliff fail to perform as obligated under the contract, Tenant will prevail against Cliff for breach of contract.

And in case you're wondering where in the cahoots that question came from, you have just analyzed another question which appeared on the feared California Bar Examination!

Okay, time for another humdinger. This problem is also from the California Bar Examination, and is probably much more difficult than the typical midterm or final examination given in the first year of law school:

Contracts Formation Example #6: Pat v. Don

On December 26, of last year, Pat received at his store in York a letter which Pat noticed was postmarked in Kent three days earlier, reading:

"Answering your inquiry on labels the same as previously furnished, I quote you in lots of 100 dozen or more monthly, yellows at 15 cents per dozen, stripes at 12 cents, to include all of your requirements for your York store for the next calendar year. Shipments are to be made on the first day of each month, terms 30 days net, f.o.b. Kent."

"I intend to discontinue the production of stripes. If you will order 300 stripes for York for January delivery, I will furnish you with all the stripes you wish for your Dover store on the same terms until my supply is exhausted."

You have seven days to study this proposition, (signed) Don Distributor, December 23."

Late in the afternoon of December 29, Pat telephoned Don, saying: "I accept your proposition for stripes next year, also I order the 300 dozen stripes for January delivery. Today at noon I mailed you a letter on the yellows." Don replied: "Didn't you get my telegram?" Pat answered: "No, but I'll come to your office early tomorrow." The letter Pat had mailed to Don read: "Not interested in yellows, price is too high." The course of mail is one day between Kent and York.

As promised, Pat went to Don's office and interrupted Don who was about to open Pat's letter. Pointing to the letter, Pat said to Don: "I accept your proposition for the yellows for next year. Please forget what I said in the letter, but I do think that you ought to stand the freight, the same as always." Pat paused, Don made no response, and Pat continued: "I'll take 200 dozen yellows now, also 100 dozen stripes for Dover."

Don told Pat that the proposition had already been withdrawn and handed Pat a copy of the telegram Don had sent to him, showing filing time 10:00 a.m., December 29, at Kent telegraph office and reading: "Disregard mine 23rd. Withdrawn." Pat never received the telegram.

Don is amply supplied with both kinds of labels.

Does Pat have an enforceable contract for stripes? If so, for how many? Discuss.

Does Pat have an enforceable contract for yellows? If so, who pays the freight? Discuss.

Stripes

December 23: Don mails offer re: stripes
December 25: Pat receives Don's letter
December 29: (10:00 a.m.) Don telegraphs revocation
December 29: Pat telephones Don, accepting stripes proposition and ordering 300 dozen stripes for January.
December 30: Pat visits Don and orders 100 dozen stripes for Dover

Model Answer #6: Pat v. Don

The issue is whether there is a legal relationship between Pat and Don for the sale of stripes. A legal relationship requires an offer, acceptance and consideration. This transaction is ruled by the U.C.C., since a sale of goods is involved.

December 25: Don's letter re: stripes

The issue is whether Don's letter regarding stripes is a valid offer. In order to constitute an offer, the offeror's communication must (1) manifest a present intention to contract; (2) be certain and definite as to all essential terms; (3) be communicated to the offeree.

Don clearly specified that he was quoting prices and quantities for stripes for sale in response to Pat's inquiry. Don included all terms of the offer, and therefore manifested a present intention to contract. All essential terms were included: price (12 cents per dozen), subject matter (stripes), quantity (output contract or lots of 100 dozen), time for performance (first day of each month) and shipping costs. Finally, the offer was communicated to Pat, the offeror. Therefore, Don's letter constituted a valid offer.

December 29: (10:00 a.m.) Don telegraphs revocation

The issue is whether Don's attempted revocation terminated the December 26 offer. A revocation is effective upon receipt. Although Don telegraphed the revocation before Pat's acceptance, Pat never received the telegram, and therefore Don's attempted revocation was ineffective.

Under the U.C.C. firm offer rule, a signed, written offer to buy or sell goods that expressly states it will remain open is irrevocable for the period stated. Because Don is a merchant in stripes and the offer was in writing and signed by him, the firm offer rule applies. Here Don stated that Pat had seven days to study this proposition. Arguably, the inclusion of this clause gave Pat seven days to decide whether to accept Don's offer. If the clause is so interpreted, then Don's offer was irrevocable for the time period stated in his offer, seven days. Assuming that the seven days ran from December 23, the date the offer was sent, as of December 29, Pat would have had an additional day to consider Don's offer, and Don could not revoke the offer on December 29.

Therefore, Don's attempted revocation was without legal effect.

<u>December 29: Pat telephones Don, accepting stripes proposition and ordering 300 dozen stripes for January.</u>

The issue is whether Pat's telephone call of December 29 constituted a valid acceptance. An acceptance must be unequivocal, communicated to the offeror, accepted by the offer's terms and made with knowledge of the offer. First, Pat unequivocally accepted the offer by stating, "I accept your proposition for stripes," and "I order 300 stripes for January delivery." Pat communicated his acceptance by telephone and obviously had knowledge of Don's offer. He also accepted Don's offer by its terms, agreeing to purchase stripes in accordance with Don's offer. Hence, Pat validly accepted Don's offer.

Consideration exists since each party incurred a legal detriment (Pat's act of paying for stripes; Dan's act of giving up stripes) and received a legal benefit (Pat's receipt of stripes; Dan's receipt of money).

December 30: Pat visits Don and orders 100 dozen stripes for Dover

The issue is whether Pat validly accepted Don's offer to provide the Dover store with stripes. On December 30, during Pat's office visit, Pat stated, "I'll take 200 dozen yellows now, also 100 dozen stripes for Dover." By this statement, Pat accepted Don's offer to "furnish [Pat] with all the stripes you wish for your Dover store on the same terms," until Don's supply was exhausted. Pat unequivocally accepted Don's offer by its terms, had knowledge of the offer through Don's letter, and communicated his acceptance to Don. Therefore, Pat validly accepted Don's offer for stripes for his Dover store.

Thus, Don is obligated to provide Pat with all the requirements needed for Pat's York store, regardless of Don's supply, and 300 dozen stripes for January delivery. Furthermore, Don must provide Pat with whatever stripes he "wishes" for the Dover store, until his supply is exhausted, including the 100 dozen stripes he ordered on December 30th.

Contract for Yellows

December 23: Don mails offer re: stripes and yellows
December 26: Pat receives Don's letter
December 29: (10:00 a.m.) Don sends telegram revoking offer
December 29: (noon) Pat mails letter rejecting offer re: yellows
December 30: Don receives Pat's December 29 letter
December 30: Pat accepts proposition for yellows and orders 200 dozen yellows

December 26: Pat receives Don's letter

Don's letter constituted a valid offer for the same reasons as in the stripes analysis above. Don responded to Pat's inquiry re: yellows, and quoted prices and quantities of yellows for acceptance by Pat; Don also requested an acceptance within seven days. All essential terms, including quantity (100 dozen or more or output contract), subject matter (yellows), price (15 cents per dozen) and time for performance (first day of each month). The offer was also communicated to Don. Thus, Don's letter constituted a valid offer for sale of yellows.

December 29: (10:00 a.m.) Don sends telegram revoking offer

As stated in the stripes analysis, because a revocation is effective upon receipt and since Pat never received Don's telegram, Don's attempted revocation was ineffective.

December 29: (noon) Pat mails letter rejecting offer re: yellows
December 30: Don receives Pat's December 29 letter

The issue is whether Pat's letter of December 29 constituted a rejection of Don's offer. In his letter, Pat stated, "Not interested in yellows, price is too high," clearly rejecting Don's offer. However, although Don had received the letter, Don had not opened it before Pat's acceptance. In some jurisdictions which strictly construe the rejection rule, the offer was terminated when Pat's letter was received by Don; however, some states would hold that the rejection was not effective until it was actually read by Don. Pat could also argue that he may revoke his rejection and accept Don's offer, because the seven day period given to him by Don in the offer had not yet passed, and Don had not detrimentally relied upon Pat's rejection.

December 30: Pat accepts proposition for yellows and orders 200 dozen yellows before Don opens Pat's December 29 letter

Assuming that the rejection is not effective, Pat clearly accepted Don's proposition for the yellows and ordered 200 dozen yellows in accordance with the terms of Don's offer, with knowledge of the offer. Pat communicated his acceptance to Don on December 30. Thus, Pat accepted Don's offer, and Don is obligated to provide Pat with yellows for his York store, and 200 yellows.

As to the issue of freight costs, under U.C.C. 2-207, unless the offer makes clear that no change is allowed, modifications of an offer are viewed as proposals for additions to contract, and the contract is deemed accepted. The additional proposal is made part of the contract if the offeror is a merchant and does not object, the proposal is not inconsistent with contract and does not materially alter it. Because both Pat and Don are merchants, and Don's offer is not limited to its terms, U.C.C. 2-207 applies. The shipping costs are not material to the contract, since Don has paid for such costs in the past, and are not inconsistent with an acceptance of the terms of the sale of yellows. Hence, unless Don objects, the shipping costs should be borne by him.

* * *

Remember that the area of contracts formation is only one of the potential areas you may be tested on. However, almost without exception, contracts formation is the most testable area in first year contracts law, and you should expect to see a contracts formation problem on your first year contracts examination.

DEFENSES TO A CONTRACT

Once contract formation has been determined, you must then turn to the issues of defenses to a contract. As set forth in your Contracts Problem-Solving Approach, there are seven basic defenses: illegality of the contract, fraud, lack of consent, statute of frauds, capacity, unconscionable contract and mistake. Even though a legal relationship may exist, that is, offer, acceptance and consideration are present, a "defense" to the contract may be raised, which has the effect of barring the contract. For example, although a valid offer, acceptance and consideration exist, if the transaction involved an illegal act, the transaction is barred. Likewise, if fraud is employed in securing the legal relationship, no contract exists. As with Torts and Criminal Law, you must examine the facts before you in order to determine if a particular defense may be asserted.

Contract Defenses Example: Sylvester Salesman v. Grandma Moses

Sylvester "Sly" Salesman approached Grandma Moses and offered to sell her a set of encyclopedias at the reduced rate of $500 per book. Sylvester told Grandma Moses that to refuse his offer was a disservice to the educational needs of the American children. Grandma Moses, who was senile, agreed to purchase a set of sixty books two years from the date of the agreement, not

realizing that the suggested retail price per book was only $50. May Sylvester Salesman enforce the contract as against Grandma Moses?

Clearly in the above example, Grandma Moses and Sylvester Salesman agreed to enter a legal relationship for the purchase of encyclopedias. Their agreement is supported by consideration, a valid offer and acceptance. However, Grandma Moses may raise a number of defenses to the existence of the contract:

SYLVESTER SALESMAN v. GRANDMA MOSES

Defenses to the Contract

The issue is whether Grandma Moses may raise any defenses to the contract she entered into with Sylvester Salesman. A defense, if found to exist, bars the contract, thereby releasing Grandma Moses from her duty to perform.

Fraud

Grandma Moses may raise the defense of fraud. Where one party induces another to enter a contract through the use of fraud and false impressions, the contract is voidable. Here Sylvester erroneously told Grandma that the value of the encyclopedias was $500 per book and that the offered price was a reduced rate. In fact, the suggested retail value of each book was $50. Because Sylvester obtained Grandma's consent to the contract by misrepresenting the value of the books, the defense of fraud may be raised by Grandma to void the contract.

Statute of Frauds

The Statute of Frauds provides that certain agreements must be in writing which contains the names of the parties, subject matter, terms and conditions of the contract, consideration and signature of the party to be charged. There is no indication in the facts that Grandma signed any agreement, and if her agreement was oral, then the contract may be avoided on two grounds. First, a contract which is incapable of being performed within one year must comply with the Statute of Frauds. Because the agreement between Grandma and Sylvester was to take effect two years from the date of the agreement, a writing was required. Secondly, a contract for the sale of goods over $500 must be in writing, and because the contract price was for $30,000 worth of goods, a writing was required. Therefore, Grandma Moses may assert that the contract is void for failure to comply with the Statute of Frauds.

Capacity

The issue is whether Grandma may raise the defense of mental incapacity to bar the contract. A contract is voidable if a party is unable to understand the nature and consequence of the contract, unless necessaries are involved. Because Grandma was senile, presumably she was unable to understand the nature and consequence of the transaction she entered. Evidence of this fact is that Grandma agreed to purchase a set of encyclopedias for $500 per book, an exorbitant price at any measure. Further, Grandma apparently believed Sylvester's incredulous misrepresentation that the books were, in fact, worth $500 each. Because encyclopedias are not human necessities, Grandma may avoid the contract on this ground.

Unconscionable Contract

Where there is gross disparity between the parties, or the contract is one-sided or against public policy, the court may refuse to enforce unconscionable or oppressive terms. Here, both Grandma's and Sylvester's relative economic circumstances are not evident, but it may be inferred that Sylvester represents a company, while Grandma is an individual. Thus, there may be gross disparity between the bargaining position of each party. On one hand, Grandma is free to purchase encyclopedias from another salesperson or another company; therefore, it cannot be said that Grandma was coerced into entering the contract with Sylvester.

However, on the other hand, it is clear that Grandma was senile at the time she agreed to purchase the books and was at a considerable disadvantage in bargaining with Sylvester. Most important, there was no economic justification for the exorbitant price of $500 charged per book by Sylvester, when in fact, each book was worth only $50. Thus, the contract price was oppressive, and the court should find the contract unconscionable. The court may "blue line" the contract to reflect the true value of the books, or void the contract in its entirety.

* * *

As you can see from the above model answer, the I-R-A-C format is again followed religiously, in the same manner that Tort or Criminal Law Defenses were analyzed.

CONDITIONS

Have you ever made a conditional promise to another? For example, have you ever said, "I'll go to the movies with you Saturday if I study hard this week." In this example, your promise to attend the movies is conditional upon your studying hard during the week. This statement differs considerably from the statement, "I'll go to the movies with you Saturday," because in the former statement, there is no obligation to go to the movies unless your study schedule permits. In the language of contracts law, your promise is said to be "conditional."

First, it is important to determine the effect of a condition on the duty to perform. Does the condition release the promisor from a duty to perform or give rise to the duty to perform? Thus, we look to the timing of the condition in order to determine its effect.

A condition is classified as a condition precedent, condition concurrent, or condition subsequent depending on when the contingency must occur. If the contingency is to occur in the future, before the duty to perform matures, as in the above example, the condition is called a "condition precedent." If, on the other hand, the condition must occur at the same time performance must be rendered, the condition is called a "condition concurrent." For example, if Cal agrees to sell you a Rolls Royce when you give Cal $125,000, the condition that you give Cal $125,000 must simultaneously occur before Cal must perform and sell you a Rolls Royce.

By contrast, a condition subsequent is one which extinguishes or eliminates a duty to perform. In other words, the occurrence of a future circumstance releases the promisor from performing. Thus, if Madge agreed to give Bart $5 a month unless he drinks soda, Madge would have an immediate duty to pay Bart $5 which would be extinguished by the occurrence of the condition, that is, Bart's act of drinking soda.

Once this distinction is made, and the type of condition is identified, then it can be determined who has the burden of proving the occurrence or nonoccurrence of a condition. The person to whom the promise is made – known as the promisee – must prove the occurrence of a condition precedent or condition concurrent, and the person making the promise – known as the promisor – must prove the occurrence of condition subsequent.

Now, if all of that hasn't completely confused you, add this to the equation: how do you know if you have a condition? Like people, all conditions are not created equally. There are three types of conditions: express conditions, implied conditions and constructive conditions.

Express conditions are those stated in the contract or agreement. In the "Madge & Bart" example, the condition stated that Bart not drinking soda is an express condition because it is stated in the agreement.

Implied conditions are those conditions which are "inferred" from the language of the contract as necessary to the contract. For example, if Gomez agrees to accept delivery from Uncle Fester at Morticia's airport, there is an implied condition that Morticia's airport actually exists. Thus, this condition is not stated, but is implied.

By contrast, constructive conditions are those created by operation of law in the interests of fairness of justice. There are basically three situations where the court will imply a condition in the absence of an express condition to the contrary. First, where the contract provides that performance by the parties must occur at the same time and place, each party's performance is a constructive condition concurrent for the other. Secondly, where one party's performance is due in stages and the other party's may be performed instantly, the former is a constructive condition precedent to the latter's performance. Thirdly, where one performance is required before the other's, the first party's performance is a constructive condition precedent to the other.

Let's take an exam question involving conditions:

Conditions Example #1: Lon v. Les

Les Vegas signed an agreement reading, "I agree to pay Lon Shark $50,000 from my gambling winnings on Tuesday." Les Vegas then strikes it big on Tuesday, winning a $100,000 jackpot. Must Les pay Lon?

(ISSUE) The issue is whether Les must pay Lon $50,000. Under the express terms of the agreement, Les' receipt of gambling winnings on Tuesday was an express condition precedent to Les' duty to pay Lon. **(RULE)** Where performance is subject to a condition precedent, an absolute duty to pay arises upon occurrence of the condition. **(APPLICATION)** Thus, because Les received gambling winnings on Tuesday, **(CONCLUSION)** Les owes Lon an absolute duty to pay $50,000.

And now another:

Conditions Example #2: Marla Boro v. Smokey

Marla promises to give $5 per week to Smokey, unless he smokes cigarettes. Smokey refrains from smoking for four weeks but smokes one cigarette in the fifth week. Must Marla pay Smokey?

(ISSUE) The issue is whether Marla must pay Smokey. Under the express terms of their agreement, Smokey was to refrain from smoking, and this circumstance was an express condition subsequent to Marla's agreement to pay Smokey $5 a week. **(RULE)** Where performance is subject to a condition subsequent, the occurrence of that condition extinguishes the promisor's duty to perform. **(APPLICATION)** Thus, because Smokey smoked a cigarette, **(CONCLUSION)** Marla is relieved of her duty to pay Smokey $5 per week.

(ISSUE) The second issue is whether Marla must pay Smokey for the four weeks he did not smoke cigarettes. Under their agreement, Marla agreed to pay Smokey "$5 per week," which would suggest that Marla was to pay Smokey for each week he refrained from smoking. **(RULE & APPLICATION)** Because Smokey's performance was due in stages and would require at least one week, and Marla's performance, i.e., the payment of $5, could be rendered immediately, Smokey's performance was a constructive condition precedent to Marla's performance. **(RULE)** Where performance is subject to a condition precedent, an absolute duty to pay arises upon occurrence of the condition. **(APPLICATION)** Thus, after Smokey refrained from smoking each week, Marla had an absolute duty to pay Smokey $5 per week. **(CONCLUSION)** Therefore, Marla must pay Smokey $20 for the four weeks he refrained from smoking.

* * *

While the terms and vocabulary accompanying the law of conditions may at first glance sound a bit confusing, conditions simply reflect good old-fashioned common sense, combined with our old friend and hero I-R-A-C.

EXCUSE OF CONDITIONS

The next area in your problem-solving approach concerns a number of situations when a condition will be excused, because to require performance would be unfair. Again, these circumstances are all based on common sense. For example, one such situation is "Estoppel," which occurs when the promisee, by words or conduct prior to the time for satisfying a condition, leads the promisor to believe that she will not insist on satisfaction. Let's add a few facts to the Marla Boro v. Smokey example:

Excuse of Conditions Example #1:

Smokey v. Marla Boro

After Marla Boro learned that Smokey had not smoked for four weeks, Marla

called Smokey and told him it was all right to smoke just one cigarette, and that she would still pay him $5 per week. Smokey indulged himself and immediately after he took the first puff, Marla told him that the deal was off because he had broken his promise. Must Marla pay Smokey if he continues to refrain from smoking?

(ISSUE) The issue is whether Marla is relieved of her duty to perform because of the occurrence of the condition subsequent. Under the express terms of the agreement, if Smokey smoked, Marla was no longer obligated to pay Smokey $5 per week. **(RULE)** However, under the doctrine of estoppel, even the occurrence of a condition subsequent may be excused where the promisee, by words or conduct, prior to the time for satisfying a condition, leads the promisee to believe that he will not insist on satisfaction. **(APPLICATION)** Because Marla expressly informed Smokey that their agreement would be unaffected by Smokey smoking one cigarette, Marla would be estopped from being released from her duty to perform. **(CONCLUSION)** Thus, if Smokey continues to refrain from smoking, Marla would be obligated to pay Smokey $5 per week.

* * *

Another circumstance which excuses all conditions is known as voluntary disablement. Voluntary disablement occurs when the person making the promise, i.e., the promisor, has rendered himself unable to perform the contract, as in the following example:

Excuse of Conditions Example #2: Latosha vs. Mannie

Latosha entered a contract to sell Mannie her classic Porsche on September 1. On August 15, Latosha sold the Porsche to Mario. Must Mannie wait until September 1 before suing Latosha for the Porsche?

(ISSUE) The issue is whether Mannie may sue Latosha for the Porsche, or whether he must wait until the occurrence of the condition precedent, i.e., occurrence of the date September 1, before suing. **(RULE)** Voluntary disablement occurs when the promisee has rendered herself unable to perform the contract. **(APPLICATION)** Here Latosha has sold her car to another, making it impossible for her to perform. Thus, the condition that Mannie wait until September 1 is excused, and **(CONCLUSION)** Mannie need not wait two weeks before suing.

(ISSUE) However, if Latosha can demonstrate that she can still perform by either tendering another classic Porsche which comports with her agreement with Mannie, or repurchasing her Porsche from Mario, she may not be in breach. **(RULE)** Both the minority and the U.C.C allow timely restoration if the promisee gives the promisor clear notice and proof of ability to perform before the promisor detrimentally relies on the promisee's prior action. **(APPLICATION)** Thus, if Mannie did not rely on her sale of the Porsche to Mario by purchasing another vehicle, and Latosha could prove that she could perform the contract, there would be no breach and **(CONCLUSION)** the condition would not be excused.

Notice how the U.C.C and minority view are discussed in a separate I-R-A-C analysis, which adds considerably to the discussion. Extra points may often be accumulated by including discussion of important trends in the law, even though the rule is in the minority. Because we are not told in the problem which law governs Latosha and Mannie's transaction, it is well within the analysis to discuss the minority and U.C.C viewpoints as well as the majority rule.

DISCHARGE OF DUTY TO PERFORM

The next area of law on the contracts totem pole involves certain situations where the duty to perform is discharged. Again, taking it from the big picture, after you have determined that there is a legal relationship supported by an offer, acceptance and consideration, that no defenses bar the contract, and that any conditions have either occurred or been excused, the next issue is whether any circumstances have occurred which have discharged the duty to perform. "Discharge" simply means that the party discharged need not perform the contract.

One such circumstance is impossibility, which occurs when it becomes impossible for a party to perform. In order for this defense to apply, the contract must be objectively impossible to perform; that is, no one could perform the contract. Because this is a meaty area to test on a contracts essay examination, let's tackle a problem involving impossibility:

EXAMPLE #1: <u>Bugsy v. Lulu</u>

Horse trainer Lulu contracted with Bugsy to breed their respective horses, Ed and Elaine. However, on the date set for the artificial insemination, Lulu learned that Ed was sterile. Has Lulu breached the contract?

(ISSUE) The issue is whether Lulu's duty to perform was discharged by the circumstance of impossibility. Under the contract, Lulu was obligated to breed her horse Ed with Bugsy's horse Elaine, and therefore had a present duty to perform. **(RULE)** If, after a contract is formed, a party is unable to perform, that party is discharged if the impossibility is objective, i.e., no one could perform. **(APPLICATION)** Here Lulu is unable to perform because her horse Ed is sterile and cannot therefore "breed" with Elaine. Because no one could cause Ed to "perform" since Ed's sterility is a medical condition which cannot be cured, the impossibility is objective in nature. **(CONCLUSION)** Therefore, Lulu is discharged from her contract with Bugsy.

Because impossibility is a popular area to test, we'll take one more example involving destruction of goods:

EXAMPLE #2: RICKEY V. CLOIE

Cloie contracted to purchase 5,000 of Rickey Rapp's new album, "No More Hickeys for Rickey." The albums were to be delivered to Cloie's business address downtown. While in transit to Cloie's business, the entire shipment of records was destroyed in a car accident. Must Cloie pay for the records?

(ISSUE) The issue is whether Cloie is liable for the destroyed records. **(RULE)** Under the U.C.C., which governs the sale of goods, if particular identifiable goods are destroyed without the fault of the parties before the risk of loss passes to the buyer, both parties are discharged from performing. **(APPLICATION)** Under this view, both Cloie and Rickey would be discharged from performing their obligations under the contract. **(CONCLUSION)** Thus, Cloie would not be required to pay for the records if the risk of loss had not passed to Cloie.

(ISSUE: BUT WHAT IF THE RECORDS WERE NOT IDENTIFIABLE?) However, if the 5,000 records which were destroyed in the accident were not "identifiable" and the contract did not specifically identify which 5,000 records were to be supplied by Rickey, both parties would still be obligated to perform. Thus, Rickey would be required to supply Cloie with 5,000 albums, and Cloie would be obligated to pay for them.

(ISSUE: BUT DID THE RISK OF LOSS PASS TO CLOIE?) The next issue is whether the risk of loss passed to Cloie. Under the U.C.C, if delivery to a specific location is required under the contract, the risk of loss passes when the carrier places goods at the buyer's disposal at the specified location. Because Rickey was required to deliver the goods to Cloie's downtown office, the risk of loss passed only when the carrier delivered the goods into Cloie's possession at her office. Because the goods were destroyed before being delivered into Cloie's possession, the risk of loss is on Rickey, and Cloie need not pay for the destroyed records.

* * *

"Discharge" simply means that the parties are released from their obligations to perform, by impossibility, frustration of purpose, subsequent agreement of parties, impracticality and occurrence of a condition subsequent, as set forth in your Law Charts for Contracts. Let's take another circumstance amounting to discharge:

EXAMPLE #3: RICKEY RAPP v. FANS

Rickey Rapp decided to host a rap concert at the local community center. Rickey sold out tickets ranging from $10 to $20 in 10 days time. Five days before the concert, the City Council passed a bill requiring a city tax of $21 per patron at any event "involving decibel levels of 22.3 or more." Rickey's performers normally perform at levels of 200 decibels or more. May Rickey cancel the contract with the ticket holders on the ground of impracticality?

(STATE THE GENERAL ISSUE) The issue is whether Rickey Rapp's duty to perform the contract with the ticket holders is discharged by impracticality. **(STATE THE RULE)** Under common law, three elements must be met before impracticality is shown.

(ISSUE & RULE) The first is that in performing the contract, the obligor, Rickey Rapp, encountered circumstances which were unforeseen to the parties at the formation stage. **(APPLICATION)** Here Rickey Rapp had no reason to believe that the City Council would pass a bill taxing decibel levels at the time the contract was entered into. **(CONCLUSION)** Thus this element is met.

(ISSUE & RULE) Secondly, the obligor must show that expenditures from further performance are grossly disproportionate to the original consideration supporting the obligor's duties. **(APPLICATION)** Rickey Rapp sold the concert tickets for $10 to $20, and is being taxed at $21 per ticket. Prior to the imposition of the City Council's tax, Rickey Rapp's expenses would not have included a twenty-one dollar per patron tax, and because the cost of the tax exceeds the value of the most expensive ticket, the unforeseen tax is grossly disproportionate to the original consideration. The cost of the tax would clearly exceed any potential revenues, and in the case of a $10 ticket, Rickey would lose $11 per patron. **(CONCLUSION)** This element is met.

(ISSUE & RULE) Third, the obligor must not have assumed the risk of such circumstances. **(APPLICATION)** There are no facts indicating that Rickey assumed the risk that the City Council would act to tax patrons based on decibel levels, unless he had reason to believe that the City Council would act in such an irrational manner. **(CONCLUSION)** Therefore this element is met.

(STATE OVERALL CONCLUSION) In conclusion, Rickey's duty to the ticket holders is discharged, but Rickey would be required to refund any consideration paid by the concert goers.

BREACH & REMEDIES

After making it down the yellow brick road of contracts law, whizzing past contracts formation, conditions, excuse of conditions and discharge, you're ready to meet the Wizard! But don't be disappointed by the simplicity of the "breach" analysis, because all you need to do is tell your professor whether the contract was breached, whether that breach is minor or material (i.e., a biggie breach or a tiny breach), click your heels together three times, and you're home free!

SAMPLE BREACH ANALYSIS: Toto v. Dorothy

Dorothy breached her duty to Toto by failing to comply with the terms of their agreement. Dorothy's breach was material, since she violated the express purpose of the contract by failing to tender performance. Hence Dorothy is in breach and Toto may collect damages.

Depending on your professor's first year contracts curriculum, you may also be required to discuss what remedies are available to the non-breaching party in the event of breach. If so, then discuss the issue of remedies by identifying the potential remedies available, taking care to define each of the remedies named.

SAMPLE REMEDIES ANALYSIS:

> Toto is entitled to damages. The **standard measure** of damages in a contracts action is the market price less the contract price. (APPLICATION) Thus, Toto's damages are __.
>
> Toto may also recover **consequential** damages. Consequential damages are those damages arising from breach as a result of special needs or position of the buyer. (APPLICATION) Therefore, Toto may recover consequential damages for __.
>
> Additionally, Toto may recover **incidental/nominal/punitive** (rare) damages for ___.

Toto's damages, however, are subject to certain **limitations**. First, any consequential damages must be **foreseeable** under Hadley v. Baxendale. (APPLICATION) Secondly, the non-breaching party has a duty to **mitigate** damages and avoid foreseeable damages. (APPLICATION) Thirdly, damages must be **caused** by the breach. (APPLICATION) Finally, damages must be established with **certainty**.

Toto may also seek RESTITUTION/RESCISSION/REFORMATION/ SPECIFIC PERFORMANCE/ENFORCEMENT OF A PERSONAL SERVICE CONTRACT/ UCC REMEDIES.

When learning contract law, remember that awe-inspiring, mighty force which governs the law of contracts: Common sense. With a good measure of common sense, coupled with the "big picture" of contracts law, you will succeed in mastering first year contracts.

How to Answer a Civil Procedure Problem

The law of Civil Procedure is a hotchpotch of the nuts and bolts of civil practice – from the filing of a suit to the jurisdiction and power of the court and the stages of a jury trial, to name just a few. Because the law of Civil Procedure is made up of many different areas of law, it is probably the most difficult first year course to organize into a Problem-Solving Approach. But do not fear. As in all areas of law, Civil Procedure is really a series of "tests" and "rules" which determine whether a particular procedure may be applied.

It is important to distinguish early on between those rules and procedures that apply in the federal courts, and those which apply in state court, and which are common to both. There are three primary sources of the rules of Civil Procedure. First, there may be rules of your state, either in the form of a code or court rules, which govern the procedures that apply in state court. Secondly, the Federal Rules of Civil Procedure govern the procedure of the federal courts. Your professor will probably require that you purchase a copy of these rules, in addition to your course casebook. Thirdly, case precedent or decisions have established various rules and procedures. Thus, in solving a Civil Procedure Problem, you must first decide whether state or federal court rules apply. Very often, a different set of rules will be applied depending on whether the case is being heard in state or federal court.

While professors teach the various concepts and rules of Civil Procedure law in varying order, many begin with the concept of jurisdiction. As explained in the introductory section of this book, jurisdiction really refers to the power of a court to subject a person or thing to its decision. The most popular type of jurisdiction – for exam purposes – is personal jurisdiction. This refers to the court's power to render an individual to its decision. <u>In-rem</u>, meaning "in land," refers to the court's power to render a decision regarding certain property located in the state. Quasi-in-rem jurisdiction gives the court power to determine the rights of particular person relating to specific property within the court's control.

Hence, a common exam issue is whether a court has power over a particular defendant. This issue is raised in exam fact patterns and in the real world, when a plaintiff sues a defendant in Court "A" in State "X," and defendant or counsel claim that the Court is without jurisdiction or power over the defendant. The issue is stated: "Does Court "A" have personal jurisdiction over the defendant?"

The answer to this question involves a lengthy but not overly complex analysis. In essence, there are two ways to assert personal jurisdiction over a defendant.

The first is known as the "traditional bases," referring to grounds which have traditionally been used to assert the power of a court. These grounds, which are set forth in the Law Charts for Civil Procedure, include: a defendant's presence in the state at the time of personal service, defendant's domicile or residence in the forum state, express consent to jurisdiction, as where the defendant agrees to appear in court, implied consent, where the law requires that the defendant appear and defend in court, and where the defendant waives or fails to object to jurisdiction. The presence of any of these grounds creates an absolute basis of jurisdiction, conferring jurisdiction upon the court to exercise its power over a particular defendant.

The second way a court may exercise jurisdiction is if the court finds that the U.S. Constitution Due Process Clause permits it to. The Supreme Court determined long ago that a court may exercise power over a defendant if the defendant has had sufficient contact with the state to justify requiring the defendant to defend in the state. The test is an objective test where the court weighs and balances certain factors, upon which the court bases its decision whether to exercise jurisdiction.

Each of these factors is set forth in your Law Chart for Civil Procedure. But before turning to your approach and mentally reciting the minimum contacts "test" of personal jurisdiction, let's apply some good old fashioned common sense.

If you were deciding whether or not to haul a defendant into court to defend a lawsuit, what kind of information would you be interested in knowing? For one, you would ask where the incident giving rise to the cause of action occurred. You might also want to know what kind of contact the defendant has had with the state in which the court is situated. Did defendant have direct or indirect contact with the state? Were the defendant's contacts sporadic (a one shot deal) or systematic (by design)? You would determine whether the defendant received any benefits and protections from the state, and whether it was foreseeable to the defendant that he would be sued in the state. You would also factor in whether it was the defendant or plaintiff who initiated the contact with the state.

You would also consider questions of fairness and convenience. You would want to know whether it would be a great burden for the defendant to defend in the state; you might also inquire as to whether the state had any particular interest in requiring the defendant to defend in the state; you might consider the location of the evidence and witnesses, which state's law would apply and whether an alternative, more convenient location was available. Finally, you would be concerned about the possibility of multiple law suits resulting from your decision.

These factors are known as the "minimum contacts" test.

If these factors weigh in favor of the defendant, then personal jurisdiction is improper; if, on the other hand, these factors favor the plaintiff, personal jurisdiction will be found to exist.

Thus, in solving a Civil Procedure personal jurisdiction problem, you would consider (1) traditional bases; (2) any law or statutory authority providing for jurisdiction; (3) the minimum contacts test.

JURISDICTION, NOTICE & VENUE

Without further adieu, let's do a personal jurisdiction problem:

Personal Jurisdiction Example #1: Eddie v. Triple XXX & Mean Mike

Eddie Earnest, a Nevada resident, applied for a job as a bartender with "Triple X productions." "Triple X productions" is a large conglomerate which is incorporated in Delaware and has its principal place of business in New Mexico. Eddie applied for employment with the "Triple X Topless Bar" in Las Vegas, and interviewed with Mean Mike, a local employee who worked at Triple X Employment Agency. Upon seeing Eddie Earnest, Mean Mike told Eddie that the company only hired females because the bar was a topless bar and that a male had never been hired. When Eddie accused Mean Mike of sex discrimination, Mike picked up Eddie and threw him outside the office. Eddie wants to sue Triple X productions and Mean Mike for sex discrimination and assault and battery. Does the federal court sitting in Nevada have jurisdiction over the defendants?

Before solving this problem, let's look at structure and format of the analysis. Remember again that a great deal of your examination is preordained and pre-written before you step into that exam room:

P v. D

The issue is whether **[the court]** in **[location]** has personal jurisdiction over defendant **[name defendant(s)]**.

Since this action was filed in **[state/federal]** court, the problem must be analyzed under **[state/federal]** procedural requirements.

Before a court may properly hear a case, it must have personal jurisdiction over the parties. Personal jurisdiction refers to the power of the court to subject a particular defendant to its decision. Because this case involves an adjudication of parties' rights (or denial of rights), a court hearing this case must have personal jurisdiction over the defendants.

Traditional Bases

It should first be determined whether any of the traditional bases of jurisdiction exist, since these bases create an absolute basis for personal jurisdiction in most cases. **(APPLY EACH OF THE TRADITIONAL BASES).** Therefore, traditional bases/no traditional bases of jurisdiction exist.

Modern Basis

Under the modern basis, a defendant must have certain minimum contacts with the forum such that maintenance of the suit does not offend traditional notions of fair play and substantial justice. This analysis requires a three-prong test.

The first inquiry is whether there is any statutory authority for the assertion of jurisdiction. **(APPLICATION)**

The second requirement is that defendant must have "sufficient minimum contacts" with the forum state. First, if the cause of action arose in the forum state, this is a strong indication that jurisdiction would be proper. **(APPLICATION)** Secondly, if the defendant has substantial activity in the forum state, this will support a finding that jurisdiction exists. **(APPLICATION)**

Thirdly, the court will inquire as to whether the defendant purposefully availed itself to the benefits and protections of the forum's law. **(APPLICATION)** Fourthly, the court will consider whether the defendant could foresee being required to defend in the forum state. **(APPLICATION)** Fifthly, the court will determine whether the defendant initiated contact with the forum state. **(APPLICATION)**

The court, weighing each factor, would find that the defendant **has/does not have** sufficient minimum contacts with the state to warrant the exercise of jurisdiction.

The third requirement is that the court's exercise of jurisdiction must not offend traditional notions of fair play and substantial justice. In weighing these factors, the court would consider the burden on the defendant of defending the action in the state. **(APPLICATION)** In considering the choice of law, the court would determine that the law of state __________ would apply, weighing in favor of trial there. Thirdly, the state interest is **(APPLICATION)**. Fourthly, multiplicity of suits will/will not result if personal jurisdiction is exercised, because **(APPLICATION)**. Fifthly, the court will consider whether any alternative forums exist. **(APPLICATION)** Sixthly, the court will consider where the evidence and witnesses are located. **(APPLICATION)**

In conclusion, the fair play and substantial justice factors weigh in favor/against a finding of personal jurisdiction in the state.

Based on the foregoing, the assertion of personal jurisdiction by the court in the state would be proper/improper.

* * *

By providing you with this format, please do not feel like a computer, regurgitating values and filling in the blanks like pages in a coloring book. By contrast, it is your unique application of the facts which will determine your success on the examination. Also be advised that your professor's approach to personal jurisdiction may differ, and you should, of course, follow your instructor's approach and tailor a "grid" to fit that approach. This example is only offered as one possible approach to solving the problem. In the following model answer based upon the above approach, the application is indicated in **bold** type:

Eddie Earnest vs. Mean Mike and Triple XXX Productions

The issue is whether the **federal** court in **Nevada** has personal jurisdiction over defendants **Mean Mike and Triple XXX Productions.** Since this action was filed in **federal** court, the problem must be analyzed under **federal** procedural requirements.

Before a court may properly hear a case, it must have personal jurisdiction over the parties. Personal jurisdiction refers to the power of the court to subject a particular defendant to its decision. Because this case involves an adjudication of parties' rights (or denial of rights), a court hearing this case must have personal jurisdiction over the defendants.

Traditional Bases

It should first be determined whether any of the traditional bases of jurisdiction exist, since these bases create absolute personal jurisdiction in most cases. **The facts are clear that Triple XXX is not domiciled in Nevada, since its place of incorporation is Delaware, and its principal place of business is in New Mexico. Thus, it cannot be argued that Triple XXX is domiciled in Nevada. However, Mean Mike is a Nevada local, and thus, if domiciled there (i.e., if Nevada is his home or a place which he intends to make his home), he is subject to the court's jurisdiction.**

In addition, if either defendant expressly consents to suit in Nevada, the federal court may exercise personal jurisdiction over them, since it is waiveable. Either defendant will be held to have waived any personal jurisdiction objection if they appear in court.

Therefore, traditional bases of jurisdiction exist as to **defendant Mean Mike, and the court may exercise personal jurisdiction over him. However, no traditional bases exist as to defendant Triple XXX.**

<u>Modern Basis</u>

Under the modern basis, a defendant must have certain minimum contacts with the forum such that maintenance of the suit does not offend traditional notions of fair play and substantial justice. This analysis requires a three-pronged test.

The first inquiry is whether there is statutory authority for the assertion of jurisdiction. **The federal court must look to the long arm statute of the state in which it is sitting, and determine whether the statute allows assertion of jurisdiction under the facts. Since no statute is included the facts, this cannot be determined.**

The second requirement is that defendant must have "sufficient minimum contacts" with the forum state. First, if the cause of action arose in the forum state, this is a strong indication that jurisdiction would be proper. **Here the cause of action arose in Triple XXX's Nevada bar, where Eddie was subjected to assault and battery and sex discrimination, the very crux of his claim against the defendants.** Second, if the defendant has substantial activity in the forum state, this will support a finding that jurisdiction exists. **The defendant owns a bar in the forum state, and probably advertises, promotes, hires and collects revenues in Nevada. While Triple XXX will argue that one bar in Nevada does not constitute substantial activity, it will likely lose on this issue.**

Third, the court will inquire as to whether the defendant purposefully availed itself to the benefits and protections of the forum's law. **By operating a business in Nevada, Triple XXX availed itself of the laws of the state of Nevada; because the sales of liquor and topless dancing are highly regulated businesses usually requiring state licensing, Triple XXX necessarily benefitted from the laws of Nevada, where it did business.** Fourth, the court will consider whether the defendant could foresee being required to defend in the forum state. **Again because Triple XXX is doing business in Nevada, and was hiring employees, it could certainly foresee that its activities in Nevada could require Triple XXX to defend against a law suit in the forum state.** Fifth, the court will inquire whether the defendant initiated contact with the forum state. **This point could go either way, since the defendant could argue that Eddie Earnest initiated contact by**

applying for the job, and Eddie would argue that Triple XXX initiated contact by seeking employees in Nevada.

The court, weighing each factor, would find that the defendant has **sufficient minimum contacts** with the state to warrant the exercise of jurisdiction.

The third requirement is that the court's exercise of jurisdiction must not offend traditional notions of fair play and substantial justice. In weighing these factors, the court would consider the burden on the defendant of defending the action in the state. **The burden on Triple XXX to defend the suit would probably not be too great on either defendant, since Triple XXX has a business in Nevada, and Mean Mike lives there. However, Eddie Earnest could argue that it would be a burden for him to defend in New Mexico or Delaware.**

In considering the choice of law, the law of the state of **Nevada** applies because the alleged discriminatory statement was made in Nevada, weighing in favor of trial there. Thirdly, the state has a strong interest in providing a forum for its residents, and **since Eddie is a resident of the state, this weighs in Eddie's favor.** Fourthly, multiplicity of suits will likely result **if it is held that Nevada has no personal jurisdiction over the defendants because one action would be brought against Mean Mike (since he is a resident), and another action against Triple XXX in Delaware or New Mexico.** Fifthly, the court will consider whether any alternative forums exist. **Here there are no alternative forums available.** Sixthly, the court will consider where the evidence and witnesses are located. **Mean Mike and other witnesses, as well as any of Triple XXX's employment policie, are likely to be found in the forum state.**

In conclusion, the fair play and substantial justice factors weigh **in favor** of personal jurisdiction in the state.

Based on the foregoing, the assertion of personal jurisdiction by the court in the state would be **proper**.

* * *

Eddie Earnest v. Triple XXX & Mean Mike provides an excellent example of a complex analysis, which really is not that complex once the analysis is properly organized. This example requires the determination and analysis of nineteen separate issues. Yet, when the Civil Procedure *Law Chart* is applied, and each issue is dealt with one at a time, the task at hand becomes clear and the analysis much simpler.

At the risk of having even more fun, now that you are learning how to analyze complex fact patterns with ease, let's move to a personal jurisdiction problem involving more facts:

Personal Jurisdiction Example #2: <u>Harry & Natasha v. Jumping Jelly Beans Bungee Cord Company</u>

Harry and Natasha were planning to get married after a very brief courtship. Harry worked as an electrolysis hair remover in Palm Springs, California, and Natasha was a famous Broadway actress in New York, where she owned a fabulous home. While making plans for the wedding ceremony, Harry read about a bungee cord jumping ceremony in "Fascinating Lives of Newlyweds" magazine which is distributed solely in Nevada by Novelty Marital Ads, which has its principal place of business in the same state. The article was accompanied by an advertisement placed by Jumping Jelly Beans Bungee Cord Company, a Nevada business which boasted of a "Thrill of a Lifetime - Bungee Cord Jumping for Newlyweds - The Only Way to Jump Into Marital Bliss - Special Price of $99.99."

Harry contacted Jumping Jelly Beans Company and arranged for a bungee cord jumping wedding ceremony on January 1. On that day, Natasha flew into Nevada, where she met Harry, who had driven in from California where he resided. Together, they climbed the tower, attached the matching his and her bungee cords to each other's waists, embraced and repeated their vows before a minister of the peace, and jumped. Unfortunately, because of a malfunction in the machinery, both Harry and Natasha were suspended in the skies indefinitely.

Eventually, almost seven hours later, Harry and Natasha were rescued, but by that time, their romance had soured, and they quickly filed for divorce.

Harry and Natasha have filed suit for intentional infliction of emotion distress, negligence and strict products liability against Jumping Jellybeans in a federal court in Los Angeles. Jumping Jellybeans has demurred on the ground of lack of personal jurisdiction. What result?

Also, consider the following facts: (1) Jumping Jelly Beans has done business in Nevada for fourteen years and has served California clientele on only a few occasions; Jumping Jelly Beans is a sole proprietorship owned and operated by Marco Polo; (2) that Jumping Jelly Beans only advertises in "Fascinating Lives of Newlyweds" publication; (3) that the publication is not distributed in California because it does not meet obscenity standards in California; (4) That bungee cord jumping was recently made illegal in California due to safety hazards; (5) California has a "long arm" jurisdictional statute, allowing the assertion of jurisdiction on any basis not inconsistent with the Federal Constitution.

* * *

First which facts are relevant to solving the problem before you. This is the first of the

Six Steps of Exam Writing. Let's look at the fact pattern again, this time distinguishing between the relevant and irrelevant facts. The facts which are relevant to solving the personal jurisdiction problem are indicated in **bold** type:

Harry and **Natasha** were planning to get married after a very brief courtship. Harry worked as an electrolysis hair remover in Palm Springs, California, and Natasha was a famous Broadway actress in **New York**, where she owned a fabulous **home**. While making plans for the wedding ceremony, Harry **read** about a bungee cord jumping ceremony in "Fascinating Lives of Newlyweds" **magazine** which is **distributed solely in Nevada** by Novelty Marital Ads, which has its principal place of business in the same state. The article was accompanied by an advertisement placed by **Jumping Jelly Beans Bungee Cord Company, a Nevada business** which boasted of a "Thrill of a Lifetime - Bungee Cord Jumping for Newlyweds - The Only Way to Jump Into Marital Bliss - Special Price of $99.99."

Harry contacted Jumping Jelly Beans Company and arranged for a bungee cord jumping wedding ceremony on January 1. On that day, Natasha flew into **Nevada**, where she met Harry, who had driven in from California where he resided. Together, they climbed the tower, attached the matching his and her bungee cords to each other's waists, embraced and repeated their vows before a minister of the peace, and jumped. Unfortunately, because of a malfunction in the machinery, both Harry and Natasha were suspended in the skies indefinitely.

Eventually, almost seven hours later, Harry and Natasha were rescued, but by that time, their romance had soured, and they quickly filed for divorce.

Harry and Natasha have **filed suit** for intentional infliction of emotional distress, negligence and strict products liability against Jumping Jellybeans in a **federal court** in **Los Angeles**. Jumping Jellybeans has **demurred on the ground of lack of personal jurisdiction**. What result?

Also, consider the following facts: **(1) Jumping Jelly Beans has done business in Nevada for fourteen years and has served California clientele on only a few occasions; Jumping Jelly Beans is a sole proprietorship owned and operated by Marco Polo; (2) that Jumping Jelly Beans only advertises in "Fascinating Lives of Newlyweds" publication; (3) that the publication is not distributed in California because it does not meet obscenity standards in California; (4) That bungee cord jumping was recently made illegal in California due to safety hazards; (5) California has a "long arm" jurisdictional statute, allowing the assertion of jurisdiction on any basis not inconsistent with the Federal Constitution.**

Next, you must determine what questions are presented by the facts. This is the third step of the *Six Steps of Exam Taking.* In order to figure out what the issues are, simply apply your Personal Jurisdiction problem-solving approach. Here is an example of an outline of the exam answer. By drafting a quick outline before writing out your answer, you have a road map which sets forth your analysis and organization:

<u>Harry & Natasha v. Jumping Jelly Beans Bungee Cord Company</u>

i. INTRO - state general rule - Court needs PJ + notice + venue

- I. Personal Jurisdiction
  - A. Traditional bases (presence/domicile/consent/waiver)
  - B. Modern Basis - State general minimum contacts rule.
    - 1. Statutory authority: CA long arm/fed court will follow.
    - 2. Minimum Contacts:
      - C = Cause of Action - Nevada where balloon boarded.
      - A = Activity of D - no activities in CA.
      - P = Purposeful availment - bungee cord jumping is illegal - no benefits, protections available to JJ.
      - F = Foreseeability - by virtue of placing ad in Nev. NO
      - I = Initiate - Harry contacted JJ, not vice versa
      - B = Burden - equal burdens on H & N vs. Marco Polo
      - L = Choice of law - Nevada's law applies
      - I = Interest - CA's interest in regulating bungee cord jumping in Nevada?
      - M = Multiplicity - no - only 2 suits by Harry & Natasha
      - F = Forum - alternative forum in Nevada
      - E = Evidence - In Nevada
      - W = Witnesses - In Nevada, except for Harry & Natasha

Conclusion: No PJ!

MODEL ANSWER: <u>HARRY(H) AND NATASHA(N) VS. JUMPING JELLY BEANS BUNGEE CORD COMPANY (JJ)</u>

Before a federal court sitting in Los Angeles may properly hear this case, it must have personal jurisdiction over the parties. (TELL THE GRADER WHAT YOU ARE DOING IN YOUR ANALYSIS - ALSO TAKE IT FROM THE BIG PICTURE SO THAT YOUR ANALYSIS AND DIRECTION ARE CLEAR!)

PERSONAL JURISDICTION (USE HEADINGS WHERE APPROPRIATE)

There are two bases which a federal court sitting in California may assert in personam jurisdiction over Jumping Jelly Beans Bungee Cord Company, (hereinafter "JJ") - the traditional bases and the modern basis under <u>International Shoe</u>. (AGAIN THIS SENTENCE TAKES IT FROM THE BIG PICTURE AND LETS THE READER KNOW WHERE YOU ARE GOING)

A. Traditional Bases

A DETAILED ESSAY ON WHAT THE TRADITIONAL BASES ARE IS NOT NECESSARY - GET TO THE POINT BUT QUICKLY MENTION THE KEY PHRASES! NOTE THAT EACH ISSUE IS TAKEN ONE AT A TIME AND DISCUSSED; ALSO REMEMBER THAT THERE ARE ISSUES, AND THEN THERE ARE ISSUES – DISTINGUISH BETWEEN MAJOR AND MINOR ISSUES!

JJ was neither **present** in California at the time of personal service nor **domiciled** in California and there is likewise no indication that JJ ever **expressly consented** to jurisdiction, by voluntarily appearing to defend the suit in California or by agreeing in any contract between JJ and plaintiffs. However, it should be noted that JJ may **waive jurisdictional objections**, by filing a counterclaim or appearing in court to defend.

Therefore, no traditional bases of jurisdiction exist.

(ALWAYS REACH A CONCLUSION - DO NOT LEAVE YOUR ANALYSIS DANGLING IN MID-AIR LIKE HARRY AND NATASHA!)

B. Modern Basis

Under the modern basis, a defendant must have certain **minimum contacts** with the forum state such that maintenance of the suit does not offend traditional notions of fair play and substantial justice.

First, any **statutory authority** providing for jurisdiction must be considered. Because H and N have chosen to sue in federal court, the federal rules provide that absent a special federal statute, a federal court must handle personal jurisdiction as if it were a court of the state in which it sits. Therefore, California's statute would apply.

California's long-arm statute allows the assertion of jurisdiction on any basis not inconsistent with the federal constitution. Thus, the analysis turns on the federal standard of personal jurisdiction.

Under the minimum contacts test, jurisdiction would not be proper. The **cause of action** occurred in Nevada, where both H and N were suspended for seven hours due to the malfunction of the machinery. It was at this time that both H and N suffered the emotional distress and injury underlying the negligence and strict products liability actions. Thus, this factor weighs against a finding of jurisdiction.

JJ's **activities** in California appear negligible. Here JJ has absolutely no activities in California, aside from serving occasional California residents, presumably in Nevada.

If JJ engaged in systematic activities with the clients, by virtue of advertising or some other consistent business contact in California (e.g., through a travel agency or other business presence) then this factor would turn the tables in favor of jurisdiction. On the other hand, if these California clients traveled to Nevada for a bungee cord jumping ceremony as did H and S, this would weigh against finding of jurisdiction.

JJ did not **purposely avail** itself of the benefits or protections of the forum's law. Indeed, here California's law could offer no benefit or protection to JJ whatsoever because of the illegal status of bungee cord jumping.

Likewise, JJ could not **foresee** or expect to defend in California. By placing an ad in a Nevada magazine which is not distributed in California and is illegal under obscenity standards, JJ could be somewhat certain that the ad would not reach the eyes of California residents. Thus, JJ did not target a California audience for its advertising. H and N could argue that the geographic location of Nevada relative to California gives rise to the possibility that the magazine might reach California residents, but such an allegation would not meet the foreseeability test.

Finally, it cannot be said that JJ **initiated** any contact with California. Here H contacted JJ to arrange the bungee cord ceremony, not vice versa. This factor would weigh against jurisdiction.

Under the foregoing analysis, JJ has insufficient minimum contacts with California.

The second prong of the federal test is whether the court's assertion of jurisdiction would offend traditional notions of fair play and substantial justice.

The **burden** of the parties would not weigh in favor of either party. H and N would be inconvenienced if forced to sue in Nevada, but because they are both from different states (California and New York respectively) a suit in any forum would necessarily inconvenience one of the parties. On the other hand, JJ is not a huge conglomerate that could afford to defend anywhere. Rather, it is a sole proprietorship owned by Marco Polo and he would be burdened by defending in a foreign jurisdiction. It could be argued here that because Nevada is somewhat close to California, Polo would not be burdened by defending there.

As to the choice of **law**, it would appear that Nevada's law would apply to this law suit, since Nevada was the location of the bungee cord jumping.

The **interest** of the state would weigh in favor of jurisdiction. California law specifically prohibits bungee cord jumping due to safety hazards, and California has a strong interest in providing a forum for residence plaintiffs injured by such activity. However, that interest is sufficiently weakened by the fact that the activity occurred in Nevada. California does not have an interest in enforcing laws in other states.

Multiplicity of suits would not result here since there are only two plaintiffs of different forums suing a single defendant. It is possible that JJ may sue its supplier and manufacturer of machinery, but there are no facts about this entity.

As to the availability of an alternative **forum**, Nevada would seem to be a fair and convenient forum for the suit, as it is there that the cause of action giving rise to the lawsuit occurred. Again, any forum would be inconvenient for at least one of the plaintiffs since each is from a different state.

The bulk of **evidence** would be in Nevada (i.e., any business records of defendant and the condition of the machinery in question). There would be no evidence in California.

Likewise, all pertinent **witnesses** would be in Nevada since the incident occurred in Nevada. There would be no witnesses in California.

Based on the foregoing, fundamental fairness would be defeated if JJ were required to defend in a federal court sitting in Los Angeles.

C. Conclusion

Based on the balancing process in International Shoe, there are absolutely no minimum contacts between JJ and California, and the only factor in the "fair play and substantial justice" analysis in favor of jurisdiction is the interest of the state, which is remote at best. Therefore, the assertion of personal jurisdiction by a federal court in California would be improper.

* * *

Personal jurisdiction is but one of four major prerequisites to a law suit. Before a court may properly hear a case, it must have personal jurisdiction over the parties, subject matter jurisdiction over the cause of action and notice and venue requirements must be met.

Subject matter jurisdiction refers to jurisdiction over the type of cause of action before the court. For example, in state court, subject matter jurisdiction is defined by court practice and statute: some courts hear family law matters, while others hear probate matters and still others decide criminal cases.

In federal court, subject matter jurisdiction is met in one of two ways. First of all, if there is a **federal law question** embedded or contained in the cause of action, the federal court may hear the case. A federal question exists when the action arises out of the Federal Constitution or federal laws. If there is no **federal law question**, the federal court may still hear the case if the **diversity of citizenship** exists and the amount in controversy is more than $50,000. **Diversity of citizenship** exists when the domiciles of all plaintiffs differ from all defendants.

Thus, in examinations which test subject matter jurisdiction, you must determine whether either or both prongs of the subject matter jurisdiction "test" are met. Let's take an example:

Example #3: Subject Matter Jurisdiction

After the California federal court held that it did not have personal jurisdiction over Jumping Jelly Beans Bungee Cord Company (JJ), Harry and Natasha filed suit against JJ in federal court in Nevada. Does the court have subject matter jurisdiction over the action?

<u>Subject Matter Jurisdiction</u>

The issue is whether a federal court in Nevada has subject matter jurisdiction over the lawsuit between Harry and Natasha against JJ. If a federal question is embedded in the cause of action, a federal court may hear the action. Here Harry and Natasha have alleged causes of action for intentional infliction of emotional distress, negligence and strict products liability. Because none of these actions involve a question arising from federal laws, subject matter jurisdiction cannot be asserted on this basis.

A federal court may hear the action where diversity of citizenship exists, that is where the domiciles of all plaintiff differ from all defendants, and there is more than $50,000 in controversy. Both Natasha and Harry reside in New York and California respectively. JJ is incorporated in Delaware and its principal place of business is in New Mexico. Thus, JJ is a resident of both Delaware and New Mexico, both of which differ from the residences of both plaintiffs. Thus, jurisdiction may be asserted on this basis if more than $50,000 in damages are alleged.

* * *

In addition to subject matter jurisdiction, **pendent** or **supplemental jurisdiction** is used to join state claims with substantial federal claims, where both arise from the same event. Similarly, **ancillary jurisdiction** allows the court to hear ancillary matters, such as state law counterclaims, if the federal claim is substantial and the federal and state claims arise from the same transaction or occurrence. Both **pendent** and **ancillary jurisdiction** are interchangeably referred to as **supplemental jurisdiction**. **"Removal"** is a procedure which gives the defendant the option of removing a case from state to federal court if there is a federal question involved, or if diversity jurisdiction existed at the time the action was filed, and personal jurisdiction is proper in the state court in which the action was brought. Each of the tests which accompany these jurisdictional rules is set forth in the Civil Procedure *Law Chart.* Let's examine a problem which raises ancillary and pendent jurisdiction issues:

Example #4: Ancillary and Pendent Jurisdiction

After Harry and Natasha filed their law suit in federal court in the state of Nevada, they added a cause of action for violation of federal safety laws, seeking an injunction against JJ's activities. A federal statute, recently passed, prohibits bungee cord jumping on federal property, and provides a $20,000 penalty to be paid to the state or individual suing the entity. JJ counterclaimed, suing Harry and Natasha for negligence and conversion, alleging that the bridal gown worn by Natasha caused damage to the machinery, resulting in a loss of business for the seven hours Harry and Natasha were suspended in air. Harry and Natasha countersued for an unrelated incident where JJ failed to return a deposit on a wheelchair, which Harry borrowed when he served a subpoena on JJ in Nevada. May the federal court hear JJ's counterclaims against Harry and Natasha, and Harry's claim against JJ for failing to return his deposit?

Model Answer:

Ancillary Jurisdiction

The issue is whether the federal court in Nevada may hear JJ's counterclaim for property damage and loss of business caused by Natasha and Harry. If the court has jurisdiction over the principal claim, it can hear ancillary matters, such as counterclaims, if the federal claim is substantial and the federal and state claims arise from the same transaction or occurrence. First, the federal claim is substantial, since the statute specifically provides for the maintenance of a law suit by an individual in order to enforce the federal law. Secondly, the counterclaims alleged property damage arising out of the same transaction and occurrence as the principal action involving the incident on January 1. Therefore, the court may hear JJ's counterclaim.

Pendent Jurisdiction

The issue is whether the court may hear Harry's claim against JJ for return of the deposit on the wheelchair. A state claim may be joined with a substantial federal claim if both claims derive from a common nucleus of operative fact. Here, the cause of action arose when Harry served a subpoena on JJ's business in Nevada, in an "unrelated" incident not involving the bungee cord jumping ceremony. The cause of action concerns the return of a deposit on a wheelchair, which has nothing to do with the subject matter of the initial cause of action or the defendant's counterclaim. Therefore, the court may not hear Harry's claim against JJ for the return of the deposit on the wheelchair.

* * *

In addition to personal jurisdiction and subject matter jurisdiction, **notice** and **venue** requirements must be met. Both "tests" are very straightforward and are set forth in the *Law Chart.* Remember to apply common sense in learning the law. What is notice? Notice of a pending law suit is like sending out an invitation to your birthday party. Obviously, you must notify your guests so they will appear; in the same manner a defendant must be notified of the pendency of a legal action against her. The concept of venue is basically one of convenience. For example, if there are six courts, all of which have subject matter and personal jurisdiction over a defendant, there still remains an issue as to which court should hear the case. The rules pertaining to venue assist the courts in determining the "venue" in which a particular case is properly tried.

The areas of personal jurisdiction, subject matter jurisdiction, venue and notice are the most popularly tested areas on first year civil procedure examinations.

JOINDER

The next testable area concerns joinder of parties. Joinder of parties refers to the numerous procedures available by which the court may join both parties and claims upon a proper showing. Parties may be joined in a lawsuit, and are generally classified as one of three types: permissive, necessary and indispensable parties. Each category, as set forth in your Civil Procedure *Law Chart*, has a checklist of factors which must be met before joinder is proper.

Claims may be joined by either a plaintiff or a defendant. A plaintiff may generally join all claims against a defendant, subject to a few exceptions, while a defendant must join all compulsory counterclaims and may join permissive counterclaims and cross-claims. A compulsory counterclaim is a claim by a defendant against a plaintiff which arises out of the same transaction or occurrence as the plaintiff's claim. Failure to join such a claim in a law suit bars that claim in future law suits. By contrast, a permissive counterclaim is a claim which may be brought and does not necessarily arise from the same incident as the plaintiff's claim. A cross-claim is where a defendant sues a co-defendant.

Problems involving joinder of defendants and joinder of claims are usually entwined with jurisdictional problems. For example, a question may involve multiple defendants which a plaintiff seeks to join, but joinder would destroy subject matter jurisdiction, as we will see in a later problem which follows. The issue is always, "May Party X be joined as a party to the action?" or "May Party X's claim be joined in A's law suit?" Remember that the same basic I-R-A-C structure should be applied in the same fashion you applied it in solving the personal jurisdiction problems discussed earlier.

Other joinder "tools" in the area of Civil Procedure include class actions, intervention, interpleader and impleader. For example, the procedure of interpleader allows an entity or individual who is facing adverse and overlapping claims to deposit its debt with the court under certain circumstances, and requires all plaintiffs to sue in that court. If the elements of interpleader are met, an insurance company facing 100 claims for $10,000 each, may deposit the defendant's policy limit, say $1,000,000, with the court. These issues are usually obvious when raised in an exam problem, since your professor must necessarily give you the facts giving rise to the necessity of joinder. For example, in testing your ability to analyze a class action problem, your professor must give you a fact pattern where numerous plaintiffs wish to sue one or more defendants.

PLEADINGS

Somewhat less testable in essay format is the law of pleadings. This is not to say that your professor will not test you on the rules of pleading. But because pleadings involve "absolute" black and white rules of procedure as opposed to gray areas, this area is usually better tested by multiple-choice format. For example, there are two types of pleadings, fact and notice. Fact pleading requires a statement setting forth the cause of action in ordinary and concise language, while notice pleadings require a short and plain statement of the claim, showing that the pleader is entitled to relief. The rule is that plain and simple, and much more amenable to being tested in a multiple choice format. Of course where there is a will, there is a way, and nothing is absolute. The point is that you must simply memorize each of the rules of pleadings, because either you know the rule or you don't.

The one great exception in pleadings in terms of being a "testable area" is the "Relation back doctrine," which holds that a complaint which is amended relates back to the date that the original complaint was filed, thereby curing any statute of limitations problem. Let's try an example:

Simon Slowpolk filed a complaint against Goober on January 1, 1997 for battery which was alleged to have occurred on that same date. On January 2, 1998, Simon added a cause of action for assault. The statute of limitations for assault is one year.

<u>Simon v. Goober</u>

The issue is whether Simon's cause of action for assault is barred by the Statute of Limitations. The statute of limitations generally provides certain time limits by which an action must be filed. A tort action for assault must be filed within one year of its occurrence. Because the assault charge was added to the amended complaint on January 2, 1998, more than one year after its occurrence, it would be barred by the statute of limitations. However, if the assault action arose out of the same transaction or occurrence as the battery action, which was the subject of the amended complaint, the date of the filing of the assault action would relate back to the date of the original complaint. Thus, the statute of limitations would not bar Simon's cause of action for assault.

* * *

While this problem is perhaps the simplest example of an exam problem involving a "relation back doctrine" issue, again it reinforces the use of the basic I-R-A-C structure in articulating the exam answer.

RIGHT TO A JURY TRIAL

Probably the second most popular area tested in first essay examinations is the right to jury trial. The test which determines whether a plaintiff is entitled to a jury trial involves a lengthy and complex analysis. While your professor may state this test in varying order, in essence, the following issues must be addressed.

First, you must determine what the particular causes of action are and whether the case is being brought in state or federal court. The answer to the latter inquiry will determine whether the Seventh Amendment of the United States Constitution, which provides for a jury trial, applies, since the Amendment does not apply to the state courts. If the Seventh Amendment applies, (or if the State Constitution has a similar right to jury trial provision), then you must look back in time and determine if there was a right to a jury trial on the particular cause of action in 1791, the "relation back" date for the Federal Constitution.

If there was no cause of action similar to the cause of action you are analyzing back in 1791, then you may analogize the cause of action to a similar cause of action which existed in 1791. For example, in 1791, no cause of action for "sex discrimination" existed; however, an analogy might be drawn between intentional infliction of emotional distress, which did exist in 1791, and sex discrimination. Another indicator of a right to jury trial is the remedy sought by the cause of action, since money damages generally called for a jury trial, while specific performance and other equitable remedies did not. Still another factor considered by courts is whether the "gist" of the cause of action was legal or equitable; again, because equitable causes of action were traditionally decided by a judge, not a jury, if the gist of the cause of action were equitable, there was no right to a jury trial. Finally, the courts apply common sense and consider the practical abilities and limitations of the jury. For example, a jury trial might be inappropriate where extremely complex issues or evidence was involved.

Also, a corollary issue is when there are both legal and equitable issues, which issues should be decided first? As a general rule, the judge should hear the legal claims first, unless the party asserting the equitable claims would be irreparably harmed.

Sounds like a mix between "Back to the Future" and "Jeopardy?" You bet. But once you apply the test a few times, you will see that it is no different from any other legal analysis, with the old help of your friend, I-R-A-C to the rescue.

BAR EXAM EXAMPLES

Now let's wrap up Civil Procedure with a real horror show problem, again taken from the California Bar Examination, involving multiple issues of personal jurisdiction, joinder, subject matter jurisdiction and a demand for a jury trial. This problem will illustrate how to use the facts in solving a rather mammoth type of exam problem involving multiple, issues:

Round #1: Pete v. Devco

Pete, a resident of State A, saw an advertisement in a newspaper published in adjoining State B. It described a new chemical process just developed by Devco, a State C corporation, with its principal office in State C. The advertisement claimed that the new process would revolutionize the industrial dye industry and urged readers to purchase stock in Devco. Pete wrote Devco requesting more information about the new process. Devco sent Pete promotional brochures which directed persons interested in buying Devco stock to consult Bull, a stockbroker.

Bull is a State A resident, but his brokerage office is in State B. Most of Bull's business has been selling Devco stock, for which Devco has paid him a commission. Devco did no business in either State A or State B. Pete purchased 20,000 shares of Devco stock through Bull. Pete is the only Devco shareholder residing in State A.

Shortly after Pete purchased his stock, it was found that the new chemical process developed by Devco had no commercial value. As a result, the value of Pete's Devco stock declined.

Pete sued Devco in United States District Court in State A, alleging jurisdiction based on diversity of citizenship. The complaint purported to state a claim for relief based solely on common law fraud and contained a demand for a jury trial.

Devco then moved for dismissal of the complaint on the ground that the court lacked personal jurisdiction over it. Under State A law a court has jurisdiction over a foreign corporation only if the corporation is doing business in the state. The motion was denied, the district court holding that it had jurisdiction to the full extent permitted by the Fifth Amendment.

Devco moved to have Bull joined as a party defendant. The motion was granted.

Bull then moved to for dismissal of the action as to him on the ground that the district court in State A lacked subject matter jurisdiction. The motion was granted.

Devco answered the complaint and moved to strike Pete's demand for jury trial on the ground that factual issues in the case involved very complex scientific matters that were beyond the intellectual capabilities of the average juror, and therefore it had no adequate remedy at law. The district court struck Pete's jury trial demand and set the case for a nonjury trial.

1. Did the district court in State A have personal jurisdiction over Devco? Discuss.

2. Was the district court correct in ordering Bull joined as a party defendant? Discuss.

3. Did the district court in State A have subject matter jurisdiction over the action against Bull? Discuss.

4. Did the district court err in striking Pete's demand for a jury trial? Discuss.

Model Answer: Pete v. Devco

The issue is whether the district Court in State A had personal jurisdiction over Devco.

The first inquiry is whether any of the traditional bases of jurisdiction exist over Devco. However, because Devco is not domiciled in State A, has not been served in State A, has not expressly or impliedly consented to suit there or waived jurisdictional objections, no traditional bases of jurisdiction exist.

The second inquiry is whether there is any statutory authority for the assertion of jurisdiction. Under the Federal Rules of Civil Procedure, a federal court is to apply any jurisdictional statutes of the state in which it sits. Here, there is a state statute which provides that a court has jurisdiction over a foreign corporation, such as Devco, only if the corporation is "doing business in the state." Because Devco does no business in

State A, the statute would appear to prohibit jurisdiction over Devco. Because the statute would be applied by a federal court sitting in State A, the federal court would be without jurisdiction under this statute.

Pete would argue that Devco "did business" in the state by selling him 20,000 shares of stock and that this single transaction qualifies as "doing business" within the meaning of the statute. However, because Devco did no other business in State A, and Pete transacted with Bull, not Devco, Pete will not prevail on this issue.

Assuming that the court applies the state statute, the remaining issue is whether the federal court's assertion of personal jurisdiction over Devco would comport with the Fifth Amendment due process minimum contacts test. Under this inquiry, a defendant must have certain minimum contacts with the forum state such that maintenance of the suit does not offend traditional notions of fair play and substantial justice.

First, the cause of action arose in State A, where Pete read the representations made by Devco in the newspaper advertisement. Thus, this factor weighs in favor of jurisdiction in State A. However, Devco did no business in the forum state, and only sent its advertising brochures to State A on only one occasion. Thus, its activities were not systematic, and it had no contact with State A, except for this one occasion. Neither can it be said that Devco purposefully availed itself of benefits and protections of State A, since it did no business there, and not had sold stock or collected revenues in State A. Prior to contracting with Pete through Bull, Devco had no customers in State A. Hence, it received no benefits or protections in State A. On the other hand, Pete could argue that by virtue of its dealings with Pete on this one occasion, Devco availed itself of State A's securities laws and benefitted by transacting with a State A resident. Further, Bull acted as Devco's agent, and the sale of stock, while consummated in State B by Bull directly benefitted Devco. However, Devco will prevail on this issue, since Pete is Devco's only customer in State A.

The issue of foreseeability must be resolved in favor of Pete. Here Devco knowingly sent promotional brochures to a State A resident, and directed Pete to Bull, an agent and stockbroker of Devco. Devco should have known that it could be required to defend in State A if sued by a State A resident with whom it transacted. Devco could argue that the placing of the advertisement was insufficient to cause it to foresee a lawsuit in State A, since the ad was placed in State B. However, once Devco sent its promotional brochures to Pete, in State A it was extremely foreseeable that Devco might be sued there.

It was Pete who initiated contact with Devco and requested more information. Devco placed the ad in a newspaper in State B and not State A and therefore did not initiate contact with Pete.

The burden of the parties favors suit in State A. Devco probably faces less of an economic burden than Pete if required to defend in a foreign state, since Devco is a corporation and Pete is an individual. As to choice of law, State A's law of fraud will be applied because the cause of action occurred there. Thus, this factor weighs in favor of jurisdiction.

As for the state's interest, State A has a strong interest in preventing the fraudulent sale of stock to its residents, and in providing its residents with a forum to resolve such disputes. Multiplicity of suits is not a concern here, since there is no indication that other parties are contemplating suit against Devco on similar grounds. However, if Pete is allowed to sue Devco in State A, he may have to sue Bull in separate law suit, since diversity would be destroyed, and thus two lawsuits would result. This fact should not, however, be determinative because Devco may not be subject to a court's jurisdiction in State B, the same problem would necessarily result if Pete sues Devco and Bull in State B. The evidence and witnesses would probably be spread throughout State A, B and C. State B would contain evidence as to Devco's advertisement, which was placed in a State B newspaper, and any of Bull's business documents, since his office is there. All of Devco's business records and files would be found in State C. Again, because the cause of action, i.e., the reading of the ad, occurred in State A, some evidence and witnesses may be found there.

In conclusion, weighing each factor carefully, Devco should not be required to defend in State A. While the minimum contacts issue is a close one since Devco could have foreseen being sued in State A, Devco did no business there except for this one isolated transaction with Pete, which Pete himself initiated, based on an ad placed in State B's newspaper. Devco sought to do no business there and only directed Pete to transact with Bull. Thus, while the issue is an extremely close one, Devco should prevail. Weighing the fair play and substantial justice factors, again Devco should prevail, since the respective burdens on the parties are not such that Pete's ability to sue in State C would be unduly hampered.

Thus, even if the district court sitting in State A does not apply the state statute prohibiting jurisdiction over Devco, under the Fifth Amendment due process analysis, it does not have personal jurisdiction over Devco.

* * *

WHEW!! As you are reading this example, you may be wondering whether it is possible to write so much in response to so little. This example illustrates more so than others the importance of using the facts. This model answer maximizes the use of every fact, however minute, and exploits every fact in its analysis. Every point of view is considered, and yet the analysis objectively evaluates each issue, reaching a conclusion on each issue, and balancing each issue to reach an overall conclusion.

This is how a lawyer would analyze a jurisdictional question in real life, and this is what you should strive for in developing your application skills.

Also note that the issue of personal jurisdiction over Devco is an extremely close one, and you could have easily concluded to the contrary. This illustrates the point made earlier – it is not the ultimate conclusion but the application that counts.

Now, onto the next issue!

2. Joinder of Bull as a Party Defendant

The next issue is whether the district court properly joined Bull as a party defendant. A necessary party is an available party whose joinder is desirable to enable the court to grant complete relief or would avoid the risk that a party would be impaired in its ability to protect its interest. A necessary party shall be joined if available. Here Bull would be a "necessary" party, since his presence in the law suit would allow the court to adjudge his liability for fraud along with Devco, if any, if Bull contributed to or made any of the representations which are the basis of Pete's suit for fraud.

However, Bull is not an available party, because his joinder in Pete's law suit would destroy diversity jurisdiction. Because Bull is a resident of State A, and Pete is also a resident of State A, diversity would no longer exist if Bull was joined, since the residence of all defendants would not differ from the residence of all plaintiffs. For this reason, the district court's joinder of Bull was improper.

3. Subject Matter Jurisdiction Over Bull

The issue is whether the district court in State A has subject matter jurisdiction over Bull. As explained above, Bull is a necessary party, and because ancillary jurisdiction does not extend to necessary parties, the court is without subject matter jurisdiction against Bull.

4. Pete's Demand for Jury Trial

The final issue is whether the district court properly struck Pete's demand for a jury trial. It did not.

Because Pete is seeking damages for fraud, it is likely that he desires a jury trial on the issue of liability and damages.

First, because the suit is being brought in federal court, the 7th Amendment applies and jury trials are favored. The 7th Amendment provides that in suits at common law, the right to jury trial shall be preserved. The next inquiry is whether there was a right to jury trial in 1791, the relation back date of the federal constitution. Common law fraud existed in 1791, and was decided by jury. Thus, under this analysis, Pete would have a right to a jury trial on this issue.

The second inquiry looks to the remedy of the cause of action in determining whether a jury trial should be granted. Here Pete is presumably seeking monetary damages for fraud, and because money is a legal remedy, this would also weigh in favor of a jury trial. On the other hand, if Pete was seeking cancellation, rescission, or another equitable remedy, then this would weigh in favor of a judge or court trial. However, this factor alone is not determinative.

The third inquiry is whether the gist of the issue is legal or equitable. Again, because the nature of a fraud action has been historically legal in nature, this would weigh in favor of a jury trial.

Thus, under all three inquiries above, a jury trial is favored.

The final inquiry, which Devco specifically addressed in its answer to Pete's complaint, is the practical abilities and limitations of the jury. If it is indeed true that Pete's cause of action involves "very complex scientific matters" which are "beyond the intellectual capabilities of the average juror" then perhaps this factor would support the district court's ruling, striking Pete's demand for a jury trial. However, it should be pointed out that today's juries are able, with the assistance of expert witnesses and the like, to handle extremely complex matters, and it is unlikely that the case involves issues so complicated that the average juror could not understand it. Pete's cause of action for fraud involves one issue: whether certain representations made by the defendants were true or not and whether plaintiff relied on the representations in purchasing Devco's stock. Unless Devco is able to substantiate its allegations, the district court should allow Pete's demand for a jury trial to stand.

* * *

Time for a double breather. If you've braved it this far, and can handle this problem, or are at least keeping up, you are riding the high waves, and will make mincemeat of your first year Civil Procedure final examination! But as they say, practice makes perfect, so let's do it again:

Round #2: <u>Byer v. Seler</u>

Seler, a citizen of State S, and Byer, a citizen of State B, met in State B and signed a written contract by which Seler agreed to sell Whiteacre, located in State W, to Byer. The contract as written provided that the purchase price of Whiteacre was $75,000. Seler returned to State S and sent Byer a deed conveying good title to Whiteacre.

Byer did not send Seler any money, but brought an action against Seler for reformation of the contract to correct an alleged error in the contract price. Byer alleged that the agreed price was $45,000 and that the $75,000 figure in the contract was a typographical error. The action was brought in a federal district court in State B. Subject matter jurisdiction was based on diversity. Personal jurisdiction over Seler was based on service of process under State B's long-arm statute.

Seler moved to dismiss the action, alleging lack of both personal and subject matter jurisdiction. The motion was denied.

Seler then filed an answer asserting that the written contract accurately stated the agreed price. In addition, he counterclaimed for the $75,000 purchase price set forth in the contract and demanded a jury trial. The motion was denied.

Did the court rule correctly on the motion to dismiss? Discuss.

Remember to carefully apply each of the *six steps of exam taking* before putting pen to paper. As you read and visualize each fact, make sure and SEE Seler and Byer as real people. Do not let cardboard names affect your ability to visualize the fact pattern!

As you can see from your first reading of the facts, Byer and Seler are enmeshed in a dispute over whether the contract states the agreed upon purchase price. Let's go for it:

Model Answer: Byer v. Seler

1. Seler's Motion to Dismiss

The issue is whether the court properly denied Seler's motion to dismiss for lack of personal and subject matter jurisdiction.

PERSONAL JURISDICTION

The first issue is whether the court had personal jurisdiction over Seler. Personal jurisdiction refers to the power of the court to subject a particular defendant to its decision.

Since this action was filed in federal court, the problem must be analyzed under federal procedural requirements.

Traditional Bases

The issue is whether any of the traditional bases of jurisdiction exist, since these bases create absolute personal jurisdiction in most cases. Seler is a citizen of State A, and is therefore not domiciled in the forum state. Here we are told that Seler was served in accordance with State B's long-arm statute, but not whether Seler was served in the State or elsewhere. Therefore, it cannot be assumed that Seler was present in the state at the time of personal service. Seler has not waived jurisdictional objections, and has not expressly or impliedly consented to jurisdiction. Therefore, based on the facts, none of the traditional bases are present.

Modern Basis

Under the modern basis, a defendant must have certain minimum contacts with the forum such that maintenance of the suit does not offend traditional notions of fair play and substantial justice.

The first inquiry is whether there is any statutory authority for the assertion of jurisdiction. Under the Federal Rules of Civil Procedure, a federal court must apply any jurisdiction statutes of the state in which it sits. Here State B has a long arm statute, which allows jurisdiction on any basis not inconsistent with the federal constitution. Because Seler was served in accordance with the statute, the service of process was authorized by State B's long arm statute.

The second inquiry is that the defendant must have sufficient minimum contacts with the forum state. Applying each of the minimum contact factors, the cause of action arose in State B, where the contract was executed. The "activity" involved was Seler's act of contracting in State B with a State B resident for the sale of land. Seler also purposefully availed itself of the benefits and protections of State B, since the contract was likely drafted in accordance with State B's laws, and both parties relied upon State B's laws in interpreting and enforcing the contractual provisions. Furthermore, by executing the contract in State B, it was foreseeable to Seler that it might be required to defend in State B in the event the contract was breached by either party. Finally, while it is unclear which party initiated contact, Seler voluntarily went to State B for the purpose of contracting with Byer. Taken together, Seler has sufficient minimum contact with the form state to justify a finding of jurisdiction.

The third inquiry is that the court's exercise of jurisdiction must not offend traditional notions of fair play and substantial justice. Here no unequal burdens upon Seler and Byer would result because both appear to be individuals of equal resources. State B's law would apply since the contract was executed there. State B has a strong interest in providing a forum for parties who contract in the state, and Byer is a State B resident. Multiple suits will not result if jurisdiction is exercised by a State B court, because only two parties, Seler and Byer, are involved. Lastly, all evidence and witnesses would presumably be in State B, where the contract was executed. Thus, these factors weigh in favor of jurisdiction in State B.

Based on the foregoing, the assertion of personal jurisdiction by the court in State B would be proper. Thus, the court properly denied Seler's motion to dismiss on this ground.

SUBJECT MATTER JURISDICTION

The second issue is whether the court had subject matter jurisdiction over Seler. Subject matter jurisdiction exists in federal court where a federal question is embedded in the cause of action, or where diversity jurisdiction exists. A contract action for reformation does not involve any issues arising under federal law, and thus, no federal question is presented.

However, because Seler is a citizen of State S and Byer is a citizen of State B, diversity of jurisdiction exists, because the domicile of all plaintiffs differs from that of all defendants. In addition to diversity, the amount in controversy must exceed $50,000. This element is not met because the amount in controversy is $30,000, the difference between the price appearing on the face of the contract and the amount Byer claims should have been written. Because this amount does not exceed $50,000, the jurisdictional amount is not satisfied.

Therefore, the court should have granted Seler's motion to dismiss for lack of subject matter jurisdiction.

How to Solve a Real Property Problem

Real property, in my opinion, is best tested in multiple choice format, simply because it involves a great deal of very specific, absolute rules, and because of its exact nature, is more susceptible of being tested in either a true-false or multiple choice format, as opposed to essay format.

However, regardless of the examination format, the method used to solve the problem remains the same. In each of the preceding essay examinations, the fact pattern was analyzed, following the *six steps of exam taking* and an answer articulated, using I-R-A-C. To answer a multiple choice problem, you follow the same problem-solving strategy, except that instead of articulating you answer in essay format, you need only indicate your ultimate conclusion by choosing the appropriate answer. In order to select the correct answer, you must still analyze the problem and understand the reasoning behind each possible answer.

Therefore, while "Property" is commonly tested in a multiple choice format, do not dismay, for the process of solving property problems will involve the same good old fashioned problem-solving analysis.

Identifying the Property Interest and its Characteristics

For all of its strange vocabulary and complex-sounding verbiage, property is really fairly simple and straightforward. The main issue in solving a property problem is, "WHAT IS IT?" Think of yourself as an extra-terrestrial who is visiting earth for the first time. Back on your planet, you were given a book listing the characteristics of all of the things you would see and experience on earth. However, you have never actually seen these items yourself. How would you know what you were observing? Simple. You look in your little E.T. guide. For example, under "Ice cream," it said "cold, sometimes colorful, ice like substance which humans often consume in large quantities for apparently pleasurable reasons, sometimes found inside an edible container known as a cone." When you visited earth, you would look for those described qualities in order to determine whether you were observing an ice cream cone.

Like the extra-terrestrial searching for an ice cream cone, you will be asked to determine, from a set of facts, what property interests may or may not exist. For example, a property problem might read as follows:

Property Example #1: CREATURE FEE-TURE:

Uncle Fester owns Munster's castle for the life of Dracula. What interest does Uncle Fester have in Munster's castle?

The issue is what property interest Uncle Fester holds in Munster's castle. You would determine Uncle Fester's interest by studying the characteristics of the land grant he holds. From the above statement, it can easily be determined that Uncle Fester owns Munster's castle only as long as Dracula lives. Thus, because Fester owns an estate measured by the life span of another, he owns a life estate pur autre vie in Munster's castle. A life estate pur autre vie is a life estate measured by the life of another.

Once you have identified the property interest held by a party, then it is necessary to state the effect of such ownership interest on the problem before you. The "effect" of a life estate is that Fester owns Munster's castle for Dracula's lifetime.

When Dracula dies, then Fester no longer owns Munster's castle.

Let's add a fact:

Uncle Fester owns Munster's castle for the life of Dracula. Upon Dracula's death, Wolfman holds a remainder in the castle.

The new party, Wolfman, has a remainder interest in Munster's castle. A remainder is a future interest created in one other than the grantor upon the end of a prior estate. Now this raises yet another issue. Is the remainder a vested remainder, a vested remainder subject to complete divestment, vested remainder subject to open or a contingent remainder? After reviewing your Property Law Chart, you would see that it is a vested remainder, a remainder to an ascertainable and existing person, which becomes possessory when the preceding estate, owned by Fester, comes to an end. Let's change the fact pattern slightly:

Uncle Fester owns Munster's castle for the life of Dracula. Upon Dracula's death, Wolfman holds a remainder in the castle as follows: "remainder to Wolfman, but if Wolfman dies hairless, then to Igor and his heirs."

Now Wolfman again has a remainder, but it is a vested remainder subject to complete divestment, or in other words, subject to being completely taken away upon the occurrence of a certain condition or circumstance. Thus, if Wolfman dies without any hair, i.e., "hairless" not "heirless," then Munster's castle goes to Igor and his heirs.

Note that in each of the above examples, we seek to define the property interest held by the parties, and then to state the effect of that ownership interest.

Let's continue on with our hairy example:

After Dracula's death, Wolfman moved into Munster's Castle, and decided to build a road so that he could go hunting for small rodents. He gave his next door neighbor, the Mummy, the right to use the road as a driveway, since the Mummy owned many vehicles. What interest does the Mummy have in Wolfman's road?

Here the Mummy would have an easement in Wolfman's road, that is the right to go onto Wolfman's road and use the road as a driveway. Mummy would be an "easement holder." Mummy's easement would be "appurtenant" since its use is attached to the use of the adjoining land owned by Mummy, and benefits Mummy's use and enjoyment of his land. Mummy's easement would also be defined as an "affirmative" easement, because it entitles Mummy to make affirmative use of Wolfman's road.

Mummy's land would be the dominant estate or dominant tenement, because it is her land which is benefitted by the easement. Wolfman's land would be the servient tenement, since it is his land which is burdened by Mummy's easement.

These are largely "labels" but remember that this is the language you must learn and know like the back of your hand. Let's complicate things a bit more by adding a few more creepy facts:

A few weeks after Wolfman gave Mummy the easement to use the driveway, Mummy began to hold local car races on Wolfman's road. Mummy charged admission to the road, and large crowds soon gathered. One day, during a race, one of the race car driver's, Phantom Oprah, crashed, destroying Wolfman's road. Who is responsible for the damage to the road, and may Wolfman strip Mummy of his racestrip?

This fact pattern raises the issue of the rights and duties of easement holders. As set forth in your Property *Law Chart*, certain rules determine what an easement holder can and cannot do:
(1) the easement holder may only use the easement for those activities reasonably contemplated at the creation of the easement;
(2) where the scope of the easement's use is not specified, a reasonable scope will be implied;
(3) while the scope of use may change with time, change from family use to commercial use overburdens the easement;
(4) the easement user has both the right and duty to make repairs on the easement, but cannot substantially change the nature of an easement in the name of repairs.
What do you do with these rules?

You KNOW what to do. Apply 'em!

The issue is whether Mummy is must pay for the damage to Wolfman's road. While Mummy clearly has an easement in Wolfman's road, her use of the easement is subject to certain rights and duties. First, an easement holder may only use the easement for those activities reasonably contemplated at the time of the creation of the easement. Here the parties contemplated only

that Mummy would use the driveway to park her many vehicles, not to race cars. A raceway is a far cry from a driveway. Thus, Mummy has abused the easement.

Secondly, while the scope of use may change with time, change from family use to commercial use overburdens the easement. Here again, the easement was granted for the parking of Mummy's vehicles, a family use, and instead Mummy used the easement for commercial purposes, charging the public admission to observe race car driving. Thus, because this commercial use by Mummy overburdened the easement, Wolfman may seek an injuction and damages against Mummy on this ground. Finally, Mummy would have an affirmative duty to repair the easement, and to refrain from future uses which would destroy or be incompatible with the use of the easement as a driveway.

Again, it's your old friend and ally I-R-A-C! Note how the I-R-A-C structure is again employed to give you a solid and concrete analysis of each of the rights and duties of easement holders. In the above example, each issue is taken individually and addressed one at a time.

Let's go on to add another set of facts to make things even more horrific, if that's possible:

Mummy sold her land to Frank N. Stine and included the easement in Wolfman's land as part of the land transaction. Wolfman refused to honor the easement, pointing to the written instrument which expressly provided that the easement was only for Mummy's use. Can Stine force Wolfman to do so?

In order to answer this question, we must turn to our Real Property *Law Chart* and ask, "Does the easement RUN WITH THE LAND?"

The issue is whether Mummy's easement to use the road on Wolfman's land runs with the land and can be enforced as against Wolfman by Mr. Stine. The first issue is whether the easement involves a benefit or a burden. Clearly, Stine's right to use Wolfman's road as a driveway is a benefit, because it enhances the value of Stine's land. The second issue is whether the interest touches and concerns the land. Here, because the use of extra parking space and an additional egress road increases the value and worth of Stine's land, the easement touches and concerns the land. The third issue is whether the original parties intended that the interest would run with the land and that successive owners would be bound by the interest. Here it is clear from the face of the written

instrument that Wolfman intended to grant an easement only to Mummy, not successive owners in the land, such as Stine. Therefore, because this element is not met, the easement does not run with the land, and Stine cannot force Wolfman to honor the easement.

Again, this is not an attempt to teach or preach the law, but instead is another example how you can use I-R-A-C to solve a property problem. Let's take the same problem, this time using a multiple-choice format:

A few weeks after Wolfman gave Mummy the easement to use the driveway, Mummy began to hold local car races on Wolfman's road. Mummy charged admission to the road, and large crowds soon gathered. One day, during a race, a race car driver, Phantom Oprah, crashed, destroying Wolfman's road.

Which result is the most correct:

(a) Wolfman must make all repairs on the road but can order Mummy to stop racing cars.

(b) Mummy can continue to race cars on the road but is liable for any damages to the road.

(c) Wolfman can enjoin Mummy's use of the road and can collect damages from Mummy for the damage to the road.

(d) Mummy can continue her commercial activities but must legally give Wolfman a share of the proceeds, since the road belongs to Wolfman.

(e) Phantom Oprah, not Wolfman, is liable for the damage to the road.

The above example is a typical "sneaky" multiple-choice question. Notice that the interrogatory asks only which answer is the <u>most</u> correct, not which answer is in fact correct. Thus, while one or all of the statements which follow may be correct or true statements, only the <u>most</u> correct statement is the acceptable answer. Let's analyze each of the four statements, using IRAC:

(A) The issue is whether Wolfman must make repairs on the road. This is not true because the easement holder, not the owner of the servient estate, must maintain and repair the easement. Because the easement holder has no duty to maintain the easement and Wolfman is the easement holder, he has no duty to repair. Therefore, this answer is incorrect.

(B) The issue is whether Mummy can continue to race cars on the road. While it is true that Mummy is liable for any costs of repair as the easement holder, she is abusing the easement by racing cars on Wolfman's road. Therefore, she cannot continue to race cars on the easement, since such use abuses the easement, and therefore terminates the easement. Therefore, the first portion of this answer is incorrect.

(C) The issue is whether Wolfman can seek an injunction against Mummy's use of the road. The rule is that an easement holder's right to the easement may be enjoined from abuse, either from uses outside those originally intended, or overburdening the easement by changing from family to commercial use. Here Mummy abused the easement, since it was intended to be used as a driveway, not a raceway, and she used the driveway for commercial purposes. Therefore, this statement is correct. The second issue is whether Wolfman may collect damages from Mummy for the damage to the road. The rule is that the easement holder has the duty to make repairs. Because Mummy damaged the road during her racing activities, she must pay for the damages to the road. Therefore, this statement is correct in its entirety.

(D) The issue is whether Mummy may continue her commercial activities. The rule is that commercial activities overburden an easement where the scope of the easement's use changes from family to commercial. Because Mummy is using the easement for commercial purposes, and its intended use was as a driveway for her residence, she is overburdening the easement. Therefore, this statement is false. As to whether Wolfman may compel Mummy to give him a share of the proceeds, there are insufficient facts to determine whether this is true. This answer is not correct.

(E) The issue is whether Oprah, not Wolfman, is liable for the damage to the road. While Oprah may very well be liable as a joint tortfeasor for the damage to Wolfman's road, it is clear that Wolfman, as an easement holder, is liable for the damage to the road since he has a duty to repair. Therefore, this statement is untrue.

Of course, no one in solving the above problem would actually go through the process of writing down each and every analysis in I-R-A-C format, but the above analysis illustrates the thought process which every law student should undergo in solving the problem. Just for the blood-curdling scream of it, let's do it again:

Mummy sold his land to Frank N. Stine and included the easement in Wolfman's land as part of the land transaction. Wolfman refused to honor the easement, pointing to the written instrument stating that the easement was only for Mummy's use. Can Stine force Wolfman to do so?

What answer is the most incorrect:

(a) Wolfman need not honor the easement, since there was no intent that Stine would be able to use the driveway.

(b) Because there was a written instrument stating Wolfman's intent to grant the easement to Mummy, Stine cannot use the land.

(c) Stine may use the road as a driveway, if the court determines that Wolfman intended the easement to run with the land.

(d) Because the easement was a benefit to Stine's land, it probably runs with the land.

(e) Because Stine's use of the roadway will increase the value of his land, the easement "touches and concerns" his property.

Before we get started, did you get zapped? If you did, you may not have noticed that the interrogatory asked, "What answer is the most incorrect?" This is a common sucker punch, so watch for it, and do not let it get you!

Use the I-R-A-C formula again to solve this problem:

(A) The issue is whether Wolfman could refuse to honor the easement because of the lack of intent that the easement run with the land. The rule is that the original parties must intend that the interest would run with the land and that successive owners would be bound by the interest. Here the instrument granting the easement specifically stated the easement was only for Mummy's use. Therefore, this statement is correct, as Wolfman may refuse to honor the easement because of the lack of intent that it run with the land as evidenced in the instrument.

(B) The issue is whether the instrument precludes Stine from using the land. This statement is awkward, since it is not the instrument which prohibits Stine from using the land. It is rather the contents of the instrument indicating lack of intent that the easement run with the land which determines that Stine is not entitled to the easement. However, this statement is generally true, since the intent in the document controls the alienability of the easement.

(C) The issue is whether Stine may use the road as a driveway, if the court determines that Wolfman intended the easement to run with the land. The rule is as stated above, that the parties must intend the easement to run. Should the court determine, contrary to Wolfman's instrument, that he and Mummy intended that the easement run, then Stine would be entitled to use the road as a driveway. Therefore, this statement is correct.

(D) The issue is whether the easement was a benefit to Stine's land and if so, whether it "probably" runs with the land. While it is true that the easement was a benefit, since it benefitted Stine's use of his land by providing a driveway, that fact does not necessarily mean that it "probably" runs with the land, since as stated above, the parties must still "intend" that the easement run with the land. Therefore, this statement is false.

(E) The issue is whether Stine's use of the roadway "touches and concerns" his property. The rule is that an interest touches and concerns the land when it affects the quality or value of the property. Because Stine's use of a driveway appurtenant to his property increases the value of his property, the easement is said to "touch and concern" his land. Therefore, this is a true statement.

As you can see, once again I-R-A-C is employed to win out against the forces of evil and uncertainty, even if those forces come to you in the shape of multiple-choice or short answer questions! And besides, using I-R-A-C sure beats flipping a coin!

The Rule Against Perpetuities

The Rule Against Perpetuities has been shrouded in a veil of confusion, fear and mystery. The Rule is simply a device used to weed out "funky" future interests which do not vest or mature within a given time period. An analysis of one such problem involving the Rule is offered to help demystify this elusive rule.

The Rule is one of four rules governing future interests. The other rules, which are set forth in your Law Charts, include the Doctrine of Merger, The Rule in Shelly's Case and the Doctrine of Worthier Title. The approach to the Rule involves two issues: (1) Is an executory interest or a contingent remainder at issue? (2) Will the interest be owned by an existing, ascertained person and not be subject to a condition precedent, within 21 years after some life in being? In determining the answer to the latter issue, you must look at when the instrument was created, figure out who is the life in being and add twenty-one years to the life in being. Then you ask: will this interest vest or fail?

Let's analyze a problem:

Homer devises his island to Madge for life, remainder to Lisa's children who attain the age of 25. Is this interest valid?

The issue is whether Homer's devise to Madge for life, "remainder to Lisa's children who attain the age of 25," is a valid interest. The Rule Against Perpetuities provides that an interest is void if there is any possibility that it may vest more than 21 years after some life in being at the creation of the interest.

First, the Rule applies only to executory interests and contingent remainders.

Assuming that Lisa is still alive and may still have children, Lisa's children have a contingent remainder, since the remainder is created in favor of an unborn ascertainable party (Lisa's children), and their interest is subject to a condition precedent (attaining the age of 25). Thus, the Rule applies.

The second issue is whether the interest violates the Rule. Assuming that the devise is effective upon Homer's death, the life in being would be Madge's. The issue is whether the interest would vest or fail within 21 years of Madge's death. Here the interest would violate the Rule, because Lisa could have a child after Madge's death, and that child's interest would not vest or fail until it reached the age of 25. Thus, the contingent remainder to Lisa's children is void.

You see, you need not be a rocket scientist to apply the Rule. Let's try another one:

Gomer conveys "to my grandchildren who attain the age of 21."

The issue is whether Gomer's conveyance "to my grandchildren who attain the age of 21," is a valid interest. The Rule Against Perpetuities provides that an interest is void if there is any possibility that it may vest more than 21 years after some life in being at the creation of the interest.

First, the Rule applies only to executory interests and contingent remainders. Because Gomer is conveying this interest during his life, he may still have children, and those unborn children would have a contingent remainder, since the remainder is created in favor of an unborn ascertainable party, and their interest is subject to a condition precedent (attaining the age of 21). Thus, the Rule applies.

The second issue is whether the interest violates the Rule. Because the conveyance is effective immediately, the life in being would be Gomer's. The issue is whether the interest would vest or fail within 21 years of Gomer's death. Here the interest would violate the Rule, because Gomer could have an unborn child at the time of the conveyancing, and that child's interest would not vest or fail until it reached the age of 21. Thus, the contingent remainder to Gomer's children is void.

If, after all the dust settles, you cannot understand the Rule Against Perpetuities, please do not jump off a bridge – you are in good company. Knowing this Rule is not a prerequisite to the pursuit of happiness. You will get it in the next life!

Landlord-Tenant

This area of property law generally involves the all too familiar tensions between the two entities known as landlord and tenant. The landlord rents his/her property to tenant. The tenant possesses the premises according to the terms of the lease. As with all property interests, you must first seek to determine what property interest each party holds. There are five categories of lease agreements, as set forth and described in your Real Property Law Chart: tenancy for years, periodic tenancy, tenancy at will, tenancy at sufferance, and where there is no lease agreement.

Both the landlord and tenant have respective rights and responsibilities. The tenant has the duty to pay rent and avoid waste or property damage but may raise certain defenses, such as where the landlord fails to keep the building up to code. The landlord has the right to eject tenant for failure to pay rent. As you can tell, this area of real property is ripe with testable issues.

Let's take an example involving a lease agreement the tenant's failure to pay rent and any defenses he may assert against landlord:

Abner decided to rent one of Landie's apartments and signed a lease agreeing to pay $50 per month. After moving in, Abner learned that the apartment had no running water due to damaged plumbing. Abner complained to the housing authorities, but Landie did nothing to fix the plumbing. Abner refused to pay rent, since it cost him $75 to fix the plumbing. Landie sued Abner for failure to pay rent. What result?

Model Answer: <u>Landie v. Abner</u>

Abner would have a periodic tenancy in Landie's apartment. A periodic tenancy is an estate for a year or lesser stated period which automatically renews itself at the end of the stated period. Here Abner signed a lease which provided for a payment of $50 "per month." This lease would be construed as a month to month lease, since it requires the monthly payment of rent and automatically renews itself at the end of each month.

Under the periodic tenancy, Abner had the duty to pay rent, and thus is in breach of the lease agreement for failing to pay rent. Landie is within his rights in attempting to evict Abner for non-payment of rent.

However, Abner may assert that Landie breached the implied covenant of habitability. In every residential lease, there is a covenant of habitability, which requires that the leased premises be fit for living purposes. If the landlord breaches this covenant, the tenant may withhold rent. Because water is a basic human necessity of humane living conditions, Landie had a duty to maintain running water in the premises. Because he failed to maintain the plumbing, Landie has breached this covenant, and Abner can remain on the premises and withhold rent until the plumbing is fixed. In most states, Abner can withhold rent and use the rent money to effectuate repairs.

Landie cannot, however, attempt to evict Abner because Abner reported Landie to the housing authorities. The defense of retaliatory eviction provides that the landlord may not retaliate against a tenant who informs authorities of the landlord's wrongdoing. In many states, there is a presumption that an attempted eviction within a short period of the reported violation is improperly motivated. Here, Landie will face allegations of retaliatory eviction, since he is attempting to evict Abner shortly after Abner reported Landie to the authorities.

This analysis begins by stating the relationship between Landie and Abner, the nature of their lease agreement, and the rights which flow from their respective roles as landlord and tenant. We then examine Abner's rights as against Landie, and then Landie's rights against Abner. Once again, the basic I-R-A-C structure is employed to articulate a well-reasoned analysis of each issue.

Next, let's review a problem involving the tenant's duty to maintain the leasehold:

<u>Landie v. Mimi Millionaire</u>

After Abner moved out of Landie's apartment, Mimi Millionaire moved in, signing a six month lease, but paying only the first month's rent. Mimi began building a new swimming pool in the backyard without Landie's knowledge, and while digging the pool, Mimi discovered a valuable chest of gold nuggets, which she sold for millions. Mimi abandoned the apartment after one month and left the windows and doors open. Due to heavy rains, the carpets in the apartment were ruined.

Model Answer: <u>Landie v. Mimi Millionaire</u>

The issue is whether Mimi has committed waste of the premises. A tenant has the duty not to commit waste. A tenant commits amelioratory waste when she substantially alters the lease premises. Here, the construction of the swimming pool in the back yard is a substantial alteration of the leasehold and, therefore, Mimi is liable for any damages caused by her activity.

The next issue is whether Mimi committed waste by removing the valuable chest of gold nuggets from Landie's land. A tenant commits affirmative or voluntary waste by exploiting natural resources and minerals on the leasehold. A chest of valuables would be analogous to minerals contained in the ground, and therefore Mimi committed waste by removing the chest and keeping the contents. Here Mimi, as a tenant, had no right to remove the chest from the grounds, and in the absence of proof of superior title, the chest belonged to Landie, since he owned the leasehold and, presumably, the mineral rights.

The final issue is whether Mimi committed waste by allowing the carpets to be damaged. Permissive waste occurs where the tenant's omission to act causes damages to the premises. Here Mimi left the windows and doors open, allowing heavy rains to cause damage to the carpets in the apartment. Therefore, Mimi is liable for any damage to the carpets.

An additional issue is raised by Mimi's **abandonment** of the leasehold. Recall that Mimi signed a six-month lease, and yet she abandoned the premises after one month:

The issue is whether Mimi remains liable for rent after she abandoned the apartment. If the tenant abandons the premises, the landlord has no duty to mitigate damages and may still collect rent for the lease period. Because Mimi signed a six-month lease, she remains liable for the rent for the additional five-month period under the lease, even though she is no longer residing in the apartment.

Again observe how the basic I-R-A-C structure produces a comprehensive, well-organized analysis. In each area analyzed above, review the approach contained in your Real Property Law Chart, and carefully study the application of that approach to the exam problem.

Rights in Land

Exam questions involving rights to land will hit you right between the eyes, since the examiner must give you a fact pattern where two neighbors are fighting over a common wall, or the right to lateral and subjacent support of land, or rights to water. Let's look at a problem involving both lateral and subjacent support of land:

Queenie v. Blaster

Blaster constructed a huge oil pump on the edge of his property. The operation of the oil pump caused Queenie's house on the adjacent lot to sink one foot into the ground and has caused small landslides onto Queenie's land.

The issue is whether Queenie may sue Blaster for violation of her property rights. Ownership of land carries with it the absolute right to have land supported in its natural state by adjoining land (lateral support) as well as the right to underground or subjacent support. Because the operation of the oil pump has caused small landslides on Queenie's land, Queenie may sue for disturbing her right to lateral support. Queenie may also sue for interference with her right to subjacent support, since the operation of the pump has caused her home to sink one foot into the ground.

As you can see, these issues stick out like a glass of ice tea on Mars and can't be missed!

Adverse Possession

The subject of adverse possession is a favorite of law school professors, although it is rarely the subject of real life litigation. This doctrine allows acquisition of real property where one adversely possesses the land of another for a certain time period, usually five, ten or twenty years, depending on state law. As you might guess, most people nowadays are not fond of others occupying their land and do not take kindly to trespassers, not to mention the fact that it is quite difficult to occupy another's land for years without their knowledge and consent. However, adverse possession still appears on law school examinations throughout the country, because, as you might have guessed, it's a great area to test students on.

As set forth in your Real Property Law Chart, each of the "HA NO ACE" elements must be present, and tacking and tolling concerns must be considered. Let's try one on for size:

EXAMPLE: GILLIGAN'S HOUSE

Gilligan decided to build a home for him and his wife Ginger. He built his home on land belonging to Mr. and Ms. Howell after securing Mr. Howell's permission. Two years later, Gilligan ran off with Mary-Ann, leaving Ginger, who immediately married Skipper. When Mr. Howell learned that Skipper, not Gilligan, was living in the house on his property with Ginger, he told them to vacate the premises immediately. However, Mr. and Ms. Howell were shipwrecked on a desert isle for three years. When Mr. Howell returned, he found Skipper and Ginger living in the house and ejected them. However, the Professor moved in the next day and lived there without Howell's consent for two years. Professor sued Howell for the land on an adverse possession theory. The statutory adverse possession period is five years. What result?

Model Answer:

The issue is whether Professor acquired the land which he occupied through adverse possession. In order to acquire land through adverse possession, the party must adversely possess the land for the required statutory period. Such possession must be hostile, adverse, notorious, open, actual, continuous and exclusive.

Here, the statutory period is five years. While Professor only occupied the house and land for two years, he may tack on to his own possession the periods of adverse possession of his predecessors, Skipper and Ginger.

During the entire five year period, both Professor and Skipper and Ginger occupied the land with Mr. Howell's knowledge, but without his consent. Since the Howells lived next door, the Howells were aware that the land was being occupied without their consent, at least during the time period they were living next door. Both Skipper's and Professor's possession was hostile, since Howell had told Skipper to vacate the premises immediately, and yet one day later, the Professor moved in without Howell's consent. Neither the Professor or Skipper made any attempt to hide the fact of possession or occupancy, and their possession was therefore open. Both Skipper and the Professor occupied the land continuously for their respective time periods, and exclusively, as no one else lived there, other than Ginger, who was also occupying the premises without Howell's consent, at least after Gilligan left. Their possession was actual, as all parties actually lived at the premises, and adverse, being in derogation of Howell's rights to the land. Thus, because all the elements of adverse possession are met, Professor may prevail.

However, the statute of limitations does not begin to run if the true owner is operating under some disability to sue when the cause of action is first accrued. Here, being shipwrecked on a desert island would likely qualify as a disability, operating to toll the statute of limitations for three years. If the court so found, then the Professor would not prevail, because the statutory time period has not yet expired.

* * *

Of course there are many other Real Property issues you could see on an essay examination. While this section provides you with some examples of successful I-R-A-C exam answers, the key is to use this same I-R-A-C structure and Problem-solving Approach to solve each issue. In this way you will write your way to a winning score on your Real Property examination!

Preparing For Midterms & Final Examinations

Part V

Law School According to Garth

Ten Major Downfalls of Final Examinations

How to Memorize the Law

A Question of Time

Developing a Study Schedule

A Final Word

Law School According to Garth

As a writer and grader of exams, I have traveled down the weary road of exam grading more times than I care to remember. In fact, I am writing this section of the book within hours of grading nearly 100 first year examinations, the grading of which will determine whether this group of students will graduate onto their next year of legal studies.

Put yourself in the shoes of your professor. Reading 100 or more exam answers is not a particularly exciting task, even for the sadistic grader or most sympathetic humanitarian. It gets down right nitty gritty at times, even when one grades examinations during television commercials or while enjoying a good bag of ***Doritos*** (although you have to make sure the cheese does not wind up on the exam booklets). Yes, believe it or not, human beings grade law school essay examinations, and they grade those examinations under human conditions.

I am not suggesting that your professor will not take the grading of your final examination with the utmost seriousness. In fact, it is quite likely that your professor will be dead serious when he or she is reading your examination. The point here is that you do everything possible to make the grading of your examination as easy on your professor's mind and eyes as possible. You have absolutely no control over when your examination will be read, or your professor's mood when he or she is reading your paper. However, you do have control over what you write on those pieces of paper.

What follows are universal and sometimes humorous pet peeves about law school exam answers, written by Professor Garth Grader one of the world's toughest law school exam graders. These observations are offered not as critical whinings of a burnt-out exam grader, but instead a laundry list of potential downfalls for you to avoid in your exam writing. Heed Garth's warnings!

The Ten Major Downfalls of Final Examinations by Garth Grader

All right, dudes and duddettes, get ready for Garth's list of major downers on law schoolers examinations:

1. AVOID THE ENDLESS PARAGRAPH: One of the greatest law school traditions is the endless paragraph, which goes on and on, ad infinitum, and you know, it keeps going on like a bad dream, and just when you think it's going to end, it goes on a little more, and then a little more, and then there's a light at the end of the tunnel, and you think the paragraph might end, but as you turn page after page, you realize that you have encountered the awesome, bold, wild, crazy, extreme

PARAGRAPH WITHOUT AN END, and you realize that once you've begun reading that paragraph, there's no way on earth that you can stop reading it, and you find yourself reading word after word, without end, and soon learn that you have no choice but to continue reading the paragraph forever, into oblivion . . .

Says Garth: "I never saw a paragraph I didn't like."

Garth's favorite paragraph story: "Although if you took that one paragraph that the fella from law school wrote in them stack of blue books and put the sentences back to back, it would've reached to Mars and back . . ."

But Garth says four to seven sentences per paragraph is about right.

2. DO NOT REPEAT YOURSELF. I REPEAT, DO NOT REPEAT YOURSELF: Who enjoys a broken record or sitting through the same awful movie twice? Not Garth, unless Garth is singing or Garth is in the movie. Yet many law students, feels it is necessary to repeat the same phrase, again, again and again. One such mutron wrote "the facts state" 30 times on the examination. Another buttron wrote "Assuming, arguendo" 25 times, while another wrote "on the other hand," 14 times!

3. IF IT FEELS GOOD, UNDERLINE!

Yes, it's true that sometimes underlining a word can help to emphasize it and make it feel more important. So the next time you feel down and out, underline yourself, but please, on your exam, don't underline each and every word you have written. It's definitely bad news, since most graders don't have swivels attached to their necks, which jerk back and forth in a vain attempt to understand and appreciate the ultimate significance of each underlined bit of wisdom.

4. DON'T ABBREVIATE EVERY OTHER WORD

How do you abbreviate the word "the" or the proposition "to"? If you don't know, I know a couple of law students I could direct you to. Yes, these students abbreviated every other word on their examinations. A typical sentence looked like this: "D acted w/o malic. afore. and there. is n/g of 1st murd." While this is a great example of shorthand, not being as gifted and skilled in the art of the abbreviation, I made sure that he received abbreviated scores.

5. GARTH SAYETH: DON'T MISPELLETH ON THE EXAMETH!

For legal writers, a misspelling is like a fly in your soup. On an important legal brief in real life, a horrible misspelling could cost you your job, or at least add a tight grimace on your boss's face. (And you wouldn't want that, would you?) On a law school examination, it could secretly cost you a few points, even though your spelling ability or lack thereof has nothing to do with your vast knowledge of the law. In Garth's secret fantasy, it is I, Garth, who pulls the Gestalt lever along with the law school professors, to send up a few volts of electric shock for every misspelled word. So let's pull those levers.

6. DON'T CITE UNLESS YOU'RE RIGHT

Old Garth proverb: "Always cite the case of Johnson v. Smith after each sentence on law school examination." Rationale? There's always someone named Johnson who sued someone named Smith for something related to whatever you're saying. If you get caught, then cite George v. Sue. Getting caught citing the wrong case is worse than walking up to someone on the street that you think you recognize, calling to him or her by name, tapping him or her on the shoulder, and realizing that you've never seen him or her before in your life.

Listen to Garth: Don't be a Goober!

7. HOW TO CAUSE GRADER WHIPLASH

WARNING: A dangerous hazard to the health and chiropractic well being of exam graders was recently determined to be the cause of grader whiplash, causing sharp neck pains, headaches, loss of vision and in a small percentage of graders, temporary insanity. This phenomenon was determined by medical authorities to be caused by reading law school examination insertions and deletions. Graders are warned to beware of numerous arrows, pointing to various portions of exam analysis apparently left out by exam writers.
Garth's special hint: Use this technique when you want to get back at your Professor for calling on you in class on your birthday.

8. DON'T BE SQUISHY-SQUASHY

Well, maybe, perhaps you can't help being a little wishy-washy about your statements, as you're probably not real sure about what the conclusion might be, and you sure wouldn't want to be wrong about anything, would you? As Garth says at the race tracks, you can't hedge all your bets. Nothing drives Garth more bonkers than one of these answers that says "probably" this, "probably" that. Make a commitment!

Take a stand! Join with Garth and a greater number of citizens who have decided to take a stand and make a difference! "We are the world, we are the lawyers . . ."

9. DON'T MESSY WITH MY ESSAY

An essay examination means exactly that -- essay format. Not knee bone connected to the thigh bone, thigh bone connected to the fibia, etc. Yet many law students submit what looks like a skeleton outline of an exam answer in lieu of the real thing. It's like buying a fried rat at the fried chicken diner and taking a bite and realizing that it really isn't chicken.

10. WRITE AS IF THOU IS HUMAN

The final word of advice from Sir Garth: Garth hath seen evidence that primates can reason. Some of the examinations I have seen are so poorly written that they must have been written by another form of life unknown to humankind! Could it be conclusive proof of the existence of the Loch Ness Monster, or perhaps the Abominable Snowperson? The handwriting is clearly that of a being with at least one appendage with the ability to write up and down characters, but the characters are clearly out of this world! Is there a new race of alien life who live among us, who look, breathe and eat like us, but write using strange, undecipherable characters?

Until we meet again, Garth Sayeth: WRITE ON, BROTHERS AND SISTERS!

How to Memorize the Law

After you have read the cases, distilled the black letter law, diligently listened to your Professor's lectures, drafted your precious outlines, formulated your own problem-solving approaches and adopted the *Law Charts* in this book, and taken practice examinations, you might wearily ask, "Is there yet another task which awaits me?"

That final task involves memorizing the law for examination purposes. Unless you are fortunate enough to have an instructor who allows open book examinations, you will be required to memorize the law, which means memorizing the law charts.

Unlike the bar examination, while in law school, you are afforded the luxury of knowing what subject you are being tested on. Rather than facing a battery of possible exam subjects, your law school subjects will greet you one at a time. This will allow you to focus on each subject individually, rather than attempting to memorize all subjects at once.

You will be relieved to know that in real life, a lawyer is not required to "memorize" every bit of law necessary to the practice of law. While having a good memory does not hurt, most lawyers rely on law books and good research skills rather than a good memory, as it is quite impossible to memorize the great mass of law, which is impermanent and changing.

Most of us who were born without the benefit of a photographic memory memorize details by reference to generalities. For example, you might remember what a room in a house looks like by remembering the house. By visualizing the house, you are able to recall what a particular room in the house looks like. By remembering what the room looked like, you are able to remember the color of the carpet and type of furniture in the room. Using generalities as a point of reference, we are better able to recall specifics.

Memorizing the law is analogous to the process of opening doors. Think of a house you are familiar with. Take yourself on a visual tour of that house. As you open each door, you will find that you are able to remember in great detail what items are inside the room. What follows is an application of this simple principle and basic memory techniques:

Visualize a huge castle. This is the castle of Torts. After walking over the drawbridge, above the Scottish loch, you are confronted by seven huge wooden doors. The six doors read, "Intentional Torts", "Negligence", "Strict Liability", "Products Liability", "Defamation", "Miscellaneous Torts."

You approach the first door and see the words "Intentional Torts" written upon it. You open that door with a mighty push, enter a corridor and see seven doors. Each door which aligns the corridor is labeled respectively "Battery", "Assault", "False Imprisonment", "Intentional Infliction of Emotional Distress", "Trespass to Land", "Trespass to Chattels", and "Conversion."

You walk up to the first door labeled "Battery." You open the door and find yourself staring at a strange computer that reads: Battery - (1) affirmative act; (2) with the intent to touch another; (3) resulting in harmful or offensive contact." A different color button aligns each element of battery. On impulse, you push the (2) button, and suddenly you see before you the words "ACTUAL INTENT" OR "SUBSTANTIALLY CERTAIN THAT CONTACT MUST OCCUR. CHOOSE ONE OR BOTH." You press the latter button, and before you appears the case of Garratt v. Dailey, which you learned in class. You immediately recall the tiny tot Brian Dailey who pulled the chair out from under Ruth Garratt and forever established the rule of "substantial certainty." Your recollection of that case causes you to recall the concept you gleaned from that case: that the intent requirement of a battery was met if the defendant, by his act, should have been substantially certain that contact would occur to plaintiff.

Just for the heck of it, you press button (3) and are confronted with yet another choice, "ACTUAL CONTACT AND HARMFUL OR OFFENSIVE TO THE REASONABLE PERSON . . . CHOOSE ON." You select "actual contact" and immediately think of Fisher v. Carrousel, in which a patron at a cafeteria that discriminated against blacks pulled a plate out of the plaintiff's hand. The rule of law arising from that case suddenly comes into your mind. You immediately recall that battery requires "actual contact or contact with something closely connected to plaintiff's person."

This strange exercise illustrates the process of memorizing the law. You need not memorize each and every detail. What you need to memorize is the process involved in opening those doors so you will have the law at your fingertips in the exam room. You do not want to be sitting there, as each valuable minute ticks away, trying to remember what the definition of "battery" is.

In order to memorize the Intentional Torts for exam purposes, you must begin by developing a problem-solving approach that organizes the law of battery into a simple, easy to apply checklist of elements. Instead of memorizing your entire approach, you should memorize key phrases and definitions. While every person's capacity for memorizing details will vary, almost everyone can memorize the seven intentional torts. You may memorize the names of each of these intentional torts by repetition, much in the same way you memorized the seven days of the week.

If that proves confusing or difficult, you could follow the memory approach recommended in the Torts *Law Chart.* If you review your Torts *Law Chart,* you will see a cartoon character next to the mnemonic "BAF IT TC!" That cartoon is not a hallucination, but is a character that will cause you to forever remember the seven Intentional Torts. Whenever you are thinking of the Intentional Torts, whether you are studying for finals or shopping at the local mall, you will immediately see the words "BAF IT TC!" This phrase is melded into your brain, as is the cartoon which accompanies it.

This magical mnemonic will cause you to instantly recall each of the seven intentional torts faster than the speed of sound.

Once you are reminded of the phrase "BAF IT TC!" you recall that the first intentional tort is battery. Just thinking of the word battery makes you think of the rule of law you have faithfully memorized: "Battery is an affirmative act with the intent to touch another resulting in harmful or offensive contact." This rule has been committed to memory, and you can recite it as if your life depended on it. Once you have recited this rule, you instantly recall each "element" of a battery, because each element is contained within this rule you have memorized. The words "affirmative act" within the battery rule bring to mind the concept that the act must be voluntary and not the result of coercion, accident, duress, unconsciousness or mistake. The words "harmful or offensive" cause you to recall that the touching amounting to battery must be harmful or offensive to the reasonable person.

In this way, you are able to recall the rules you need to know to solve a battery problem by simply memorizing fifteen words. Likewise, for the tort of trespass to land, you memorize the following rule: "An affirmative act that invades the plaintiff's possessory interest in land." As you recall this rule, you remember the three elements of this tort: (1) a voluntary act; (2) invading P's interest; (3) in land. In this way, you open the doors to each element of trespass by memorizing a single rule of law.

This process of opening doors applies to every subject and to every course you will take in law school. While this entire discussion may appear obvious, because you will be required to memorize a great deal of detailed information, it is important that you organize the law into edible and digestible bits of information that are easily memorized.

In recalling the defenses to the Intentional Torts, you see an apparition of a police officer, shouting the phrase "COPS NA!" at the top of his or her lungs. Once that phrase is in your mind, you cannot help but think of each of the defenses to the intentional torts: Consent, defense of Others, defense of Property, Self-defense, Necessity and the privilege of Arrest. Focusing on the "O" in the mnemonic "COPS NA!" you think of the majority rule, which holds that the defendant stands in the shoes of the protected party and is only entitled to use the same amount of force that the protected party was entitled to use. You then recall the minority rule, which protects the actor's reasonable mistake, and instead asks, "What amount of force did the defendant believe was reasonable?"

As you can see, memorizing the law is like funneling the details of the law into the general categories.

The same principle applies to Contracts. Imagine being inside a human maze. You are as you are now, except that you are facing a dark hallway that splits into three passageways. The first passage way reads "Offer." The second and third passageways are labeled "Acceptance" and "Consideration."

You instinctively enter the path of "Offer" and are immediately confronted by a huge stone wall. The wall reads "Present Intention To Contract" and contains strange writing which you must decipher to determine how to climb over the wall. You decipher the strange characters and pull a secret handle, causing a rope to appear, draped over the wall. You grab the rope and begin to climb over this wall. While it requires great mental and physical abilities to accomplish this task, you are successful. As you jump over the wall, you find there is a bottomless pit just a few steps from where you have landed. In order to cross this pit, you must recite each of the essential terms of an offer: parties, price, quantity, subject matter, time and place for performance. You are once again successful in saying each of the magic passwords; a plank magically appears, and you walk over the bottomless pit. Just as you catch your breath, you feel the heat of the flames engulfing the dark corridor before you. After momentarily panicking, you realize that you must run through the flames before they engulf you. As you run through the flames, you yell, "Communicated to the offeree" at the top of your lungs, and as you recite this rule, the flames subside. You find yourself at the end of the first maze, sitting on a beautiful beach, surrounded by white sand and blue waters, sipping a Pina Colada.

While this adventure may seem a far cry from memorizing the law, it once again illustrates the process of opening doors. Like the maze that presents numerous obstacles to those who enter its pathways, an offer requires that three "obstacles" or "elements" be fulfilled before an offer is said to exist.

Your first task of deciphering the strange characters on the wall is akin to your task in solving "the present intention to contract" element of an offer. You must analyze and evaluate the language of the offer to determine what a reasonable person would think hearing those words. Once confronted with that task, you instantly recall the rule which will guide you through the obstacle in your path.

The second obstacle requires you to search for a checklist of items; the third obstacle is overcome by "communicating" in the same way an offeror communicates to an offeree.

Without belaboring the point made here any further, I advise you to apply these principles in memorizing each of the law school subjects. You will find that memorizing the law is more fun and interesting than you may have imagined.

As is obvious from the *Law Charts* in this book, mnemonics are one memory device recommended. Mnemonics are easy-to-remember codes that will help you to remember the law and checklists in your approaches. You may find that mnemonics do not work for you; if that is the case, then do not use them. If you dislike the mnemonics in this book, then develop your own. Mnemonics can also be taken to an extreme. It defeats the purpose of mnemonics to have a mnemonic for every single detail you must memorize. In addition to memorizing 500 rules, you will have 200 mnemonics to memorize as well.

Other memory aids include flashcards, the use of charts, talking to yourself, being tested by a colleague, study mate or friend, and writing exercises. A brief word about each.

<u>Flashcards</u>: The information printed on your flashcards should mimic your *Law Charts.* The purpose of a flashcard is to test your ability to retrieve whatever information is required to solve a particular problem. The blind-side or front of the flashcard should contain the general word, concept or phrase that represents the door you are attempting to open. For example, the front of the card might read "BATTERY" OR "DEFENSES TO A CONTRACT" OR "THE INTENTIONAL TORTS." On the opposite side of the card, you should list whatever rules you are required to recall.

Be realistic in deciding how much information to memorize. Do not write a 1,000 word essay on the back of the card, complete with Hornbook citations and quotations from cases. Focus instead on key words and phrases, and stick to the minimum information you will need to remember for the examinations. You do not need 10,000 flashcards. Be selective about the details you memorize.

The Survival Series' ***First Year Flashcards*** and ***Bar Cards*** provide an excellent example of flashcards which incorporate these principles. Each card is color-coded and contains an illustration which will assist you in remembering the rules of law and their exceptions. For more information, see the order form at the back of this book.

Charts: Charts provide an essential visual aid that may prove helpful. Like the charts provided in this book, devising your own charts will not only force you to understand the law conceptually, but will also give you a visual picture of the law. For example, if your mind goes blank when analyzing a personal jurisdiction problem in Civil Procedure, but you remember that your chart began with the personal jurisdiction, the traditional bases and the modern basis of jurisdiction, you are immediately reminded of what those traditional bases are. You also rememember the "CAPFI BLIMFEW" mnemonic, which has been tattooed in your mind. You remember all of this because you are able to visualize the test of personal jurisdiction.

Talking to yourself: While I would not encourage talking to yourself in public, if you are able to articulate a rule of law to yourself, chances are that you understand it. Imagine that you are explaining the concept of "Termination of an Offer" to another:

"Let's see. If there is a valid offer, I must always check to see whether the offer has been terminated. An offer is terminated in three ways: revocation, rejection or by operation of law."

"First, an offer may always be revoked by the offeror before acceptance. This means that the offeror changes his or her mind and "takes" the offer back. If the offeror revokes the offer, the offeree may no longer accept and the offer is terminated. But wait a minute. There are four exceptions to this rule. The first is that if the offeree pays consideration to keep the offer open for a certain time period, the offer may not be revoked. That means if the offeree gave $5 to the offeree on the condition that the offeror would give him five days to decide, the offeror cannot revoke the offer until that five day period is up. The second exception is that if the offeree reasonably suffers detrimental reliance that the offeror cannot revoke. This means that the offeree somehow relies on the offer, like where the offeree refrains from buying a house, and does so reasonably in relying upon the offeror's offer to buy another house. The third exception is the U.C.C. Firm Offer, etc . . ."

As mentioned, if you are able to explain the law to yourself or another person, you probably understand it, and this will also help to test your memory of that particular area of law.

Having a Study Mate Test You

One of the great advantages of having someone else test you is that you cannot cheat. You cannot flip the flashcard over or abandon the "test" in favor of your favorite TV show. Direct confrontation is often the best test of memory. This is what lawyers do in conducting cross-examination of witnesses. "Name the seven intentional torts forwards and backwards," or "What are the elements of res ipsa loquitur?" And remember, if you experience humiliation at being unable to recall a rather pointed inquiry by your colleague, you can always reverse roles and get revenge by asking him or her an even more difficult question.

The "Best" Memory Test

The best test, of course, is taking examinations without any assistance from the written materials.

Whatever memory methods you employ, make sure that you set aside sufficient time to memorize the things you need to know on the examination.

Be creative in memorizing the law. Make the process of memorizing the law fun, like a game show or a round of "Trivial Pursuit." Remember that the sky is the limit, and you must find a method that works well for you. Not everyone remembers things in the same fashion.

A Question of Time

Most law school professors impose strict time constraints on the examinations. For this reason, you must learn how to manage the available time to maximize your success on law school examinations.

As you have seen from the examples in this book, the traditional format of law school examinations is the essay question, although some professors prefer either a multiple choice or short answer format. The time estimates involved in multiple choice or short answer questions are readily determinable, because in most instances, you need only divide the number of questions by the available time. For example, if your professor tells you that 60 multiple choice questions will appear on a two-hour final examination, you know that you must allot approximately two minutes per question.

Time concerns on essay examinations, by contrast, are not as easy to gauge. Because all issues are not created equal, you will have to devote varying amounts of time to each issue, depending on the complexity of the issue presented and the facts and law involved.

There is no rule of thumb as to how much time should be spent analyzing a major issue versus analyzing a minor issue. As you learned in the Freddie Fox example, the issue of trespass should have been solved in a matter of seconds, while the issue of specific intent was deserving of perhaps five or ten minutes of discussion.

In this section, you will learn how to make time your friend and ally, rather than facing the "time monster" who viciously ticks away each minute.

First you must allot the available time between the various tasks you must perform to successfully analyze and exam problem. Let's briefly review once again the six-steps of exam taking:

Six Steps of Exam Taking

(1) **READ THE QUESTION** - Read the question carefully for content and determine what facts are relevant to solving the problem.

(2) **VISUALIZE THE PROBLEM** - See the fact pattern come to life and commit these facts to memory.

(3) **DETERMINE WHAT QUESTIONS ARE PRESENTED, APPLY THE PROBLEM SOLVING APPROACH AND CREATE AN OUTLINE** - Determine what particular issues are presented by the problem, apply your problem solving approach (or LAW CHART) and organize your analysis (e.g., outlining).

(4) **MAKE A QUICK JUDGMENT CALL AS TO HOW MUCH TIME TO SPEND DISCUSSING EACH ISSUE** - Divide the number of issues by the available time according to the relative importance of each issue.

(5) **WRITE OUT YOUR ANSWER** - We will focus on basic I-R-A-C to express your answer.

(6) **REACH A CONCLUSION, MOVE ON TO THE NEXT PROBLEM/ISSUE** - Always conclude one way or another; don't be wishy-washy! Also, once you have completed the problem, move on to the next issue or problem once your allotted time is up.

Each task is essential and must be performed within the time frame given to you to complete the problem. You would therefore divide the available time by each of the tasks before you. For example, if you had one hour to complete a particular examination, you might spend 20 minutes reading and visualizing the fact pattern, 10 minutes drafting an outline, and 30 minutes writing your answer.

But how much time should you spend analyzing each issue presented? Following the six steps of exam taking, you should have taken the time in Steps Three and Four to write out at least a skeletal outline of the issues you are required to analyze in solving the problem. You must then make a snap judgment as to how much time to spend analyzing each issue before you begin writing the examination.

For example, in analyzing the Gifford Gangster burglary problem discussed earlier in this text, your outline might appear as follows:

<u>People v. Gifford Gangster</u>

I. Burglary

State the general rule & issue
1.<u>Trespassory</u> - w/o true owner's consent; here premises leased to David & Mattie, who did not consent to Gifford's entry
2. <u>Breaking</u> - GG uses glasscutter to cut hole in window.
3. <u>Entering</u> - slightest entry sufficient - Iron hand used to enter premises and actually penetrates structure.
4. <u>Dwelling house</u> - C/L required that the structure be a residence - here David occasionally slept in offices; modern law abrogates.
5. <u>Of Another</u> - office leased to David & Mattie but owned by GG's boss.
6. <u>At Nighttime</u> - 6:00 pm - nighttime? Modern law abolishes this requirement.
7. <u>With the specific intent to commit larceny or felony</u> - GG intended to steal Maria's file at time of entry; file contained movie owned by VC.

Again, the detail you include in your outline might differ substantially but should at least contain a checklist of the elements you intend to discuss in your exam answer.

After outlining your answer, you will see that the major issues are (1) trespass; (2) breaking; (3) entering; (7) specific intent. The issues of (4) dwelling house; (5) of another; (6) at nighttime are fairly straightforward and require less discussion.

Let's assume that you have 90 minutes to complete this examination. Depending on how fast you read, you might spend 30 minutes reading and visualizing the problem. If you spent an additional 15 minutes drafting an outline, you would have 45 minutes remaining to write out your exam answer.

Following these time constraints, you might spend 35 minutes analyzing the four major issues, roughly nine minutes for each, and 10 minutes discussing the minor issues.

This is not to suggest that you should spend five or 10 minutes of your valuable time to figure out mathematically how much time you can afford to spend analyzing each issue before you. That would be a tragic waste of time and energy. What I am recommending is that you get into the practice of making a quick snap decision as to how much time to spend analyzing a particular issue before you write it, and more importantly, that you stick to any time constraints you set.

If, on the other hand, you had only 60 minutes to complete the Gifford Gangster problem, you would set different time parameters. Instead of spending 30 minutes reading and visualizing the problem, you would limit yourself to no more than 15 minutes. You would spend no more than 10 minutes outlining the answer, leaving 35 minutes to write out the answer. The minor issues would be discussed in five minutes, leaving 30 minutes for the major issues.

If you were analyzing additional issues, such as other crimes in the Gifford Gangster example, then you would similarly decide how much time to spend analyzing each issue. For example, if you were required to analyze Vito Corleone's "Solicitation" or "Conspiracy," you would allot sufficient time to the discussion of both issues.

Let's take the example of Dennis, Frank, & Conco discussed in the Torts section in Part VI of this book. Your outline to that exam might appear as follows:

1. <u>Frank v. Dennis</u>

    <u>Trespass to Land</u> **(5 minutes)**
    Affirmative act/invades P's interest/in land
    <u>Defense of Necessity</u> **(5 minutes)**
    Public Purpose? D acts to save heavy equipment

    <u>Frank v. Conco</u>

    <u>Vicarious Liability</u> **(10 minutes)**
        Employer liable for employee's torts if within course of employment.
        D employed by Conco as draftsman
        Involved in personal errand
        Sunday morning - not a workday
        D works in downtown office
        Frank might argue that employee has duty to act
        Conco will win

2. Dennis v. Frank

False Imprisonment **(5 minutes)**
Act/Omission/with intent to confine someone/resulting in actual confinement of P/actual awareness of confinement or injury
all requirements met

Defense of Consent **(10 minutes)**
Express consent? D "agrees" to enter office
Consent exceeded? D initially agrees, but is not told he must wait an hour for the president arrived until he is already in the room.
Effect of presence of four employees?

Again remember that the detail you include in your outline may differ. After having read, visualized and analyzed the problem, you then make a snap decision as to how much time to spend analyzing each issue. Clearly, the major issues, that is, the issues that raise the most questions and require the most discussion, are vicarious liability in the first part of the question and the defense of consent in the second part.

Assuming that you had an hour to complete your answer, you might apportion your time as follows: 15 minutes to read and visualize the question, 10 minutes to outline your answer, leaving 35 minutes to write your answer. The major issues may be worthy of 10 minutes each, leaving 15 minutes to analyze the minor issues, or roughly five minutes each for your discussion of trespass to land, necessity and false imprisonment.

What is important is that you set rough time limits – for that is only half the battle – - and follow them. An undisciplined writer might spend 20 minutes analyzing trespass, which is a minor issue, as there is little question that Dennis committed trespass by moving the heavy equipment, 10 minutes would be spent on necessity, and the remaining five minutes on vicarious liability. Not only would this exam writer fail to address any of the issues raised by the second interrogatory, but his or her analysis of the first interrogatory would be uneven and incorrectly analyzed.

While it is indeed possible to write a 20 minute essay on trespass, the question does not require it. The writer should spend the majority of the time allotted to the first interrogatory discussing the meatier issue of vicarious liability. Such an exam answer is like running in a race and quitting half way through.

Remember that getting to the finish line means everything. You should have that finish line clearly in sight while you are writing your exam answer. While you must strive to be comprehensive and complete in your analysis, an unfinished exam answer represents an incomplete answer to the problem. The objective is to complete the examination within the given time frame and to maximize the time parameters available to you.

Professors sometimes give students examinations not capable of being fully analyzed in the allotted time period. These are called "race" exams, as the student must race to complete the examination. Even on these type of examinations, if you carefully plan out your analysis by outlining your exam answer before you begin writing, you will find that you will be able to apportion your time accordingly so that you complete the examination.

There is no magic rule as to how much time is required to write a winning examination. But if your professor gives you three hours to complete the examination, and you complete your answers in 30 minutes, chances are that you missed the boat on more than one occasion. While substance always prevails over time, use the time given to you to maximize your success on the examination.

As I recommended to you earlier, get your hands on every past examination authored by your professor. Check to see how much time your professor allots for the examination, and ask your professor whether she or he intends to follow the same time parameters. This simple task will help you immensely in preparing to deal with the time constraints you will be operating under in the exam room.

If you are reading this section before you have attempted to write examinations, do not focus on time considerations alone. It is more important, at least initially, that you learn how to properly write a law school exam answer before you attempt to write that examination within time constraints. Ideally, you should begin writing examinations without regard to time, slowly building up your speed and analysis skills. However, be extremely mindful of time in the month or so before final examinations. You will find that as your problem-solving skills improve, the speed with which you solve problems will increase as well.

If you are having problems with time management, then use an alarm clock or other timing device to constantly reinforce the time constraints you are operating under. In this way, you will learn how to write winning examinations under time pressure.

Developing a Study Schedule

You may feel somewhat overwhelmed by the many different tasks before you. Indeed, between reading class assignments, briefing cases, keeping an outline, developing a problem-solving approach and taking exams, you will be a very busy bee.

The best way to attack each of these tasks is a little bit at a time. Rather than briefing all Torts in one week, keep up with the class assignments each day, and brief the cases as they are covered in class. Likewise, keep a running outline of class materials, and then you will not have to spend an entire one or two weeks writing your Torts outline.

Do not allow yourself to fall behind. As a lawyer, managing your time is one of the most important things you must learn to do, and failure to manage your time will contribute to job-related stress as well as loss of money and clients.

Keep a daily schedule of activities. Most lawyers, much like business people, keep a date book of daily activities to manage their schedules; it is suggested that you follow this practice as well.

Of course, every student's studying habits will vary. One student might study eight hours a day, while another might study four hours, depending upon each student's individual attention span and discipline. While there is no firm rule as to how many hours you should study each day, it is safe to say that if you are studying over 10 hours a day – or under three – you are probably doing something wrong.

When you develop your study schedule, vary the activities, exercises and tasks as often as possible. This will not only make studying more fun and bearable, but will also break up your day as well. For example, your typical weekly schedule might begin as follows:

Monday

7:00 -8:00: Exercise gym and breakfast!
8:00 - 9:00: Study for Torts
9:00 - 10:30: Torts Class
10:30 -11:30: Study Session with Booboo
11:30 -12:30: Lunch
12:30 - 1:00: Meet with Torts Professor
1:00 - 2:30: Criminal Law
2:30 - 3:30: Study for Contracts - Brief Cases
3:30 - 5:00: Contracts
5:00 - 6:00: Basketball with Michael J.
6:00 - 7:00: Dinner
7:00 - 8:00: The Simpsons
8:00 - 9:00: Criminal Law Practice Examination
9:00 - 11:00: Free time!
11:30: Zzzzzzzzzz!

Tuesday

7:00 - 8:00: Exercise gym and breakfast!
8:00 - 9:00: Study for Criminal Law
9:00 - 10:30: Civil Procedure
10:30 -11:00: Study Session on Criminal Law
11:00 -12:00: Work on Criminal Law Outline
12:00 - 1:30: Lunch at the park

1:30 - 3:00: Contracts Outline & Law Charts
3:00 - 5:00: Contracts Study Session
5:00 - 6:00: Read the "National Enquirer"
6:00 - 7:00: Dinner
7:00 - 10:00: Movies!
10:00 -11:00: Contracts Practice Examinations
11:00 pm: Good night!

This is not to suggest that you must have something to do every breathing moment of the day, but by planning your activities throughout the day, you will find that you will have more than enough time to study, and to have fun!

A Final Word

Let's recap the law school learning experience and exam writing skills you have learned in this book and put it all together:

The Law School Learning Experience

- Read the cases and complete all reading assignments.
- Brief each case using F-I-R-A-C format.
- Incorporate class notes, case briefs and other relevant information into an outline.
- After each major section is completed, develop a problem-solving approach or adopt the *Law Charts* in this book.
- Memorize the *Law Charts* for the purpose of exam taking.
- You are ready to take examinations!

Writing Law School Examinations

- Read the question.
- Visualize the fact pattern.
- Determine what questions are presented and outline your answer.
- Make a snap decision about how much time you will spend analyzing each issue.
- Apply the *Law Chart's* Problem-Solving Approaches to the facts and write out your answer using I-R-A-C.
- Follow the "Ten Rules to Write By."
- Be Mmindful of Garth's "Ten Major Downfalls."
- Reach a conclusion, smile and move on!

Solving a legal problem is really this simple. But the key is that you apply this system to real-life exam problems. Even the best of theories is useless if not applied. That is why you must take practice examinations as often as possible and apply each of the strategies and techniques in this book. This book contains over 50 examples of model questions and answers. Practice using the exams in this book, and write and re-write each examination until your exam answers are better than the answers contained in this book. Remember that it is not enough to simply read the model examinations in this book. You must put pen to paper and write examinations like Mozart wrote concertos. Only in this way, will you learn how to write winning examinations!

As I leave you, let me say that it's been a great pleasure to be your coach and tutor in law school. The challenges which await you as you finish law school and begin in your legal career will be well served by the time and energy invested you are doing now. Once you have mastered the skill of problem-solving, it is a skill you can apply to a myriad of situations and tasks which face you each day.

It our hope that this book will help you achieve whatever goals and objectives you have set for yourself in law school. Good luck on your legal career!

Appendix

Part VI

Case Briefing Forms

Glossary of Abbreviated Terms

Glossary of Terms by Subject

General Vocabulary

Civil Procedure

Contracts

Criminal Law

Real Property

Research & Legal Writing

Torts

Case Brief Form

____

(Case Title) **(Year)** **(Cite)** **(Subject Area)**

Facts: ____

____

____

____

____

Issue(s): ____

____

____

____

Rule: ____

____

____

____

____

Application and Rationale for the Rule: ______________________________

____

____

____

Conclusion: ____

____

____

____

Concurring/Dissenting Opinion: ____________________________________

____

____

____

____

____

Professor's Comments: ____

____

____

____

Case Brief Form

(Case Title) (Year) (Cite) (Subject Area)

Facts:

Issue(s):

Rule:

Application and Rationale for the Rule: ______________________

____

____

____

Conclusion: ____

____

____

____

Concurring/Dissenting Opinion: ______________________

____

____

____

____

____

Professor's Comments: ______________________________

____

____

____

Glossary of Abbreviated Terms

Glossary of abbreviated terms used in Law Charts: The following abbreviations are explained immediately preceding their use in the *Law Charts.* However, for your convenience, they are set forth here in alphabetical order.

ABAMR – American Bar Association Model Rules

Amd - Amendment

BER - best evidence rule

BFP - bona fide purchaser

CODE - American Bar Association Code

C/L - common law

Corp - corporation

C/P - community property

D - defendant

FED - federal

FMR - felony murder rate

FRE - Federal Rules of Evidence

GC - general considerations

govt. - government

hrg - hearing

juris - jurisdiction

juvie - juvenile

K - contract

L - landlord

L/E - life estate

MAJ - majority view

MIN - minority view

M/L - modern law

N/A - not applicable

Obj - objective

π - plaintiff

PJ - personal jurisdiction

Q/CP - quasi-community property

RaP - Rule Against Perpetuities

SH - shareholders

SMJ - subject matter jurisdiction

SoF - Statute of Frauds

SoL - Statute of Limitations

S/P - separate property

st. - state

TES - time, energy & services

T - tenant/testator

UCC - Uniform Commercial Code

UPC - Uniform Probate Code

V - victim

Glossary of Terms by Subject

General Vocabulary

appellant - party appealing to a higher court.
appellee - party against whom an appeal is taken.
application - explanation of legal reasoning.
black letter law - informal term which is used to describe the basic principles of law
brief - concise statement summarizing a case decision.
case - a legal action.
cause of action - the legal basis of the lawsuit.
common law - that body of law which originated and developed in England.
contra - Latin word meaning "contrary to" or "on the other hand."
defendant - the party or persons against whom a legal action is brought.
dicta - the Latin word taken from "ober dicta" which refers to those portions of a case or legal opinion which are unnecessary to the decision in the case and therefore are not binding precedent on future decisions.
elements - component of a cause of action or defense.
en blanc - when all judges are present and participate in a case decision.
exception - that which is excluded from application of a general rule or principle.
FIRAC - standard abbreviation for Facts, Issue, Rule, Application, Conclusion.
intent - refers generally to a person's state of mind.
issues - questions presented by a legal problem.
law chart - charts that contain problem solving approaches.
majority rule - refers to rule adopted in majority of states.
minority rule - refers to rule adopted in minority of states.
modern law - a recent legal trend or rule.
motion - formal request made to have an issue pertaining to a pending lawsuit decided by the court.
opinion - a written legal decision explaining why a court reached a particular conclusion.
outlines - summaries of materials which generally contain a conceptual review of the law.
plaintiff - party instituting legal action.
per curiam - a case opinion where the author is not identified.
problem solving approach - a checklist approach used to solve legal problems.

red herring - refers to a fact or circumstance which misleads or deceives the reader
rule - rule of law.
six steps of exam taking - 1) read the question, 2) visualize the problem, 3) determine what questions are presented and create an outline, 4) estimate how much time to spend discussing each issue, 5) write out your answer, 6) reach a conclusion and move on!
Socratic method - teaching method which begins with a general principle agreed upon by all, and employs deductive reasoning and specific examples to explore the correctness or depth of general principle.
stare decisis - common law doctrine which holds that courts of law are bound by general principles of law which have been previously decided. Stare decisis means "to stand by."
substantive law - law which establishes the obligation and rights of persons.
trial court - court in which the case of action was tried.

Civil Procedure

additur - where defendant agrees to greater damages to avoid court's granting of plaintiff's new trial motion.
amount of controversy - prerequisite in diversity suit to bringing case in federal court.
ancillary jurisdiction - gives the court power over ancillary matters such as counterclaims where court has jurisdiction of the principal action.
answer - defendant's written response to plaintiff's complaint.
citizenship - refers generally to place of abode or residence.
class action - lawsuit where one or more members of a numerous class have a common interest in the subject of a lawsuit and sue or defend on behalf of the class.
collateral attack - permits defendant to challenge default judgement against him on grounds that the court lacked jurisdiction.
collateral estoppel - doctrine which prohibits relitigation of a factual issue which was already decided on its merits.
complaint - plaintiff's pleading setting forth causes of action against defendant.
compulsory counterclaim - counterclaim which arises from the same transaction or occurrence as the plaintiff's claim; claim is waived unless asserted by defendant.
counterclaim - cause of action asserted by defendant against plaintiff.
court trial - trial decided by judge.

deposition - an oral or written examination of a party or a witness under oath that takes place out of court.
directed verdict - motion is granted when evidence reveals that one party must prevail over the opposing party who has presented its case.
diversity of citizenship - requires that the domiciles of plaintiffs must differ from that of all defendants.
domicile - place of residence.
Erie doctrine - holds that federal courts must apply state statutes and case law to non-federal causes of action.
federal rules of civil procedure - rules of procedure which apply to the federal court system.
forum - court.
full faith and credit clause - provision in the United States Constitution which requires that public acts, records and judicial proceedings of one state be honored by the other states.
garnishment - legal action which allows a debtor's wager, money or property to be applied against a debt owned to a third party.
general appearance - where defendant appears in court waiving all jurisdictional objections.
habeas corpus - application to obtain the release of a person unlawfully imprisoned.
indispensable party - unavailable party whose absence will prevent the court from rendering an effective judgement.
interrogatories - written questions which must be answered under oath by the party to whom they are sent.
in personam jurisdiction - gives the court power over a defendant.
in rem - gives the court power over property located in the state.
interpleader - person who holds property subject to conflicting claim may bring all claimants into court in order to avoid double liability.
intervention - procedure where a third party (the intervenor) is permitted on his own motion to join the pending lawsuit.
joinder - procedure of jointing parties or claims in a lawsuit.
jurisdiction - power of the court to make legally binding decisions and determine the geographic area in which the court's decision is binding.
jury instructions - instructions of law give to the jury.
jury selection - process by which the jury is selected.
jury trial - trial by jury.
limited appearance - allows defendant to appear in quasi-in-rem case and limit judgement against him by the property attached by plaintiff.
local action rule - jurisdictional rule that holds where an action involves injury to real property; the action must be tried in the forum where the property is located.
local rules - rules of the court which govern procedure of locality.
long arm statute - state law which sets forth when a court's jurisdiction

may be exercised.

minimum contacts test - the criteria by which it is determined whether a defendant may constitutionally be required to submit itself to a court's decision.

necessary party - available party whose joinder is desirable to enable the court to grant complete relief or would avoid risk that party before court would be impaired in its ability to defend.

nonsuit - motion which is granted where plaintiff has presented its case by failed to show a right to relief.

notice - requirement that interested parties be informed of pendency of an action.

pendent jurisdiction - gives the court power to decide non-federal claims where there is proper federal subject jurisdiction over a related claim.

permissive counterclaim - counterclaim which may be asserted by defendant.

permissive party - available party who has some interest in the action and would be convenient to settle their rights in action.

personal jurisdiction - refers to the power of a court to subject a particular defendant or items of property to its decision.

pleading - the complaint, answer, responses to counter-claims/cross-claims, responses to defenses; two types are: 1) **fact pleading** which requires a statement of the facts setting forth the cause of action or defense in ordinary and concise language, 2) **notice pleading** which requires only a short and plain statement of the nature of the claim.

prayer for relief - statement of pleadings setting forth relief sought.

pretrial conference - meeting between the parties, their attorneys and the judge prior to a trial to familiarize parties and the court with the issues involved in the case.

protective order - order which protects a party or witness from annoyance, embarrassment, or oppression.

quasi-in-rem - give the court power to determine rights of particular persons relating to specific property within the courts' control.

quo warranto action - civil suit brought to decide by what authority a person holds an office or presumes to act.

real party in interest - party who has the right to enforce the claim that is the subject matter of the action.

relation back doctrine - allows amendment of the complaint to relate back to the date of the original pleading if the allegations contained therein arose out of the same conduct, transaction or occurrence set forth in the original pleading.

remittitur - where plaintiff agrees to lesser damages after a jury verdict to avoid courts granting of defendant's motion for a new trial.

removal - procedure which allows the defendant to remove a case from state to federal court when certain conditions are met.

res judicata - Latin phrase meaning "a thing decided;" rule of law preventing parties from relitigating the same cause of action or from splitting a cause of action.
special appearance - where defendant appears in court only to challenge jurisdiction without waiving jurisdiction.
stakeholder - person in interpleader action seeking to institute interpleader action.
standing to sue - requirement the plaintiff have a stake in the subject matter of the lawsuit.
subject matter jurisdiction - gives the court power to determine a certain type of case.
subpoena - legal document summoning party or witness to appear in court.
subpoena duces tecum - legal document used to compel a witness to produce specific documents for inspection.
summary judgment - judgement where no triable issue of material facts exist a matter of law.
variance in proof - occurs when what has been proven a trial differs from the pleadings.
venue - location of the court proceedings.
verification - affidavit under oath or penalty or perjury stating that allegations in pleading are true.
work product - materials prepared by an attorney for trial that disclose the theories, mental impressions or litigation plans of the attorney.

Contracts

acceptance - voluntary act by offeree exercising power to create a contract; an acceptance is effective upon dispatch to the offeror.
agent - one who acts legally on another's behalf.
assignment - where one party assigns a right to receive performance from another party.
bilateral contract - an agreement with is accepted by a promise, i.e., "I promise to give Ed $5 when he mows my lawn."
blue pencil - term of art describing court's power to excise words or phrases or terms from a contractual agreement and give the effect to the contact without the phrases which have been removed.
breach - failure to perform contractual duty or obligation.
condition - an event or circumstance which must occur before the duty to perform arises. Three types of condition: express, implied or constructive. Express condition arise from the express language of the contract; implied condition are those factually inferable from the contract as necessary or as matters of good faith and cooperation; constructive condition are those

created by operation of law, in the interest of fairness and justice.
condition concurrent - contingency which must be satisfied at the time that performance occurs, i.e., "I agree to give Jose my car when he give me $5,000."
condition precedent - contingency other than passage of time which must occur before a precedent contract duty matures, i.e., "Yuri must perform if she earns money this year."
condition subsequent - contingency which releases party from performing a matured duty, i.e., "I agree to give Beth $50 a month unless she date Mark."
consideration - requirement that a legal agreement be supported by value given and received by both parties.
contract - an agreement for consideration between competent parties to do (or refrain from doing) a lawful act.
counteroffer - offer which "counters" or is made in response to a rejected offer.
damages - award of money damages is the normal remedy for breach of contract.
defenses to a contract - includes illegal contracts, fraud, lack of consent, statute of frauds, lack of capacity, unconscionable contract, mistake.
delegation - where one party delegates his duty to perform to another.
detrimental reliance - where party reasonably relies on a representation or promise to his/her detriment.
discharge - occurs where some circumstance releases or discharges a party from performing a contract obligation. Circumstances include impossibility, frustration of purpose, subsequent agreement of the parties, impractically and condition subsequent.
disclaimer - provision in contract purporting to absolve party of liability or clarifying terms of contract.
duress - defense to a contract where contract entered into due to threat or force.
excuse - where the occurrence of a condition is "excused," releasing party to whom performance is owed. "Excuses" include prevention of performance, anticipatory repudiation, waiver, disablement, impossibility, and estoppel.
firm offer - under the UCC, a signed written offer to buy or sell goods which expressly states it will remain open is irrevocable for period stating (or if none) for a reasonable time not to exceed 90 days.
fraud - defense to a contract where party entered into contract based on false impression of contract terms induced by the other party.
guaranty contract - a written promise to answer for another's debt.
illusory promise - unenforceable promise where promisor may avoid suffering any legal detriment, i.e., "If I feel like buying one, I will."
incapacity - defense to a contract where the party to the contract is under

legal age to contract or mentally unable to understand nature and consequences of a contract.
indirect revocation - where offeree learns of acts of offeror which are inconsistent with the offer.
invitation for an offer - where a party request or invites an offer.
K - accepted abbreviation for "contract."
mailbox rule - rule of "acceptance" which holds that acceptance is effective when placed in mailbox – and revocation/rejection is effective when mail received – unless offer provides otherwise.
merchant - one involved in the business of the sale or purchase of goods.
mistake - defense to a contract where mistake is mutual or where unmistaken party knew or should have known of error.
moral consideration - unenforceable promise based on a sense or honor and moral duty.
offer - proposal manifestation a present intention to contract and creating the power of acceptance in the offeree; a communication which a reasonable person would conclude is sufficiently specific and serious to manifest the communicator's willingness to be bound by the acceptance of the person to whom the offer is made.
offeree - the party to whom the offer is made.
offeror - the party making an offer.
option contract - contract whereby value or consideration is paid for a promise not to revoke the offer.
output contract - contract where party agrees to purchase entire production output.
parole evidence rule - rule of construction that holds where parties have entered a written contract – oral evidence is not admissible to varying terms. Exceptions to the rule exist.
promisee - party to whom a promise is made.
promisor - party making a promise.
promissory estoppel - substitute for consideration where one party reasonably incurs a detriment or loss.
quasi-contract - an implied contract (and therefore, not a good contract) whereby party may sue for the reasonable value of work done or good transferred where other party has been unjustly enriched.
reformation - equitable remedy whereby court reforms a written contract.
rejection - where either offeror/offeree refuses or rejects offer.
rescission - equitable remedy where court cancels the contract.
restitution - equitable remedy where court restores non-breaching party any benefit conferred on the breaching party.
revocation - where offeror takes back or rescinds the offer; a revocation of an offer is valid upon its receipt by the offeree.
service of process - act of serving a subpoena.

specific performance - equitable remedy where court orders party to perform.
statute of frauds - defense to a contract which requires that certain agreements be in writing.
third party beneficiary - where one party enters a contract for the benefit of a third party.
transfer - describes transfer of a case from a court where venue is improper to a court where venue is proper.
UCC - the Uniform Commercial Code which applies to the sale of goods.
unconscionable contract - contract which is one sided and inherently unfair.
unilateral contract - an agreement which is accepted by the act of performing, i.e., "Pay me $5 when I mow your lawn."
ultra vires - defense to a corporate contract where subject matter of contact outside legal powers of a corporate party.
widget - an item or thing.

Criminal Law

accessory before/after the fact - common law theory of criminal liability where one party acts in concert with another is held to be an accessory either before or after the crime. **Accessory before the fact** is one who solicits, encourages or aids the perpetrator in committing a crime; **accessory after the fact** is one who assists know criminals to avoid apprehension or conviction.
accomplice liability - theory of liability which holds that a party, though not a perpetrator of crime, is vicariously guilty of a crime.
actual intention to commit a crime - state of mind described as intentional, purposeful, knowingly, willfully, or deliberately; requires that the actor actually intended to commit the actus reus, or know that it is substantially certain to result from this conflict.
actus reus - the "act" requirement of a crime.
affirmative act - act performed voluntarily.
aiding and abetting - the theory of criminal liability where one party who acts in concert with another is held criminally responsible for the foreseeable acts of the other.
age - defense to a crime; person under 14 is presumed incapable of realizing wrongfulness of an act.
arrest - the act of physically placing a person into police custody.
arson - malicious burning of dwelling house or another.
assault - the act of perpetration with specific intent to commit an act which would be a battery or menacing act or gesture with specific intent to

produce in another fear or an imminent battery.

attempt - act in the direction of perpetrating an intended crime.

battery - intentional or criminally negligent application of unlawful force to person of another.

burden of proof - in a criminal case, proof beyond a reasonable doubt must support an accused's conviction.

burglary - at common law, the tresspassory breaking and entering into the dwelling house of another at nighttime.

causation - the requirement that defendant's conduct must be the legal cause and proximate cause of the criminal act.

concurrence - requirement that the mental element of a crime must occur at the same time as the required act.

conspiracy - agreement for an unlawful purpose.

criminal homicide - killing of a being by another with criminal intent.

criminal negligence - state of mind, also referred to as "culpable negligence," "gross neglect," or "recklessness," which requires that at the time the actus reus is performed, the defendant should have been aware that his conduct created a high probability that the actus reus would occur.

duress - also called coercion; defense to a crime not involving serious violence where crime committed as a result of threat of death or serious bodily harm.

embezzlement - conversion of personal property of another by person in lawful possession (resulting from fiduciary relationship) with specific intent to defraud.

entrapment - defense to a crime where one commits an act at the instigation of police.

extortion - use of threats of future harm with specific intent to induce another to give up property.

false imprisonment - the intentional use of force to confine person of another.

false pretenses - fraudulent misrepresentation of past of present fact causing the victim to pass title to personal property, made with specific intent to defraud.

felony - designated serious crimes which carry state prison sentence or sentence which exceeds one year.

felony murder rule - theory of liability which holds that even the most accidental killing is murder if committed as a result defendant's commission of a dangerous felony.

forgery - making of a false writing having apparent legal significance with intent to defraud.

general intent - state of mind when one commits the actus reus without justification or excuse; general intent crimes include rape, battery and other crimes which require the defendant only to intend the act which causes the actus reus.

insanity - defense to a crime where mental illness has affected the accused's mind; the four rules are: **M'Naughten Rule**, defendant adjudged insane if at the time of the criminal act, mental illness prevented defendant from knowing the nature/quality of act or that the act was wrong; **Irresistible impulse test**, mental disease makes defendant incapable of controlling his/her conduct; **American Law Institute Substantial Capacity**, defendant insane if mental illness causes defendant to lack substantial capacity to appreciate criminality of conduct or conform conduct to the requirements of the law; **Diminished responsibility**, mental illness short of insanity may be asserted in homicide case to mitigate the charge.
intoxication - defense to a crime where actor is either involuntary intoxicated though force, mistake, or fraud, or where actor's voluntary intoxication negates the specific intent element of a crime.
intoxication - defense to a crime where actor is either involuntary intoxicated through force, mistake or fraud, or where actor's voluntary intoxication negates the specific intent element of a crime.
kidnaping - false imprisonment accompanied by asporation (movement) of the victim.
knowledge - state of mind when one either perceives a certain fact or deliberately avoids discovery of the fact, i.e., crime of receiving stolen property requires that defendant knew or should have known that property was stolen.
larceny - tresspassory taking and carrying away of another's personal property with intent to deprive him/her of it permanently.
larceny by conversion - conversion of personal property by person in lawful possession with specific intent to defraud.
larceny by trick - use of fraud to obtain temporary delivery of possession of another's property with intent to deprive him of it permanently.
lesser included offenses - one who is charge with a crime may also be convicted of any lesser offenses. A lesser offense is one in which each element of the crime are included in the charged crime, i.e., larceny or theft is a lesser offense of robbery because each of the elements of a theft are included in the crime of robbery.
malice - actual intent or wantonness without any justifying or mitigating factors.
malum in se - crime which is inherently wrong, i.e., murder.
malum prohibitum - crime which prohibits morally neutral activity which is proscribed by legislature as a means of prohibiting some other evil, i.e., driving under the influence of alcohol.
mayhem - maiming or disfiguring another with malice.
mens rea - the "intent" requirement of a crime.
merger - describes concept whereby one offense whose elements are included in a second offense merges into that second offense, i.e., solicitation merges into conspiracy.
misdemeanor - class of criminal offenses which carry a possible jail sentence

of one year or less.
mistake of fact - defense to a specific intent crime if supported by an honest belief; a defense to a general intent crime only if the mistake is reasonable.
mistake of law - not a defense to crime unless the mistake is honest and specific intent crime involved or where mistake based on reliance on government pronouncement or failure of government to inform public of law or where knowledge of the law is a defense.
modus operandi - a criminal's method of operating.
necessity - defense to a crime when crime committed in order to avoid a greater evil.
negative act - where a defendant is punished for failing to commit an act, i.e., reporting taxes to the IRS.
rape - sexual intercourse with another without consent.
receiving stolen property - receiving of property knowing it to be stolen with specific intent to permanently deprive the owner thereof.
robbery - larceny from the person or presence of another by the use of force or intimidation upon him.
solicitation - inciting another to commit any felony or misdemeanor involving breach of the peace.
specific intent - some crime require a double intent – both an intent to commit the actus reus and a specific intent to accomplish a further goal. For example, burglary requires the actor perform the acts constituting the burglary and also that the actor have the specific intent to commit a felony or theft inside the structure at the time of the entry. Specific intent crimes also include assault, murder, attempt, conspiracy, theft and solicitation.
statutory rape - sexual intercourse with a person under age specified by law.
strict liability - crimes which have no means rea or intent requirement, i.e., bigamy, statutory rape, adultery, traffic violation.
transferred intent - doctrine which holds that defendant who aims criminal act at one person but cause it to another will be treated as if he intended to injure that other person.
uttering - offering known as a false instrument as genuine with intent to defraud.
wantonness - know alternatively as "wanton," "reckless," and "willful." This state of mind requires the actor commit an act which creates a high probability that the actus reus will occur. Some state require that the defendant be subjectively aware of this risk.

Real Property

adverse possession - method by which non-owner may obtain ownership of land which he occupies adversely.
affirmative easement - allows easement holder to make affirmative use of a servient estate.
bonafide purchaser - good faith purchaser of land who pays valuable consideration for land.
condominium - describes manner of ownership whereby units are separately owned and each owner possesses an undivided share of the land and common areas.
constructive eviction - occurs where the landlord's conduct substantially interferes with the tenant's enjoyment of the property.
contingent remainder - remainder subject to a condition precedent or taken by an unborn or unascertained person.
covenant - agreement between two parties relating to land; covenants may either be "personal" or may "run with the land." A "personal" covenant does not transfer down to a successive owner of the estate, whereas a covenant which "runs with the land" is binding and enforceable against a successive owner of the land.
conveyance - transfer of the land.
curtesy - husband received a life estate in wife's property upon her death.
deed - written document transferring title to land.
defeasible - estate subject to the possibility of being taken away.
delivery of deed - grantor's intention that the deed shall operate as a conveyance.
devise - to give.
dominant tenement - land whose owner is benefitted by an easement.
dower - wife receive life estate in one-third of husband's property acquired during marriage.
easement - right to use another's land.
easement in appurtenant - easement which is attached to a piece of land and benefits the owner of such land in his/her enjoyment and use of the land.
easement in gross - easement which is unrelated to any land owned by easement holder, i.e., easement giving holder the right to remove gravel from the land.
eminent domain - power of government to take private property for public purposes.
equitable servitude - agreement between two parties not to do something which can be enforced without privity of estate.
estoppel by deed - if grantor conveys land which he does not own but later

acquired, the land goes to the grantee upon acquisition.
executory interest - future estate in a party other than the grantor which becomes possessory when a grantee of a vested remainder or defeasible fee is divested of her estate.
fee simple - estate of absolute ownership.
fee tail - estate which passes by descent only to lineal descendants, abolished at modern law.
fixture - personal property which is regarded as part of real property that passes with the property to which it is attached.
grantee - person receiving a grant of land.
grantor - person making a land grant.
grantor-grantee index - method of recording land interests which is an alphabetical index listed under the last name of the grantor or grantee.
implied covenant of habitability - implied agreement in residential lease that the premises are fit for living purposes.
implied reciprocal servitude - describes an implied restriction on land where there is a common plan (if one lot is restricted in some fashion). A similar restriction is implied on the remaining land.
interstate succession - statutory scheme setting forth inheritance rights of survivors where testator dies without a valid will.
inverse condemnation - where severe land use restrictions constitute a taking and entitle the landowner to damages or compensation.
joint tenants - jointly owned estate where each tenant owns the entire estate subject to the right of survivorship.
landlord - lessor of land.
lateral support, right to - right to have land supported in natural state by adjoining land.
license - personal privilege to use land granted by a landowner to another.
life estate - estate owned for life.
marketable title - title reasonably free from doubt that a well-informed, reasonable prudent buyer would accept.
merger, doctrine of - rule which holds that if two successive estates are held by the same individual, the merge.
mortgage - financial relationship where the mortgagor borrows money to purchase land from mortagee who may satisfy debt from land if loan is not repaid.
negative easement - prevents owner of servient tenement from using the land in a certain manner; five negative easements in include light, air, subjacent or lateral support and flow of an artificial stream.
partition - physical division of property.
party wall - wall which is built along boundary lines between two properties used by both owners of the properties.
profit - the right to take something from the land of another.
profit in appurtenant - profit is attached to a piece of land and benefits the

owner of the land in his/her use and enjoyment thereof.
profit in gross - profit is unrelated to any land owned by the profit holder.
pur autre vie - life estate measured by the life span of one other than grantee.
quitclaim deed - document which releases whatever interest the grantor has in land.
recording acts - laws which requires a party to publically record interest in land; three major types include notice, race-notice, and race statutes.
remainder - future interest created in one other an the grantor upon the termination of a prior estate.
retaliatory eviction - where the landlord vindictively evicts a tenant because tenant informed authorities of alleged wrongdoing.
reversion - remaining estate when an estate less than a fee simple absolute is granted.
right of re-entry - right of grantor to re-enter land and take possession
right of survivorship - characteristic of joint tenancy and tenancy by the entirety in which the estate goes to the surviving court.
rule against perpetuities - no interest is good unless it must vest, if at all, not later than 21 years after some life in being at the creation of the interest.
servient tenement - land whose owner is burdened by an easement.
Shelley's case, the rule in - if a grant creates a freehold estate in the grantee and remainder in the grantee's heirs, the grantee instead has a fee simple absolute. Thus, if a grant is "to *A* for life, the remainder in *A*'s heirs" then under the rule, *A* has a fee simple absolute.
shifting executory interest - jointly owned estate between husband and wife with the right of survivorship.
subjacent support, right to - right to have underground support of land.
tenancy by the entirety - jointly owned estate where each tenant owns a separate, alienable interest.
tenancy in common - jointly owned estate where each tenant owns a separate, alienable interest.
tenant - lessee of land.
tract index - method of recording land interests organized by lot and block number.
vested remainder - remainder to an ascertained and existing person.
vested remainder subject to open - remainder to a group of people at least one of whom exists and can be ascertained.
waste - damage or injury to real property.
worthier title, doctrine of - grantor cannot give a remainder to his own heirs.
zoning power - power which allows division of land into districts where certain uses of land are prohibited or permitted in order to segregate incompatible uses and protected established uses from economic loss caused by new uses.

Research and Legal Writing

advance sheet - recent case opinions which are issued immediately after a case is decided and are later incorporated into case book series.
affidavit - declaration of facts made by a person, usually made under penalty of perjury or take before one qualified to take statements under oath.
annotations - summaries of the law and/or facts.
blue book - nickname for book titled, " A Uniform System of Citation," published by the Harvard Law Review Association.
brief - legal document containing statement of facts, points of law, and arguments raised by counsel.
citation - legal citation which usually indicates in shorthand the location of a particular case or section within a book, i.e., the citation for People v. Finder might be 135 State App. 3d122.
demand letter - letter written by attorney informally advising opposing party of the cause of action and requesting redress prior to the filing of the lawsuit.
form books - books which contain examples of various legal documents and written instruments.
holding - decision or conclusion of the court.
infra - Latin word which refers the reader to an upcoming citation or part of a book or document.
inter alia - Latin word meaning "among other things."
Lexis - a legal research system developed by Mead Data Central which organizes legal documents including statutes and cases.
memorandum of points and authorities - legal document setting forth law and arguments of a party.
sheparadizing - trademark property of Shepard's Citation, Inc. describing the manner in which their publications are used.
slip opinion - individual case opinion published immediately after case is decided.
supra - word which refers the reader to a previous citation or part of a book or document.
Westlaw - a legal research system developed by West Publishing Company which organizes legal documents including statutes and cases.

Torts

affirmative act - voluntary act, absence of mistake, coercion, duress or accident.
arrest - defense based on probable cause to arrest for crime.

assault - act with intent to place plaintiff in apprehension of an immediate harmful or offensive touching.
assumption of the risk - defense to negligence action where one knowingly and subjectively accepts the risk of a particular act.
battery - act with intent to touch another resulting in harmful or offensive touching.
breach - where one party fails to fulfill a legal duty to another.
business torts - torts for injury to business relations; includes torts of injurious falsehood, **interference** with contract rights and interference with economic advantage.
but for rule - rule of causation which determines whether "but for" the defendant's act, a particular injury would or would not have occurred.
Cardozo, Judge Benjamin - judge who decided the Palsgraf case and many other seminal tort cases.
causation - refers to the requirement that a party cause the tortious injury or damage.
chattel - French word meaning property.
common carrier - business which transports people.
consent - defense whereby party agrees or is said to agree to tortious conduct.
comparative negligence - defense to negligence action which compares negligence of plaintiff and defendant in terms of blameworthiness.
contributory negligence - defense alleging that party bringing negligence suit was in fact negligent, contributing to the injuries complained of.
conversion - act with intent to assert control over a chattel which in fact belongs to plaintiff resulting in substantial injury to chattel.
damages - financial measure of injuries in tort law.
defamation - publication to a third person by defendant defaming plaintiff, capable of bing understood by third persons in defamatory sense causing damage to plaintiff's reputation.
defamation per quod - where a statement is not defamatory on its face but must be explained to demonstrate injury to plaintiff.
defenses - excuse or justification raised by defendant barring defendant's tort liability against plaintiff.
dram shop acts - laws which hold sellers of alcohol liable for injury caused by intoxicated customers.
eggshell theory - rule holding that the defendant takes plaintiff as he finds her; in other words, plaintiff's handicap or special circumstances causing even unforeseen injury to plaintiff is no defense. Based on case where plaintiff had a thin "eggshell" skull.
false imprisonment - act or omission with intent to confinement someone resulting in actual confinement of plaintiff.
family purpose doctrine - owner of vehicle is liable for the negligent acts of family members using the vehicle for family purposes.

governmental immunity - body of law which immunizes state and federal governments from tort liability.
guest statutes - laws which determine liability of automobile drivers for torts committed against a guest or passenger.
Hand, Judge Learned - famed New York Judge who wrote many groundbreaking tort decisions.
immunity - removal of liability for tortious conduct.
indemnity - where defendant who has paid all or part of a claim recovers payment from a third party.
intention infliction of emotional distress - intentional tort involving the intentional causing of emotional distress to another.
joint enterprise - doctrine which hold those who act in concert vicariously liable for the torts of others committed during the course of an enterprise.
last clear chance doctrine - defense to negligence action which holds several defendants who tortiously cause one harm may be held either jointly or severally liable for such harm.
libel - written defamation.
licensee - one who has a license in property interest or another.
misrepresentation - torts of intentional and negligent misrepresentation provide remedy where plaintiff justifiably relies upon defendant's misrepresentation.
necessity - defense whereby actor's tortious conduct is privileged to avoid a greater evil.
negligence - careless conduct; breach of duty of due care which is the actual and proximate cause of plaintiff's injuries.
nuisance - cause of action for substantial interference with plaintiff's right to use and enjoy land.
omission - failure to act.
others, defense of - defense where one party acts to defend another.
Palsgraf case - leading case where "duty" issue in negligence actions resolved.
prima facie case - what plaintiff must prove to prevail on cause of action.
privacy torts - cause of action for invasions of privacy' includes tort of intrusion, public disclosure of offensive private facts, placing plaintiff in false light; appropriation of plaintiff's name or likeness.
products liability - area of law involving tortious injuries caused by use of products; includes the separate torts of Misrepresentation, Breach of Express Warranty, Strict Products Liability, Breach of Implied Warranty, and Negligence.
property, defense of - defense whereby actor acts to prevent injury to real or personal property.
Prosser's Hornbook on Torts - famous hornbook on torts law.
proximate cause - rule of causation which determines whether the act in questions was the legal cause of plaintiff's injuries.

reasonable person - refers to hypothetical reasonable person used to objectively evaluate conduct (i.e., how would a reasonable person act?)
release - occurs when plaintiff surrenders a claim against a party receiving it.
res ipsa loquitur - the thing speaks for itself; refers to a manner of proving negligence when defendant is in exclusive control of instrumentality and type of accident does not occur unless someone is negligent.
respondeat superior - doctrine which holds employer liable for torts committed by employee within course of employment.
restatement of torts - code of tort law.
satisfaction - plaintiff's acceptance of full compensation for injury.
self-defense - defense where party acts to protect itself from bodily harm.
slander - oral defamation.
standard of care - sets forth defendant's duty to act reasonably in a negligence action.
state of the art - defense to products liability tort which permits the fact finder to consider evidence of the state of scientific and technological knowledge at the time the product was made.
statute of limitations - statute which limits the time in which a cause of action may be brought.
strict liability - basis of tort liability where part is held strictly liable regardless of the absence of any mental requirement; in other words, the party is held liable based on conduct alone. This basis is used where a dangerous activity, such as nuclear power, is involved.
substantial factor - rule of causation which holds that if either one or two acts cause an injury it is sufficient that the defendant's conduct was a substantial factor in causing such an injury.
tort - a private wrong.
tortious - conduct involving a tort.
transferred intent - concept whereby actor's tortious intent toward one party is transferred to injured party.
trespass to chattels - act which invades plaintiff's possessory interest in land.
vicarious liability - liability for the actions of another.
wrongful death - lawsuit based on claim that another's life was tortiously or wrongfully terminated.

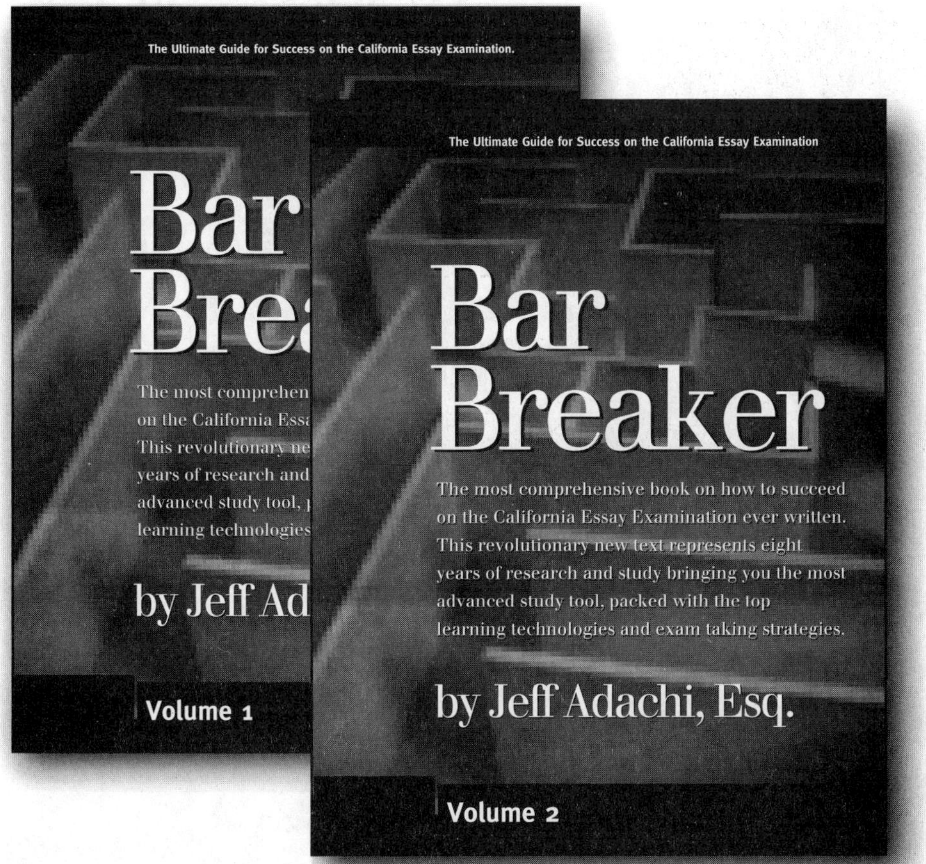

FINALLY!

A self study Bar review course for under $100

The Bar Breaker is the most comprehensive book on how to succeed on the California Essay Examination. This book contains:

- ♦ Written by a former bar exam grader & question writer
- ♦ Now used in some Bar/Bri Essay Advantage Courses!
- ♦ 100 actual Bar Exam questions with answers & commentary
- ♦ Examples of good & bad essay writing
- ♦ How to master time saving strategies
- ♦ How to write a 90 answer
- ♦ How your exam will be graded

PRAISE FOR THE BAR BREAKER

"If you feel apprehensive about the essay portion of the Bar, this is the book for you. When I sat for the exam, I felt confident I knew what to do & how to approach each question." - Susan Kalra, Esq.

"*Bar Breaker* contains a wealth of exam writing tips & strategies & a systematic approach to problem solving not taught in the regular Bar course. It was instrumental in my passing the Bar the first time!" - Mark Sollitt, Esq.

"A masterpiece...absolutely indispensable in preparing for the Bar. I recommend it to anyone who can't afford not to pass." - Matthew Dubuque, Esq.

ISBN 1-882278-04-6

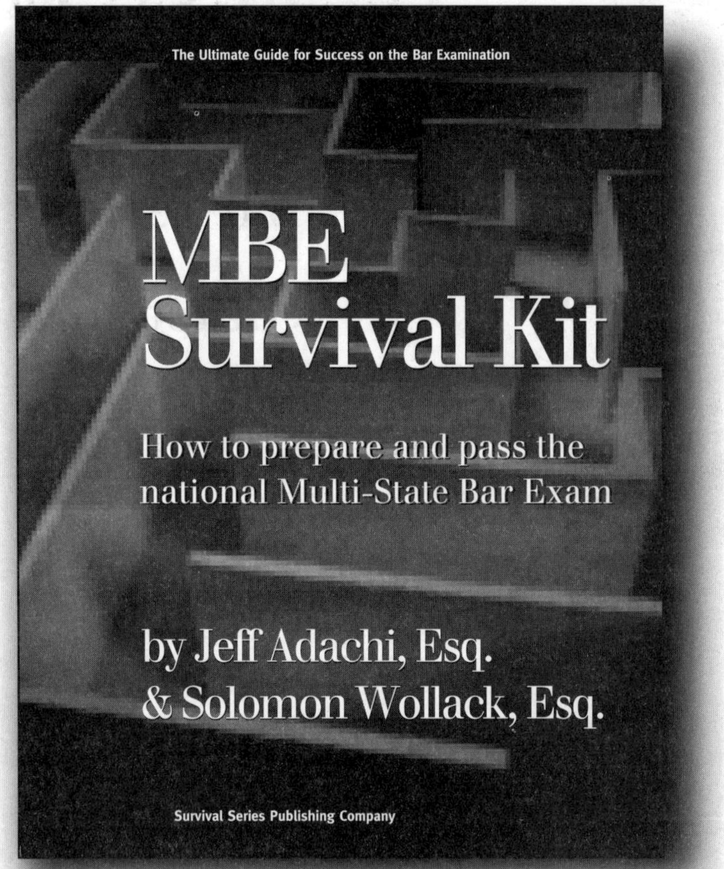

Whether you are preparing for the Bar Exam or the "baby" bar, this book gives you the tools you need to succeed...

The multi-state bar examination (MBE) is one of the most difficult challenges you will ever face. Consisting of 200 questions administered over a six-hour time period, you will have less than 1.8 minutes to complete each question.

- ♦ **Written by a Bar/Bri author & professor!**
- ♦ **Over 300 simulated practice questions and explanations**
- ♦ **Includes contracts, constitutional law, criminal law & procedure, evidence, torts and real property**
- ♦ **The 4 Step MBE Attack Plan**
- ♦ **Multi-State Bar Exam Diagnostic Test**
- ♦ **10 Rules of the MBE**

"There are many study guides that provide sample questions and answers, but this book goes beyond the simple explanation of the answers; it is more focused and detailed!" - Jae Kim, Esq.

"The book was very helpful in reinforcing the rules, and the ties were great and put everything in perspective. I raised my score 20 points and passed the Bar!" - Robert Trent, Esq.

ISBN 1-882278-08-9

ABOUT THE SURVIVAL SERIES PUBLISHING COMPANY

Survival Series is authored by *Bar/Bri* professor and author, **Jeff Adachi, Esq**. Adachi is a former bar exam grader, bar exam question writer, and a certified criminal law specialist. He was recently elected San Francisco Public Defender. *Survival Series* is a complete series of law and bar exam books that has earned the praise of leading law schools professors and students nationwide!

For more information, visit **www.survival-series.com**!

Law School Survival Kit (327 pp.): A comprehensive guide to law school designed to give students practical advice and problem solving skills necessary to succeed in any state. This book includes Law Charts, memory mnemonics and illustrations, comprehensive strategies for case reading, briefing and exam preparation and over 50 model essays.

Bar Exam Survival Kit (217 pp): The complete bar preparation book, containing attack strategies and Law Charts for all multi-state subjects and other common bar subjects. Learn how to prepare for the bar exam in any state and how to analyze and write essay questions. Now used by some *Bar/Bri Essay Advantage* bar review courses!

Bar Breaker (2 vol., 1100 pp.): Contains over 100 past bar exam questions and model answers with analyses. Hailed as the "Bible of the California Essay Exam," this book is used by some *Bar/Bri Essay Advantage* bar review courses!

MBE Survival Kit (450 pp.): Contains over 300 multi-state, multiple choice questions and analyses for the bar exam in any state. Includes a diagnostic test, the four step MBE attack plan, and the ten rules of the MBE.

Bar Cards (460 cards): The only flashcards designed specifically for the Bar Exam! Each color coded card contains a humorous illustration, comprehensive coverage of black letter law and memory mnemonics. Bar Cards includes: torts, contracts, contracts remedies, evidence, real property, constitutional law, criminal law and criminal procedure.

Complete Bar Cards (960 pp.): Contains the multi-state subjects and also includes: community property, ethics, civil procedure, wills, corporations, and trusts.

Legal Limericks (100 pp.): Forty clever and humorous limericks about some of the most controversial and fascinating legal cases and law suits recorded in American jurisprudence.

ORDER FORM

TITLE	QUANTITY	PRICE	(QTY) x (PRICE) = TOTAL
Law School Survival Kit		$29.95	
Bar Exam Survival Kit**		$29.95	
Bar Breaker, Vol. I & II**		$99.95	
MBE Survival Kit		$34.95	
Bar Cards		$29.95	
Complete Bar Cards		$49.95	
Legal Limericks		$7.95	
Add shipping & handling *Call (800) 200-7110 or (323) 526-7110 for quote*			
(CA Residents please add 8.5% **sales tax** to total)			
Please allow two weeks for delivery Overnight service available by telephone		***TOTAL:***	

** Now used in some Bar/Bri Essay Advantage bar review courses!
(Prices are subject to change without notice)

Name: ____________________

Mailing Address: ____________________

City: ____________________ State: _____ Zip: ____________

Telephone: ____________ Email: ____________ Fax: ____________

Law School: ____________________ Year in School: ____________

Method of Payment: cash ( ) check ( ) money order ( ) credit card ( )

Credit Card (circle one): Discover Visa Mastercard

Card Number: ____________________

Signature: ____________________ Expiration Date: ____________

Please mail or FAX this form and allow 2 weeks for delivery. Thank you!

Legal Books Distributing, 4247 Whiteside Street, Los Angeles, CA 90063
(323) 526-7110 or (800) 200-7110 tel., (323) 526-7112 or (800) 689-1749 fax.
www.survival-series.com

FEEDBACK FORM

We care what you think!

Did the book(s) help you with your studies?

Did you pass the bar exam?

Please fax, or mail comments to: SSPC, P.O. Box 77313, San Francisco, CA 94107. Fax (415)664-6463. Or use the mailing list page at www.survival-series.com.

(Print clearly or type)

Book Title: ______________________________

Name of store purchased from: ______________________________

How did you hear about us? ______________________________

Comments (please be specific):

May we use your name and comments in future SSPC advertising?

If so, please sign and date here:

Name: ______________________________

School: ______________________________

Signature: ______________________ Date: ____________

ORDER FORM

TITLE	QUANTITY	PRICE	(QTY) x (PRICE) = TOTAL
Law School Survival Kit		$29.95	
Bar Exam Survival Kit**		$29.95	
Bar Breaker, Vol. I & II**		$99.95	
MBE Survival Kit		$34.95	
Bar Cards		$29.95	
Complete Bar Cards		$49.95	
Legal Limericks		$7.95	
Add shipping & handling *Call (800) 200-7110 or (323) 526-7110 for quote*			
(CA Residents please add 8.5% **sales tax** to total)			
Please allow two weeks for delivery Overnight service available by telephone		***TOTAL:***	

** Now used in some Bar/Bri Essay Advantage bar review courses!
(Prices are subject to change without notice)

Name: ____________________

Mailing Address: ____________________

City: ____________________ State: _____ Zip: __________

Telephone: __________ Email: __________ Fax: __________

Law School: ____________________ Year in School: __________

Method of Payment: cash ( ) check ( ) money order ( ) credit card ( )

Credit Card (circle one): Discover Visa Mastercard

Card Number: ____________________

Signature: ____________________ Expiration Date: __________

Please mail or FAX this form and allow 2 weeks for delivery. Thank you!

Legal Books Distributing, 4247 Whiteside Street, Los Angeles, CA 90063
(323) 526-7110 or (800) 200-7110 tel., (323) 526-7112 or (800) 689-1749 fax.
www.survival-series.com